D1572217

BOHEMIANS WEST

BOHEMIANS WEST

Free Love, Family, and Radicals in Twentieth-Century America

SHERRY L. SMITH

Heyday, Berkeley, California

Copyright © 2020 by Sherry L. Smith

All rights reserved. No portion of this work may be reproduced or transmitted in any form or by any means, electronic or mechanical, including photocopying and recording, or by any information storage or retrieval system, without permission in writing from Heyday.

Library of Congress Cataloging-in-Publication Data

Names: Smith, Sherry L. (Sherry Lynn), 1951- author.
Title: Bohemians West : free love, family, and radicals in
  twentieth-century America / Sherry L. Smith.
Other titles: Free love, family, and radicals in twentieth-century America
Description: Berkeley, California : Heyday, [2020] | Includes
  bibliographical references and index.
Identifiers: LCCN 2020015153 (print) | LCCN 2020015154 (ebook) | ISBN
  9781597145169 (cloth) | ISBN 9781597145176 (ebook)
Subjects: LCSH: West (U.S.)--History--1890-1945--Biography. | United
  States--History--1901-1953--Biography. | Field, Sara Bard, 1882-1974. |
  Wood, Charles Erskine Scott, 1852-1944. | Man-woman
  relationships--United States--History--20th century. |
  Radicalism--United States--History--20th century. | United
  States--Social conditions--20th century. | United States--Politics and
  government--1901-1953.
Classification: LCC F595 .S666 2020 (print) | LCC F595 (ebook) | DDC
  978/.03--dc23
LC record available at https://lccn.loc.gov/2020015153
LC ebook record available at https://lccn.loc.gov/2020015154

Cover photo courtesy of the Huntington Library, Art Collections and Botanical Gardens, San Marino, California.

Cover and Interior Design/Typesetting: Ashley Ingram

Published by Heyday

P.O. Box 9145, Berkeley, California 94709

(510) 549-3564

heydaybooks.com

Printed in East Peoria, Illinois, by Versa Press, Inc.

10 9 8 7 6 5 4 3 2 1

For
Robert W. Righter

CONTENTS

PREFACE

Sara Bard Field and Charles Erskine Scott Wood's love affair began the day Clarence Darrow came to town. Darrow, a nationally renowned attorney for the underdog, visited Portland, Oregon, in October 1910 on business. He also made time for pleasure, bursting into Erskine's office and insisting he join him for dinner that night. Darrow wanted Erskine to meet Sara, a reluctant newcomer to Portland. He knew her from the Midwest, where they shared a commitment to progressive politics and the love of a particular woman. Sara's sister, Mary Field, was Darrow's mistress.

At first, Erskine declined. He planned to take his wife to dinner at the Portland Hotel. But Darrow would not be denied, and when Erskine pressed for more information about this woman, Darrow admitted she was the wife of a Baptist minister. What, Erskine thought, could he, a self-proclaimed atheist, not to mention a philosophical anarchist, possibly have in common with her? Darrow promised, "Listen, she's one of us."

Sara, too, resisted Darrow's invitation. Erskine was a wealthy lawyer who lived on Portland Hill, an upscale neighborhood above the town's commercial center, where he traveled in the highest social circles. He was much older than Sara, and besides, she had no decent clothes to wear. Darrow persisted, however, so Sara and her husband, the Reverend Albert Ehrgott, joined Darrow and Erskine at the Hofbrau, a bohemian eatery, while Wood's brother escorted Mrs. Wood to dinner elsewhere. Thus began a passionate and tumultuous relationship that lasted thirty-four years.

This book tells the story of that relationship and its connection to early twentieth-century American radicalism in the American West. It focuses on people who fought for far-reaching change not only in union picket lines and at suffrage rallies but in homes and bedrooms, in public arenas and in private lives. It charts their determination to transform the nation not from the vantage point of New York's Greenwich Village, normally seen as the epicenter of radical/bohemian America, but from the West. And it does so through the lives of Charles Erskine Scott Wood, Sara Bard Field, and their circle of friends and colleagues—a constellation of radicals that spanned the continent. The tale spins out over one hundred years of American history, from Erskine's birth in the antebellum 1850s to Sara's death in the mid-1970s. Coursing through its pages are tensions between capitalists and labor organizers, militarists and pacifists, suffragists and sexists, politicians and poets. It also explores friction between men and women, parents and children, love and loss, passion and power, freedom and responsibility, selfishness and sacrifice.

In falling in love and pursuing a life together, Erskine and Sara challenged deeply rooted social conventions as they dove into the radical politics of intimacy. They did not do so recklessly, thoughtlessly, or quietly. In fact, they wrote hundreds of letters explaining themselves and their purpose. They declared marriage obsolete and themselves as pioneers in free love. They advocated a new progressive form of partnership that exalted individual freedom and women's emancipation. Sara and Erskine knew they were ahead of their time and thought their example could be helpful. So, they saved their capacious correspondence, believing a chronicler would someday tell their story and give others the courage to chart their own course for freedom.

In some respects, they proved prophetic about the fate of marriage in the United States. The institution has fallen increasingly out of favor over the last century, and divorce rates have grown steadily, recently plateauing at nearly 50 percent of marriages. Few have thought as deeply or written as extensively as Erskine and Sara about marriage's pitfalls or shared the most intimate details of their experiences as free lovers so candidly, with people they would never know. They lived lives of emotional intensity, reflection, and deeply ingrained self-consciousness. But they did not advocate thoughtless or irresponsible promiscuity. Instead, Sara and Erskine attempted to craft a purposeful relationship that joined commitment with freedom. At least, that was the intention. It proved a challenge. The pair differed on issues of timing, levels of commitment, sacrifice, and monogamy. Ultimately, tensions percolated down to which person exercised greater power—a calculation that shifted over time.

Family commitments, too, thwarted their ideal love. Sara and Erskine were married with children when they met. Consequently, this is a story as much about those families as about the couple. Both operated in webs of relationship and obligation they could not easily shed. Their love led to heartbreak for spouses, offspring, and other lovers. It tore deep wounds from which some never recovered. For all its light and joy, their affair cast long shadows. And Sara and Erskine were not themselves oblivious to the suffering they unleashed; neither escaped heart-wrenching pain of their own. In choosing to prioritize their desires over those of family members, they wrestled with whether self-realization or responsibility to others, self-expression or self-sacrifice, should prevail. Both believed their lives, for too long, had been defined and constrained by others. They chose one another because they wanted to express their true, authentic selves, even though that meant breaking bonds. They agonized over ending commitments, made in early adult life, to people for whom their love had faded. They wrestled with whether marriage vows and parental responsibility trumped everything else.

Sara especially struggled. So many new opportunities opened to women in journalism, literature, politics, and sexuality in the 1910s, yet the costs to grasp them proved heavy. In seeking a fuller life, she faced greater social pressure to nurture her family, as well as greater stigma should she put self first. Her awakening to new possibilities was dramatic, her personal transformation profound.

Erskine—a prominent, wealthy man—was more experienced, worldly, and committed to philosophical anarchism and free love than Sara. He did not undergo the same transformation during the course of their affair, nor did he face the same level of social pressure or risk the same potential costs that Sara did. Erskine was not indifferent, however, to the pain he caused. He, too, struggled with loosening family ties. He loved his children and grandchildren and retained deep affection for his loyal wife and an equally loyal mistress of many years. For all of them he felt a strong sense of responsibility and remained committed to providing for them economically throughout his life and theirs.

The story, however, goes beyond Erskine and Sara's unorthodox love. It also involves the couple's commitment to, and active involvement in, leftwing, or progressive, politics. This book weaves together their affair and the era in which it took root. Turmoil and sweeping change rattled the United States in the 1910s as entrenched ways of everyday life faced fierce challenges. The nation condoned racial segregation in every region. Corporations crushed labor organizations with bloody violence and the consent of an aggressively hostile judiciary. Congress severely restricted Asian immigration. Women could vote in only a few places, while husbands exercised enormous power over wives, and governments policed women's bodies and sexuality. The United States pursued exploitative, imperial policies, from Puerto Rico in the Atlantic to the Philippines in the Pacific.

Yet far-reaching change was in the air. Workers and women demanded bold, innovative political solutions to injustice. People experimented with new social interactions, sexual and gender relations, and artistic expressions. Fresh ideas, some borrowed from European immigrants with roots in their homelands' radicalism, inspired native-born Americans to live up to this nation's values of liberty, equality, and justice. To be radical in 1910s America—perhaps especially to be a woman radical—was to be despised in many quarters. Yet it was exhilarating to dream big, be hopeful, and make the break for something more.

Nineteenth-century radical reformers—engaged in abolition, suffrage, and temperance, among other issues—often rooted their work in religious belief and moral calling. In contrast, twentieth-century radicals, witnesses to a world unraveling traditional social structures at a brisk pace, grounded themselves differently. They believed political and personal liberation went hand in hand. They leapt into all kinds of experiments and, in the process, took great risks. In art and literature, they championed modernism over Victorian styles. In politics, they supported labor unions, socialists, and anarchists, and opposed policies that protected the privileged. Some eschewed private property and capitalism altogether. They fearlessly denounced American imperialism at home and abroad. The suffragists among them roiled the nation, demanding not only votes but equal political rights in a democracy that had failed them for so long. Some chose militant methods to capture attention and allies, taking the issue to the streets and sometimes ending up in prison for their efforts. Others took risks with love, transforming homes and marriages—occasionally forsaking both.

Erskine and Sara participated fully—Wood as a philosophical anarchist, Sara as a socialist and ardent advocate of women's suffrage, emancipation, and empowerment. They involved themselves in nearly every major leftist cause of the first half of the twentieth century: birth control, free speech, civil rights and civil liberties, Native American rights, labor unions and workers' rights, government restraints on the excesses and exploitive nature of corporate capitalism, and anti-Japanese internment during World War II. They opposed militarism and American imperialism, stretching from the nineteenth-century wars against Native Americans to Vietnam.

They consequently offer insight into the much-overlooked story of radicalism in the West. Most of it took place in Oregon and California, flavored by these regions' particular characters, issues, and people. Yet their experiences and connections reached well beyond the West, illuminating the wide geographic reach of radicalism and cultural/literary bohemianism across America. This generation of left-leaning movers and shakers all knew one another. Modern communication and transportation networks made interaction and exchange easier than ever before. New ideas, values, and a willingness to experiment and challenge convention were not limited to Greenwich Village or a handful of eastern locales. They popped up across the country, staking positions and establishing communities of progressive-minded people that remained a vital part of the American fabric thereafter. The time has come to tell the complete story.

That said, as soul mates Erskine and Sara yearned—above all else—for a life of the mind, a place of solitude away from the political cacophony where they could write poetry. They dreamed of a remote spot, far from the discord of family and the turmoil of revolutionary change, where they could live together quietly and write. It might seem a little paradoxical that feminist Sara's ultimate goal in life was simply to live with one particular man. After all, she eschewed marriage and exalted independence and autonomy. Yet, throughout the whirlwind of suffrage politicking and the ups and downs of her affair with Erskine, she remained unwavering about her ultimate goal. To be with him remained her steadfast and primary purpose.

And paradox also riddled lawyer Erskine's life, as his radicalism rested upon a financial foundation that was funded by his representing corporations and capitalists in court. To be sure, however, genuine commitment to social and economic justice, freedom, and peace underwrote the couple's radical politics. More than dilettantes, Sara and Erskine devoted significant treasure and time to these causes. Nevertheless, the freedom they sought ultimately focused on personal fulfillment and material accumulation that few working people could ever afford. The couple's prospects of achieving these "anarchistic" goals depended upon Erskine's privileged position of whiteness, maleness, wealth, and land ownership. Their form of bohemianism rejected poverty and embraced material richness.

Further contradictions multiply from there. Erskine criticized imperialism in the West and abroad while simultaneously enjoying its benefits. Sara and Erskine supported the labor movement but found actual working people distasteful. They preached equality while unconsciously protecting and perpetuating their status as socially superior, refined, and sensitive souls. Their attitudes regarding people of other races failed to meet twenty-first-century standards.

Such inconsistencies also characterized the politics of their love. Conflicts over truth, power, equality, freedom, responsibility, and money arose between them. When one looks at the couple as thinkers and practitioners of free love, one sees how quickly ideology and principle broke down. For all their talk of "Truth," lies often accompanied their actions. For all their political commitment to equality between men and women, their experience as a couple demonstrated the difficulty of achieving equity.

Still, they persevered, even as they changed over time. Sara, especially, grew as she learned lessons and gained confidence from participation in the suffrage movement and applied them to her relationship with Erskine. She slowly bent him to a more equitable love. They did not win all their public battles, but Sara and Erskine did achieve a hard-won personal relationship of intellectual and emotional companionship, reciprocity, shared power and work, and mutual sexual satisfaction.

———————

The twists and turns of Erskine's and Sara's experiences, and how they negotiated the dilemmas they faced, were distinctly their own. So, why does *their* story matter? They are not well known, yet fame matters little in an intimate story of the heart. They offer extraordinary insight into the lived experience of their era—a perspective of American radicalism on a granular scale. There is something compelling about looking at the subject from a vantage point from which you can see personal desires, choices, and consequences up close rather than only in large-scale panorama. Value comes through probing the individuals' struggles to carve out a life of meaning, on *their* terms. They dared to challenge convention by crafting new philosophies of love and politics. They jumped in, took risks, made choices and mistakes, admitted weaknesses and failures, and lived with the consequences. Their relationship transcends the distant or abstract. By drilling down into the particulars, their story becomes more human, comprehensible, and interesting.

The aim of this book is neither to venerate nor to judge Erskine and Sara. It is to illustrate, and to understand, how difficult it is to set a new path, negotiate freedom and responsibility, balance love for self with love for others, and live up to one's ideals—whatever they may be. Digging deep into this couple's experience is instructive for its reminders of the endless intricacies and inconsistencies in the human heart and within human relationships.

In the course of writing this book, and talking about its central characters with friends and family, I have often been struck by how quickly and intensely listeners react to them. This couple seems to strike a chord . . . or a nerve. Their bittersweet saga, I have come to understand, prompts people to ponder their own loves and losses, life-changing experiences and missed opportunities, risks and regrets. This can be difficult territory. It can unearth disappointment, pain, mistakes, and personal flaws we might prefer to keep buried. Sara and Erskine did not deny their failings but instead shared them with us. I am grateful they left such a complete record in an effort to achieve an honest story.

However one feels about Sara and Erskine and the choices they ultimately made, the challenges and dilemmas they faced remain current. The complications of modern life regarding marriage, family, and relationships of power between men and women continue to confound people. So too do profound inequalities in the larger economic and political spheres. Ongoing assaults on civil liberties and civil rights, conflicts between workers and corporate power, profound inequality between the extremely rich and the rest of us, and the consequences of past and present imperialism remain vexing problems. Their world seems remarkably familiar. More than one hundred years after Clarence Darrow introduced them, Sara and Erskine still have something to say to us about the choices we make.

Their story, then, begins in only the narrowest sense on that evening Darrow brought them together. Who they were, what they longed for, and what they rejected had shaped their lives up to that fateful meeting and set them up for what was to come. Three decades separated Sara and Erskine in age and experience, yet they discovered a shared yearning for a more meaningful life and a willingness to risk much to achieve it, in spite of the odds and in spite of the costs.

One

ERSKINE'S ROAD TO RADICALISM

THE UNITED STATES MILITARY ACADEMY IN THE 1870s WAS HARDLY A NATURAL incubator for a radical, anarchist, and poet. Nor did Charles Erskine Scott Wood turn out to be your average West Point cadet. He enrolled there only at his father's command, for William Maxwell Wood, Surgeon General of the Navy, decided his son would pursue an army career.

As a first step, Wood arranged an interview for Erskine with the president of the United States. Shrouded in cigar smoke, Ulysses Grant talked mostly about Erskine's father. No discussion of the young man's interest in, or suitability for, military service, or even the purpose of the conversation, cropped up. In fact, not until the family dinner that evening did Erskine learn his father's intent. Equally surprised, his mother expressed concern about an education that trained men for the "killing trade," to which her husband curtly replied that he wanted this for their son. Neither parent sought Erskine's opinion, and so by fall 1870, the young man found himself marching with the other "plebes" on the ramparts above the Hudson River.[1]

A formidable man, William Maxwell Wood shouldered multiple roles: husband, father, medical doctor, and naval officer accustomed to commanding others. He displayed supreme confidence in his own judgment. Certainly in his family, he ruled. Yet the stern patriarch did not completely intimidate Erskine. At age eighteen the boy did not yet know his heart or calling, so he did not balk at West Point. As Erskine grew into young manhood, though, the rigidity of academy life sparked rebellion . . . not enough to get expelled, but enough to rouse the wrath of a father who never hesitated to chastise him for falling short of his high expectations. When authorities arrested Erskine for leaving his post to seek shelter from the cold, for example, his father fell into paroxysms of despair. The episode inflicted "the greatest wound my happiness can receive," he wrote his son. Erskine blithely continued to receive demerits, accumulating ninety-five in the first six months of his second year—five short of dismissal.

Erskine's growing rebellion against a military career proved more troubling. He preferred a literary one, an inclination inspired by the rich library of classic works his father encouraged Erskine to read. That the boy suggested this alternative profession to his father indicated a degree of fearlessness, as he surely knew the proposal would not be welcome. Initially, William Maxwell muffled his normally sharp rhetoric, dismissing Erskine's ambitions as the "follies of youth." The rebuff did not succeed, however. When Erskine next floated the idea of joining the Egyptian Army or starting a plantation of orange trees in Florida—anything to spare him the drudgery of American army duty—his father unleashed a barrage of angry ridicule. Erskine's "monomaniacal and boyish desire" to find a more romantic vocation reminded him of something dreamed up by "academic cloistered school girls whose imaginations [were] inflamed by fairy tales, the Arabian Nights, and maudlin novels." His son's concern for self rather than duty to God, country, and family especially disturbed him. If released from the army, Erskine imagined he would have a life of freedom, but his father warned, "That will never come to you." Nor should it be a goal. Obedience to a constitutional government and the military is the "mildest and best subordination." Although he, remarkably, claimed he did not intend to control Erskine's life, Wood concluded his son showed neither the mental nor moral fitness to make good decisions on his own.[2]

Erskine followed his father's orders. He stayed at West Point, graduating twenty-fourth in a class of forty-one, while ranking fourth highest in earned disciplinary demerits. The young man's charm, humor, high spirits, and extemporaneous speaking abilities made him popular among his comrades. His misgivings about the military, however, remained.

Erskine's years at West Point and his relationship with his father provided both the foundation for his adult life and his longstanding resistance to it. It set the seeds of his radicalism. Although he served in the army for a decade, Erskine continually defied its regimentation. He went to war but denounced conquest. He shot at the "enemy" but wrote poetry that valorized Native Americans as free people who fought tyranny and oppression. He put duty to family and country, if not to God, before self, even as he resented doing so. He rejected his father's belief in subordinating individual freedom to government, developing a reputation as a philosophical anarchist. He married but deplored the institution, becoming a champion of free love and pursuing affairs with a string of women. Nor would he follow William Maxwell's advice to cultivate habits of fiscal austerity rather than debt. Erskine embraced life with gusto, borrowing large sums of money along the way. For much of his adulthood he sustained a divided self and soul: soldier, legal advocate for the wealthy and powerful, and family man on the one hand; bohemian, poet, radical defender of the downtrodden, and free lover on the other.

———————

Born February 22, 1852, in Erie, Pennsylvania, Wood spent his early life in a household with an often-absent father and a loving, gentle mother. When at home, William Maxwell meted out discipline under a rule of "joyless tyranny," but he was not unloving. His stern admonitions laced with sarcasm mostly derived from a deep sense of responsibility for his children's future. He always ended his letters with notes of genuine affection.[3]

Erskine's father instilled also a passion for literature. He read his favorite poets aloud to his children and familiarized them with the Bible for its literary qualities. He taught Erskine to have contempt for the idea that wealth was the sole object of life and encouraged him to see thoughtfulness toward the weak as the mark of a gentleman. He chastised his son for anti-Semitic remarks and for joining other West Point cadets when they ostracized an African American colleague. Rose Wood, an abolitionist, and her husband treated their African American employees with respect, even if they could not always shed condescending racial attitudes. A Free Soil Democrat, Wood held in contempt an aristocracy based on slaveholding.[4]

William Maxwell Wood traveled the world, bringing home from far-flung, exotic ports of call red silk damask curtains, Chinese rugs and porcelain, pewter dishes, and a large ebony armchair from Ceylon. His salary, never substantial enough to support his taste for fine things, left William Maxwell in perpetual debt. According to Erskine, he was "too much the Bohemian and reckless Naval Officer" to be otherwise. Erskine replicated this behavior as a cadet, going into debt to secure sashes, buttons, boots, and other extravagances that added flair to his military uniform.

While posted to Washington, D.C., as surgeon general, Wood purchased a farm about a dozen miles from Baltimore. Erskine, fourteen when the family moved there, loved to lie in the house's screened-in porch at night, watching the fireflies and listening to the whip-poor-will call. Faced with mandatory retirement from his position as surgeon general at age sixty-five, William Maxwell hoped the property would support his family, but he could not make the farm pay. A sailor and a doctor, not a farmer, he drew deeper into debt and began to drink more heavily. Alcohol had been a part of his seafaring life, and now it became more reckless and degenerating. Wood grew increasingly abusive and ill-tempered with his wife and family, although Erskine, by this time, lived away at West Point.

It was at this Maryland house where one other childhood experience took place that portended Erskine's later relations with women. When Erskine was eight years old, his father sent him to bed without dinner as punishment for some transgression. The family's nanny smuggled bread, milk, and cookies into his room, then locked the door from the inside and lay on his bed. Under the pretense of a game she called "Bridge" she "irritated [him] into a juvenile erection and used [him] for her sexual gratification." Many times, he claimed, older girls made sexual advances toward him because of his good looks, an experience that continued into his adult life.[5]

As for his education at West Point, it was not simply an endless stream of duty, demerits, and drudgery. Outlets for his artistic and romantic impulses emerged through his friendship with J. Alden Weir, son of the head of the Drawing School. Only six months older than Erskine, Weir went off to Paris to study painting not long after they met. When duty brought Erskine back to the Academy years later, the two reconnected and Weir introduced him to many emerging, yet still unknown, artists in New York City, including Childe Hassam, Olin Warner, and Albert Pinkham Ryder. Weir, in fact, became Erskine's ticket to bohemian America.

Young men training for the officer corps also received equestrian training, fencing, and dancing lessons. Erskine especially loved dancing and the company of women. During the summer of 1872, he returned home on furlough and met a neighbor's cousin, Nanny Moale Smith, from Washington, D.C. She arrived in a basket-like carriage made of willow, drawn by a white horse and driven by an African American boy outfitted with tailcoat and stovepipe hat.

Two greyhounds raced alongside. What an entrance. The stepdaughter of a wealthy medical doctor, Nanny's long brown hair swept all the way down her back. Erskine found her beautiful, spirited, and irresistible.[6]

When, in summer 1874, Erskine eventually asked for permission to marry Nanny following graduation, her stepfather did not forbid it, though he convinced Nanny to wait. Having already endured two years of a mostly long-distance courtship, the young couple parted in tears. Returning Erskine's affections and ardor, Nanny presented him with a locket containing her photo and a snippet of her luxurious hair. Erskine gave her a small ring. Then he turned west to take up his post.[7]

A winter 1875 train ride across the continent proved a revelation to the brand new Twenty-first Infantry second lieutenant. He had traveled up and down the Atlantic seaboard but never to the West. The country's vastness dazzled him. Assigned to remote Fort Bidwell in Northern California, Erskine had little to do besides drill the enlisted men.[8] He did not play cards or drink. A less imaginative and curious person might have despaired, but Erskine explored the outdoors. The landscape's natural beauty, though subtle, seduced him.

The Harney Desert, with its brilliant star-saturated night skies and magnificent birds, particularly captivated him. Thrushes in sagebrush and blackbirds edged with red epaulets on their wings or yellow on their heads "sang as if their hearts would break . . . away out there in the middle of the world amidst utter loneliness." Erskine called the cuckoo owl, who emerged from his burrow at night to trespass on small badger hills and gather nesting materials, "a minstrel of the moon." Dipped in silver moonlight, this "little tiny bit of beauty and loveliness" saluted "the stars and all those unknown things of this world" through its song.[9] He found it all breathtaking. It sparked his poet soul. The wide-open West took hold of Erskine and never let go.

In addition, he became acquainted with at least one Native American family when a Paiute named Debes invited him on a swan hunt. Erskine stayed with him, his wife, and their child in their home, where, he later remembered, they "turned in like a happy family," which "should be the way if Indians were treated properly." The experience marked the beginning of Erskine's emerging sensitivity to Indian peoples' humanity.[10]

As much as he enjoyed his time at Fort Bidwell, when he received orders to transfer his company to Fort Vancouver, Washington, just across the Columbia River from Portland, Oregon, Erskine welcomed the change. Portland served as headquarters for the army's Department of the Columbia, which had jurisdiction over Washington, Idaho, and Alaska and was nearer to "civilization."[11] Appointed judge advocate of the department, he traveled around the Pacific Northwest attending to legal disputes. Not particularly stimulating or fulfilling work, it at least allowed more freedom than most officers experienced. He received even greater release from tedious military duties when General Oliver Otis Howard, who commanded the entire department and had taken special interest in Erskine, selected him to accompany a private citizen, Chicagoan Charles H. Taylor, on an exploring and mountaineering expedition to Alaska Territory. Erskine's role would be to gather military information, but the trip offered the imaginative young lieutenant something more—potential for literary inspiration and expression.[12]

The United States had purchased Alaska from Russia in 1867, but much of it remained unexplored and unknown to Anglo-Americans. The central aim of Taylor's expedition: climb Mount St. Elias. In Sitka, Taylor engaged a huge canoe, three Native American men, and a local prospector to serve as crew, and then, with Erskine, paddled to the Gulf of Alaska. When they encountered turbulent weather and seas, however, the boat's owner, Tah-ah-nah-lekh, refused to go any farther, forcing Taylor to end the expedition. Erskine wanted to stay, so he requested a three-year leave of absence to explore the interior of Alaska.

While waiting for a reply, Erskine spent time in an Asonque settlement, collecting tribal history, tales, and other information. He then moved on toward Sitka. Along the way a Native man asked him to look at his ailing son. Relying on what he had picked up from his father's medical practice, Erskine prescribed hot baths and a dose of bubbling digestive powder. Luckily, the boy recovered.

Meanwhile, a young woman from the village invited Erskine to stay in her lodge, which was replete with bear and seal skins. He accepted, an aspect of his adventure he did not share with Nanny. The Native woman was, he later recalled, "young, plump, [and] good looking (as the round faced Thlinkit [*sic*]

Indian are good looking after their fashion)." Erskine, at twenty-five, wore "sky blue army trousers." Resorting to sentimental stereotype, he called her a "princess" who, "after the simple frank fashion of her sex among her people[,] made love to me." The woman, whom he never named, offered to help him search for the Yukon's headwaters up the Chilkat River. But first, he had to go to Sitka.

As fate would have it, he never returned to her. "Honestly, to this day," Erskine wrote nearly fifty years later, "it is one of my regrets that the Nez Perce War sudden and unexpected made me break my word to this girl and add one more example to the long list of mans and white mans perfidy." In truth, Howard had already approved Erskine's extended leave. He could have remained in Alaska, but the southeastern part of the territory had become less stable after the army evacuated Forts Sitka and Wrangell, and Russian and American settlers feared Tlingit attacks on those who remained. Erskine probably doubted the wisdom of staying too, and so he left. Only when his steamer docked in Port Townsend, on the Olympic Peninsula, did Erskine actually begin to hear rumors of war, and only when he reached Fort Canby, at the mouth of the Columbia River, did he confirm military conflict with the Nez Perce. Howard did not recall him from Alaska to join the fight. It is noteworthy that in telling the story many years later, Erskine either misremembered these details and chronology or lied about them. His regrets about breaking his word to the young woman most likely came retrospectively in the highly romanticized tale he told as an old man.[13]

He did, however, return to the village and the woman in another way. Five years later, he published "Among the Thlinkits in Alaska" in *The Century Magazine*. Based on journal notes and salted with Mark Twain–inspired humor and lighthearted commentary, Erskine finally realized *his* ambition: to write and publish, and in a leading American journal, no less.[14]

Meanwhile, Erskine's regiment entered the fight against the "non-treaty bands" of Nez Perce. The violence had erupted as so many conflicts between the United States and sovereign Native American tribes did: over American settlers' insatiable demand for land and their government's willingness to oblige, even if it meant dishonorable, deceitful practices. In this case, that meant signing treaties with some groups or bands of the tribe and then holding the entire tribe to those promises. When the U.S. government came for the eastern Oregon homeland of the Wallowa Valley band of Nez Perce, brothers named Ollokut and Hin-mah-too-yah-lat-kekt (the latter more famously known as Chief Joseph) tried for five years to reverse the terms of the 1863 treaty that ceded their homeland—a treaty they had never signed. But peaceful negotiation and diplomacy failed, and by 1877, war sparked between white settlers in the Wallowa Valley and a handful of the young Nez Perce men. Understanding that the actions of a few implicated them all, Joseph and others fled rather than move to the Nez Perce reservation near Lapwai. The army followed in pursuit.

The Nez Perce case proved particularly troubling because relations between that tribe and the federal government had been friendly for years, beginning with the Lewis and Clark Expedition. Local white settlers felt little compassion for the Native peoples, but the history of peaceful relationships elicited some sympathy for the Nez Perce elsewhere in the nation, even as tribe members fought the army while trying to flee across the Canadian border.

Erskine headed into combat for the first time, serving as General Howard's adjutant during the expedition.[15] As he neared the theater of war, he mused on the prospects of his own death: he was, as he wrote in his diary, "fearing the field" and full of a "peculiar nervous feeling of going to death." A few days later, while burying the dead after the Battle of White Bird Canyon, the stench and horror of blackened and mutilated bodies deeply affected him. Now Erskine expressed eagerness for the fight: "only want a crack at an Indian and feel no disposition to show any quarter." That mood too, however, passed when, several weeks later, while guarding some Nez Perce prisoners and reflecting on "the fate before them," he acknowledged having "thoughts on the Indian as a human being, a man and brother."[16]

After a long chase across Idaho, Wyoming, and Montana, and several victories in battle, about 450 Nez Perce men, women, and children surrendered just short of the international border, where the Seventh Cavalry, under Nelson Miles's command, surprised and intercepted them. Two hundred others escaped into Canada. Erskine witnessed Chief Joseph's formal capitulation. He then sought him out, listened to his explanation of the conflict, and drew sketches of

Joseph and his baby daughter. Erskine found Joseph dignified, and the incredible saga of the Nez Perce journey heroic. The two men exchanged saddles, became friends, and in the years to follow renewed their battlefield-born tie.[17]

Erskine realized Joseph could become a rich literary subject, and almost immediately he began writing sympathetically about the charismatic leader. He handed a newspaper editor a "verbatim transcript" of Joseph's words of surrender that was lengthier than other eyewitness accounts. It conveyed Joseph's distress. "I am tired . . . . My heart is sick and sad. From where the sun now stands I will fight no more forever." Some scholars now attribute elements of Joseph's famously poetic "Surrender Speech" to Erskine. For the remainder of his life, however, Erskine insisted the words came from Joseph. Whatever the truth of their authorship, these words, printed and reprinted across the nation, helped catapult Joseph into national celebrity and earned additional sympathy for his people.

In the end, the war reinforced Erskine's views of Indians as men and brothers. It also provided an outlet for his creative and literary impulses, through published articles in nationally known periodicals and in his poetry. Finally, it fostered Erskine's nascent but evolving radical critique of American government, society, and imperialism.[18]

———————

During these years of military service, Erskine's interest in marrying Nanny never waned. True, he enjoyed the company of other women—from the Alaskan Native woman to actress Lotta Chissold, a member of a bohemian opera troupe he met while sailing up the Columbia River in 1878. Nanny, meanwhile, had her own bevy of suitors during Erskine's long absences. Still, the couple remained committed. That his beloved did not read challenging books or demonstrate intellectual interests only once elicited criticism from the young lieutenant. And if Nanny found Erskine's tendency to correct her spelling a tad annoying, she never mentioned it. Nor did their marriage plans fade as Erskine railed against economic factors that delayed the nuptials and then admitted that his spendthrift habits explained his failure to save adequately for marriage.[19]

One other concern loomed. Nanny's Catholicism became a heated issue in December 1877, when Erskine wrote a raging anti-Catholic letter, possibly sparked by Nanny's stepfather's concern that Erskine would not promise to raise his children in the church. Erskine believed Roman Catholicism was "an outgrowth of early darkness and superstition" so clearly antithetical to reason and thoughtfulness that anyone who believed its tenets was "narrow & contracted in mental caliber." Who could possibly accept the infallibility of the Pope or see purgatory as anything but a "religious money grab"? Catholicism reflected the Dark Ages out of which it arose. Its "dogmas are to me such drivel . . . so narrow, mean and bigoted . . . that [I] am almost becoming a bigot myself against the worm-eaten old institution."[20] His fervor suggested he was, in fact, on the edge of that very thing.

The issue created a crisis in the relationship. Erskine stopped all correspondence. After several months, Nanny broke the silence, asking why he had never spoken about religion before. After two years apart, perhaps he had found a new love? Maybe he had outgrown her "in all things," but until he looked her in her eyes and took back the ring he gave her, she remained committed to him.[21] The letter revealed glimmerings of Erskine's growing skepticism toward religion and radical antipathy toward authority in any form. If he held the Roman Catholic Church in greatest contempt, he had little good to say about any religion, concluding that no institution, sacred or secular, should interfere with individual freedom. These ideas eventually became the bedrock of his commitment to anarchism.

Erskine's letter differed qualitatively from earlier ones, emphasizing ideas rather than emotions, arguments rather than endearments. Reflecting a tone reminiscent of his father's, he expressed absolute certainty concerning the rightness—and righteousness—of his position. Supreme confidence, even arrogance, appeared in the lines. Further, it revealed a fundamental difference between Erskine and Nanny. Her Catholicism rested on unexamined early education and acceptance of others' points of view. She was not introspective or intellectual. Neither was she, one might add, dogmatic. Erskine's viewpoint, on the other hand, came from reflection on and rebellion against received ideas, and when he made up his mind, he fiercely dug in his heels. He would not bend, not even for her. In the end, Nanny capitulated. She never renounced her Catholic upbringing, however.

On November 26, 1878, a Reverend Randolph of Emanuel Church—rather than a Catholic priest—married Erskine and Nanny in her grandmother's Washington, D.C., parlor. It had been a six-year courtship. A belle like Nanny proved an asset to army post society as well as a fetching companion to Erskine, who certainly loved her. "I wonder how much you will be to me in the rest of my life," he wrote. "Trouble there will be . . . but no more separation." After the ceremony, they traveled to Fort Vancouver, Washington Territory, and the following year, on September 1, 1879, Nanny gave birth to their first child, a treasured son named Erskine. Six months to the day later, the baby's grandfather, William Maxwell Wood, died. No longer the son, C. E. S. Wood took on the mantle of father.[22]

Erskine's discontent with his army career deepened, although when General Howard accepted the position of Commandant of West Point and took Erskine along, things brightened a bit. One of his duties was housing visitors who came to the campus. In preparation of one such visit from literary giant Mark Twain, Erskine painted the ceiling of his attic, where the author would sleep, with quotations from Shakespeare and Chaucer. During their lengthy chat about literature, Twain mentioned his unpublished work titled *1601, or Social Conversation as it was by the fireside of Queen Elizabeth*, which skewered royalty and included obscene language and scatological references. When Twain remarked that publishers would not touch it, Erskine, on the spot, offered to print it secretly on the Academy's printing press. Twain accepted. This act of rebellion appealed to Erskine, as did the opportunity to ingratiate himself to Twain. Nanny found the writer less appealing. His primary topic of discussion with her: his hatred of babies.[23]

Most days at the Academy provided less sparkle. Howard came to Erskine's rescue once again, allowing him to enroll at Columbia University to study for a bachelor's of philosophy and a law degree. Finally in his element, Erskine made the most of the opportunity by hanging out with bohemian types, especially artists. These were his people. This was where he belonged. Erskine also experienced incredible personal freedom for a married man. During his time at Columbia, Nanny and their two children (daughter Nan had been born in summer 1881 at West Point) lived with her family in Baltimore. In letters, Erskine occasionally mentioned his attraction to other women, adding that he did not have time for flirtations.[24] To promise fidelity while simultaneously relating real-life temptations might have been meant as good-natured teasing, but whatever the motive, he seemed unable to self-edit.

At the end of the idyllic sojourn in bohemian New York, Erskine returned to the army. Assigned to Boise Barracks, Idaho, with regular company duty, he despaired. To make matters worse, General Nelson Miles now commanded the Department of the Columbia. The two men clashed because Erskine had made publicly clear that Howard, rather than Miles, deserved credit for the surrender of the Nez Perce. Things came to a head when Miles blocked Erskine's requested transfer to Fort Canby, on the Oregon coast, and a six-month sick leave. He suspected Erskine wanted to use the time to investigate business opportunities as a civilian in Portland. The charge outraged Erskine, who brazenly complained. Miles threatened court-martial. Finally, General William Sherman intervened, although by that time Erskine had decided to resign from the army. In spring 1884 he opened a law office in Portland and bid adieu to the army forever.[25]

Not that Erskine aspired to a law career. For the time being, however, it offered some advantages. If successful, he could earn enough money to support his growing family and indulge in the acquisition of paintings and other beautiful things. If industrious and energetic, he could find time to engage in politics and, more importantly, poetry. If charming and witty enough, he could publish his own rebellious, radical points of view and suffer no harm to his law firm or his social life. If discrete, he could engage in flirtations and even affairs with other women. He had not suppressed his growing radicalism or forsaken his dream of a literary bohemian life; he just had to postpone it. In the meantime, he could dabble in it occasionally. For the next two and a half decades, that is exactly what Erskine did.

Portland was a young city of just over twenty thousand people when the Woods moved there. Once President Polk secured Oregon Territory for the United States in 1846, settlers established a town where the mighty Columbia and Willamette Rivers met. A few years later, the California Gold Rush provided the town's first economic boom, supplying miners who had moved up the coast. Rapid expansion followed in the years after the Civil War, led and controlled by a handful of families, including that of William S. Ladd and his grandson Henry Corbett. Benefiting from a system virtually free of regulation and a continent of public lands and riches ripe for the taking, the business elite flourished.[26]

Erskine had cultural, though not financial, capital. Portland offered robust opportunities for a well-educated man with charm, taste, and ambition. With ready-made connections from his Fort Vancouver days, he joined a thriving law practice headed by politically and socially prominent partners. The firm's collection of lucrative clients, and its potential to grow, turned out to be gold for Erskine, who developed particular expertise in maritime and corporate law.[27] Clients included the Port of Portland, the Great Northern Railway, Portland Flouring Mills, the Ladd and Tilton Bank, and many elite families.[28]

Much of Erskine's time and talent focused on a railroad land grant. In the nineteenth century the federal government donated huge swaths of federal lands to private companies as incentive for them to construct transportation networks. Railroads then attracted farmers who, in turn, enriched the entire nation. Building railroads required enormous capital, however, so government enhancements smoothed the financial process. This was federal subsidy on a gargantuan scale and, in the context of the Gilded Age, opportunity for gargantuan graft. The Willamette Valley and Cascade Mountain Wagon Road Company received nearly eight hundred thousand acres of land in eastern Oregon in exchange for the promise to build a toll road to the Idaho border. Proceeds from their land grant sales would reimburse construction costs and provide significant profits. When the company built a shoddy road, however, the people who had purchased their lands expecting something better became outraged. The company quickly unloaded the remainder of the land grant property before the settlers' lawsuits eroded their profits.

The French banking firm Lazard Frères purchased the land. When Congress and the Justice Department began to sue road companies for slapdash or nonexistent roadways, Lazard Frères defended their title to the property as fair and square, simultaneously claiming they were not to blame for the road company's failures. They should not be punished. They hired Erskine and his law firm to help secure that position and their property.

The land grant case required significant chunks of Erskine's time for more than twenty-five years. In 1892, courts upheld Lazard Frères's legal ownership of the land without responsibility for the poor road, but the task of turning property into profit remained. Erskine oversaw the drawn-out legal aspects of its sale. He stood to gain a significant commission for all his labor, but just *when* the payout would materialize remained uncertain. For the duration, Erskine secured a separate office, specifically for this case, in the Chamber of Commerce Building. It consisted of two rooms: one for the land grant work and the other his private office for literary writing and entertaining guests. He hired an attractive young divorcée named Kitty Seaman Beck as his secretary.[29]

Busy as his legal work kept him, Erskine still found time for politics. A Democrat, he opposed the concentration of wealth in the hands of the few (even if they were his friends or clients) and supported economic reform to end special privilege (even as he personally benefitted from it). He openly criticized robber barons and corporations who looted the nation's public lands, coming quite close to biting the Lazard Frères hand that fed him. Erskine supported progressive political reform to bring more power to the people through initiatives, referendums, and the direct election of senators. Voters put this "Oregon System" in place by 1912, and it became a prototype for reform in many other states. Erskine also actively campaigned for women's suffrage.

Inspired by his experience in the Nez Perce War, Erskine lambasted warfare and corruption in Native American affairs and lobbied for justice on their behalf. His critique of conquest at home also extended to American overseas expansion. Erskine opposed the United States' control of the Philippines, finding its war against insurrectionists inconsistent with American democracy. An outspoken anti-imperialist, he denounced the nation's drive for economic power in the Pacific and demanded self-government and self-determination for Filipinos.

Through public speeches and essays in newspapers and periodicals, particularly the *Pacific Monthly*, Erskine touted his more radical positions, including commitment to philosophical anarchism. What he had in mind was a system that allowed the greatest freedom for the individual. Or, as he once explained it to a friend, "by anarchistic I mean the lessening of the powers of government and the freeing of the individual for a perfect individual expression of his life, compelling that collectivism which is essential to the social life to be based on self-interest or voluntary cooperation." He preferred anarchism to socialism, as the latter called for government control of industry and, consequently, curbed liberty.

His was not a revolutionary brand of anarchism but a more benign form—one that evolved through time and from "the propagation of ideas" rather than through violence, which "only obscures the ideas and retards [anarchism's] acceptance."[30] Of course, he understood people associated anarchism with bomb-throwers and immigrant radicals, but he did not hesitate to use the word. Actually, he used it precisely because it caught peoples' attention. The shock value of the word appealed to Erskine's personality, style, and sense of self. Embracing anarchism made his credentials as a rebel in lawyer's clothing more obvious.

He certainly attracted the attention of Emma Goldman, an anarchist of more radical stripe who advocated overthrow of the current economic system. She planned to lecture in Portland in 1908, but the YMCA reneged on its contract to allow her to speak in their building. So, Erskine swooped in to help. He raised money and then found a lecture hall where Goldman could speak. On the night of her appearance, he introduced her to the audience, his remarks focusing less on anarchism and more on free speech. What mattered was not what Goldman said, he insisted, but that she had the *right* to say whatever she wanted. Although Goldman found Erskine's anarchism a bit too genteel, she appreciated his efforts on her behalf and thought his introduction brilliant.

Other anarchists, birth control advocates, labor organizers, and suffragists found their way to Erskine's legal office. He did what he could to support them, providing bail or pro bono legal aid when possible. Erskine also supported the Industrial Workers of the World (IWW), or "Wobblies," who aimed to create a single labor union to unite all workers for the purpose of taking over the means of production. Erskine did not support their willingness to use violence, but he endorsed their overall goals. After one particularly brutal confrontation in Spokane in 1909, when local authorities rounded up and jailed more than one hundred IWW members, Erskine outspokenly defended the right to free speech of the members of the profoundly unpopular organization. This took courage.

Publicly identifying himself as an anarchist made Erskine fodder for the

Portland press, which reveled in the opportunity to point out inconsistencies between Erskine's philosophical/political position and his livelihood. He declared himself an anarchist, the *Oregonian* noted, yet he worked as an attorney for one of the biggest land monopolies in Oregon, not to mention Portland's gas monopoly, big banks, and the wealthy elite with whom he socialized. How did he reconcile these contradictions? Erskine, it concluded sarcastically, was "an unusually elastic, versatile man."[31]

Erskine shrugged off the criticism. Accepting the mantle of unconventional rebel, he sincerely embraced progressive and radical positions but also had huge debts and so practiced law to support his family, his causes, and his artistic appetites. Erskine lived generously and extravagantly, beyond his means. He knew the Lazard Frères work would eventually pay huge commissions, but he was not willing to wait to enjoy life to its fullest. At one point, he told his friend J. Alden Weir, he was $100,000 in debt.

Happily, most clients tolerated his radical politics. They valued his legal skills and put aside any ideological differences. Plus, he had significant social cachet in Portland. Erskine and Nanny made an attractive, charming couple and they had a lovely growing family. Erskine's taste, self-assurance, and style attracted the Portland scions who felt less secure about their own such qualities. He was college educated, a published writer, an artist, a clever and talented speaker, and an indisputably attractive man who dressed with flair—opal-studded cufflinks, black flowing capes, and soft rather than crisp white shirts. The touch of the bohemian added to his allure.[32] If he seemed inconsistent or hypocritical, it mattered little to most. He was an asset to Portland.

Yet, the paradoxes in his life sometimes troubled Erskine or, more accurately, he felt deep frustration that he could not live as he wished. Thirty years out of West Point, he still had not achieved "perfect individual expression." Two things particularly gnawed at him: mortality and marriage. By his forties, the discontent became palpable. Thoughts of death depressed him. "Last night I lay awake . . . my thoughts all of death and the fear of death—that dreadful rebellion of annihilation," he wrote in August 1893. Oblivion, he believed, followed death.[33]

Prospects of premature death especially disturbed him; he was undone by the idea that death could arrive before a person had fulfilled his or her life's potential or destiny. Friend Olin Warner's demise at age fifty-two, for instance, devastated him. Run over by a cab after collapsing on a street corner, Warner had been at the time engaged in creating paneled doors for the Library of Congress, an enormously important commission. Then death had ended it all.[34] In Warner's loss, Erskine saw his own opportunity for artistic expression slipping away. A few years later, while in the Harney Desert with his artist friend Childe Hassam, he made that point explicit. Fearing he had lost his creative and imaginative powers, dispiriting thoughts of death crept in. Then age fifty-six, he said, "I have done so little of what I wanted to do and of what was in me." Some of this despair reflected common enough middle-age anxiety, but for Erskine it felt like much more. He believed his responsibilities to others had stymied his opportunity to express his true self.

Erskine also expressed discontent with marriage, not just his marriage to Nanny but with the institution. For the first fifteen years or so after their wedding, Erskine and Nanny had been happy. They had more children: William Maxwell, or Max, born in 1884, Lisa in 1885, and Berwick in 1887. A sixth child, named Katherine, died several months after her birth in 1891. By his forties, however, Erskine decided monogamous marriage was antithetical to Nature, and to men's nature in particular, and certainly to his own.

Still, he enjoyed his home and family. The Wood house befit his social and economic status and served as a showcase for Nanny's flower garden. Erskine filled the interior with paintings by Hassam, Ryder, Weir, and Joshua Reynolds, as well as medallions of Wood family members and Native American headmen that had been created by his friend Olin Warner. He added rich tapestries, porcelain and glass figurines, Alaskan Native pieces, Indian masks, Oriental rugs, and Chinese and Japanese art pieces. The variety of exotic objects resembled Erskine's father's collections. And, of course, there were books—wonderful literature in beautifully bound volumes of rich paper.

Erskine was a generous, indulgent, and affectionate father. His literary attributes made him a dazzling storyteller. Anarchistic tendencies led to permissive parenting, in sharp contrast to his own father's ironhanded discipline.[35] Importantly, he encouraged his children to pursue *their* interests. When Max and a friend created a hand press in the attic, Erskine provided a cluster of Indian tales for a lovely little book they produced. He purchased a share in an elite duck-hunting club just for his sportsman son, Erskine. Most notably, in 1892 and 1893 he sent this oldest son for months-long visits with his friend Chief Joseph at the Nespelem Agency in northeastern Washington. Where Erskine's father sent him to the army, he sent his son to the Indians; what a contrast. Dressed in buckskin and moccasins made by Nez Perce women, young Erskine lived the ideal boy's life, participating in the fall hunt, riding bareback, living in Joseph's household, and learning the Nez Perce language. Joseph acted as a father to the boy, guiding and, on occasion, reprimanding him. For the rest of his own long life, the younger Erskine, who knew even then that Joseph was a great man, felt deepest gratitude to his father for having made the experience possible.[36]

But the elder Erskine could not shed all of William Maxwell's tendencies. When his oldest son headed to Harvard, he wrote him a twenty-seven-page letter reminiscent of—yet far exceeding—his own father's lengthy missives. Noting its long sections on health, diet, exercise, and alcohol, one could be forgiven for assuming the naval doctor had written the letter from the grave. Erskine echoed William Maxwell in his admonition that because his "life blood" had purchased his son's Harvard education, the boy was consequently "honor bound" to get as much good out of the investment as possible. Yet, Erskine veered from his father's script in several important ways. He made clear he wanted his son to get pleasure from life and, most importantly, he wanted him to decide his own profession. If the young man wanted to be an artist, poet, or sculptor, that would be fine. Above all, Erskine wanted his firstborn to find out what he loved doing and then do it.

As to sharing advice on matters of morality and marriage, Erskine cautioned that love was a luxury. His son should look for a woman who would provide healthy offspring, for the purpose of marriage was to produce children. Shared tastes, values, habits, and even tempers were more important for sustaining a lifelong partnership than love, which he said inevitably dies.[37] Erskine made clear his disillusionment regarding marriage to daughter Nan, too. Days before her wedding, he wrote a twenty-one-page letter summarizing his unorthodox views: "Nature is a persistent free-lover" rather than the current "fossilized, fixed and unchangeable" system created by society and religion, which does not allow for the transformation many people undergo between ages twenty and forty. Another "law of Nature" is that "life should be happy." When marital happiness ends, he told Nan, divorce should follow, for an unhappy marriage is "prostitution." Erskine offered to draw up a contract for the couple in which they would agree to separate should love, on either side, end. This probably did not shock Nan. Her father had published essays in the *Pacific Monthly* that had made these points quite publicly. She did not, however, take him up on the offer of a prenuptial agreement.[38]

While Erskine's love for his children remained steadfast, his ardor for Nanny diminished. He retained affection and respect for her and they shared commitment to their children, who were fast leaving home, but after fifteen years of marriage, the sexual attraction had disappeared. Twenty years after they met and six pregnancies later, Nanny had become matronly and stout. "When a woman breakfasts in curlpapers," Erskine wrote in his diary in 1894, "love has ended and marriage begun." On another occasion he noted, "The end of life is marriage and marriage is the end of life." To compound the problem, Nanny did not share Erskine's intellectual acumen or radical politics.

Erskine meanwhile continued his long practice of cultivating friendships with beautiful, intelligent, and artistic women. He did not pass up opportunities for greater intimacy, declaring in his journal, "I am sensuous . . . . I am a man. I have senses. I love to pleasure them. I know not if I will ever have any other joy. I am *sensuous*."[39]

Nanny suspected infidelity and Erskine denied it.[40] But of course her worries had merit. Sometime after 1895 he had embarked on an affair with Helen Ladd Corbett, a member from one wealthy Portland family who had married into another. Widowed at age thirty-six—and rich, beautiful, and very interested in Erskine—Helen showered him with luxurious gifts, encouraging his taste for the finer things. She also bestowed extravagant presents upon Erskine's children.[41] In a small city with two such outsized figures as Erskine and Helen, Nanny inevitably learned of the relationship. She also knew about her husband's intimacy with Kitty Beck, his secretary for the Lazard Frères land grant case. Comparatively quiet and socially inconspicuous, Erskine's relationship with Kitty caused Nanny less public humiliation, but the heartbreak remained nevertheless.

Nanny told her son Erskine about the Corbett affair, claiming Helen had stolen her husband and wanted her children, too. Young Erskine immediately terminated his friendship with his mother's rival. "My duty is to my true, self sacrificing loving Mother and so it had to end," he told his father, who replied that Helen was not solely to blame. Erskine agreed. He *did* blame his father, "but thank God . . . I love you as I always have—just as I always have."[42] The son did not want to choose between his parents, yet allegiance to his mother took precedence.

By 1910, various paradoxes and frustrations had beset Erskine's life. He longed to leave the law for a poet's life. The contradiction between his radical politics and his professional duties to conservative clients could not be easily resolved as long as he felt responsible for his family's economic well-being and incurred further debt through lavish spending. The contradiction between his free-love philosophy and his marriage loomed. Erskine felt imprisoned in a false relationship, one based on dishonesty, hypocrisy, and a great deal of pain. He did not want to continue living this way. Nanny, of course, knew Wood's position on marriage and divorce, and she made him well aware of hers: she would never agree to divorce. Part of this stemmed from her Catholic upbringing, part of it reflected concern about the social stigma attached to divorce, and part of it rested on her love for Erskine. She hoped that somehow—if she could weather his affairs—he would eventually return to her.

Nanny had not counted on Sara Bard Field entering the picture.

Two
SARA'S ROAD TO PORTLAND

SARA AND ALBERT EHRGOTT WERE ON THEIR HANDS AND KNEES, DIGGING IN THE dirt, when a dark shadow fell upon them. It was not a cloud that cast it but the large, lumbering body of Clarence Darrow, who had come to invite them to dinner. They were putting in a garden at their recently purchased home in Rose City Park, a new Portland suburb with unpaved streets. In fact, the roads were quite muddy that autumn day. When they had arrived in the city earlier that year, the Ehrgotts found Albert's church-sponsored parsonage impossibly small, ugly, and crowded, and since Sara simply had to have more space, they took out a mortgage and invested in this three-bedroom home with a yard.

Sara's journey to Portland and that fateful dinner started in the American Midwest. Nothing in her background portended the trajectory of a new life that had its beginnings that evening—one lived outside conventional boundaries, framed by concepts of free love and feminism. In her youth, Sara's most influential, life-shaping relationships revolved around men, including a domineering, tyrannical father, who was then followed by a sometimes rigid and overbearing husband. These became the forces against which she chafed and from which she eventually broke. Like Erskine's, Sara's radicalism took root in resistance to patriarchal power. When she struck out for liberation, however, it was yet another man who provided the incentive, encouragement, and money she needed to realize it.

Beyond freedom, Sara wanted happiness—something in short supply in her childhood home. Born in Cincinnati, Ohio, on September 1, 1882, her earliest memories centered on Detroit, the place George and Annie Field moved in 1885. Sara was the middle child of the five who survived to adulthood.

The Fields practiced thrift, sobriety, and self-denial befitting a middle-class, semi-cultured, semi-genteel family. George, a distant and dictatorial father, made the Baptist Church the center of his life. He began each day with Bible reading, followed by prayers that went on for such long stretches of time that Sara and her siblings had to surreptitiously lace their shoes under the table so that as soon as their father finished they would be ready to dash for the door and reach school on time.

George's severe discipline ignited the rebellion of his second daughter, Mary. Once, when her mother placed a huge boiled potato on Sara's plate and the young girl blurted out, "Oh my, I couldn't eat all that," George sharply replied she *would* eat it and everything else on her plate. Mary, noticing Sara's tears, quickly assured her, "Never mind, Sara, pretty soon you'll be grown up and you can do as you please." Furious, George sent Mary to her room and kept her on bread and water for two days, "like a prisoner," while Sara slipped her sister food and special treats, careful to avoid George's wrath. Sara remembered George expressing warmth and affection only once, when she had decided, at age thirteen, to be baptized. He took her onto his lap and asked why she wanted this. She replied, "Oh, I want to be good." Nothing could have pleased her father more: obedience to him and to his God.[1]

Whenever George left home (he traveled frequently as a buyer for a Cincinnati-based wholesale grocery business), the children would go through "an almost bacchanalian dance" as the door closed behind him. Sara's mother loved literature, and in the evenings while she and her four daughters sewed, Sara read aloud. It resembled a scene out of Louisa May Alcott's *Little Women*. They devoured Dickens, Thackeray, Sir Walter Scott, Jane Austen, Lew Wallace, George Eliot, Longfellow, Whittier, Shelley, Keats, and Oscar Wilde. In this small company of women, Sara lost herself in literature. She also began writing. One essay focused on the ideal father: kind, understanding, generous, and tolerant—in short, the antithesis of George.[2]

When their father returned, so did tyranny. Rebellion followed. George threw oldest child Alice out of the house for disobeying over some trifling thing. Mary, her father's favorite—smart, witty, whimsical, imaginative, lively, and not the least afraid of him—went next. Mary had provided George the most joy but also caused the most trouble. George funded her education at the University of Michigan, where Mary studied history, philosophy, and biology, all of which led her to question the orthodox Christian ideas her father held dear. When Mary's growing intellectual independence became apparent, George announced he would no longer pay her tuition. Certain that her religious faith had been weakened and mortal soul endangered, he refused to invest further in such an outcome.

Equally certain that this education liberated her from her father's narrow path, Mary sought an alternative money source. A friend of her mother's provided a monthly stipend that allowed her to continue school, and Mary agreed to repay it after she graduated and found employment. Furious, George barred Mary from his home. Ever resourceful, however, she found other places to stay, and she also found work, including at a home for unmarried mothers. She delighted in bringing some of the so-called illegitimate babies to the Field home when George was away—directly defying him, albeit in absentia. Eventually Annie's pleas to allow Mary back home reopened that door, but the strain between father and daughter endured as Mary's religious doubts turned into certainties.[3]

It is not surprising, then, that Sara would try a different approach. She opted for cooperation. But it did not work. Sara wanted to attend the University of Michigan too, but George indicated that he would pay tuition only for a Baptist college in Kalamazoo (today's Western Michigan University). This devastated Sara. She had faithfully attended church and never disobeyed him, but now her dream of a university education at the school of her choice had vanished in an instant. Sara cried herself to sleep the night she received his dictum and then decided to reject the orthodox Baptist school. Determined to get away from her father's home at all costs, Sara chose marriage to a Baptist minister instead.[4]

Just a few weeks after her father closed off Sara's hope for liberation through education, the Reverend Albert Ehrgott visited Detroit for a convention. He stayed with the Fields, who knew him from their days in Cincinnati. Ehrgott had black hair, piercing black eyes, and a black moustache. His voice filled the Field home with "basso profundo comments" and a deep stage laugh. It was the month of May. The spring air and light seemed to conspire as he quickly fell in love with Sara, now a lovely young woman of seventeen. One evening, after another in a long series of church meetings, the couple sat on the Fields' porch while the aroma of white wisteria wafted round their heads. Ehrgott told Sara his plan to resign from his pastorate in Springfield, Ohio, and take up one in Rangoon, Burma. To leave a secure position for life in a foreign land struck her as romantic and brave. He then asked Sara to join him as his missionary wife.[5]

Susceptible to the flattery that this man thought her capable of such a charge, she thrilled at the prospect of travel to an exotic destination. The romance of an older man's admiring gaze and the depression caused by her father's refusal to fund an education at the University of Michigan help explain Sara's willingness to accept Albert's proposal. Her parents suggested she marry Ehrgott after he returned from Burma. She refused to wait, and so they agreed to an immediate wedding.

To characterize this marriage as "rebellion" probably occurred to Sara only later. At the time, it must have seemed to all that she chose a most conventional life, one that would not only be sanctioned but enthusiastically applauded by her father. What could be more submissive than exchanging life in her father's home for one with Reverend Ehrgott, a man nineteen years older than Sara and who shared George's religious commitments and fundamental values? Crushed by her father's intransigence and feeling trapped, a youthful Sara thought release through marriage an acceptable form of escape.

Mary, however, believed her beloved younger sister unwittingly chose conventional domesticity and dependence over freedom. A few days before the wedding, Sara asked Mary what she thought was the greatest development of the last century. Her answer: "The realization that a woman has a soul, a personality and an individuality." Men and women working together, and outside the narrow confines of marriage, was the future. Sara's acceptance of the traditional role of wife and, eventually, mother seemed to Mary . . . well, a failure of character.[6] On September 12, 1900, just four months after they met and eleven days after Sara turned eighteen, the couple joined their lives. Mary stood up as maid of honor. Disappointed as she was over Sara's choice, she nevertheless loved her sister and would never boycott the event. The next day the newlyweds headed to Asia. As it turned out, Mary was right: Sara had exchanged one trap for another.

Ehrgott, born in Cincinnati in 1863, came from a musical and artistic family of German Bohemian ancestry. His father, a lithographer, died during Albert's boyhood. His oldest brother, Louis, worked as a leading vocal teacher in the Midwest. A second brother, Oscar, had a beautiful baritone voice and accompanied on piano well-known operatic contralto Madame Ernestine Schumann-Heink during her concert tours. In fact, the entire Ehrgott family, with one exception, made music, entertained guests, drank beer, and recited German poetry.

Albert was the exception. Lacking both artistic spirit and musical talent, he studied accounting at New York's University of Rochester and found employment in a glass and china firm. He then came under the influence of a young, magnetic minister who believed Albert would make a wonderful clergyman as well. After an intense conversion, Ehrgott leapt at this advice and attended New York's Rochester Theological Seminary. This led to family conflict. Albert no longer joined their parties and, more, he chastised his brothers for drinking beer, shocking and baffling them. Albert's mother asked Sara to convince Albert that drinking beer was acceptable and that his brothers remained good people, but the minister had taken on an entirely new frame of reference, new standards, and a new life and would not budge from his disapproval.[7]

Sara hardly knew the man to whom she had committed herself for life. She knew even less about sex. Her mother provided no prenuptial education, only thrusting into her daughter's hands the book *The Physical Life of Woman* as the young bride left on her honeymoon. The first night, on a boat trip from Detroit to Cleveland, Sara became sick. It petrified her to be alone with Albert, and he, no doubt sensing her fear, did not press for intimacy. The next night, however, they consummated the marriage. When Sara found herself bloody, she rushed to the bathroom and wept over how dreadful marriage had turned out to be. That initial abhorrence gradually passed as Sara learned more about the female body, sexuality, and the basic facts of procreation. She eventually discovered early married life had some pleasures. In one letter to her sister Alice she gushed, "I am just the happiest woman alive." Ehrgott, too, claimed to be "on the heights of matrimonial bliss," adding that they attributed their joy and love "supremely to our devotion to our Lord Jesus Christ."[8]

The couple threw themselves into preparations for Burma. As agents of the American Baptist Missionary Union, Albert and Sara visited churches to speak—or, Albert spoke and Sara demurely and silently accompanied him— about their plans and to presumably raise financial support. Then it was off to India, scheduled for a fall arrival in order to avoid the hot plunge of summer. Weeks on a cattle ship, the animals below and the people above, and the roughness of the swells doomed Sara to constant seasickness. A British couple that befriended Sara and Albert proved to be a saving grace. Mrs. Tilly, wife of the Official Collector of the Port of Burma, was a motherly figure, and she took Sara aside to ask if her sickness might be due to pregnancy. Sara thought that prospect impossible because she had only been married for six months. Mrs. Tilly assured her pregnancy could occur anytime after marriage. Ten months after their wedding, Sara gave birth to their first child.[9]

The Tillys hurried on to Rangoon while the Ehrgotts explored India. There, Sara's encounter with profound poverty became one of the great turning points in her life. In Calcutta and Bombay, she witnessed, for the first time, people literally starving in the streets while men loaded grain, rice, wheat, and tea onto ships for export. She came face-to-face with a colonial system that allowed wealthy British landowners to sell food overseas for profit while people of the land remained destitute. Up this point, the teenaged Sara had given little thought to her fellow man. Now, she was witnessing—up close—social injustice, the huge gap between wealthy and poor, and the indifference of the former to the latter. It shocked and upset her. Albert concurred about the wickedness of colonialism. When Sara expressed her indignation to others, including Englishmen and -women, however, they responded with anger: "This is the way life is and we don't discuss it." Mrs. Tilly unsatisfyingly responded that the poor will always be with us.[10]

Of course, their criticism of economic disparities did not stop Sara and Albert from taking some advantage. Their own tiny household of two included a staff of five: a cook, a housekeeper, a valet for Ehrgott, a water boy, and an errand boy—all at less than the cost of one servant in the United States. After their son's birth, they added a nurse to help with the baby. The Burmese did not seek employment in service jobs, according to Sara, so she and Albert hired Indians. Sara accepted the belief of many British colonials that white people could not engage in physical labor in Burma because of the heat and humidity, thus making domestic help imperative. Moreover, Sara claimed, servants lost respect for employers who did their own housework. In short, she quickly adapted to a class and labor system that privileged her. Even in later years she seemed unaware of the racist assumptions at work, noting that upon her return to the United States she had a difficult time finding maids as talented as her Indian household staff.[11] Yet, Sara's horror at social inequities was sincere, at least in her own mind, and it laid the foundation for a more sophisticated understanding of economic issues and the progressive, and even radical, political positions she eventually embraced back home.

Sara experienced two other awakenings in Burma that loomed increasingly large in her later life. She noted the difference in status and power between Indian women and Burmese women. While Indian women seemed submissive and subservient, never sitting down at the table with their husbands but rather serving them and then eating separately, Burmese women struck her as amazingly free and assertive. They not only managed their households, they took charge of economic affairs and businesses at the nation's bazaars. They shared equal status with their husbands—a sociological insight that impressed Sara as she began to experience her own stirrings of independent thought and appetite for equality. These ideas developed almost simultaneously with the first glimmerings of Sara's resistance to her husband's religious orthodoxy.

The Ehrgotts did not truly serve as missionaries. Their purpose was to minister to the already converted—the Eurasian Baptists of Rangoon—rather than to evangelize among the non-Christian Burmese. One Sunday the Tillys, members of the Church of England, came out of friendship to hear Albert preach. It happened to be a Sunday when he served communion. To Sara's horror, an usher informed the Tillys that as non-Baptists they could not take communion. Shocked and indignant, Sara quarreled with Albert over the incident—the first serious disagreement in their marriage. It stunned Albert that his young bride would react so strongly and, more importantly, challenge his view. Sara, who had sought baptism into religion out of girlish emotion rather than intellectual understanding of church doctrine, now began to doubt that doctrine. Realization of the church's fallibility broke upon her with traumatizing force.[12]

Sara's awakenings came through personal experiences, not through books or the academic education that had inspired Mary, and these new ways of thinking cut deep grooves in her emerging consciousness. Lessons in capitalism and colonialism, women's freedom, and religious orthodoxy provided the first cracks in Sara's heretofore unexamined worldview. Bright, open, eager to learn, and at a highly impressionable age, she felt things deeply. Never again would Sara assume she could live a life free from responsibility to other humans. She must reach out, help, take action. No longer would she meekly serve at her husband's side and unquestioningly accept his religious dogma. She would contest the parts she disagreed with. Finally, Sara began to understand that women as well as men could obtain freedom. In Burma, she later said, "I was sitting on a whole nest of eggs of experience," and when those eggs started to crack open, they startled her and frightened her off the nest. "I didn't go back to sit on them until they had hatched into full-fledged knowledge. That was to come much later, but it was the beginning."[13]

The birth of their son, Albert Field Ehrgott, on July 20, 1901, suddenly altered the Ehrgotts' plans for an extended stay in Asia. The baby's delivery proved complicated. The doctor in attendance, fearing the chloroform would give out before the baby emerged, used forceps, which did not harm the infant but wreaked havoc on Sara's body, tearing the perineum back into the sphincter muscle of the rectum, and damaging Sara's uterus as well. No one in Burma would undertake the necessary surgical repairs, and so the couple conceded that Albert's seven-year commitment to his Rangoon church would have to end prematurely. It upset Sara that her physical ailments harmed her husband's career. Albert did not hide his bitter disappointment, but there was no alternative to returning to the United States. After a nightmare trip by sea, with the added anxiety of an infant to care for, the couple arrived in Detroit.

Mary, teaching high school in Michigan at the time, came to the rescue. She rushed home for Christmas vacation to care for the baby while Sara underwent an hours-long operation. Meanwhile, Aunt Mary determined that Albert Field, who loved lights, would have a Christmas tree. Never before had the Field family decorated a tree, George considering it a pagan custom, but Mary flouted the rules of her father, who, by now, was a grandfather and wavering a bit on the custom. A tree they had. When Mary carried the baby into the room and he reached for the lights, Sara realized his delight made all the trouble worthwhile.[14]

Ehrgott meanwhile searched for employment. During summer 1902 he temporarily replaced a minister friend at a pastorate in Wallingford, Connecticut.

When that job ended, he enrolled in courses at Yale to brush up on his Hebrew and biblical exegesis. Wives of students could audit classes, and so Sara attended a nineteenth-century poetry class taught by English professor Robert Lounsbury. She found the poetry mesmerizing and reveled in the opportunity to simply *think*. Although Sara did not take the course for credit, she wanted to write and submit papers along with the regular students, and Lounsbury—a Browning specialist, a great lecturer, and a generous human being—agreed to evaluate them.

Sara's work impressed Lounsbury. Probably knowing her status as a minister's wife with little money, he asked her to read to him several afternoons a week for pay, as his eyesight had deteriorated. Although this relationship lasted only a short time, it left a deep imprint on Sara. Not the least of its dividends came when Lounsbury commented: "I have an idea you're a poet. Have you ever tried to find out?" Imagine the power of such a question, and coming from such an eminent person to one who saw herself as quite inconsequential. The simple encouragement of the Yale professor planted in Sara's mind the possibility of becoming a poet.[15]

The Yale sojourn ended when Albert received a call from a church in Cleveland. In 1903 that city was among the most politically progressive in the nation, although the Ehrgotts' church, located in a very poor neighborhood, was decidedly not progressive. Sara and Albert decided to address the social needs of the congregation anyway, establishing a free kindergarten and soup kitchen in the church. These efforts attracted the attention of progressive reformer and mayor Tom Johnson, who invited Sara to visit him in his office. He told her about his tent meetings, where people of all incomes and backgrounds could congregate and listen to lectures on social and economic justice. A disciple of Henry George and his book *The Single Tax*, Johnson brought the author to Cleveland to present his taxation system as a way to redistribute wealth in America. Sara attended. She also heard socialist Eugene V. Debs speak and took son Albert along. After his speech, Debs, mingling with the crowd, paused in front of Sara, put his hand on the boy's head, and said, "Young man, may you live to see these wrongs that I have talked about tonight righted." Such experiences quickly caught Sara up in progressive politics and thought. The books of George Herron, especially *The Social Meanings of Religious Experience*, particularly spoke to her. Herron criticized the church for supporting an evil economic system antagonistic to Jesus's teachings.

Sara shared these books with her husband. Impressed, Reverend Ehrgott became a Christian Socialist, too. Preaching this new gospel to his congregation, however, displeased the few wealthy members who kept the church economically afloat. They told him to stop, Albert refused, and so they fired him. Once again, Sara thought Albert terribly brave. Standing up for his socialist beliefs became perhaps the bravest thing he had ever done.

On other matters, though, the couple continued to drift further apart. These new social theories in no way altered what Sara saw as Albert's otherwise "fossilized" religious orthodoxy. One particular incident underscored this view. A wealthy young man seduced, impregnated, and then deserted a young girl from the congregation. Albert and others decided to expel the girl from the church for her moral failure, which outraged Sara. Albert's heartless position underscored Sara's growing belief that she and her husband no longer shared spirit, sympathy, and understanding. Meanwhile, Albert objected to her growing political activism. He thought she should confine it solely to the church. Sara, using her second pregnancy and the birth of daughter Katherine in April 1906 as an excuse, increasingly avoided church services altogether as she came to realize she had married into the wrong profession . . . and the wrong man.[16]

Soon, Albert had found employment in yet another church and the family was headed to Portland. Before they left, however, Sara made one more important contact in the Midwest: Clarence Darrow. Her sister Mary made the introduction. Mary had moved to Chicago to work in a settlement house. She met and worked for Jane Addams but felt Addams saw her as "too saucy and irreverent," so Mary moved on. As Director of Girls Clubs at the Chicago Common Residence, Mary witnessed firsthand real poverty, not unlike Sara's experience in India. Mary had studied socialism in college and heard Debs speak about it, but until that point she had dismissed it as utopian and unrealistic. Now, she became convinced socialism offered the best chance for a remedy. She gravitated increasingly toward the intellectuals and radicals swirling around Chicago. In that context, wealthy friend and social worker Helen Todd introduced Mary Field to Clarence Darrow. By 1908 Mary and Darrow had became lovers.[17]

It is not clear if Sara understood, at least initially, the full nature of her sister's relationship with the famous lawyer. When Sara met Darrow, they talked at great length about labor, social welfare, and other liberal causes. It astonished him that a Baptist minister's wife shared his point of view, let alone engaged in leftwing activities. They became firm friends, and he visited her in Cleveland when there on legal business. He found the Ehrgotts' marriage strange, Mary later told Erskine. They were ill suited, since Sara was a broad thinker and Albert was not. Darrow doubted their marriage would last.[18]

In 1910, the family packed up for Portland. Sara confessed to Darrow her fears that the city lacked Cleveland's progressive spirit and would prove a desolate setting for the likes of her. He promised her, "There is one man out there that I think you will like, and you'll surely meet him." He was, Darrow explained, a liberal thinker—a philosophical anarchist with many gifts: painting, poetry, and lawyering. That man was Erskine Wood.[19]

Three

THE AFFAIR BEGINS

In 1910, Portland—tucked into the confluence of the Willamette and Columbia Rivers, and ever green under the rain-saturated clouds that frequent the Northwest—bustled. October can be dreary, though, as hours of daylight shorten and inches of rainfall rise, and the inclination to turn inward and join friends in cozy places such as the Hofbrau, where the bohemian set met, deepens. That is where Clarence Darrow hosted the Ehrgotts and Erskine Wood on an evening that put into play events that would upend the lives of most of those assembled there.

It surprised Sara that no "Mrs. Wood" joined them. Instead, Erskine brought his private secretary, Kitty Beck. Darrow made sure he seated Sara next to Erskine.

She was just barely twenty-eight, attractive but not beautiful, honest, unpretentious, intelligent, and serious-minded. Erskine probably noticed her brown eyes and slender frame.

In return, Sara found him instantly and absolutely captivating. Erskine was fifty-eight, striking, a presence. Wherever he went, people turned around to look at him. They assumed he was a person of some creative distinction, perhaps a musician, painter, or poet, as he had the flair and personal style of an artist. Some of this was calculated, some of it a simple fact that the man was handsome and confident in the power of his attractions. He had a beard, a beautiful complexion, curly gray hair, and the "kindest eagle blue-gray eyes" Sara had ever seen. In retrospect, poor Albert never had a chance.[1]

Hungry for conversation of substance, Sara had been a stranger in a strange land for months. Cut off from the excitement and purpose of midwestern progressivism, and far from the stimulation of Yale, she grabbed this opportunity to connect with the first really thoughtful people she had met since moving to the West. In fact, she took the initiative, launching into a discussion about modern literature by asking Erskine if he had read H. G. Wells's new book, *Ann Veronica*, which advocated greater freedom for women.

No, Wood admitted, he had not. He rarely had time for reading beyond that required for his law practice. When he did take the time, Erskine said with a smile, he read poetry. Way back in Cleveland, Sara now remembered, Darrow had told her Wood was a poet.

As dinner ended, Darrow suggested the entire group retire to Wood's private office so Darrow could read one of British writer John Galsworthy's short stories aloud to them. Sara wanted to go, but her husband could not, as he had another engagement. Understanding the importance of this evening to his young wife, however, Ehrgott amiably encouraged Sara to join the rest. So all except Albert trooped over to Erskine's place.

The room astounded Sara. Exquisite Oriental rugs, expensive English furniture, and many lovely art objects set the space apart from anything she had ever seen. She immediately grasped something about Erskine: he insisted on surrounding himself with sumptuous beauty in the places he inhabited for his personal and artistic life. He would not tolerate ugliness. His law office could be all business and spare, but the place where he worked on what mattered most—this room of his own—had to be splendid, sparing no expense to decorate it. This was where he wrote poetry and his true self surfaced. As Darrow read the Galsworthy story, Sara only partly listened. Instead, she drank in the surroundings and watched Erskine, who nodded in appreciation of the story. This beautiful man fit perfectly within his gorgeous surroundings.

A few hours later Ehrgott fetched Sara. At that moment, her delight turned to despair. The magic of the evening evaporated as she realized, taking Albert's arm, that she had glimpsed a life that would never be hers. She had peered in and even stepped over the threshold for a few hours, but that was all. In her heart she believed these were the people with whom she belonged—spiritually and intellectually—not with Albert and his congregation. She also knew implicitly she was not Darrow's and Wood's economic or social equal. A deep chasm separated her from these dazzling men. That insight left her feeling utterly alone. To have entered briefly this sanctum of artistic and cerebral life only underscored the poverty of her own existence.

It was not about the things in the room, or the money that provided them, but the sensibilities, warmth, richness of feeling and thought. She loved the evening and believed Erskine a "great man." She wanted to return but doubted its likelihood. After months of intellectual and aesthetic deprivation in Portland, and sensing a growing, gnawing apprehension that she was not meant to be a minister's wife, it was heartbreaking to experience such fullness and simultaneously realize it was unattainable. It was not love at first sight for Erskine that caused her pain; it was understanding that his way of living represented the kind of substance and depth she wanted but that lay beyond her reach.[2]

Several months passed, during which the evening certainly loomed larger for Sara than for Erskine. He did not contact the Ehrgotts, and it did not occur to Sara to contact Erskine until Darrow wrote asking about the friendship. Encouraged that Erskine might accept an invitation to meet again, Sara hesitantly called and invited him to dinner. Well aware that it could be a recipe for disaster to combine her husband's religious orthodoxy and Erskine's iconoclasm and well-known radicalism, she warned her visitor about Ehrgott's views, presenting the potential for conflict as a way out.

Erskine nevertheless accepted. He arrived, again without his wife, on the Ehrgotts' modest doorstep with a box of candy for the children and a generous spirit that led him, an epicure, to praise the badly burned roast beef. To make matters worse, the post-dinner conversation turned to religion. Erskine angered Ehrgott by challenging Christ's divinity. Why not present Jesus as a great and marvelous teacher but also human—just like us? he said. Why deify him and thus set him apart? Indignant, Albert took the bait. A great argument ensued and, Sara concluded, "Well, that was that."[3]

Surprisingly, however, it was not. Sara and Erskine next crossed paths when Darrow returned to Portland, this time in the employ of the liquor industry, to present a lecture against Oregon's consideration of a prohibition law. Albert favored prohibition and did not attend, but Sara opposed it, believing prohibition would simply encourage bootlegging and violence. She had been reading about the Scandinavian experiment of state-sponsored and -regulated liquor sales and found that system the better option. To her delight, Darrow mentioned the approach in his lecture. Afterward, when Erskine discovered that Sara already knew about the Scandinavian system, it impressed him.

Gradually, Sara came into his focus as a woman of intellectual depth matched with a commitment to liberal, even radical politics. She was not like any other woman he knew. Erskine then invited the Ehrgotts to his home for dinner. Once again, Nanny Wood was not present, and Erskine's younger daughter, Lisa, cohosted the evening. After the meal, Albert stayed at the table with the other guests while Erskine took Sara on a tour of his den. He showed her his collection of beautiful objects, including terra-cotta Tanagra figurines from ancient Greece, opalescent mortuary glass, and rare books. But when he picked up one particular book to read to her, it was a new one: a treatise on free love.

What was behind that choice? Possibly Darrow had alerted Erskine to Sara's increasingly unsatisfactory marriage, or maybe Erskine simply sensed the growing gap between minister and wife. To an inveterate womanizer who never let marital status get in the way of potential seduction, perhaps the book was his opening salvo. Maybe he saw Sara as a kindred soul, unhappy in marriage and yearning for freedom. Or perhaps the issue simply mattered to him as a concept and Sara seemed as good an audience as any.

Whatever the motive, it deeply affected Sara. The book's author argued that love was not something one could honestly promise for a lifetime. If and when love dissipated, it made no sense to maintain the marriage for the sake of the children. Staying together out of duty destroyed homes, and it was also unnecessary when it was possible for the mother and father to live apart and yet share the children. As Erskine read, Sara realized he was describing her situation perfectly. She knew the growing, "almost violent" differences between Ehrgott and herself poisoned their home, and she believed sustaining the marriage for the sake of their offspring would become increasingly untenable. It seemed remarkable to Sara that Erskine chose a book that so astutely addressed her troubles and offered a resolution to her problems.[4]

This revelation came at a time when Sara was increasingly shaking off the received wisdom of father and husband and replacing it with ideas of her own. She did not do this impulsively but as a result of reading widely and carefully contemplating the issues. In the process, she gravitated toward radical positions on a range of matters from socialism to sex. Ehrgott, meanwhile, questioned nothing. Although sympathetic to socialism and women's suffrage, he remained steadfastly, conventionally conservative, especially when it came to religion. Sara realized they now stood "continents and worlds apart." They could never reattach.

The implications frightened her. She would have to find a way to support herself, to be an independent person. But how? And what about her children, nine-year-old Albert and four-year-old Katherine? Sara loved them as much as any mother loved her children, and hoped that if she obtained autonomy, they would benefit as well. In seeking personal liberation, Sara believed she was not selfish but rather preparing a better life for a son and daughter who could be raised in an atmosphere of liberal ideas. She should not have to sacrifice her role as mother to live fully. That was the very message Erskine shared with her in his study. A mother—even one with a growing mind and a radical bent—had a right to raise her children in freedom.

At first, Sara kept these thoughts to herself; only rarely did she engage her husband in debates about controversial topics. One evening over dinner, though, she defended the out-of-wedlock relationships of the British poet Percy Bysshe Shelley, philosopher and feminist Mary Wollstonecraft, and novelist George Eliot. Alarmed, Albert angrily feared she was becoming a heathen. This was not the woman he had married. Sara replied that he was not the man she thought she had married either. Such conversations, however, did not alert Ehrgott to the realization that his marriage was in trouble. He had no idea Sara considered leaving him, nor did he imagine Erskine could be party to such an outcome. In fact, as the internal stress took its toll on Sara and she lost weight, Albert reached out to help the wife he loved. Perhaps some intellectual work would help her, a bright, intelligent woman who needed stimulation and a purpose beyond the roles of wife and mother. And so, unwittingly, he turned to Erskine. He knew Sara admired him, and he innocently thought encouraging their interaction would satisfy her yearnings.

In early 1911 Reverend Ehrgott stopped by Erskine's office to see if he could help Sara find work. Erskine agreed to try to secure writing assignments for her with the magazine *Pacific Monthly* and Portland's daily *Oregonian* newspaper. In the meantime, he would hire her to edit his poetry. To Albert, this seemed the perfect arrangement: Sara would earn money for the family while exercising her poetic skills; Wood would obtain a sympathetic and talented editor; and Ehrgott would restore peace to his household. Everyone wins. The potential pitfalls never occurred to him.[5]

At first glimpse, Sara offered little to Erskine. She had no experience as a writer or editor. The gap between their literary accomplishments replicated the other disparities between them. Erskine had published in some of the nation's most prestigious periodicals and regularly contributed to the *Pacific Monthly*. A chest full of his poetry awaited editing and possible publication. Erskine's literary connections—not only on the Pacific coast and in the East, stemming from his days at West Point and Columbia Law School—brought him into contact with some of the most talented poets, painters, and writers, a hub of bohemian activity. He resided and made his living in Portland, but the place neither defined nor contained him.

Sara, on the other hand, had been to Burma, briefly, and spent some heady days in New Haven and Cleveland, but those experiences had led to little beyond personal discontent about her life. She demonstrated ambition—without which she would not have sought out Professor Lounsbury's poetry course at Yale or engaged with progressive mayor Tom Johnson in Cleveland—but she did little with that energy. The Lounsbury relationship produced no manuscripts, let alone published poetry, and her political actions remained linked primarily to her husband's church. That Erskine believed her capable of providing useful editing advice seems a stretch. That Sara believed herself capable of providing it was equally unlikely. Yet, Sara displayed confidence in her poetic sensibilities and literary judgment. Professor Lounsbury's encouragement had certainly reinforced this self-assessment. Besides, Erskine had no one else in Portland to help him. He felt isolated in his creative work. *Pacific Monthly* and the political periodical *Liberty* published his work but offered no editorial guidance. This young woman, who began her very first conversation with him by pronouncing judgments on contemporary literature, seemed a breath of fresh air. Why not give her a try? She might have exactly what he needed: a critical eye matched with a sympathetic soul. So, Erskine handed over a collection of his sonnets, titled *Maia*, and waited to see what Sara would do with its themes of free love and living with, rather than in opposition to, nature.

Sara thought the verses had potential but found them monotonous, repetitious, and lacking a larger narrative trajectory. They needed pruning and rearranging. She boldly suggested Erskine create a greater sense of story. That pleased him. He appreciated her honesty and took heart in her conviction that out of the sonnets' random poetic sentiments something solid could be shaped. He delighted in this person who took his poetry seriously and believed in him. He had self-confidence in spades and a healthy ego, but he saw no harm in a little additional burnishing.[6]

Poetry, then, provided the foundation of their relationship, but what was initially a simple matter of employment for Sara quickly became much more. Both revered poetry, seeing it as the most refined human expression that addressed the most vital aspects of life. To them, poetry mattered more than anything, and certainly more than politics. So, Sara threw herself into the work, convinced that, with her editing help, Erskine's poetry could compare to the best verse in America. It also provided a useful and unique way to carve out a place for herself in Erskine's life. No one else in Portland seemed interested in, or capable of, serving as his editor. Poetry provided them both a close friendship and a professional partnership.

If Albert hoped the editing work would relieve the family of some of its financial woes, Sara of her depression, and his marriage of its strife, he miscalculated. The unhappily married Sara now found herself not only in the inner sanctum of Erskine's opulent private office but in intimate contact with his profoundest thoughts and yearnings. She might not be his social or economic equal, but she was something more important: a potential soul mate. Erskine provided Sara a conduit to the world of ideas, both poetic and political, that better fit her growing sense of self. This remarkable man listened to her and trusted her judgment. He validated the person she was becoming. He encouraged her to think anew and be independent. In turn, Sara was lovely, something the womanizing Erskine certainly appreciated, but not *just* lovely. This woman linked physical attractiveness with mental acuity, intelligence, literary taste, and imagination. Those qualities made her unique and undeniably desirable.

For the first few months of their collaboration, their growing mutual attraction remained unacknowledged and unspoken. Erskine's wife, Nanny Wood, though, took note and feared it. She realized that her husband would find Sara's combination of attributes irresistible and he would not deny himself the pleasures of a sexual relationship if the opportunity arose. One day while working at the Wood home with Erskine, Sara was standing close to him when Nanny unexpectedly entered the room with some guests. Seeing her husband and Sara together, Nanny fell into a swoon and fainted. As her friends gathered around to offer help, Nanny said about Sara, "Don't let that woman in, put her out."[7]

Even as she was enjoying her work with Erskine, Sara continued to lose weight and remained distracted, distant, and unhappy when at home. Ehrgott undoubtedly noticed, and Erskine, too, observed that Sara seemed troubled. So he broached the subject of her health, fearing she suffered from tuberculosis but could not afford medical help. He offered to pay for an examination and X-rays, to which Sara replied, "No, I don't think I have tuberculosis. I'm troubled about my home life and how any departure from it, breaking up the marriage . . . , would affect the children." Then, unable to contain her feelings any longer, she confessed, "I'm in love with you," and began to cry. Erskine rose from his chair and responded, "Well, I would never have dared to tell you this . . . under the circumstances of our life, but I know that I have never found a companion like you, and I love you." And so it was out. Sara later claimed that this moment, when they mutually confessed their love, initiated "a matter so vital that we were willing to make almost any sacrifice on earth to establish a life together."[8] Actually, that is doubtful. The likelihood that Erskine, at this early juncture, envisioned this nascent love affair becoming a lifetime commitment was slight. While Sara lost no time in expressing her hope for that very thing, Erskine remained considerably more guarded and cautious.

Sara now found herself in totally new emotional and psychic territory. She opened herself completely to Erskine without hesitation, discretion, or, possibly, good judgment. She had never experienced love like this before nor been so intensely connected to a handsome, accomplished, wealthy man. Adoration came pouring out. At times she seemed out of control, over the top, adolescent-like in her enthusiasm although nearly thirty years old.

Erskine, on the other hand, had had many lovers. Sara was alluring, but Erskine was not likely to sacrifice everything—including not just his wife and family but any other women he was seeing on the side—for her. Undoubtedly he had told other women he loved them, and he probably meant it, at least in the moment, but those words did not signal eternal commitment for him. The nature and depth of Sara's and Erskine's affections, then, diverged: hers were boundless, while his were circumscribed, cloaked more in philosophical principle than emotional connection. Moreover, Sara's claim of a mutual willingness to sacrifice all for a life together preceded consummation of the affair. A man of Wood's appetites and inclinations would not have made such a commitment to a woman he had not yet taken to bed.

By June 1911, however, they had become lovers, and Sara's emotional attachment, already near fever pitch, deepened. They made love in the sanctum of Wood's private office. As Sara described it in her overwrought prose, "Then indeed did the Gates of Life swing open and my soul . . . Oh! The sublime glory of it sweeps over me as I write." The contrast with her marital lovemaking was profound. The sensual, sensitive, much experienced Erskine introduced her to pleasures she had never known. Now, added to all the other attributes he displayed, and that Sara hungered for, came the most intimate physical joining of their bodies to match the joining of their souls. After the first occasion of lovemaking, Erskine left her to attend a meeting and Sara lay a long time in the darkness unable to move, conscious of only one thing: "He loves me, we have met." She finally collected herself, "as in a dream," found the streetcar home, and went to bed. All night she repeated the words: "He loves me, we have met." She, of course, revealed none of this to her husband.[9]

The outpouring of passion and ardor in her letters to Erskine was so extreme during this period that it is a wonder he did not flee in a panic from her. She worshipped him, her Ideal Man, and did not hesitate to tell him so. "You are all men's goodness melted into one with none of their badness," she wrote. She never imagined one man could be a poet, prophet, and perfect lover. Sara hoped she did not weary him by "my constant emptying of the box of adoration at your feet!," but she could not help herself. She loved him beyond "fear of death, or ambition of life" or, she tellingly added, "beyond my children." She called him "my universal, my God, my All-in-All." She began christening him with nicknames such as Poet Man, Poet Prophet, and Poet Lover, and she gladly accepted his name for her, Sappho, after the Archaic Greek poetess, not realizing he had bestowed the same name on other women before her.[10]

Sara's early letters, often written in Erskine's private office and left for him to read before he went to bed, revealed Sara's ambition not only for her lover's poetic productivity but for the life she intended to make with him.

Bold, aggressive, and single-minded, Sara asserted herself into his present and his future. She found what she most wanted and doggedly pursued it without regard for her marriage, let alone his. In this heightened state of infatuation, Sara could think only of the two of them.

She made sure, however, to emphasize what *she* offered *him*. He needed time to write and someone to inspire and oversee his work; she carved out a place for herself by urging him to devote more time to his creative work, with her help. She understood his unrealized dreams and ambitions and assured him it was not too late to achieve them. Shrewdly, Sara was not above playing on Erskine's anxieties about dying before he had realized his artistic potential. "The cold fact is time is pursuing, relentlessly, insistently," she warned. Look at Goethe, Sara advised. He did some fine work after sixty, but not much. Erskine must prioritize writing now, with Sara as indispensible editor, or forever forfeit the possibility of success.[11] She compared their relationship to that of poet Elizabeth Barrett Browning and writer Robert Browning, musing on how sweet it would be to not only work but live together. Daily companionship would strengthen, not dissipate, their love.

Sara fantasized about living with Erskine in a small cottage far enough from the city to have privacy and peace for work, yet close enough to visit interesting people and attend lectures for intellectual stimulation. They would devote days to literary work and evenings to friends engaged in invigorating conversation. All of it, of course, revolved around Erskine's personality and poetry. "Now does that appeal to you, Mr. Poet-Man? How do you know that we may not see it realized some day?"[12]

Sara also made clear her desire to conceive a child with Erskine. By August, barely two months into the affair, she regretted that she was not yet pregnant. Describing their child in most remarkable terms, she wrote: "He will come—the new little Christ-Child with your face and your soul to make atonement for the sins of humanity." She added, "We will conceive him in such a love heat as will fire his soul." On another occasion she offered a more secular justification, in keeping with Erskine's attraction to Darwinism and eugenics, by claiming science and ethics demanded they have a baby, for their child would be a combination of their best selves and a monument to a love greater than literature.

To express her longing to bear Erskine's child by deifying Erskine himself was a strange approach to take with a man who doubted Christ's divinity, but to reach for such language came as second nature to Sara. Quite simply, Erskine had replaced her religion—odd, she admitted, but appropriate because everyone yearned to connect their souls with an Infinite Being greater than themselves. Few found perfect love with another human, so they "stretch out hungry hands to a mythical God or a long dead, unsubstantial Christ." Sara, however, had found the perfect man in Oregon and needed no other.[13]

Erskine tried to dampen her adulation, enthusiasm, and expectations. He did not reciprocate with equally effusive declarations of love but instead cautioned her, more than once, that he might not love her very long. He repeatedly reminded her of the transient nature of love, and he ignored the issue of having a child with her. Sara shoved his warnings aside, claiming that if a few months of joy turned out to be all they had together, it was worth it, particularly if it resulted in Erskine's published poetry. She did not imagine that she had "hooked [him] with nonforgeable [*sic*] chains." All she cared about was "the blessed heavenly now," the exhilarating intoxication of their complete harmony and the thrill of being together.[14]

Sara nevertheless did beg Erskine for one thing: a real love letter with the emotional intensity and devotion she was constantly offering him.[15] Erskine did write her a letter, but he showed greater interest in philosophizing about and justifying free love than in singing a particular lover's praises. He did not deify Sara or empty a "box of adoration" at her feet. As she noticed, he hardly mentioned her at all. Only after much metaphysical rambling did he turn briefly to his "mad longing" for Sara, for the thrill of her body, and for her "dear sweet flesh . . . lighted by the spark from [her] sympathetic soul." It was something, at least, but it was not the passionate declaration Sara wanted. Mostly the letter summarized the intellectual context of their affair.[16]

When he did turn to Sara, Erskine acknowledged what she gave him: understanding and stimulation. True, they shared "almost hysterically ecstatic nights," and he promised she was "first in his heart." He simultaneously made clear he would not acknowledge these things openly, however, because it would hurt another woman. (Sara probably thought he was referring to his wife.) Although blameless for a love that came "without excuse, apology, reason or pity," he said that loving Sara meant lying and hurting others, and so their affair must remain secret. Deception was the lesser evil to desertion.

Free love, Sara should have realized, meant the opposite of exclusivity to Erskine. He would not cut off ties with other lovers. He unambiguously told her this, and cautioned against any expectation that she would ever be his sole lover. He did not operate that way. Her dream of a cottage together appealed, but Erskine explained that he would not easily or quickly extricate himself from entanglements with, and responsibilities for, others, although he wished he could, like Faust, be remade and "young again for you." Erskine acknowledged that she was buried deeply within him and hoped their affair would not turn into "just the common place tragedy."[17] But he made no promises for the future. Meanwhile, such warnings made not a dent in Sara's devotion.

She did, however, occasionally express unease about hurting and lying to her husband, even as she went through normal routines to evade suspicion. When Albert begged her to attend church one morning, she agreed to the "unpleasant mockery." It seemed a small favor to render in light of the coming pain she intended to inflict. Weary and bored by the service, Sara passed the time daydreaming about Erskine. Housework and cooking, which now fell to her as they relied on a minister's sparse salary, frustrated her more than ever. Meals now consisted of one or two simple courses, using as few plates as possible, to reduce the need to wash them. She would no longer allow "a brainless society to dictate [her] habits and rob [her] of life's real food." The children barely merited mention, appearing only once in her early missives to Erskine.

Sara did, though, confide in Mary about the affair. Her sister expressed concern not about its moral implications but about her fear Sara was losing her self, her "personality," in a mad rush toward Erskine. To this, Sara claimed that in Erskine she had finally *found* herself. She did not subordinate her talents for his benefit but joined them together to make not only art but life itself.[18] Still, at times, she sounded exactly like a woman who had lost sense of her self in her insatiable hunger to be near Erskine. Even Sara once acknowledged the difference in the intensity of their love, telling Erskine that with his "man's makeup and [his] *full* life," she represented only a small niche in his complicated world. She expressed scorn over her endless yearning. Then she fell back on Erskine's ideas (derived from reading about evolution) that personality was biologically determined rather than a matter of choice, and it could not be altered: "I am as I am, that I love as I love . . . . So don't be disgusted with my woman's heart which has conquered even my intellect, but tell me you understand."[19]

Sara had much to gain if she could extract him from his other entanglements. She also had much to lose. In throwing herself at Erskine, she had no guarantee he would catch her. His reputation as a womanizer, and his clear admonition that he would not forsake other lovers, would give most women pause. And even if he agreed to her terms, she—as a wife who left an upstanding husband, and a minster no less, for a married man—would find little support in Portland or elsewhere. Most would sympathize with Reverend Ehrgott and Nanny Wood, and Sara would face social ostracism. Further, adulterous women had little legal standing. Sara risked losing her children, as very few judges or courts would grant custody to the cheating spouse over the righteous one. Lastly, Sara had no money of her own. Although she believed in her literary skills, she had no experience writing for pay or any evidence she could succeed as a writer. The economic risk, if Wood turned away from her, was sizeable.

He, on the other hand, risked little. His long-suffering wife had already proven she would not leave him over his dalliances with other women, nor would he lose his children. They might disapprove of his choices, but they would not stop loving him. His reputation in Portland as a notorious womanizer also did not threaten his social standing or economic position; had that been the case, both would have been sacrificed long before. Erskine's work and wealth remained secure. The only thing he risked was causing pain to others if he chose Sara alone. And that, he told her, he would not do.

If Sara seemed aggressive, brazen, and selfish in building a relationship with Erskine, she also demonstrated courage. She found herself living in an emotional vortex during the early fall of 1911 but decided to continue on this course because she felt she must. Her life, up to this point, had reflected the values, interests, and desires of others. Now she made the first moves in choosing the life she wanted for herself. Prior to moving to Portland, she had taken the occasional baby steps toward self-assertion, yet because they didn't measurably alter her circumstances, they left her unhappy and unfulfilled. Her decision to marry had only entrapped her. Her pursuits of a literary education and political activism had left her bereft when she was forced to follow her husband and move to a new city. When she met and fell in love with Erskine, he was to be sure yet one more father figure, but with a difference: He opened the door to an alternative existence—one of self-realization, poetry, love, and sexual expression. Sara determined to walk through this door and knew that, once she did, there would be no turning back.

One September day she rode a streetcar across a bridge and then later turned the moment into a metaphor, finding it "typical of my own life position at present—about to pass over from dependence, captivity, conventional modes into independence, freedom and unconventional expression of self! Will my bridge break? Will I have courage to go from the known to the unknown? A man can scarcely realize what a leap it is for a long housed woman!"[20] In the meantime, her first step on that path to freedom depended on finding work and a wage. For now, at least, Erskine helped smooth the way.

Four

TRIALS

ALMOST ONE YEAR TO THE DAY AFTER SARA AND ERSKINE FIRST MET, A SMALL band including Sara's family and Wood's secretary, Kitty Beck, accompanied the couple down to the Columbia River. There, Sara boarded the steamer *Rose City*. Her destination: Los Angeles. It was a perfect autumn day for a journey by sea, with gentle winds blowing in from the southwest. In taking this voyage, she did more than travel; she embarked on a new career—or, at least, that was the hope. Erskine, in his role as patron, had secured an opportunity for Sara to write about the sensational McNamara trial for the *Oregon Daily Journal*.

Sara and Erskine harbored several secrets that day, the biggest, of course, being their affair. They also planned the trip as a test of Sara's readiness for liberation. Proving she could make a living as a journalist would be the next step toward ending her marriage. Albert and their children, of course, had no inkling. Only Kitty knew everything, and she could be counted on for discretion.

As the steamer pulled away, Sara focused not on husband, son, or daughter but on "a man in gray—a Poet-Man whose eyes have searched my soul and into whose keeping I have placed myself, body and soul." On the dock, Albert Field watched his departing mother so intently that he claimed he could see her waving a handkerchief even as the ship nearly faded from sight. Then the farewell party sauntered down to Washington Street, little Katherine at the fore, refusing to be led.

Erskine walked alongside Ehrgott, who confided that he wanted to quit the ministry and find employment as a teacher. He hoped to throw off the fetters of church life and exercise greater control over his time and activities. Erskine empathized with the man's desire for freedom. He also mused on the pain Ehrgott would face when Sara revealed she no longer loved him and wanted to leave him. Eventually, Erskine predicted, men and women will "give the beloved one freedom it shrinks from taking," although Nanny had not yet evolved to that point and he doubted Albert had either. For now, the oblivious Reverend Ehrgott announced that Sara would be homesick, particularly for her family.

Erskine, Kitty, and the Ehrgotts stopped at Coffman's for ice cream. Katherine began to cry, not because her mother had left but because the adults had "invaded her freedom" by ordering without asking if she wanted ice cream or ladyfingers. Erskine characteristically solved the problem by providing both. Afterward, Ehrgott collected his children and went on his way, a moment Erskine captured in a drawing of the reverend leading two goats and carrying a shepherd's crook.[1]

––––––––––

The McNamara trial pitted against each other two of the largest forces of early twentieth-century America: big business and labor. Workers demanded the right to unionize in order to advance and protect their interests, and businesses, determined to protect their profits, fought unions using whatever tools they had at hand, including espionage and violence. Some workers returned the violence. By the turn of the century the nation seemed entrenched in warfare between capital and labor.

On October 1, 1910, that violence reached Los Angeles. James B. McNamara, an unemployed printer and the brother of John J. McNamara, treasurer of the International Association of Bridge and Structural Iron Workers Union, planted a bomb in the alley behind the *Los Angeles Times* Building. It exploded at one o'clock in the morning, with over one hundred employees working inside. The initial blast ignited gas and barrels of flammable ink, setting off a huge conflagration that enveloped the structure and it occupants. Twenty-one people died, incinerated on the spot. Others escaped the horrific inferno only to die soon after.

Retired general Harrison Gray Otis, owner of the newspaper, immediately suspected the labor movement was behind the bombing. He hated unions and had led the charge against them in Los Angeles. Although he had once been a union printer himself, military service in the Civil War and the Spanish-American War, along with his entrepreneurial experiences, had transformed him into a staunch supporter of the open shop. Otis skewered socialists, Democrats, and liberal Republicans with heightened—and some would say scurrilous—rhetoric. He stocked his newsroom with rifles and shotguns in anticipation of attack.

On the union side of the conflict, Bay Area residents Olaf Tveitmoe, of the Building Trades Council, and Anton Johannsen, a Chicago labor leader and friend of Clarence Darrow, organized a General Campaign Strike Committee to take on Otis's and other nonunion shops in Southern California. Their tactics included picketing, attacking nonunion workers, and bombing nonunion job sites.

Industry-paid detectives and Los Angeles police, catching a little luck as well as the bombers' mistakes, soon uncovered the involvement of the International Association of Bridge and Structural Iron Workers. A disgruntled informant from within that union then led police to Chicago, where they found James McNamara in the company of Ortie McManigal, who was carrying a suitcase of dynamite. The pair was on their way to the next bombing. At the same time, authorities in Indianapolis seized John McNamara at the ironworkers' union headquarters. An accommodating judge provided an illegal extradition order to ship him to Los Angeles, outraging labor supporters, who saw the move as kidnapping an innocent bystander.

Labor leaders believed no one could better defend the McNamaras than the celebrated Clarence Darrow. In 1907, he had secured an acquittal for William Dudley "Big Bill" Haywood, leader of the Western Federation of Miners and later founder of the Industrial Workers of the World, who was on trial for his alleged role in the assassination of former Idaho governor Frank Steunenberg. The huge victory burnished Darrow's reputation as a champion of labor. Although he harbored misgivings about the McNamaras, Darrow took their case.[2]

The fierce conflict between capital and labor captured everyone's attention, and journalists covered it all. It was, in fact, something of a golden age for journalism, when writers such as Ida Tarbell, William Allen White, Ray Stannard Baker, and Lincoln Steffens proved almost as famous as the robber barons, labor leaders, and politicians they covered. Moreover, women made significant inroads in the field, Sara's sister Mary among them. Mary, on her way to cover the McNamara trial for the *American Magazine*, suggested Sara join her in Los Angeles. The invitation offered Sara respite from her stifling marriage and a chance to test herself as a writer.[3] Erskine, seeing the trial as a path toward Sara's independence, encouraged friends at the *Oregon Daily Journal* to hire her as a special correspondent. The editor would not have engaged a total novice without input from someone who knew and would vouch for her, and thus Erskine's intervention (and probable financial support in covering her expenses on the trip) was critical in helping Sara snare the assignment.[4]

Sara's first taste of freedom proved intoxicating. She sat on the deck at night watching the stars "silently take their place in the heaven," and she remembered it as a glorious experience overall, except for the men and women who spent the voyage drinking and smoking instead of passing the time as Sara did: gazing at the tireless ocean, reading books, and talking with fellow passengers about substantive issues, including women's emancipation and suffrage.

One man in particular found Sara captivating. The ship's telegraph operator, an Irishman with one arm, overheard her debating suffrage and returning arguments as quickly as her opponents delivered their "senseless objections." He listened but said nothing. Later, he invited Sara to learn about the ship's wireless system. In the midst of conversation about telegraphs, he suddenly stopped and blurted out that she was "the most interesting little lady ever came on board and I'm dead in love with you." She quickly informed him she was married with two children, which settled him down. Ehrgott would have had a fit if he learned of this interaction, but Sara told Erskine, certain he would enjoy the story. She also wanted him to know that other men found her attractive and he risked losing her if they remained apart for long.[5]

Otherwise, Sara left little doubt Erskine was the only man for her. As distance between them grew, she longed for him and the freedom that would allow them "with our rare love [to] face the world as fearlessly as I face these stars." Erskine had provided her with some reading material for the journey: Shakespeare, Elizabeth Barrett Browning's *Sonnets from the Portuguese*, and a few of his own verses that, he told her, she had inspired. She loved them because she knew "the hidden meaning of each line—the precious memory that every flight immortalizes." They fueled her yearning to have him near so they could enjoy days of comradeship and "nights, ah! The nights—a rapture of closeness . . . . I'd like to have us free to go into one of those little rooms together and alone and—well, would *you* want an upper berth while I had a lower or vice versa or would one narrow, low bed do for two? I'd be willing to be your berth and then you would have an *upper* berth after all," she added, with a dash of ribald humor reflecting her newly discovered sexuality.

Back in 419, Erskine's private office, he only briefly touched on the sensual in his letters. Sara's "flavor" lingered where her body had lain, but he missed her more because she interested him, brought new thoughts, stimulated him intellectually. He missed her because her soul "mated" his. True, he found her "so responsive, so tremulous" that he would "like to crush [her] sensitive body out of all existence, till we were one—and dropped so into eternity." Yet he preferred not to write of passion in "cold ink." Instead, they should "reserve the sparks of soul contact till we can give and receive them in all spiritual force." Then, he turned to the issue of Sara's poor spelling and urged her to send any dispatches to him before passing them along to her *Journal* editor.[6]

Once in Los Angeles, Sara found many things to distract her from her obsession with Erskine. The McNamara trial loomed. So too did the more immediate "trial" posed by sister Mary and her lover, Clarence Darrow. Watching them up close provided Sara with an intimate view of another couple's experience in free love. Its highs and lows could have served as a cautionary tale about love outside of marriage, but Sara did not see it that way. Darrow, she believed, was no Erskine, and Mary's relationship with him bore no resemblance to the rare, pure, spiritual love Sara shared with Wood.

Initially, Darrow discouraged Mary from coming to Los Angeles, claiming her presence would either "expose or divert" him. Under public scrutiny, he would not be able to spend time with her. Mary ignored the warning, however, and soon after he arrived in Southern California, he "summoned" her, as Sara put it.[7] Three years before, thirty-year-old Mary had met fifty-one-year-old, married Darrow and fallen for him, hard. True, Darrow had none of Erskine's refinement or apparent outward attractions. He often appeared in rumpled, baggy clothes, and his face featured a prominent, almost bulbous nose. Yet he had undeniable appeal. Darrow was smart, witty, compassionate, creative, charismatic, and a famous advocate for workers, the powerless, and the poor. Over the course of his flamboyant career, he took on big business, fundamentalist Christians (in the Scopes trial and other cases), and proponents of the death penalty (most notably in the Leopold and Loeb murder case).

When Mary met Darrow he had also established a reputation as a rake and a rascal, particularly among Chicago's "new women," who gravitated to progressive causes and found employment in social work and journalism. Many of these professionally ambitious, intelligent, and self-reliant women proved susceptible to Darrow's charms, and some pursued free-love relationships with him based on sexual and emotional compatibility and equality. They rejected marriage as a necessary prerequisite to intimacy, while Darrow enjoyed the chase and loved the sex. Others, however, may have hoped for more, and still others may have been less willing partners. Darrow could be boorish and aggressive, as Sara learned, and quite possibly not all of his targets successfully fended off his unwanted advances. Divorced from his first wife, Jessie, in 1897 he married a journalist named Ruby Hammerstrom in 1903. Ruby understood Darrow would never be faithful, but he promised no one would ever usurp her standing as his legal wife.[8]

Mary met Darrow when he spoke at a 1908 political rally to support his client, the exiled revolutionary Christian Rudovitz, who faced extradition to Russia. Darrow's address, with its deep empathy and electric intelligence, impressed Mary, but it did not leave her speechless. When her friend Helen Todd introduced them, Mary and Darrow fell into rapid-fire repartee. Darrow told Mary he preferred journalists to social workers (her current occupation) but he imagined she could string words together fairly well. She replied that she preferred radical poets to old-fashioned lawyers. Delighted, Darrow assured her that within every lawyer she would find "a wrecked poet." Mary thought he looked "more wrecked and poetic than any attorney she had ever seen." He laughed heartily, and before long they became lovers.[9]

Darrow publicly squired Mary around Chicago and, at least on one occasion, hosted his mistress and his wife at the same dinner. At one point that evening, Darrow pronounced Mary the most clever woman he had ever met. Ruby turned to Mary and said, "You're the thousandeth!" When Mary seemed merely amused by Ruby's reaction, the latter angrily added, "No, you're maybe the thousandth-and-first woman he told that to." That Darrow allowed, let alone created, such a social encounter between wife and mistress seemed unnecessary, insensitive, and cruel to both women. Mary, however, had entered the relationship knowing Darrow had committed to never leaving his wife, and she accepted those terms. Ruby's terms: she suffered his dalliances in exchange for a secure, though hardly happy, marriage.

And yet that did not make the experience painless for either of the women. The many days and nights Mary spent alone, and her gradual realization of the ephemeral nature of the relationship with Darrow, took their toll. Her life might sound "gay," she told Sara, but the reality was otherwise. Sometimes she experienced flashes of futility and even "the longing to end it all under the cool twinkling waves or to sleep forever with the drug that eternally soothes." The problem? "It's having no one who cares a damn, no one interested *personally*." It was "the sudden and blinding realization that my life meant nothing to any one in particular."[10]

Still, the relationship was not merely a fling, nor did Darrow exploit her with the intention of hastily discarding her in favor of another. He respected Mary and took genuine interest in her talents. He helped her, as he had his other lovers, both professionally and financially as she moved from social work to journalism. Notably, Darrow provided her with a letter of introduction to the famous novelist Theodore Dreiser and later financed Mary's move to New York City, where she began to publish short stories in *The Delineator*, a magazine for which Dreiser was an editor. The writer mentored her while Darrow encouraged from afar. Mary thrived. She had found her niche. By the summer of 1910, her "talent, social concern, the desire to be of some use in the world and the wistful little itch for admiration and possibly even fame, all work[ed] together smoothly and flourish[ed] in the sunlight of editorial receptivity," her daughter later remembered. Magazines clamored for her work, including the leading muckraker journals of the day—*McClure's*, the *American Magazine*, and *Everybody's Magazine*. She championed labor and immigrants, while getting paid for it.

Her new work also offered opportunities to befriend fascinating and sometimes wealthy radicals. In July 1910 socialist Ida Rauh, the wife of writer and editor Max Eastman, hosted Mary at Provincetown, Massachusetts, which was fast becoming a haunt of the Greenwich Village literati, all radical and bohemian types. A warm, affectionate, rich, and generous woman, Rauh presented Mary with a stylish sailor suit "much as if she were sticking a one cent stamp on a letter." Although Mary proudly celebrated earning her own money, including her first literary paycheck of $150—she did not hesitate to accept cash and other gifts from Darrow or Rauh.

Riding high, Mary hoped to write a piece for *McClure's* on anarchist Emma Goldman. Theodore Dreiser promised he would "make [her] literaturely" and gave her enough work to stay financially solvent, for a time. Writing for a living was invariably precarious, she told Sara, but "the books, the talks, the meetings, the mental world is open to you, and though I sometimes starve for the more material things, still there is a great deal of joy in the beautiful things that are written and painted, and dreamed of." What she most aspired to achieve was the power to move peoples' hearts by writing a socially useful and beautiful novel.

Midsummer 1910, Darrow wrote Mary an affectionate note of congratulations: "I watch you on your road up . . . . You have gone so far I can't see you any more . . . . We will have to stop praising you pretty soon or you will lose your head." He ended with, "Damn if I wouldn't like to see you Molly dear— Ever C.D."[11] Just a few months later, Mary alerted her younger sister about Darrow's impending visit to Portland and encouraged her to meet with him. Sara's prospects for self-realization and success were at a low point. Be sure to see Darrow, Mary repeated to Sara, to talk about your future. Mary knew he would help.[12] Now, a little over one year later, as the McNamara trial geared up, all three congregated in California. Darrow *had* helped Sara by introducing her to Erskine. Erskine *had* helped her get this journalism job. Now it was up to her to make something of the opportunity.

Soon after Sara arrived at the tiny apartment in Los Angeles where the sisters shared a Murphy bed, Darrow invited them to dinner at a fashionable restaurant. His earlier misgivings about Mary's presence vanished, and Mary soaked in the pleasure of the moment. As Darrow walked the sisters home, he draped his arms around both. Uncomfortable, Sara dropped her handkerchief and, after picking it up, remained beyond his reach. Mary brushed off the half-embrace of her sister as harmless "boyishness." Sara believed it too familiar.

A few days later he came to their apartment, and Sara left them alone for several hours of sexual intimacy. When she returned, Darrow followed her into the tiny kitchen, where he hugged her "like an old grizzly to my unspeakable discomfort." Sara shrugged him off, indicating her unavailability. On another occasion, she visited his office for an interview and he locked the door behind her and attempted to seduce her. She later reported to Erskine, "You, who have made love to Sappho at furnace heat, have no idea what it is to try it on her when she's at refrigerator temperature!! I wonder if he ever had quite such a freeze out." She walked to the door, unlocked it, and, telling him she would interview him on another occasion, left. Offended by these passes but not wanting to alienate Darrow entirely, Sara tried to focus on his affection for her sister and the confidence he gave Mary, which "put her into the groove of victory."[13]

But other things bothered her. Darrow could be lively and gregarious yet also temperamental, depressed, and unpleasant. He exhibited dramatic mood swings in very short periods of time.[14] Sara found his supposed disdain for women's suffrage and emancipation upsetting. He told Sara, in jest, that he opposed women's suffrage on biological grounds and teased her that the issue, on the California ballot that fall, might fail. Actually, Darrow, a longtime advocate of women's rights, had publicly advocated women's suffrage as early as the 1880s, but on this issue, Sara proved humorless.[15]

Sara also disapproved of Mary and her friends' propensity to drink and smoke cigarettes. Her distaste, in turn, annoyed Mary, who thought Sara's attitude spoiled the lively fellowship her journalism, labor, and lawyer companions shared. Darrow's indelicate commentary about Sara's relationship with Erskine, however, was the thing that bothered Sara most. When Darrow asked about Erskine, she evaded answering. The lawyer then smiled a "slow, insinuating smile and said, 'Oh hell, Sara. You don't have to lie to me. I'd be ashamed of Wood if he didn't think everything of you[,] and more ashamed of you, if you didn't think the same of him.'" Preferring not to lie, and also not wanting him to know she understood his meaning, Sara quickly changed the subject. Inwardly, though, she seethed at his coarseness, "insinuat[ing] about matters that every instinct ought to teach him are sacred and fine—and for him to do so on absolutely no foundation is too vulgar for words!" Sara could forgive

Darrow his dirty fingernails but never his "soiled actions."

That Darrow brought into the open something she tried to keep hidden unnerved her. In addition, it suggested—to her horror—that her hallowed relationship with Erskine was not so rare, ideal, or different from Darrow's relationship with Mary and other women. Both lawyers and married men, Wood and Darrow advocated free love and shared reputations as renowned philanderers who preferred much younger women. They both also served as generous patrons to the Field sisters. However, differences existed: Mary was single; Sara, a married woman with children. Darrow and Mary carried on their affair in a comparatively public and honest way, while Erskine and Sara kept theirs hidden, championing "truth" in their correspondence but practicing deception daily. In the face of much evidence, Sara refused to acknowledge any parallels between the couples, insisting her relationship with Erskine was "sacred" while Mary and Darrow's lacked refinement and spiritual depth.

Wood responded to Sara's missives about the Darrow/Mary saga with uncharacteristic venom directed at the attorney. In a thirty-page letter written in his signature green ink, Erskine pronounced Darrow a vain, selfish, avaricious man who reveled in the attentions he received from his swarm of idolizing admirers. He did not respect women. "He only cares for a woman as a hot water bag—mental or physical." Darrow would use Mary only as long as she paid him adequate tribute. If she stopped, Darrow would "turn her off like a dog." And that, of course, would be the eventual outcome anyway, because "a woman's body is nothing more to Darrow than to a sultan—a delicious morsel to be taken everywhere found and forgotten. A woman's mind is nothing to him except that the adoration of a brainy woman is more subtle flattery. But he'd take flattery from a chorus girl." When his appetite for Mary waned, he would drop her.[16]

Wood then turned to his friend's professional life. Darrow took the McNamara case, Wood said, not to fight for justice but to gain personal glory and profit, although admittedly "in this he is like . . . most of us lawyers." Darrow was known to have resorted to unscrupulous practices including bribery, perjury, and intimidation to win cases. His confession that the McNamaras were "guilty as hell" particularly rankled Erskine. An attorney should never betray a client's confidence or confession. Finally, if Darrow truly believed in labor's cause, he would encourage workers to repudiate violence. By taking this case, he encouraged bloodshed and "the poor generations to come will reap the whirlwind . . . . He *knows* it." Sara should keep her distance from both Darrow and Mary, Erskine warned. Avoid their influence. Escape their moral tyranny, browbeating, smoking, and drinking—adding that Mary (whom he had never met) was addicted to both cigarettes and alcohol. Sara should not tell Mary anything she would not want Darrow to know. Just as Darrow had not kept his clients' confidence, Mary would not keep Sara's.[17]

Wood's advice about steering clear of Mary proved difficult to follow. The sisters shared a rock-solid connection. True, Mary tried to shape Sara's thinking about the trial, which Sara resented, and yet they still enjoyed each other's company. They had long talks about books, ideas, "universal themes," and, undoubtedly, men. Still, Sara tried to follow Erskine's advice and not tell all.[18] The anger and bitterness at the core of Erskine's depiction of Darrow, however, unnerved Sara, in part because she had fed him the details that elicited the outburst. It would certainly have surprised Darrow, who saw Wood as a friendly colleague, having invited him to join the McNamara defense team. Erskine turned him down, claiming participation would hurt his law firm's business, although the real reason, he confided to Sara, was Darrow's willingness to use illegal tactics. But that does not explain the unusual vehemence here. Possibly Erskine envied Darrow's fame and success and coveted the Chicago attorney's access to big cases and their consequent big fees. Maybe he feared comparisons of himself to Darrow on another level, knowing the two men were not as distinctive in personal conduct as Sara believed.

On the matter of free love and Darrow's insinuations about Sara's extramarital relationship, however, Erskine defended Darrow. True, Darrow could be coarse and impertinent, but he did not realize it, and he would likely be surprised to learn she thought this of him. Further, he knew that Darrow would not judge Erskine and Sara's affair, and so Sara need not lie to him about it. Where Darrow failed, Erskine explained, was not seeing "that in the most perfect state of freedom these things will be even holier than now and nobody's business."[19] At this point, Sara backpedaled, and she focused again on Darrow's redeeming qualities, which included his admiration of Erskine's poetry. She remembered him reading Erskine's sonnets aloud one evening, with great feeling and understanding, and noting, "There's a great man for you." Darrow could not be totally villainous if he recognized the "superlative expression" of Erskine's life and literary work.[20]

————————

For all the diversion Mary and Darrow's affair provided, Sara devoted most of her time and effort in Los Angeles to the purpose at hand: conveying the flavor and feel of the McNamara trial. A complete novice in journalism and the law, Sara often found herself confused by the court proceedings. She felt unfit to do justice to the story, unable to adequately express what she witnessed. As other reporters blithely dashed off stories, she envied that skill even as she strived to create more meaningful, less superficial pieces. Sara saw herself as an astute observer and remained hopeful she could learn to communicate her impressions with verve and depth.

The trial's first order of business, selecting a jury, unfortunately did not lend itself to riveting reporting. Clearly sympathetic to the defense, Sara sensed that the prosecution preferred nonprogressive, unreflective men—an opinion Erskine encouraged her to keep to herself. She must report objectively, without favoring one side or the other. Sara's greatest challenge remained finding a narrative hook or compelling human-interest story to elucidate this stage of the trial. One potential juror offered a possible prospect. Wearing a seedy-looking black suit, he quietly awaited his turn for the lawyers' questions. When later asked about capital punishment, however, he rose up and announced that, as a Quaker, he opposed it. After his dismissal, possibly on that response, he walked out of the courtroom "with his face lighted as if by a blaze of revolt." Sara had to restrain herself from jumping up and shaking his hand. Her mother's family had been Quakers, an affiliation Sara was proud of and frankly preferred to her Baptist upbringing.[21]

What thrilled her most was working in a man's world. Mary and Sara, the only female reporters covering the trial, were pleased to find that most of their male colleagues accepted them. Some could be condescending, but many others were helpful. Earl Harding, of the *New York World*, believed Sara needed someone to look after her. So, he provided guidance and an occasional dinner. Sara seemed less offended than amused. She told her husband that

Harding took an interest in her "newspaper talent," but she did not reveal his interest in her as a woman. At the end of the trial, Harding returned all personal notes she had written to him; sensing she was having second thoughts about their friendship, he did not want her to worry about it becoming public and misunderstood. Harding treasured the letters as the "essence of a sweet comradeship," adding, "dear sweet good little woman, I love you—love you tenderly and dearly."[22] Of course, she informed Erskine about Harding.

Women reporters clearly labored under distinct disadvantages, and Sara and Mary were not immune. Male journalists lived together, attended smokers, and mingled freely with sources who shared valuable information in hotel lobbies and saloons. Meanwhile, Sara and Mary boarded away from it all, and convention and modesty barred them from the same access to sources. Still, Sara reveled in the trial experience, which was so much more expansive than the "woman's world" she had known. She delighted in "the deep current of the world's doing; I love to get the influence, the swells if you please, from the big men, the ships in mid stream. It is exhilarating to me. I hate dishes and sewing and everything but my beloved babies." This brush with a world outside home and family electrified her.[23]

Her peak moment of professional acceptance came on a late October evening when nationally acclaimed journalist Lincoln Steffens invited Mary and Sara to a lecture he was presenting on the future of journalism. About 150 attended the event, including all the out-of-town journalists covering the McNamara trial. Sara and Mary were the only women who received invitations. After Steffens's speech, Darrow addressed the crowd, and then the chairman asked Sara to say a few words about women and journalism. That Sara received the impromptu call to speak, rather than the much more experienced and deserving Mary, is puzzling. But Sara, taken by surprise and not a practiced orator, steeled herself to say a few words. Her remarks, hardly revolutionary, underscored a traditional view of women: Female journalists amplified men's work, she explained, because they had a "peculiar psychology" that offered color, theories, and interpretations that men missed. They related facts to "the ideal"; they "spiritualize[d] fact," reflecting their emotional approach to life. One wonders what the more worldly, cynical Mary thought of all this. Sara, meanwhile, believed she had made "a hit with the men," who admired her bravery in speaking at all. Steffens told her she struck the right, new tone in journalism—"that is relating *fact* to the *ideal* which is *art*."[24]

Erskine commented on neither Sara's newest admirers nor her exhilaration at the taste of freedom and the thrill of working in a man's world. Instead, he critiqued her writing. Since he had recommended her to the *Journal*, Erskine wanted to make sure she turned in acceptable work. His own reputation was at stake, so he insisted she send her dispatches to him first, allegedly to correct her spelling. Erskine proved a rough critic, and his comments ranged from close editorial correction to more substantive advice regarding content. He pronounced her first effort a "scramble" and offered six pages of corrections and advice. After an overwhelmingly negative letter, though, Erskine encouragingly lauded the essay's "substance" and "philosophy." She had successfully captured the "flavor of the drama."[25]

A few days later, Erskine hand-delivered the heavily revised manuscript to the newspaper. It appeared in the next day's issue, and he mailed a copy to Sara. Erskine did not claim to have "made" her, as Darrow had made Mary, but he had played a role and believed in her, and this published article vindicated those feelings. Erskine reacted more positively to Sara's next dispatch, announcing she had treated the situation exactly right. Given this positive reaction, it then surprised him when, ten days later, the editor had yet to publish it. Erskine advised Sara to contact the editor to ask why and also to propose a series of dispatches that would be published on a regular basis. He further urged Sara to send her one published piece to other newspaper editors who might print it. She should write something for the *Pacific Monthly*, too. Persist, he encouraged, even if he turned out to be her only fan and patron.[26]

In the end, the *Oregon Daily Journal* published six of Sara's articles. Her writing, initially stiff and formal, eventually loosened up. Beyond descriptions of events and people, Sara made asides that offered a woman's perspective on the court, including her observation that "nerves are not an affliction of women alone." She worked at evocative imagery, writing of Darrow: "The constant activity of his brain finds a match in the ceaseless motion of his huge body. He is never still a moment . . . . When interrupted by the prosecution . . . he shrugs his great shoulders impatiently, shakes himself like a Newfoundland dog coming out of the water and smiles a sarcastic smile." She also noted social issues, such as the class distinctions found in the jailhouse. Prisoners who could afford the $5 weekly charge, such as the McNamaras, ate meals on white table linens and nice plates, while the rest ate in their dingy cells.[27]

Sara's biggest break came when she scored the first interview with Ortie McManigal, the union saboteur and coconspirator who had turned state's evidence against the McNamara brothers. In return for his damning testimony, the state promised freedom and a job, and the steel industry awarded him an additional, sizeable sum of money. He lost, however, his family. McManigal's wife and uncle tried to dissuade him from testifying, but he held his course and so they repudiated him. Sara painted a fairly sympathetic portrait of McManigal, emphasizing his hard life, which included poverty and the death of his mother when he was a child. She urged readers to consider those factors before judging him.[28]

The *Journal*'s editor thought it the best dispatch yet and placed it on the front page. Ehrgott agreed, but Sara dismissed the piece as pure sensationalism, lacking literary merit or introspection. It reinforced her growing fear that she had no talent for journalism. She concluded she had produced nothing of value and hoped her newspaper work would become mere preparation for magazine work, an outlet with greater regard for literary expression. No one knew better than she, "with [her] ideals resting on the spikes of stars and trailing into moons and suns, that [she had] flown very close to the ground" in these journalistic ventures.[29]

Sara's foray into journalism and experiment in freedom came to an unexpected halt in early December 1911, when the McNamara brothers changed their plea from innocent to guilty. From the start, Darrow knew the defense would be tricky. The state had overwhelming evidence against his clients, but he took the case nonetheless, because—regardless of what Erskine might have said about the lawyer's questionable personal motives—he believed in labor's larger cause. He was certain big business corrupted the state and that together these forces colluded to destroy the rights of workers. Darrow wanted to weaken that partnership. Further, labor leaders had pressured him to represent the McNamaras and promised to provide the $300,000 Darrow insisted he required to mount an adequate defense. He said only $50,000 of that total would count toward his personal fee. In debt because of bad investments, Darrow needed the money. He had accepted the job for worthy enough reasons, but once in Los Angeles, he soon became convinced that the brothers would not only be convicted but would hang. He deployed intermediaries to see if prosecutors might be receptive to a plea deal.

Nothing came of this plan until Lincoln Steffens arrived in town, not to cover the trial but to write about the reasons labor had turned to violence. Learning from Darrow that the case against the McNamaras was solid, Steffens then determined to help save their lives. An opportunity arose with the surprising success of the Socialist candidate's victory in the Los Angeles mayoral primary. Steffens and Darrow knew that Otis and the other civic leaders who supported the prosecution feared a Socialist victory in local government even more than they desired revenge for the bombing, and thus this shifting political situation unbolted the door to a deal. Darrow's plan then became to trade two guilty pleas for lesser sentences, and in turn the prosecution would benefit from the consequent blow to the labor movement while severely damaging the Socialists' chances for victory in the mayor's race. The prosecutor required both men to admit guilt—James to the *Los Angeles Times* Building bombing and John to ordering the 1910 bombing of the Llewellyn Iron Works. In return, their lives would be spared and the state would not prosecute any of the California labor leaders who might have eventually been implicated in the case. The brothers took the deal. John received a sentence of fifteen years behind bars, James got life in prison, and the Socialist candidate lost the mayoral election.

This turn of events stunned many labor leaders. Some censured Darrow for engineering the plea deal. They wanted him to stick to the principles he set out to defend at the beginning of the trail, even if it meant the brothers were sentenced to death. At least they would have become martyrs to the greater cause. Darrow told a *Los Angeles Times* reporter, "I did the best I could. I am very tired, worn and sorrowful . . . . I hope I saved a human life out of the wreckage." Even then, however, Darrow emerged from the trial facing more than disapproval from the labor community. Besides the fierce antipathy directed toward him from the group he once sought to support and defend, he now faced indictment for bribing a member of the jury. The man's world, Sara was suddenly learning, could be down and dirty.[30]

The trial over, Sara's sojourn in Los Angeles, which lasted about two months, also came to a swift end. During her final evening there, her mood darkened. She now thought the world a "sorry place." Her experiment in freedom certainly had its high points, but it also proved troubled, flawed, imperfect. Life in the midst of labor wars and legal battles fell far short of her idealistic expectations. That the McNamara trial ended in a nest of deception, betrayal, ill will, treachery, and possible criminality was bad enough. It also dashed her hope for a Socialist electoral victory and the change it would bring to the people. Paralleling all this, Sara now marked Mary's love for Darrow as "hopeless" and "heart-rending." It was blemished, sad. While still insisting Mary's affair differed greatly from her own, doubts about free love wormed their way in . . . even if they remained unstated and suppressed.

With the great adventure over, Sara headed back to Portland—not to a life of openness and freedom with Erskine but to one of dishonesty with Ehrgott. Just at the moment she longed to turn toward Erskine, she would have to return to "prison" with her husband.[31] One more concern weighed heavily on Sara as she packed her bags and headed north. Erskine had recently revealed the presence of another lover in his life. Her perfect Poet-Man had proved imperfect, after all. Sara learned that he had deceived not only his wife but Sara, too. Sara was not his only illicit lover; his life was even more complicated than she had been willing to admit. Even *their* love fell short of ideal.

Five

TRIBULATIONS

SARA DREADED THE RETURN TO PORTLAND. REPORTING ON THE McNAMARA trial and tasting freedom from home and husband had confirmed her conviction that she must leave Ehrgott and make a new life for herself. Turning conviction into practice would be arduous and painful. Every aspect of Sara's plan demonstrated a radical departure not only from her past but from formidable societal norms—challenge enough. It also entailed a number of specific obstacles. First, Erskine had not yet committed to breaking his family ties, and her power to force his hand was limited. Then Sara learned Erskine had another mistress whom he did not want to put aside. Most difficult, Sara had yet to inform her husband of her plan. She dreaded causing him heartbreak. She also knew he would fiercely fight against divorce.

To date, Ehrgott had generously supported Sara's efforts to reshape her life in new ways. While she tested her writing talent in Los Angeles for two months, Ehrgott managed job and home, church and children, without her help, a remarkable sacrifice for a husband to make in that era. Married middle-class women with professional husbands rarely worked outside the home, and married middle-class mothers of young children who also had their own careers were even more exceptional. Single or widowed women made up the vast majority of women in the workforce, laboring out of economic necessity rather than self-fulfillment. The reverend's support of his wife's venture into journalism, then, had been incredibly bighearted.

Albert offered it without complaint and only rarely hinted that he needed her help—reminding her once, for example, that she had promised to make five pounds of candy for a church fundraiser. From Los Angeles, Sara replied that he should find someone else, adding with a touch of condescension, "The issues of my life are too big to mourn over a sale when others . . . can make candy." Hobnobbing with Clarence Darrow and Lincoln Steffens while chronicling a nationally significant trial and redefining yourself turned out to be exhilarating; church bake sales and children's everyday needs paled in comparison.[1]

Ehrgott backed Sara's ambitions for several reasons. Although religiously conservative, he supported progressive political positions, including women's suffrage, socialism, and a woman's right and ability to work outside the home. He also encouraged Sara's personal growth—every bit as much as Erskine— but lacked the lawyer's deep pockets with which to stake her in the journalism gambit. Ehrgott took pride in her abilities and achievements, and he hoped this work would satisfy her intellectually and emotionally and that these things, in turn, would strengthen their marriage. He believed his wife when, in California, she expressed longing for their children and love for him. Not being privy to her passion for Erskine, he did not realize the difference between her burning lust for the lawyer and the lukewarm notes of affection she sent her "dear old brave Preacher-Man."[2]

The prospect of enhancing the family's meager coffers through Sara's writing also appealed. She justified her 1911 trip to Southern California, and arguments to prolong it once there, precisely on that basis. Sara left home less to realize her own ambitions, she told her husband, than to help the family financially. If she could syndicate some of her articles nationally she would gain the "vision of disappearing debts and wrinkles of care from blessed Preacher-Man." To that end, Sara sent off a flurry of letters to newspapers, offering her articles. Unfortunately, no takers materialized. Still, she told her husband, "All this I write with but one thing in view—*our financial situation.*"[3]

Indeed, the couple was experiencing money troubles as the bank pressured Ehrgott for payments on their debt. Sara urged him to fend them off but said that, if all else failed, he should "go to dear Mr. Wood" for a loan—a remarkable and frankly inappropriate suggestion given the secret love affair. Earlier in 1911 Erskine had encouraged her to let him know if the family was "in a tight fix." He would help. Ehrgott eventually followed Sara's advice, borrowing money from Wood. In one promissory note, Albert addressed Erskine as "my dear true friend" and ended with "Let my much love and esteem flow to you." Sara surely realized the unseemliness of her husband borrowing money from her lover, and she knew that when Albert eventually discovered her true relation with Erskine, his humiliation would be almost unbearable. She proposed it nevertheless, and then quickly turned away from its distasteful aspect, lashing out at "horrid $ $ $—the ever necessary." She longed for the day when socialism triumphed, people shared everything, and earning a living was no longer a "feverich [*sic*] fight, an insane struggle, but [instead] an assured platform upon which men rise to gaze at the stars."[4]

Although dishonest about her relationship with Erskine and her motives for going to Los Angeles in the first place, Sara did not conceal from her husband her enthusiasm over working outside the home and discovering the new person she was becoming, finally "in the groove," doing something right for herself. Sara claimed she did not completely understand the physical and mental transformations under way, yet she welcomed them. The only downside: they would likely bring "misery and pain to others," an oblique reference to her long-range plans. For now, Sara assured Albert, even as women found employment in the public world, home would always remain the center of their lives. Freedom for women had one great purpose: to make them better mothers. "Always [their] supreme mission [is to] bear and rear a noble race of noble sons." If he had any trepidation, these declarations probably had a calming effect on Ehrgott. They did not, of course, reflect Sara's true motivations. In fact, her letters home seemed designed to mask her actual ambitions and intentions. Focus on family finances and the responsibilities of motherhood did not reveal what she secretly held in her heart.

Sara did, though, genuinely appreciate her husband's willingness to "make it possible." It distressed her that he had to take their children along on his ministerial rounds and that he found his job unsatisfying. She hoped he would find release from it. His cooperation also deepened Sara's guilt over her deceit, and she went so far as to tell Ehrgott she wished she was "a different sort of a woman—more worthy of your unselfish love and stalwart devotion," these words now coming closer to an honest confession of her true feelings and future plans. He was "a dear, dear man," Sara told him, with a "great soul."[5] Such expressions of affection and respect, however, could not hold twenty-nine-year-old Sara to a man for whom she felt no passion, particularly after she discovered such pleasures and fulfillments with another. The "great river of [her] passionate love ben[t] its course" solely to Erskine and no one else. She wanted only to lose herself in it.

To that end, while in Los Angeles, Sara relentlessly pressed Erskine to join her while simultaneously discouraging a visit from Ehrgott, who trotted out the idea of lecturing there. Sara thought a Christian Socialist organization might fund him and promised to look into it, but she never did.[6] Erskine, meanwhile, did not scurry down. Only in late November 1911, as part of a trip to San Francisco on business, did he finally come to Los Angeles, where, one splendid evening, Erskine, Darrow, Steffens, Mary, and Sara dined together. "I wish you were here," Sara disingenuously wrote Ehrgott.

Mary and Darrow respected the couple's wish to keep the affair secret, and Mary approved of the romance, noting that Sara and Erskine brightened the atmosphere of any room they shared and seemed in perfect harmony; "I think I never saw two people who had as much subconscious understanding between them as you two." She also understood the inherent difficulties Sara faced in loving him. As Erskine departed, Mary accompanied the couple to the train station and then walked home with Sara, "caressing [her with] an understanding silence."[7]

During Sara's two-month California sojourn, she rarely mentioned her children. She missed them, but she missed Erskine more. "Perhaps that is inhuman and I ought to be ashamed, but I am not," she confessed to Erskine while continuing her campaign to carry his child. He consistently ignored the issue until she indicated she had a secret to share with him, at which point Erskine bluntly replied that he hoped she was not "in any delicate situation because that at once precipitates matters for which you are not prepared." Sara replied that the secret was a matter related to the trial, not her health or a pregnancy. Erskine probably heaved a sigh of relief. Sara must have found his response disappointing.[8]

———————

It was soon after this that Sara discovered Erskine had a secret of his own. Erskine and his private secretary had remained lovers throughout his relationship with Sara, but Sara had been unaware of it (or perhaps just in denial). It is difficult to know how much Sara knew about the history of Kitty Beck's relationship with Erskine. While Erskine's philandering was common knowledge in Portland, and Sara undoubtedly heard such gossip, and while she may have known Kitty and Erskine had been lovers in the past, she assumed (or chose to believe) that once her affair with Erskine began, he put other women aside.

That her perfect lover would sustain intimacy with several women simultaneously was unthinkable to Sara. She was beginning to learn that Erskine's definition of free love diverged a bit from hers. Both agreed that love and sexual intimacy did not require sanction of church or state, but on matters of monogamy and sexual exclusivity they disagreed.

Everything came out into the open in late November, then, when Kitty Beck and a Dr. Lloyd Irvine arrived in San Francisco right on Erskine's heels. Kitty surprised Wood, who was there on legal business, by announcing she intended to marry Irvine immediately. This precipitated a crisis. Erskine, having little experience with women ending their love affairs with him, felt abandoned. That Erskine had another, concurrent lover blindsided Sara, and she struggled to get the right footing, sound the right notes, reassure a suddenly insecure Erskine, and find a way to strengthen her own position with him. Sara viewed his distress not as a troubling weakness but as an opportunity.

For ten years Kitty had worked closely with Erskine, becoming his lover and building her life around him. Now, Irvine wanted to marry her. Kitty told Erskine she preferred having both men, in full free-love fashion, but Irvine found the idea scandalous and rejected it. The doctor could be jealous, selfish, and arbitrary. Kitty dreaded "marriage slavery" and hurting Erskine, and although she considered suicide, she ultimately chose marriage instead, a fate not quite worse than death. Kitty's sister Emily, or "Sissy," who also worked in Erskine's law office, offered an alternative explanation for the sudden wedding plans. Kitty realized Sara had eclipsed her position with Erskine; his visit to Los Angeles confirmed for her that Erskine had found a "truer mate," so she in turn found a new companion.

Kitty's decision to break off her affair with Erskine pained him "to the core," he told Sara, who was in Los Angeles and with whom he shared every detail of the drama through lengthy letters. He became convinced Irvine's sexual attractiveness explained Kitty's decision to pull "away from me, her idol." Admittedly, the sex between lawyer and secretary had never been "powerful." His kindness to her and the "bright youthfulness" she brought him, rather than physical passion, were the things that had held them together. Now, he felt like "a monarch who sees his Kingdom invaded," a remarkable metaphor for a man who disdained marital ownership of women and the privileges of feudalism.

He did not, however, attempt to dissuade Kitty from her decision or promise to give up Sara, outcomes Kitty may have wanted to provoke. Instead, Erskine told her to marry Irvine if she did so joyfully. She could always return to him if the marriage soured. He advised the secretary to obtain Irvine's written promise to free her without question or reproach should she ever ask for a divorce. Then, he invited Kitty and her fiancé to dine with him the next night.[9] Over what must have been an incredibly awkward and uncomfortable meal at the St. Francis Hotel, Erskine agreed the marriage would succeed only if Kitty felt no divided allegiance. Irvine seemed pleased and Erskine gave his blessing, in fatherlike fashion. As he watched the couple leave, however, he felt "desolation." He would lose daily contact with a person to whom he felt closer than any member of his own family.

Kitty and Irvine hurriedly wed in a San Francisco judge's chambers and afterward stopped by Erskine's room. Kitty fluttered around him as he finished dressing and surreptitiously left him a note. He did not mind secrecy, hypocrisy, or lying when necessary, but it hurt him to see the instant transformation marriage now required of the formerly free Kitty. "I feel it a badge of slavery and degradation," he told Sara.[10]

In the days that followed, Erskine obsessed over Kitty's supposed desertion. Clearly he was most bothered by the role sex played in Kitty's decision. When Kitty mentioned she and Erskine might someday renew their intimacy, he now replied he could never share a lover with another man—a puzzling position from a man who had engaged in a series of adulterous affairs with married women. But, Erskine explained, he did so only when the wife no longer loved her husband and no longer shared her body with him. He would never take Kitty back as a lover.[11] Free love had its limits. Erskine expected lovers to be faithful to him, and he would not rekindle former flames, particularly if the woman had initiated their breakup. Within a day or two, however, he was vacillating. Certain Kitty's marriage would fail and she might commit suicide if that happened, Erskine decided he must maintain an open door for her.[12]

By indicating that sex had played an important role in her choice to marry Irvine, Kitty played upon Wood's growing doubts about his own virility. She must have known this was a sensitive point. Irvine's prowess as a lover may have been simple fact or perhaps a weapon Kitty selected to wound Erskine, who worried about the effect of aging on his sexual performance. Erskine once told Sara their love was not "right" because he was "old" and declining in "those sex powers which burn you up and mean so much as well they ought." Sara hastily moved to dampen such concerns: "You are fresh and sweet as dewy moon itself; you have all the sparkle of the noon day sun, and yet the calm rest of the evening shadows; you have the vivacity and vigor of youth with the balance and weight of years." As for *her* sexual appetites, he had first awoken them, and when he no longer needed or cared for her, they would go dormant. "My passion as my spiritual love goes out to you only, nor desires another," she wrote.[13]

Erskine's distress over Kitty, however, corroded Sara's confidence. She had believed she was his one and only true love. Now, learning about this new complication while still in Los Angeles, she was "wild with desire to fly" to Wood in San Francisco. He refused her, wanting only a sympathetic listener from afar. Erskine also expected Sara to accept the possibility of Kitty remaining his lover. Initially, she did not object, as to do so might risk her position with Erskine. She chose to follow the simpler course of sympathizing with his pain and agonizing over Kitty's sad choice of marriage. No one understood better the agony of being wed to the wrong man. After some time, however, she shifted gears. Clearly, Kitty would no longer be the same to Erskine, and that provided Sara an opportunity that she very much intended to take: *"Now you need me in that place I do occupy more than ever,"* she wrote to him. The circle around their lives had narrowed, and the issues at hand became supposedly less complex. "I am ready to live with you . . . . Heaven forbid you should falter." Then she played the age card: "Only the young could afford to wait or be patient."

When Erskine, then, suggested Sara reprise her role as his literary secretary, she jumped at it, while boldly proposing something more: a much larger position as his official secretary (formerly Kitty's job). This full-time function would require daily presence at his side.[14] Sara pressed for this place "in 419," his personal office, and all it implied. The balance of power—which up to this moment had heavily favored Erskine—now began to tip, ever so slightly, toward Sara. He had lost one woman; he did not want to lose another. His love letters began to more closely resemble Sara's: "My soul quivers for you. The only double of my soul I ever found." He interspersed paragraphs about Kitty with renewed fervor for Sara, "bride of my soul." He must have her, "secretly or openly." When she was ready to create a splendid life together, he would be ready too, "sparing no one and defying everything."[15]

Such promises, however, reflected the emotional fervor of the moment rather than a cool, calm commitment. Almost immediately he began equivocating. Regarding the expanded secretary role, Erskine offered only, "I am considering it." Nor could he leave his wife at this time, even as Sara indicated a willingness to leave her husband immediately. Erskine's timetable for leaving Nanny and his family rested on a self-imposed commitment to create financial trusts for them that he was not yet fiscally able to accomplish. But, in this instance, he claimed to care more about the implications for Sara's children should she leave her home—concerns that ring false, since he usually argued the children would not be harmed by their mother's actions if done in the spirit of freedom. Truth be told, Erskine acted more out of selfishness than sympathy for Sara. He was not ready for a dramatic disruption in his life. Most significantly, he backed away from any responsibility for her decision to break for freedom. Sara must take her own course for her soul's sake—not for him. Lamely, Wood hoped they "could at least live in daily companionship" as poet and literary secretary.[16]

Sara thrilled at the tidbits of devotion and ignored the rest. She continued to push for the secretary job. If her husband objected, she would insist on her right to do it anyway, even though she lacked qualifications for legal work. As it turned out, when Erskine lunched with Ehrgott in early December, he "nearly asked" how Albert would feel about Sara "partly" replacing Kitty, but then decided against it. He was not ready to make this particular "plunge for freedom" for himself or for Sara.[17]

Soon after their wedding, Kitty and Lloyd Irvine visited Sara in Los Angeles, providing yet another twist to the melodrama. Kitty handed Sara a letter for Erskine, reading a few lines out loud before collapsing on a bed in sobs. She claimed Erskine had advised her to marry Irvine, a very different version of events than what Wood had related to Sara. Given Erskine's aversion to marriage and his emotional breakdown in reaction to the wedding, it seems unlikely that Kitty's account of the story was reliable.

Then, all three headed north. Kitty, Irvine, and Sara, her venture into journalism now over, shared the same hotel in San Francisco and the same ship back to Portland. On board, Irvine was "boozy, maudlin and disgusting." The newlyweds quarreled a great deal. Her husband demanded to see every letter Kitty received. Most importantly, Kitty hinted she intended to maintain a relationship with Erskine. In response, Sara promised to "keep in the background" and even offered to go away altogether, to which Kitty replied, "Oh Sara, no. You must be so much to him now." The two women, united in their love for the same man, embraced and wept. Not a spark of jealousy existed between them, Sara insisted.[18]

To a less poetic woman, the sordid aspects of the Kitty/Erskine saga would have raised serious concerns. She might also have taken lessons from Mary's heartache and cynicism, which Erskine and Sara believed derived from her affair with Darrow. Yet in some ways, Erskine's behavior was worse than Darrow's. For all the latter's faults, he had never engaged in duplicity with Mary, and certainly not on the scale that Erskine had in most of his romantic relationships. Mary always knew Darrow had other women, and Darrow did not make promises he would not keep. Erskine's record of honesty paled in comparison.

An idealist and a wildly optimistic romantic, however, Sara reveled in the sweet ecstasy of true love. She would not deny herself its benefits. She embraced the "calm sweet assurance" that her purpose in life was to be Erskine's helpmeet. As for Erskine's weaknesses—his self-pity, propensity toward deceit and secrecy, and total insensitivity with regard to how his despair over Kitty's "desertion" affected Sara—she willfully turned a blind eye. Both partners in this relationship engaged in denial and deception, yet Sara remained resolute, reminding Erskine they must embrace "the wondrous claim . . . to live together, to love together, to work together and, if it so please fate, to give the world in flesh and blood our second selves—our love incarnate." Erskine also continued to side-step Sara's unrelenting dedication to bearing his child. If she got pregnant, he promised to do anything she asked, but he also said, "It is your problem my darling," meaning it was her decision to make whether to have the child or not. He expressed no enthusiasm for the prospect himself.[19]

Extricating themselves from their marriages, particularly figuring out the timing, loomed not only as a gut-wrenching prospect but as a potentially divisive issue between Sara and Erskine. The matter of Sara's young children was equally vexing. The chances of Ehrgott agreeing to give custody of his son and daughter to an adulterous woman who deserted the family seemed exceedingly slim. Courts and public opinion would fully support him. Further, Sara needed employment to underwrite her release from marriage and create a measure of economic independence. This last matter, at least, turned out to be the easiest to address in the short term. Journalism had not worked for her, but as prospects of becoming Erskine's secretary also dimmed, another possibility emerged. The suffrage movement—the foundational crusade of the larger effort to expand women's freedom and power—became the perfect match, at the perfect time, for Sara.

Six

SUFFRAGE

ON A MID-APRIL EVENING IN 1912 SARA CLIMBED INTO THE PULPIT OF THE
First African Methodist Episcopal Zion Church, a small wooden structure in
Portland with an "awe-inspiring name." She surveyed the audience of African Americans, then launched into a ten-minute stump speech promoting
women's suffrage. Sara had arrived at 8:30 p.m. and grumpily noticed that no
one seemed in any hurry to begin the evening's event, which included five
other speakers. That her trip home by streetcar would take at least an hour
made her anxious to get things under way. When they did, she insisted on
going first. Before the speeches, however, came singing—a rousing version
of "The Battle Hymn of the Republic." Resorting to unfortunate stereotype,
she told Erskine the congregants sang with "all the fervor and feeling of their
emotional racial temperaments," which was underscored by their tragic history as a people who lived in a hostile world.

Then Sara began her pitch. Sixty years ago, she told them, some of the
people sitting in this church sought freedom. White men in blue uniforms
went to war to break their bondage, and white women supported those men,
leaving their sheltered homes to publicly stand against slavery. In the process,
they "found their souls" and gave birth to the "movement in which your liberty was born." Some of these stalwart women—Harriet Beecher Stowe, Julia
Ward Howe, Lucy Stone, and Susan B. Anthony—not only joined the emancipation movement for slaves, they began one for women. They achieved their
first goal but failed to attain the second. Now their daughters needed help
from African Americans in their bid for freedom. "You owe us a debt," she
presumptuously pronounced, mistakenly implying that the North had fought
the war primarily to free slaves, while also overlooking the role of black people as soldiers in the war and in other abolition efforts.

Sara asked the audience to support women's suffrage for an additional
reason: as a step toward "unifying the race of men," by which she meant all
people. The suffrage movement offered the prospect for such unity as part of

"the great spiritual battering ram that is shattering the walls of race prejudice." "No race," she went on, "will profit more by this lesson well learned than your race which has suffered untold tragedy." For the speech's final crescendo, she mentioned that her father carried a bullet in his arm, received as a drummer boy when he had fought for the emancipation of "your people." In his name and those of thousands who shed blood to set black people free, and in the memory of the women who had helped save them but could not save themselves, she asked the people before her to reach across the generations. Repay that debt with votes for suffrage. "We know you cannot refuse us."[1]

Silence momentarily enveloped the sanctuary. Then riotous applause swept the small space. Women wept. The other speakers surrounded Sara, congratulating her on the magnificent speech. "I think in its way it was a little classic," she told Erskine. Among suffrage presentations, it was particularly noteworthy for its emphasis on race, a topic clearly tailored to this audience. In fact, not all suffragists shared Sara's ideas on race. Many not only ignored race issues but perpetuated racism and actively compromised racial justice by practicing political expediency at the expense of the black community. Knowing that some Southern men feared that women's suffrage could also enfranchise black women, who would then press for racial justice, Susan B. Anthony and the National American Woman Suffrage Association promoted a "Southern strategy" designed to reassure white men that the association did not advocate racial equality or votes for black people. Other suffragists resorted to race-baiting, urging white men to support suffrage for white women as a way to counter the votes of African American men. Some used the same argument with followers of the nativist movement, who feared the increasing influence of immigrant men. Enfranchising white women would offset the threat these groups supposedly posed.

Sara, to her credit, did not resort to such arguments. In western states, justice and expediency were not polar opposites but sometimes even conjoined, as Sara's speech demonstrated. Of course, few African Americans lived in Oregon, so concern about their potential power did not weigh as heavily on the white community there.[2] Also, Sara offered this message regarding racial solidarity only to an African American audience; she did not present women's suffrage as an antidote to racial prejudice when speaking to white audiences.

Nor, sadly, did she shed her own prejudices. "I am sorry to add after all this 'local color' of last night that they *did* smell and . . . it made me sort of sick," she reported to Erskine. "Too bad that such black tragedy was spoiled by a foul odor."[3] Too bad Sara could neither see nor shake her own racism. In this she typified white people of her era and place, but it is nevertheless disappointing. She embraced radical ideas about marriage, love, suffrage, and socialism, but her attitudes about race remained conventional and coarse.

Sara's private sentiments compromised her commitment to shattering the walls of race prejudice, but no one could charge her with failing the cause of women's suffrage. She believed in it heart and soul. She also discovered that suffrage provided a ticket to employment. Not long after she returned to Portland from her work on the McNamara trial, her friend Emma Wold recommended that the Oregon chapter of the College Equal Suffrage League (CESL), of which she was president, hire Sara as a state organizer. Wold, the daughter of Norwegian immigrants, a cousin of playwright Henrik Ibsen, a graduate of the University of Oregon, and a teacher, had worked on the suffrage struggle in Great Britain. According to one source, she had joined Emmeline Pankhurst's Women's Social and Political Union (WSPU) and experienced arrest, imprisonment, and forced feeding while in custody. Back in the Pacific Northwest, she became Sara's first close friend and, with this job, offered Sara a lifeline. Sara would not heave rocks or break windows, as the more assertive suffragists of the WSPU did, but she would give speeches and organize local suffrage clubs.[4]

In the November 1912 election, Oregon's male voters would decide whether to enfranchise women. The CESL and the Oregon Woman Suffrage Association (OWSA) mounted a campaign to lobby for the vote. Wold thought Sara would be a particularly effective advocate because of her experience in progressive causes, her sharp mind, her attractive and youthful appearance, her excellent public speaking skills, and her dedication to the cause.[5]

Women's suffrage in Oregon had been a long time coming. Its first major proponent, Abigail Scott Duniway, began advocating in 1871. She toured the region with Susan B. Anthony, traveling more than two thousand miles from the Willamette Valley to British Columbia and back. The pair believed in grassroots leaders and organizations, so they established suffrage clubs wherever possible. Duniway bravely endured harsh crowds who sometimes pelted her with eggs, and she withstood hostile reporting from the Oregon press. She also lost support by vocalizing her animosity toward the Women's Christian Temperance Union, whose efforts in favor of prohibition Duniway thought not just distracted from the suffrage effort but actively damaged it. She further rejected alliances with the labor movement, not wanting to alienate business interests. Her autocratic management style put off still others. Consequently, under her leadership, the suffrage campaign failed to win in Oregon.

By the 1890s, the movement had experienced significant successes in other western territories and states, however. The Wyoming, Utah, and Washington Territories had granted women the vote in 1869, 1870, and 1883, respectively. These victories derived in part from fluid "frontier" environments, small legislatures, and constitutional conventions at which women pushed for suffrage on the basis of the Reconstruction era's Fifteenth and Sixteenth Amendments to the Constitution. In 1893, Colorado adopted women's suffrage, and then Idaho followed in 1896, before a fifteen-year gap brought votes for women to California in 1911. The Arizona and Alaska Territories followed in 1912; then Montana and Nevada in 1914. Most midwestern, eastern, and southern states did not enfranchise women until ratification of the Nineteenth Amendment in 1920.

Several factors explain the renewed momentum in the West in the 1910s. Innovative alliances with progressive farm-labor reformers and partnerships with working-class people, while often fraught with condescension emanating from the middle-class and elite, helped considerably. Workers understood the value of women's suffrage in their larger fight against industrial capitalism, and they formed coalitions with suffragists to offset the power of big business. In addition, a fresh generation of educated and professional women adopted more assertive tactics, including parades and speeches in public spaces. Understanding the power that the consumer and mass-media cultures offered, they also used modern advertising techniques and transportation technologies. Partnerships sometimes arose between groups normally separated by race, although these relationships were rare and could be especially tricky. Sara's visit to the First African Methodist Episcopal Zion Church is but one example of how the suffrage movement sought to reach across that chasm. On another occasion, white and Chinese women suffragists shared a lunch in Portland, and suffragist La Reine Helen Baker, just back from Britain, claimed she had never seen social lines between Chinese and English women obliterated as they were at this event.[6]

The value of strategic alliances and innovative methods became obvious when Washington and California passed women's suffrage in 1910 and 1911, and these victories in turn invigorated the Oregon suffragists.

Duniway continued to exercise her influence in the movement, even as she was no longer able to travel the state due to age. (She was in her seventies by 1912.)[7] Sara, seeking Duniway's support for the CESL position, carried a bouquet of yellow roses to the matriarch of Oregon suffrage and was pleased when Duniway bestowed her approval. Sara believed this experience—akin to "some kind of priestess giving . . . a blessing"—smoothed her acceptance into the movement.

The CESL job appealed to Sara for many reasons: It provided an income. It burnished her self-confidence to find employment through her own connections and friendships, not Erskine's. And the work allowed Sara to channel her talents and personal ambition into something bigger than herself, something important to all women and men. It was not the perfect situation, however. It meant more time away from Erskine, although their nearby downtown offices allowed rendezvous possibilities. The suffrage job also required Sara to leave her children, although she seemed more concerned about childcare issues than the emotional cost of separation from them. That first issue found resolution in a "perfectly wonderful maid." These were, Sara later noted, "those halcyon days when help from Europe came over not at all despising domestic service and capable of taking a great deal of burden off women who had something else to do"—the unstated implication here being that Sara had something *more important* to do. Sara did not give a second thought to the fact that her venture into the political world rested upon her own class privilege and the labor of a poor immigrant in need of domestic work.

The benefit of physical separation from her husband also appealed. Happily, Ehrgott encouraged the job. Sara's salary replenished family coffers and, more importantly, Ehrgott believed in the cause. In fact, Duniway appointed

Albert, a member of the Men's Equal Suffrage League, to the state executive committee for the suffrage campaign.[8] His congregation at the East Side Baptist Church, however, did not approve of his political activities or those of his wife. Members already criticized Sara for refusing to participate in churchwomen's organizations. This new position relieved her, even more, of religious duties, and that added to the growing, ominous friction between her husband and his congregants. Her professional gains amplified his professional problems, yet Ehrgott did not stall her ambitions.[9]

Almost immediately Sara ventured out in search of street corners and sanctuaries, halls and homes, to stump for suffrage. Oregon was an agricultural state—Portland and Salem aside, most people lived on farms and ranches or worked in mines—and since rural voters tended to be more favorable to suffrage than urban ones, mobilizing them was particularly important. The CESL determined the entire state must be canvassed—no town too small or insignificant—for the cause to succeed.

The pace proved grueling. Sara worked twelve to fourteen hours a day for three days in just one locale. She usually traveled via railroad, and sometimes the only available option was a dusty, smelly cattle train trailing a single coach for passengers. Hotel accommodations and restaurant fare in small towns fell far below the standards of even a modestly paid preacher's wife. Sometimes a local hostess helped Sara generate an audience, but she couldn't always count on that, so the sizes of audiences varied greatly.

Sara especially loved speaking from the top of an automobile. British suffragists were known to use cars as podiums and imported the practice to the United States. Formal meeting places attracted the already converted, but street speeches reached those who had never thought much about suffrage or who might be ambivalent, or even hostile, yet open to changing their minds. Roadside events also attracted bigger crowds. Sara would first gather a cluster of local suffrage supporters to form the audience core, then climb upon a car and start speaking around 5:00 p.m., just when the men were leaving work. Apparently, when a woman spoke from the top of an automobile, people stopped. If the novelty did not catch their attention, Sara's personal attraction might. People lingered and listened.

The technique worked in cities, too. A Jewish boys' club filled up several automobiles with "lusty youngsters" to help Sara attract a big crowd on Washington and Seventh Street in Portland. On another evening, a Salem man who never would have attended a suffrage lecture stopped as he was walking by. Afterward, he approached Sara and told her he had never considered the justice of the movement before hearing her speak. Now he did not see how anyone could argue against it and wondered that it had taken so long for the issue to come to the forefront. In Portland, another man approached to ask if she was Mary Field's sister, noting a resemblance. It turned out Mary had been his student at the University of Michigan and made a lasting impression. And a woman asked Sara if she had ever heard of C. E. S. Wood. Something about the way Sara spoke reminded her of his style.[10]

Not all listened politely. Some heckled and ridiculed her, though none heaved the battery of rotten eggs that had greeted Duniway in earlier years. Mostly Sara's efforts generated support and kindness at best, bemusement and condescension at worst. Her enthusiasm and youth helped; an attractive, slim woman aflame with passion for suffrage appealed. That she did not reinforce stereotypical expectations regarding suffragists led one headline writer in Pendleton to announce, "Mrs. Ehrgott Is Not Fat Woman," "Offers Pleasing Appearance," "Contrary to Prejudiced Opinion, Organizer . . . Is Charming and Possessed of Modest, Convincing Views." When a group of local men and women created an organization to promote suffrage and the local newspaper trumpeted it as Sara's triumph, she boasted to Erskine, "I must say Pendleton is at my feet."[11]

She always spoke extemporaneously, tailoring her arguments to her audience. To African Americans she emphasized racial justice. To the Mothers and Teachers Club of Portland's Brooklyn School she argued suffrage would make women better parents. Among a mother's most important duties, she explained, was to prepare her children for citizenship, and enfranchisement would help achieve that goal. Sara assured audiences everywhere that voting did not threaten traditional gender roles or the home. Suffragists did not shirk their duties as mothers or become less feminine.

Actually, she explained, suffrage allowed women to shape the economic conditions that had heretofore forced them out of the home and into the workplace. With the vote and consequent "remedial measures," mothers would no longer have to work outside and neglect their children. Besides, many of the critical issues of the day—child labor, water pollution, impure foods, inadequate schools, and lack of public parks, among others—mattered to mothers. They had a right to address them in the voting booth. In sum, she insisted, "We women are merely asking if we cannot come to the assistance of you men, not that we may leave the home, but that we may stay here . . . . There are one million working women in America who want to nurse the baby. They must deny its pitiful calls because they have not the time. They must work to live." This was hardly revolutionary, fire-breathing feminism. She meant to calm fears.[12]

Her approach proved effective. The *Bend Bulletin* noted that there were three kinds of suffrage speakers: militants, illogical and hysterical "sob sisters," and the middle ground between these extremes. Sara represented the last. Her speeches offered no broadsides but rather came across as "clever, convincing, concise [and] calm." She avoided sentimentality or anger. The reporter found it a rare relief to hear a woman speak on a big issue as Sara did, calling her "eminently womanly and yet soberly masculine." In La Grande, another journalist noted he and most men had always opposed suffrage, but, after listening to Sara, he changed his mind. Enfranchising women, he now concluded, was "the only graceful thing to do."[13]

Sara particularly enjoyed attention from men. In one town she found a group of men from Harvard and other colleges among her most ardent admirers. They represented "the period in young men's lives when they give a sort of adoring devotion to an older yet still young woman." Two or three of them chauffeured her around town, and one wrote a most "clever" account of her visit. In another town, she hung some suffrage posters, created by Wood himself, around the train station as "awkward country lasses, large bellied men and raw youths gazed at me in open mouthed wonder." She turned to them and said, "It's true isn't it?," referring to the appropriateness of extending suffrage to women. One young man replied, "You bet!" and then turned "a fiery red" as he "retired into his celluloid collar." This set off a rigorous discussion among the informal assemblage. Sara, having stirred up "the suffrage soup," left them to work it out.[14]

She experienced particular satisfaction regarding her suffrage work in

Eugene. She wondered at her own versatility, giving addresses to clubwomen, sorority girls, a huge crowd in a theater, members of a church, and passersby on a street corner, never giving the same talk twice. One man told her she was "far more wonderful" than nationally known suffragist Anna Shaw "because you become one with whatever people to whom you give yourself in speech." There, too, young men showered her with flowers and escorts around town, including one fellow who had no interest whatsoever in suffrage yet attended every one of her meetings, sent her a basket of violets, and testified he was a better person for knowing her.[15]

Sara enjoyed meeting women, too. She reveled in opening the possibilities of suffrage to them, from the minister's wife in Stanfield, the one with soft gray hair and gray eyes who met her train and presided over a meeting of bright, intelligent women, to those who gathered in a "bare ugly little Christian Church" in Madras. And the job provided Sara a chance to deepen her relationship with Emma Wold. They talked about all things "great and holy," with the exception of Sara's affair with Erskine, which remained secret.[16]

As much as Sara enjoyed certain aspects of her job, suffrage work and constant travel could be draining, dispiriting, and tiresome. Sometimes, Sara became depressed and struggled to keep her broader purpose in mind. Obtaining the vote represented merely the first feeble step in a long path that stretched ahead. Then there were challenges to the body, including personal hygiene and safety. In Bend, her hosts lodged her in a horrible hotel—"dirty, dingy, unkempt and buggy!"—with peeling wallpaper, a filthy floor, and cheap rugs. The paper-thin walls meant she could hear sounds from other rooms. Just as she finally fell into a fitful sleep, a man walked into her room because she had neglected to lock the door. Frightened, Sara managed to say calmly, "Guess you've got the wrong room, pardner." Mumbling an apology, he withdrew. Then she felt an insect crawling on her. She sat up the rest of the night, determined to find another hotel the next day. Several months later, while stumping at the state fair, Sara complained about the noisy crowds and said she found the public "wearing." She was sick of it all.[17]

Yet the travel paid dividends. It took her out of her cloistered city home and into the beautiful countryside. If the towns often disappointed, the landscape did not. One spring day Sara's hostess took her on an eighteen-mile automobile ride. She thrilled at the distant sight of Mounts Jefferson, Hood, and Adams, and the Three Sisters. In other places, she sat alongside rushing rivers to write love letters and dream of a future with Erskine. Nature's beauty and the fresh air cleansed her. Of course, even those moments would be brightened considerably if Erskine joined her. She tried to lure him to her, or, once when she was headed home, she suggested telling Ehrgott she was arriving one day later, in order to steal twenty-four hours with Erskine. But the risk of discovery blocked such plots from coming to fruition.[18]

More possible, ironically, was the opportunity for Sara and Erskine to appear together on the same stage. They both spoke at a Portland event teeming with the city's society people. Sara considered it a triumph, although some people snubbed her afterward because of growing gossip regarding her relationship with Erskine. They also shared the stage at a huge outdoor meeting in a Portland park. One report claimed ten thousand people in attendance; another estimated twenty-five thousand. The *Oregonian* thought the pair served as effective foils for one another: Sara provided the passionate plea while Erskine followed with a practical, nuts-and-bolts strategy for achieving suffrage. At least once, in Salem, Sara, Erskine, and Ehrgott combined forces. Ehrgott spoke last, offering scriptural support for equal rights and assuring the audience that women's suffrage was consistent with the divine order of things.[19]

To share the stage with a man of Erskine's prodigious talents and renown and still hold her own—to appear before audiences as a speaker in the same league as, if not equal to, this powerful man—boosted Sara's confidence. She delighted in her newfound self-esteem. The work helped her "prove to myself that I am able to be something beside a parasite." Yet, the satisfactions the suffrage movement provided did not alter her foremost ambition. More than the vote, equality, or emancipation, Sara simply wanted Erskine.[20]

———

Erskine had a campaign of his own in 1912. He supported women's suffrage, but it was presidential politics that mostly moved him to action, specifically stumping for Woodrow Wilson. Although Wilson's positions fell far short of Erskine's philosophical anarchism, they came closer than those of Theodore Roosevelt, who wanted to regulate trusts and implement protective tariffs.

Wilson wanted no protection or privilege for corporations and promised to break up cozy relationships between government and private business. Erskine abhorred tariffs and preferred no federal involvement in business or industry. He realized Wilson would not fundamentally alter the economic and political system but thought the man offered the best chance of achieving other important goals: labor unions, free speech, voting rights, and enhancement of individual liberty. Erskine the anarchist might have dismissed American electoral politics, but Erskine the practical lawyer did not. He believed Wilson the best man for the job.[21]

For a time, the Wilson campaign considered bringing Erskine east. He wanted to go. An eastern trip would allow him to visit publishers and friends in New York and, if Wilson won, give him standing with the president. In the end, the Democratic Party decided to use him regionally. Erskine believed travel costs explained the decision, but actually it was more a reflection on the limited nature of his fame and potential influence; audiences in the Pacific Northwest were simply more likely to have heard of him than those in the rest of the nation.

Following a schedule not unlike Sara's, and visiting many of the same small towns, he subordinated work, family, women, and poetry to the presidential campaign. He was sixty years old, but that did not slow him down. Campaigning invigorated him. Plus, sharing the barnstorming experience with Sara, on parallel though separate tracks, provided another bond, another indication of the potential power in the couple's partnership.[22]

He, too, experienced moments of both triumph and discouragement. Although he could not offer the novelty of being a woman speaker, his personal attractions, learned references to Shakespeare and Classical writers, and his soaring rhetoric brought accolades. He never tired of receiving them or reporting on them to others. On a mid-October evening in Baker City, Erskine followed senatorial candidate Harry Lane's one-hour-long, "badly disjointed—very low grade" speech. Erskine did not begin speaking until 9:30 p.m., yet "not a soul moved" during his presentation. It pleased him that a tired audience, seated on hard wooden chairs, could be inspired by his vision of the working poor's hard life, caused not by God but by "tyranny of man."

Speaking extemporaneously rather than from script or notes, Erskine, who had been struck earlier that day by the beauty of the countryside, decided to work this moment into his remarks. What he said that day was later crystallized as the speech he gave throughout the rest of the campaign. As much the work of poet as politician, his theme was "Beauty is after all the one eternal truth." The gist was that man exists in a setting of natural beauty that is there for his enjoyment and inspiration. The needlessly ugly, debased life of the poor reflected their disinheritance, their separation from this universal wealth. Wilson, presumably, would help restore that birthright. The next morning, a man on the street stopped him. "That speech was great—greatest thing ever heard in Baker City," he enthused, wondering aloud if Erskine could repeat some of it. He said, alas, he could not, but it pleased him that he had fed the "soul hunger" of the masses. Erskine found satisfaction in reaching rural people. They were honest, he thought. They listened to new ideas, and the advantages of "the close personal touch" of small-town campaigning made up for the absence of large audiences.[23]

The next day, however, his spirits lowered considerably as he reflected on his tiny audience in Weiser, Idaho. Local organizers had rushed him to the opera house, where he found the group he would be speaking to. "After [the audience] was pointed out—I [realized I] never would have discovered it myself," its size was so miniscule. When he told his handlers they should cancel his next engagement at Twin Falls and save them all embarrassment, they insisted on putting him on a 2:15 a.m. train to Idaho anyway. They would not release him from his commitment, regardless of the low turnouts.

Erskine by now concluded his valuable time could be used more effectively at home, where he thought his campaigning could do some good. To be "trotted around to a handful of people at these out of the way places" irritated him. It felt more like vaudeville than serious politics. He was no longer cut out for "one night stands." He needed his sleep. To make matters worse, when he arrived in Twin Falls, the local hosts failed to meet his train, so he had to walk to the hotel, where they later found him. When he jested that they probably had expected him to be a young man, they responded in all seriousness that, yes, they had.

This comment hurt his vanity, as did the growing realization that his assignment to the Pacific Northwest was better explained by his relative obscurity than by the limited campaign budget. When a judge tried to secure speaking engagements for him in Indiana and Illinois, the campaign demurred. "So as a desperate resort," Erskine wrote Sara, "Montana, Nevada and California were to be victimized." But even there, towns wanted bigger names. Montana and California turned him down—the latter, having had William Jennings Bryan, was not interested in "Woods."[24]

When election day arrived in November 1912, the men of Oregon voted in favor of Woodrow Wilson and women's suffrage. The *Oregon Daily Journal* reported Abigail Scott Duniway's delight in becoming the first woman in the state to register to vote. Sara Bard Field, however, told the reporter she felt more "obligation . . . than elation." Now women needed to work on better legislation for everyone. The reporter, apparently, did not ask Erskine's opinion.[25]

During the campaign, their demanding schedules meant Erskine and Sara saw less of one another. The greater distance provided opportunity to reflect on, and write to one another about, the thorny problems of their future. Believing their love rare and ideal, they also acknowledged it led to commonplace deception, despair, and suffering. One major wrinkle revolved around Kitty, who, her recent marriage notwithstanding, was not ready to remove herself from Erskine's life, nor did he want her to. No sooner had Sara left Portland on her March suffrage tour than Kitty returned to work at 419. Sara did not want to share him, but, more importantly, she did not want to lose him—a risk if she pressed Erskine on the issue of sexual fidelity.

Erskine, too, danced delicately around the issue. He wanted both Sara and Kitty but hoped to avoid hurting either of them. Erskine saw his relationship with Sara as supremely important, but he now made crystal clear that he would not give up Kitty. No one could replace her, he told Sara.[26] Pained by this declaration, Sara wondered how Erskine would feel if the circumstance was reversed: "I cannot help but feel that you would want a certain supreme place in a woman's life—a certain holy of holies upon which no other soul came! That seems to be very natural." Yet she backed off, claiming she needed to grow on the issue of sexual sharing and would not demand exclusivity.

She did, however, raise concerns about Erskine's honesty. He had withheld information about Kitty before. If Erskine renewed a sexual relationship with his secretary, Sara asked only that he be forthcoming about it. To lie anymore would taint their special love.[27]

Erskine promised total candor. As to sharing Sara with another man, it would hurt, he said, but he could do it for the love of her. Ultimately, he believed, men and women were "naturally" nonmonogamous. Erskine loved Sara—craved her sexually and mentally—but, in the end, he would not promise fidelity and would not demand it of her.[28]

As the implications of sharing Erskine settled in, Sara became more adamant about asserting her rightful place at the forefront of his life. If she had to share him, she insisted on being "first," and on his acknowledging that primacy. She reminded him that, without her, he would not have returned to his poetry. That loss would have been the world's loss. She had come to him "for no light purpose" in the "evening time" of his life. She came to help him complete his destiny, for a "poet's work is greater than anything else—his loves, his 'duties,' his family, his friends." Theirs was not a mere "affair"; they produced poetry for the ages. She probably believed this. It certainly appealed to Erskine's deepest yearnings and deepest fears.[29]

Something else came into play. In June, around the time of their first anniversary as lovers, Sara's tone took a darkly pessimistic turn. No longer breathless with anticipation of their future together, she began to doubt that time would ever come. Things had deteriorated by July, when she had to force herself to eat and drink, and she slept only fitfully. She hinted several times at suicide. By August she had abandoned the possibility of bearing Erskine's child, lamenting that they would only conceive "children of the brains . . . to carry on your name and our unity forever." The fruit of their intimacy would not be an infant but poetry.

That summer Sara experienced either a miscarriage or an abortion; we cannot know for certain which it was. We do know it was the second such loss she had experienced since their affair began. In an undated letter she spoke of her "physical agony and mental tragedy." Erskine might not have understood it, but Sara's words seem clear enough: "The mother in me is all torn to palpitating sores as I contemplate this second loss. With every drop of blood I shed I feel you are passing from me in the form I most crave—you reincarnated in our child." Sara knew he would see the pregnancy's end as desirable, and she grudgingly agreed, while adding, "The mother love is in pain." And Sara did not reveal her despondency to Erskine alone. Mary came through Portland in September and grew alarmed at her sister's mental and physical state. Mary pleaded with Sara to be willing to continue living, even if apart from Erskine.[30]

Sara's somewhat cryptic comments about the situation are not surprising. To speak about, let alone seek, an abortion in the early twentieth century was not only taboo, it was illegal. This had not always been the case in the United States. Through the seventeenth and eighteenth centuries, women could obtain legal abortions up to the time they could feel the fetus move. The rules changed in the mid-nineteenth century, when physicians, eager to strengthen their professional position vis-à-vis other care providers such as midwives, encouraged criminalization of birth control and abortion. The move toward greater restrictions on women's healthcare rights was enhanced by arguments from the nativist and white supremacist movements, which maintained that white women must continue to procreate as a way of fending off the supposed threats from immigrants and people of color, who presumably gave birth to greater numbers of children. By 1900, most states had passed laws that not only outlawed birth control and abortion but criminalized those who shared information and advertising about them. The result was that women sought abortions "underground," making the procedure not only more dangerous but more secret and shameful. Not until the 1973 Supreme Court case *Roe v. Wade* was this ban partially reversed, although opponents have since dedicated themselves to outlawing abortion again.[31]

Sara's experience, though devastating, seemed to strengthen her resolve to push for sexual exclusivity and fidelity from Erskine. By September, she announced she was an indisputable monogamist—"an intense monogamist" to Erskine's "polygamous soul." No matter how much she loved a man, if he loved her as one of two or three women, she could not live with or be sexually intimate with him. Sharing partners might be acceptable to Kitty and Erskine, but not to her. She had discovered what she loved more than any man, child, or life itself: her ideals. "Just as I would not marry any man on Earth again because it would give the lie to my principles and ideals, so I could not live with you if you wanted me as one of two mistresses in the full sense." To do that "would be laying my ideals in the coffin and then of what use is life." Surely, she hoped, he would see how ready and willing she was to live or die for him, as long as he did not ask her to violate this most sacred principle.[32]

At first, Erskine seemed unmoved by Sara's despair. Of the miscarriage or abortion, he made no mention. He met with silence her hints of suicide and her newly expressed resolve regarding monogamy. Of course, Sara was just one of his concerns. He juggled legal work, poetry, the Wilson campaign, his family, Kitty, and his annual late-summer trek out to eastern Oregon for a visit to Hanley's P Ranch and his beloved Harney Desert. There, he turned his attention to streamside reveries as he tossed flies from his fishing rod onto the rolling Blitzen River. The overhanging willows and alders, the dragonflies, grasshoppers, trout, herons, ducks, kingfishers, and the occasional track of an otter, mink, or beaver in the sand delighted him. The murmur of the river calmed him. He loved the solitude, meditating "after the manner of Isaak [sic] Walton and all good fishermen."[33]

For two days Erskine luxuriated in being alone at the ranch house, free of worry about others' welfare. He sketched, painted, and wrote poems he would send to Kitty, who typed them and then handed them over to Sara for editing. His affectionate letters differed greatly from the passionate, storm-tossed, desperate letters Sara sent. Only after receiving a number of letters from her did he finally respond to one of her concerns. He would make no pledge of faithfulness or sexual exclusivity, he said. This issue remained nonnegotiable.[34]

Then, in mid-September, the couple rendezvoused in Baker City. In the aftermath, Erskine finally wrote the kind of love letter Sara longed to receive. Separating from her now caused him suffering, he claimed. He felt like a planet hurtling through space, finally meeting his twin, experiencing "one long flash of meteoric light" and then passing again "into the ages of desolation." He wanted her warm, soft, sweet body, which "thrills like the captured trout"—a metaphor that may not have particularly thrilled Sara. More than her body, he loved her soul, their stimulating conversations, and what she could do to promote his literary legacy. "I want you to live after me—gleaning my field and making the world to know what manner of man I was," including his "faults for Truth's sake."[35]

Why this renewed ardor in a moment when they appeared to be pulling apart? One possible explanation: Sara, having learned the lesson from Kitty that Erskine's reaction to a rival could be intense, told him, while in Baker City, about the incipient arrival of another suitor, a friend from Cleveland who also loved her. A Mr. Osborne begged to see her and she had agreed. Apparently rumors about Sara's disenchantment with her marriage had reached him and, believing her break with Ehrgott imminent, he hoped to take the reverend's place. Although Osborne had asked Sara to keep this completely confidential, she shared it all with Erskine.[36]

A few days after Wood's departure from Baker City, Osborne arrived at the same hotel. She shared every detail with Erskine, starting with the comment that the Ohio man's "subconscious egotism" led him to assume he could have any woman he wanted and that, in discouraging him, she had unintentionally encouraged him—perhaps an expected reaction from a man who realizes "he loves a woman who does not return it."[37]

Osborne secured a room across from Sara's. When he wanted to talk, she invited him to her room—a "sacrilege, blasphemy," she told Erskine, to have him in the space they had shared only a few days before. Osborne then explained his visit. Having heard from mutual friends that Sara was in love with someone other than her husband, and believing it must be him, he dropped everything and raced across the country to confirm it. When Sara then revealed it was someone else, Osborne wept "like a child—the proud, reserved man for whose slight attention women have given much!" She tried to comfort him with promises that she and her lover would eventually welcome him to their home, but Osborne rejected that idea. This would be their final goodbye.[38]

Before departing Baker City, however, he told Sara she had taught him what a marriage of the soul and the sensual could be. He hungered for her body although they had never been lovers. Sara realized, as Osborne talked, that she was "in the presence of a great love such as comes to few women." Even as he sat there, "tall and strong and young and beautiful," though, Osborne did not measure up to Erskine's deeper wisdom, poetic soul, and handsome visage. Osborne seemed unimaginative and insufficient.[39]

Sara shared these details ostensibly as an indication of her dedication to truth telling.[40] She also meant to arouse Erskine's jealousy, though that did not seem to work, at least initially. To Sara's lengthy report about the melodrama, he replied that Osborne would quickly adjust, as would any man. Further, Erskine said that, "vital and tragic as it is[,] I have no time for it now"; his train would be leaving in an hour and he needed to get home. Trains did not wait for tragedies to be resolved.[41]

Several nights later, however, Sara and Erskine reunited in Hood River and it became clear something had changed dramatically between them. In fact, for years afterward they would harken back to that "bridal night." Osborne's appearance seemed to inspire in Erskine greater passion for Sara than he had ever expressed. Other factors also played a role. Her growing self-confidence, matched with her tragic experiences of lost pregnancies, probably made her appear more experienced and mature. And there was one more thing: Sara had finally written a letter to Ehrgott demanding her freedom, a bold move that then amplified her determination to elicit more solid assurances from Erskine.

Whatever the reasons, at Hood River Erskine finally gave Sara the words of commitment she sought. Under the shelter of an oak along the riverbank, they kissed and exchanged poems. Sara believed Erskine offered "holy words . . . spoken not in vow but in a religiously poetic prophecy 'till death do us part.'" She leapt at the phrase, which she interpreted not as the routine vows of the world but as a poet's promise of a lifetime together. "As you said beloved," she wrote afterward, "all our nights are bridal nights. So may it ever be—all the dark way strewn with a starry path of bridal nights."

Only one half hour after leaving her, Erskine penned a similarly ardent note: "I love you. I miss you. I want you . . . . You are my life . . . . Touch me, it will save my life." A few hours later Erskine wrote again, describing their love as "primal and primeval." Sara's strongest hold over him came through the "great things" he could do with her—not in odes and sonnets but [in] "the eternal longings of the imagination toward the beautiful." He continued: "Once you asked me for a love letter. Is this a love letter? Ah let us be done with letters. Let us mould into one and never part. Let us be happy. Let us not violate Nature . . . . Come to me."[42]

In reply, Sara returned to those words most associated with marriage vows, a dramatic departure from Erskine's earlier insistence on freedom and exemption from pledges of lifelong faithfulness, and indeed an ironic twist for a couple committed to free love: "'Till death do us part,' here in this quiet room I seem to hear your voice again as you said those great prophetic words," she wrote. Sara thrilled to that assurance precisely because it signaled a vow very much like marriage. "You are mine. I am thine. We are one—for me forever and I believe for you also." What stood in their way? The people to whom they had already made those very same promises.

Seven

SEPARATION

DURING 1912, WHILE SARA'S SELF-CONFIDENCE THROUGH SUFFRAGE WORK blossomed and her relationship with Erskine deepened, the Reverend Albert Ehrgott's world unraveled. His East Side Baptist Church congregation fired him in the spring. Several months later, his wife of eleven years confessed she no longer loved him. She sought freedom and life with another man—a person Ehrgott had believed a good friend.

How quickly his fortunes had turned. Two years earlier he had strode into Portland, answering a call from the Central Baptist Church. The *Morning Oregonian* had welcomed Ehrgott's arrival, touting his business degree from the University of Rochester, his studies at a theological seminary in the same city, his postgraduate work in biblical literature at Yale, and his missionary activities in Burma. It made no mention that the pastor's socialist leanings had led to his recent dismissal from his pulpit at a Cleveland church.

Immediately Ehrgott jumped into Portland's social problems, criticizing city officials for failing to adequately fight against vice and crime. The problem was not lack of laws but lack of enforcement, he said.[1] He also publicized his belief that socialism harmonized with Christianity. Both advocated brotherhood, cooperation over competition, and democracy over aristocracy. The two forces should be joined, Ehrgott argued. Too often Christians dismissed socialism, associating it with the scrappy, "often profane" speeches of soapbox propagandists. They failed to see the "scientific" political ideas underneath, which, if applied, would eliminate many injustices. Socialism encapsulated the "expression of our Lord's golden rule in the economic sphere," he explained. On the other hand, socialists incorrectly believed that capitalists controlled churches, which Ehrgott saw as a demonstration of their ignorance about Christianity. Practicing what he preached, Ehrgott secured the free use of vacant lots in East Portland so families could plant vegetables. He opened a cooperative store in an old church building and sold staples at cost, helping needy families buy inexpensive food and keep their self-respect. He initiated a "People's Hall" at the church with a free employment bureau.[2]

Going further, Albert had befriended Erskine, a well-known radical and atheist. When Ehrgott invited him to speak at the People's Hall, some church members, already uncomfortable with their new minister's leanings, balked. "We did not believe that a man who stands against nearly all that the church means should have been invited to speak there," one church member told a reporter. Ehrgott angrily dismissed his critics. He would socialize with, and invite to his church, anyone he wanted.

Things heated up. By March 1912, while Sara was traveling the state stumping for suffrage, a group of discontented congregants moved to fire him. It all came to a head one evening when Ehrgott assembled the church's "prudential committee" to plan activities for the next year but then went off to a lecture with Wood instead of participating in the meeting. Unaware of the members' growing dissatisfaction, Ehrgott, as he went out the door, asked the committee to consider raising his $1,800 annual salary (comparable to $47,000 today). He clearly misread his congregation. The committee members not only declined the salary boost, they asked for his resignation. Stunned and furious, Albert demanded that the entire church—not just a committee of gossipy disgruntled dissidents—be allowed to decide his fate. Several days later, after a tumultuous four-hour-long meeting, sixty-five members voted for dismissal and forty-nine for retention.

Ehrgott believed his socialist sympathies cost him the job; not his personality but his politics had led to this outcome. Instead of evangelizing, saving souls, and visiting sick church members, he had devoted his time to people beyond his flock—the poor and unfortunate of Portland. In this he simply followed Christ's model, convinced that churches would fall into "spiritual death" unless they acted upon Christ's social message. In firing him, Ehrgott told a reporter, the East Side Church had "sinned against God, man and society, against the practical in Christianity and democracy in the church." His dismissal represented not merely a strike against a minister of God but a strike against God himself. In May Albert presented his final sermon, "A Minister's Valedictory," in which he lodged one last condemnation of his congregants. Their actions had become "contaminated by the heartless commercial methods of the day." To turn out into the world a man and his family with few financial resources was, he thought, a replication of corporate practices in which, "in place of a heart of love to cherish, is found only the iron heel with which to crush out [a man's] very existence."[3]

Newspaper coverage of Ehrgott's firing indicated that his friendship with Erskine had been a factor in the minister's dismissal. Erskine, unable to restrain himself, dashed off a satirical response, which the *Morning Oregonian* obligingly published. He went after "these medieval Christians [who] have burned [Ehrgott] at their mistake." By doing so they also robbed atheist Erskine of his chance at salvation—"Now[,] there is malice for you." Clearly the people of this congregation thought themselves better than Christ, who had consorted with sinners and mingled among the poor. These Portlanders preferred their pastor limit himself to saving the souls of "respectable" people rather than those of the destitute and powerless. Christ, they believed, never made trouble, and neither should their minister. Erskine admitted his letter would do little to help his "really and truly Christian friend Albert Ehrgott," but the matter had become a personal affair, and he wrote with tongue in cheek about how his own soul must now go to hell "because of the spiritual cave dwellers of the East Side Baptist Church."[4]

Perhaps he meant well in writing this defense of Ehrgott, yet it must have been humiliating for the minister. The public nature of the controversy was embarrassing enough, and the loss of a paycheck devastating, but to have Erskine defend him was close to unbearable. If some of the church members' gossip included speculation about his wife's relationship with Erskine, the papers kept it out of their columns, but Ehrgott himself may not have been able to keep it out of his mind, and soon enough he would receive indisputable confirmation that his friend had undermined not only his living but his very life.

It is difficult to know how much Albert knew about Sara's extramarital affair, or when it was that he finally realized Erskine had encouraged and enabled it. One wonders if Sara and Erskine's secrecy was effective or if Ehrgott was a victim of self-deception. Of course, a man of religious conviction and conventional morality did not expect his wife—even a suffragist—to leave her husband and young children over an amorphous longing for freedom.

Erskine had his attractions, but could he, at his advanced age, truly seduce a woman half his years? Besides, he had a wife, children, and grandchildren, who expected his allegiance and support. Surely Erskine would not desert his family. To do so not only risked deep alienation from those he loved but endangered the social life and legal practice he had built.

Erskine's wife, Nanny, notably seemed nearly invisible as this drama unfolded over the summer and autumn months. She barely warranted a mention in letters between Sara and Erskine, and her name stayed out of the newspapers. Her social status protected her. She was a quiet, seemingly ineffectual figure—or so it appeared. A proud Southern lady who had suffered the humiliations of her husband's affairs in silence, Nanny maintained her dignity in spite of the indignities her husband heaped upon her. She knew about Erskine's other women, Kitty's role in his life, and probably Sara's. About one thing she was abundantly clear with Erskine: because of her Catholic faith, she would never agree to a divorce. In 1912, of course, Erskine gave no indication of planning to leave her or their marriage in the immediate future. She simply and silently bided her time, a tactic she had exercised for years.

By summer, however, as Erskine's ardor quickened, the couple agreed that Sara should take the first step toward their shared goal of liberation and life together. She must extricate herself from her marriage and "*possess [her] own soul.*" That meant leaving Ehrgott and possibly her children, now ages eleven and six. Even they, Wood believed, "were not too high a price to pay for freedom."[5] She made it clear that she was all in. Whatever the cost, she would go forward. The only questions: when and how?

Ever since her return from Los Angeles in late 1911, Sara had continued to share a home with Albert, although she slept in a separate bedroom. By spring and summer of 1912, when she was back from long stretches of time away on the suffrage campaign, the Ehrgotts were living in an atmosphere of tension and deceit. Meanwhile, Erskine was growing tired of the deception, for Sara and Albert ensnared him in it too, particularly when Ehrgott asked for financial loans from his supposed friend, a move that drew Erskine into an even greater thicket of lies. Dishonesty, Erskine told Sara, was "an outrage on Nature. Truth. Art." Paradoxically, he simultaneously counseled her that when she did finally confess to Ehrgott that she no longer loved him, she should do so "without too direct and intimate connection with me." Ehrgott might take the news more calmly if he believed there was no other man involved. So much for Truth.[6]

Sara procrastinated, shrinking from the prospect of hurting Ehrgott, an excuse Wood frequently employed in explaining his own delays in ending relationships. She thought it best to wait until Ehrgott settled in a new job, or when the suffrage campaign was over, or when her husband's financial state improved. Postponing the break, however, carried costs. "You and I are *not* chaste," she told Erskine (using an interesting choice of words for someone having an affair), "[and] particularly [not] me because I do not bring my body into harmony with the desire of my soul"—citing "last night for instance and the long night of humiliating remorse and spiritual disgust which followed," a probable reference to recent intimacy with Ehrgott.[7]

At one point Sara suggested Erskine break the news to Ehrgott. He declined. In another moment of anguish, she wished her husband would die a natural death so she could spare him the pain of the truth and herself the agony of inflicting it.[8] The fact that Albert loved her and had always been kind, gentlemanly, and "unselfish to the point of sacrifice—a tender, thoughtful husband, a good father," only made the prospect of revealing her plans more difficult.[9]

Surely Ehrgott had some inkling of Sara's obsessive love for Erskine. People who did not know her nearly as well were aware of it, and in fact, several tried to warn her away from him. La Reine Helen Baker, who shared Erskine's radical politics, surprised Sara with unwelcome advice. When Sara, attempting a joking tone, told her, "Oh yes, everybody falls in love with [Erskine]. I have myself," Baker quickly turned serious, warning Sara not to let emotion overpower reason, and reproaching her for falling in love with a man twice her age. Scorched by the comments, Sara quickly changed the subject.

Several months later, another woman took Sara aside to tell her she knew about the "triple friendship" and to warn Sara about Erskine's womanizing. This time Sara was ready with an impassioned response, offering a treatise on the tragedy of a marriage bond that denied each individual's right to pursue his or her own ideals. The conversation turned from the supposedly sordid aspects of an extramarital affair to a "splendid unfolding of ideas" the woman "had never dreamed of. She became the listener; I the informer," Sara boasted.[10]

On another occasion, Sara let her guard down while visiting Judge Thomas Burke and his wife, Frances, in Baker City. Their wide-ranging discussion of art and science, social problems, music, and poetry led to talk of Erskine. Sara raved about his verses and how, once published, they would be widely appreciated. Her enthusiasm getting the better of her, she added, "It will be said of [Erskine, as it was] of Jesus, . . . the world was not worthy." The comparison to Jesus stopped the conversation cold. The Burkes glanced at one another. Sara caught a reflection of her own face in the mirror and saw that, with flushed cheeks and eyes brimming with tears, she had revealed her passion for Erskine. Embarrassed, she tried to lightly brush it off. The judge, hoping to smooth over the uncomfortable moment, declared Erskine the bravest man he knew.[11]

In July, Sara finally revealed to Albert her intention to leave him. She wrote a letter rather than discussed it face-to-face. What she disclosed and what she kept hidden is unknown, since the letter has not survived. She did not, however, follow Erskine's advice to keep him out of it. We do have Albert's anguished reply, seemingly written in a state of shock and responding in the only way he knew how: through his faith. "My soul is crushed . . . . Only my undying devotion to God sustains me. He gave you to me and will restore your spiritual love when you let Him." Insisting he cared more for Sara's return to a love for Jesus than for him, he begged her, with the help of God, to control her life even if she could not control her love.

A few days later, after wrestling with "the awful reality of an unutterable sorrow," and with his spirit "fathom[ing] the depths of this awful soul tragedy," Albert recovered a measure of equilibrium and undertook a more lengthy and assertive response. Ehrgott admitted he had suspected her feelings for Erskine. For weeks her conduct had been "eating [his] soul like a cancer," even as he simultaneously bore the "rebuffs" from his congregation. Her desertion proved to be the more crushing blow. Admittedly they had their differences, which Sara always "strangely exaggerated," yet he remained devoted to her and loved her more than ever, "refined by the intense heat of affliction."[12]

He asked her, then, to renounce her choice of freedom over marriage, Erskine over husband. Ehrgott saw his wife as innocent, "the victim of a false philosophy, the prey of a fatal code of ethics." She currently lived "in the grip of an hallucination" and mental instability. People who followed the path she now sought ended up bitterly disappointed. To make matters worse, her choices affected many others. This was *not* just about her.[13] He rejected Sara's appeal that she had been helplessly swept along by love and the forces of Nature, an Erskine-inspired explanation that Ehrgott swatted away. She had consciously and willfully made choices and must accept responsibility for this crisis in their marriage. As to Sara's comment that she now felt peacefully calm, having made her "confession," he replied the admission did not "change the fact of grave error and of guilt." To reveal sinful conduct did not justify it nor wipe the slate clean. Her actions were "contrary to the highest, and purest, and sanest ethics"—by which he meant his own.

Then he turned to Erskine, whose "fatherly" interest had turned into something "baneful." If Sara was the victim, Wood was the perpetrator. Ehrgott had believed Erskine a friend and, putting aside salacious rumors, trusted him with his wife. Assuming Erskine had initiated the romance, Ehrgott now realized Wood had bought, through gifts, the family's affection for his own nefarious purposes. It also explained why Erskine shared his passionate poems with Sara—verses that expressed a "looseness between the sexes" and "set my soul on fire with righteous indignation"—even after Ehrgott had asked him to desist.

Surely, Ehrgott argued, Erskine would not continue this behavior at the cost to others "who have prior God-given claims!" Surely Sara must see that her current course served no one's interest. The "precious lives" of their children, Albert and Katherine, would be "tainted and warped." She would bring shame upon husband and family. She should also think of Erskine's wife, children, and their families. And more: "Think of what a blight would be upon . . . the great economic movements & the suffrage cause with which we are so vitally and prominently allied." Sara's disgraceful behavior would bring even "national, widespread insult and set-back" to the social movements they worked so hard to promote. Perhaps Ehrgott truly thought their influence that important, or maybe he simply grasped at any argument that might stick.[14]

Finally, Ehrgott, begging her to come back, promised his door would always be open and his love would never cease. Her welfare concerned him, not his own. If he truly thought it in her best interest, he would surrender and give her up. But his affection for her, their children, and even for Erskine "forbid my yielding to that awful step [separation] which you have spoken of in that soul-sending letter." Come back to your own circle of "God-given dear ones," he wrote. Once she did so, there would be no restrictions on her friendships . . . except for contact with Erskine, which would be forbidden.[15]

Ehrgott made his appeal less to Sara's heart than to her head; he wrote less about his own devotion and sacrifice, or their children's love and need for their mother, and more about philosophy and ethics. It seems an odd choice, to try to reason someone out of a clearly emotional state. Perhaps it reflected the nature of their relationship or the nature of his personality. Maybe Ehrgott believed a rational rather than impassioned plea would be more persuasive to Sara. The consequence: Ehrgott sounded more like a patronizing preacher than a wounded husband.

The minister's approach did not alter Sara's resolve to end their marriage. The nature of his arguments only underscored the deep chasm between them. To argue that the righteous path would lead her "into the higher, saner[,] purer love of God's ideals" could not sway a woman moving away from the church. To paternalistically insist Erskine had manipulated her was an insult to an intelligent feminist. To assume Erskine pursued Sara rather than the reverse denied Sara's agency and determination to grasp what she most wanted in life. For Ehrgott to divulge, albeit just below the surface, his deep, searing anger toward his wife's lover was understandable but not attractive to Sara. He allowed her explanations no credence; they carried no weight, had no credibility. He presented himself as wiser and more ethical—the one who knew best. It smacked of condescension. It was also a heartbreaking, heartfelt, and, from Albert's point of view, a calm, even self-possessed response to Sara's sins.

Ehrgott then opened a second front in his battle to regain his wife. Writing to Erskine, "my dear friend," Albert simply asked him to stop seeing Sara. That would allow her to regain self-control and "swing around to me in love." Erskine replied that only Sara could decide what she wanted. It was not the answer Ehrgott had hoped for. The clergyman then explained the ultimate redemption in this terrible mess would come only through Sara's return to "our personal God and Heavenly Father." Ehrgott had found mental, physical, and spiritual salvation during times of great crisis, and he believed the same would be true for his wife.[16]

Amazingly, Sara's revelation and her husband's response did not lead to an immediate break. They continued to live together. It must have been torturous. Ehrgott hoped to save the marriage. He tried tenderness. Before Sara headed out to eastern Oregon and the fateful "bridal night" in Hood River, for instance, he accompanied her to the train station and, with tears in his eyes, pinned a pink rose on her jacket. Only later did she read the note he gave her: "I pinned the rose on you Wednesday in memory of our wedding day, that full-flood time of my life—You remember it was the eleventh." No, Sara had not remembered.[17]

Other times Ehrgott expressed anger. His rage toward his wife came pouring out in front of Emma Wold on one occasion after all three had attended a Wilson campaign rally. Ehrgott seemed surly, refusing to talk except in short, cold tones that made Emma uncomfortable and embarrassed Sara. When the women began praising Erskine's speech, however, Ehrgott lost control, charging Erskine with demoralizing Sara, and then upbraiding his wife for her "unwomanliness" and "indecency . . . in running after him in a most indelicate manner." It was a situation no woman, let alone one as sensitive as Sara, could endure, according to Wold. When they returned home, Emma shared Sara's room and bed as Sara sobbed through half the night.[18]

Not long after, Sara presented her husband with a "letter of final decision." The time had come to end permanently Ehrgott's hopes for their marriage. A few days later, Ehrgott visited Erskine. He appeared stressed, embarrassed, and unaware that Erskine knew about Sara's letter. Admitting his wife wanted out of the marriage, he nevertheless refused to accept defeat. He believed overwork, nervous exhaustion, and a woman's "physical condition" explained Sara's current state. The end of the suffrage campaign and distance from dangerous ideas regarding free love would help Sara regain her sanity. How could she do otherwise? Ehrgott had done nothing wrong. He was not a drunkard or a cruel man but rather a considerate, kind husband who had given his wife tremendous freedom. Finally, Ehrgott told Erskine, he intended to leave Portland, hoping to snare a position with the YMCA in Southern California, because Sara liked it there. If that failed, he would seek a position in Detroit, near Sara's parents. Then Ehrgott revealed this bombshell: If she persisted in pushing for separation and divorce, he would keep their son and daughter. Sara would not win both her freedom and the children.[19]

That set things into motion. Erskine counseled Sara to be patient and to practice cunning. She should move to San Francisco, live with Mary, and take six-year-old Katherine with her. He could not join her immediately, however, for Ehrgott would use that as proof Sara was a morally unfit woman and mother, allowing him to permanently secure custody of both children. For now, she should simply flee, relying on Erskine to cover expenses. Once she had settled somewhere, they would figure out the next step. Sara agreed to the plan. Not entirely unsympathetic to Ehrgott, Erskine offered to help him, too. They both understood that meant money. "Let it be my compensation for the sorrow I have brought you," Erskine said during one meeting. Albert shook his hand, thanked him, and accepted money from Erskine several times over the following months.[20]

Sara found Ehrgott's arguments and assessments infuriating. That he thought her insane, preposterous. "I suppose he will have me in a straight jacket next. Ah me! What egotism. I no longer love *him* hence I must be insane."[21] She knew his wrath would be terrible when he realized she would never return. He would settle into a "hard, bitter, I'll-see-this-thing-through at any cost" state of mind. As for her children, she had never told Erskine how much she loved them. She always understood the "holy obligation of motherhood" and the highest responsibility that the role required. Yet, she put Erskine first.[22] He, on the other hand, promised only more waiting. She pointed out the difference in their willingness to act. She would not hesitate to leave Ehrgott, for instance. "I only need courage to live Truth. I really can see where in the future this consuming passion to live honestly may mean more to me than even my love for you."[23]

By late November, with the suffrage campaign now successfully completed, Sara broke down not only emotionally but physically—possibly from tuberculosis. Ehrgott, Sara, and Erskine all agreed she needed good medical care, so she left for California with daughter Katherine while Albert Field stayed behind with his father. Unbeknownst to Ehrgott, however, Sara, Erskine, and a small group of friends had planned this as not only a medical trip but a permanent escape. Sara never again lived with Ehrgott.[24]

Tuberculosis is an infectious disease spread through airborne particles often carried via coughs and sneezes. The incubation period varies among patients, but it can become chronic. Not usually a quick killer, it can take a long time to destroy a body, but kill it can. In the late nineteenth and early twentieth centuries, in fact, it was the leading cause of death in the United States. No drugs existed to treat, let alone cure, tuberculosis until the discovery of streptomycin in 1940. Before that, the treatment of choice—for those who could afford it—focused on rest in a sanitarium, preferably in a dry desert or high-altitude climate. The Southwest and California became popular destinations for patients, and a major industry developed. Sanitariums provided complete bodily and mental rest, nutritious food, sunbaths, and encouragement of a positive attitude.

Ehrgott supported Sara's departure from the damp, cold Pacific Northwest for medical treatment. As an extra benefit, she would get some distance from Erskine and his coterie of radical friends who encouraged Sara's rebellion. He also agreed to Katherine going along, assuming the family would reunite in California. He must have known Erskine would pay all bills, as unemployed Ehrgott had no money. He silently accepted the financial help.

When Sara reached San Francisco, she began hemorrhaging. Katherine hovered over her, demonstrating a concern and sympathy far exceeding her years as she took on the maternal role—perhaps not unusual for a child from a home in which the parents' traumas overshadow their children's needs. Sara longed for adult companionship, however, so Emma Wold came to help take care of Katherine. Erskine paid Emma's expenses, too.[25]

In early January 1913, Sara moved into Pasadena's Southern California Sanitarium for Nervous Disorders, known today as Las Encinas. Sara's case of tuberculosis (if, indeed, she had it at all) was determined to be noncontagious, and so she was allowed to stay there, where the focus would be on treating her emotional difficulties. At the sanitarium, founder Dr. James McBride worked to advance the revolutionary idea of treating mental illness through rehabilitation rather than isolation. His facility offered a cheerful twenty-seven-acre campus with its own cows, chickens, pigs, goats, and rabbits.[26] The serene setting included brown-shingled bungalows set among a garden of brilliant colors, and the grounds, with their orange trees and bamboo, reminded Sara of Burma. She lived in her own private cottage a short walk from the main building, and the sun, warmth, delicious food, and many books available to read provided just the tonic for her physical and emotional recovery.

Katherine and Emma took an apartment close by. Expenses added up, costing Erskine $200 (comparable to $5,000 today) per month to pay all the bills. Sara fretted about this, but Erskine impatiently swept money matters aside, telling her she was "Mrs. John D. Rockefeller—understand. Let up on this economy business—Do you think I can lose you because of dollars?"[27] Sara began to eat and gain weight. She rested, edited Erskine's poetry, and enjoyed Katherine's visits. This taste of freedom inspired her dream of creating a home with Erskine in California.

Meanwhile, back in Portland, Albert informed Erskine he was seeking work in San Francisco and intended to fetch Katherine. Claiming that he was acting the role of lawyer as well as friend on Sara's behalf, Erskine told Ehrgott his threats to take the child could hasten Sara's death. Initially this warning seemed to have no effect, but before departing for California Ehrgott visited Erskine's office one last time. He seemed chastened, promising not to deny Sara access to the children should she sever the marriage, and insisting he was not the controlling monster people thought him to be. Erskine believed the worst was over. When Albert and Albert Field headed for the train station on their way to San Francisco, where Ehrgott had found employment at the YMCA, Erskine accompanied them. In a strange, sad scene, he gave the father $70 (only enough to get to San Francisco) and the son $5.[28]

It humiliated Sara that Ehrgott borrowed money from Erskine: $350 in June, $500 (equal to about $13,000 today) in November, and $70 in December.[29] That he accepted loans and financial favors from the man whom he held responsible for seducing his wife and destroying his marriage is perplexing. Perhaps it revealed his desperation. An unemployed husband and father with a mortgage, Ehrgott had nowhere else to turn. Yet it seems a particularly unsavory choice. Beyond the cash loans, he asked Erskine to buy their Rose City house and property, valued at $6,000, for $5,500 ($143,000 today). The cash would help Ehrgott pay off his debts, and Erskine would presumably recoup the money by selling the house. Erskine consented. In short, Ehrgott suppressed his anger in order to maintain access to his rival's coffers. Mean-while, he, too, had kept secrets, hiding from Wood the full extent of his knowl-edge about the affair that had destroyed his marriage. He, too, engaged in manipulative and dishonest behavior. He did so for money.[30]

Erskine may have convinced himself the loans eased the burden of grief on Ehrgott and guilt upon himself. But even from this vantage point, the trans-actions seem ill-advised. He had entangled love and money, sex and indebt-edness before, including in his relationship with Helen Ladd Corbett. At the height of their love affair, he had been the recipient of her largesse. Then, in the midst of his affair with Sara, she reappeared several times to request money from him, as she had experienced a dramatic reversal of fortunes. Although she reminded him of her great generosity in the past, Erskine refused to help. Clearly, bestowing money and gifts could represent the best of intentions and symbolize love, but they also—inevitably—carried messages regarding guilt, obligation, and power.[31]

Including Erskine's considerable financial support of Sara, the total sum he lent, or gave, the Ehrgotts came to many thousands of dollars. That Ehr-gott took Wood's money disgusted her; that she took it wounded her pride. A woman could not claim emancipation if she was economically dependent on a man. To make matters worse, Wood earned the money through work he despised. He should be writing poetry instead of practicing law, she believed, even knowing that the law undeniably financed the choices they now made.[32]

Also, Sara was not Erskine's only dependent, although she did not give this much thought. Erskine remained deeply committed to, and economically supportive of, his own Portland family, including his grown son Berwick, who ranched in eastern Oregon. Continually in debt, Berwick sought bailouts from his generous father.[33] Actually, Erskine spent freely and lavished gifts and loans on many people, family and friends alike, leaving him in no position in 1912 to abandon his livelihood and run away with Sara. Too many people depended upon him.

Sara led a sheltered, severely circumscribed life in the Pasadena sanitar-ium. She spent her days talking about literature with Emma, worrying about Erskine's other women, entertaining occasional guests (including Clarence Darrow), writing long letters, editing Erskine's poetry, and reading. She found

Havelock Ellis's book *The New Spirit* especially interesting, particularly as the author identified Whitman, Ibsen, and Tolstoy as representatives of their age with their scientific and "back to nature" orientations. Sara believed Erskine—with his intense belief in individualism, revolt from Puritanism, and ideas of cosmic unity—belonged in this company as the "next link after Whitman in the poetic chain." Actually, Sara concluded, Erskine surpassed Whitman in his spiritual essence, exquisite writing, and subtle spirituality.

Erskine, however, knew he was no Whitman. The famous American poet—a "bold pioneer . . . a great mountain, rugged, full of seams, boulders . . . grand and beautiful"—was an original. Erskine, on the other hand, knew he leaned too heavily on Greek antecedents, and although he thought himself better than the "petty poet," he was aware that he still fell short of greatness. Erskine trusted Sara's critical faculties, but in this case she was obviously letting love get the better of her literary judgment. It did not matter. He cared less for critical acclaim and more for self-expression. Erskine simply wanted to "sing freely as larks do."[34] Meanwhile, Sara trotted out the idea that she, too, should write poetry. Some of her friends also encouraged it, worrying that Sara completely subverted her talents to Erskine's. About her poetic abilities or ambitions, Erskine said nothing. She did not seem offended.[35]

One issue, however, did catch his attention. In mid-December of 1912, Sara dropped the news of another pregnancy. Anticipating his unhappiness, she assured Erskine she wanted a "miscarriage" and understood it might have to be forced. She tried to remain calm and rational but admitted it would be "a terrific blow to me to lose another," having had two failed or aborted pregnancies earlier in the year. "Oh don't you want him or her," she asked Erskine, "with all your soul?"

Erskine urged an immediate abortion. He did not believe she could withstand a pregnancy and knew the tirade Ehrgott would raise against her should she keep the child. His greatest concern was Sara—"the child[,] I care less about." Then he added, "Not that I am indifferent to *our* soul-created child . . . . Only to me *you* are all . . . . Your life is my life." He knew she wanted to have his child, but this was not the right moment. That time would come, he promised, when they lived in their "own retreat where the winds blew health to you daily and nightly."[36]

By the time Sara received Erskine's response, the crisis had passed. On December 18 she experienced a burning fever and a coughing fit so severe Sara believed it brought on a miscarriage. Afterward, she saw "the tiny pathetic little fetus," surprisingly large for one that was only four to six weeks old. She wept for the "possibility that was no more—that hope *dead*. Who knows what genius, what power, what liveliness will never flower! And *you* the Father—Ah! . . . you, too, must feel the aching loss. Surely I do not weep alone!" Actually, Sara knew the news would make Erskine's Christmas a happier one, and, true to form, he did not deny his relief. Only once did he have a slight desire to have another child, he told her, and that was when he had considered the possibility of perpetuating Helen Corbett's "physical robust beauty" comingled with his own—a tidbit of information that probably brought Sara no solace or comfort. For him, Sara was necessary, children were not: "Without you—no life, no world, no work, *nothing*." In the end, Erskine's poetic ambitions took priority.[37]

Within a few days of the miscarriage Sara announced she was getting along "beautifully." She did not want him to feel any remorse. The horrible pain seemed to her "like a glorious atonement for such beautiful, sinful risks as we had run." She would do it all again. She had always wanted a love to which she could give herself completely, body and soul, without fear of consequences. Now she had it. Yet her mood swings continued. On Christmas Day she wanted to know when he was coming to see her. "Don't make me *send* for you," she pleaded. "Come of your own glad impulse."[38]

As 1912 ended, Sara must have reflected upon it as a year of mostly suffering. True, she had traveled widely and successfully on behalf of an important social movement, receiving acclaim along the way. But she had also left her husband, deeply wounding him in the process and risking the loss of her children forever. Sara had been away from her children often over the course of 1912, and now she remained apart from her beloved son. She had experienced several pregnancy losses (whether through miscarriage or abortion) and now was in the midst of a physical and emotional breakdown. In her first days at the sanitarium, she lay about weak and dependent upon a man who, she insisted, owed her nothing, even as the doctors told her she would never be strong enough to make her own living, a crushing blow to Sara, for whom financial dependence was antithetical to liberty and independence. Her future with Erskine remained uncertain. He might never join her in California. He might find happiness with someone else. She believed, nevertheless, that her suffering was the greatest gift she could give Erskine, for it would strengthen her character and would produce better poetry from Wood.

On the last day of the year she reminded him that her love was "like the spaces between the stars—immeasurable—infinite." She loved him not because he had a beautiful face and body but because "when I first met you I saw a soul lovlier [*sic*] than that of any other man I had ever met—a soul like an alabaster chalice and when I looked within I found it full of golden, shining stars, ideals, thoughts, hopes, aspirations, tenderness, generosity, justice, mercy, love, each one wrapped in a cloud of exquisite fancy which marked them the possession of the poet." She had sacrificed much for the mere hope of making a life with such a man. Her hopes remained firmly fixed upon him.

Eight
CROSSROADS

IN SPRING 1912 CLARENCE DARROW HAD RETURNED TO LOS ANGELES TO FACE charges of tampering with the McNamara jury. Mary, covering this bribery trial for a union periodical, came down from San Francisco, where she now made her home, and provided moral support to Darrow. For Mary, the trauma of the bribery charge and the pain of practicing free love with "the wife" nearby cast a shadow over her time with Clarence. But the invigoration of joining in solidarity with others who believed in the righteousness of the labor cause, and its legal champion Darrow, offset these troubles.

Not long after the McNamara brothers' admission of guilt in December 1911, Clarence Darrow had appeared at Mary's apartment, morose and suicidal. One of Darrow's lieutenants had been caught offering cash to a juror on a Los Angeles street while Darrow stood nearby. The aide turned state's evidence, to the delight of prosecutor John D. Fredericks, who then indicted Darrow for bribery. Darrow arrived on Mary's doorstep with a bottle of whiskey in one hand and a pistol in the other. She talked him out of suicide.[1]

Darrow faced a grim situation. If found guilty, he could be sentenced to thirty years in a penitentiary and lose his profession and honor. He could not afford to fund his own defense, and organized labor leaders such as John L. Lewis, head of the United Mine Workers Union, and Samuel Gompers of the American Federation of Labor initially refused to help, as they were still angry over the McNamaras' plea bargain. So, Darrow turned to personal friends, including Erskine. If acquitted, Darrow promised to repay him; "if not, I don't know." Three days later, however, Darrow expressed second thoughts. He did not want Erskine's money unless he could truly spare it. "I will get along in some way," he said. Erskine sent $500 (about $13,000 today), even though he believed Darrow guilty. Darrow thanked him, hoped his friend would be repaid, and added, "I believe you will."[2]

While in San Francisco on legal business in April, Erskine joined Mary, Darrow, and Fremont Older, editor of the progressive *San Francisco Bulletin*, for a ride in Older's automobile. Talk turned to radicalism and labor. Erskine confessed he loved "the masses" in the abstract but found them distasteful, "smelly, ignorant, uninteresting" in the flesh. When the poor came to his office with their "hollow eyes, pale cheeks, ugly clothes," he had to air out the place afterward. Mary undoubtedly found his snobbery troubling.[3]

More upsetting to Mary, however, would have been Erskine's recent conversation with Anton Johannsen, a militant labor organizer and public supporter of Darrow. Johannsen thought Darrow had the right philosophies but was "too weak to abide by them." Though committed to a "piratical course," Darrow was "too flabby to be a pirate." Johannsen told Erskine he thought Darrow had convinced the McNamaras to plead guilty *not* to save their lives but to save his career. James McNamara would have willingly gone to the gallows on labor's behalf, but Darrow, knowing the prosecution had "the goods on him" regarding bribery, sacrificed labor for self. It would "cut Mary to the bone," Erskine wrote Sara, to know Johannsen "holds these contemptuous views of D[,] for she talks so fondly of the labor leaders' loyalty to and love for D." In the end, labor leaders put their misgivings aside and helped finance Darrow's defense, as to have him convicted or plead guilty would have been ruinous to the larger cause.[4]

Mary, meanwhile, stood loyally by Darrow, thoroughly and unquestionably devoted to his vindication. His sensitivity along with his egotism had twisted him up like a rope that "cuts him cruelly," she told Sara. When proceedings finally commenced in May 1912, Mary was there, along with the "awful" Ruby Darrow—an "ignorant, cheap, tawdry little creature."[5] Darrow, meanwhile, had bigger problems than jealousies among women.

His case, though, was not hopeless; the prosecution's argument not airtight. It lacked corroboration of the supposed conversations between Darrow and his aide about bribing jurors, and the trail of money proved murky. Still, a jury trial always carried risks, and initially Darrow appeared nervous and grim. His savvy defense attorney Earl Rogers and, of course, his own commanding presence in the courtroom helped change the dynamic. So, too, did Lincoln Steffens's testimony. By the time Darrow testified in his own defense, the prosecution's case had crumbled. Darrow put on an outstanding performance. He was a "master hand of narration," a *Los Angeles Times* reporter (who was hardly a Darrow partisan) noted.

Darrow's greatest triumph came in his closing remarks. Approaching the jury box with both hands in the pockets of his signature gray suit and his hair in disarray, Darrow told those dozen men he was not on trial for bribery but rather "because I have been a lover of the poor, a friend of the oppressed, because I have stood by labor for all these years, and I have brought down upon my head the wrath of the criminal interests of this country." He deftly changed the narrative from tawdry corruption to a fight against oligarchy and oppression. Darrow's only crime was standing for "the weak and the poor . . . for the men who toil" and against the owners of big business, who saw in this prosecution their chance for retribution.[6] Even prosecutor Fredericks admired Darrow's eloquence before quickly reminding the jury that eloquence had no bearing on guilt or innocence. On August 18, three months after the trail began, it took the jury only thirty-five minutes to find Darrow not guilty.

Throughout the ordeal, Mary buoyed the spirits of her beloved Clarence. If Darrow found sexual solace in the arms of other women, he still turned to Mary for moral support. Both found comfort in the rousing company of fellow labor advocates. One evening Mary joined Darrow and a cluster of these men for dinner, drinking, and poetry. Olaf Tveitmoe, of the Building Trades Council, loomed particularly large. A militant organizer known as "The Viking," he spoke with a booming voice. Anton Johannsen, his private thoughts about Darrow's guilt notwithstanding, joined the group too. He represented, Mary thought, the spirit and quicksilver of labor; Tveitmoe, the iron. When the latter rose to quote western poet Richard Neihardt's "Battle Cry," Johannsen burst out: "God! That's a God damn son of a bitch of a poem! Say it again!" Tveitmoe obliged as the others joined in, as if repeating a prayer. With a "God damn it!" in place of an "Amen," Johannsen called for someone to pass the whiskey. All drank, including Darrow, who, Mary noted in her diary, sat quite close to another woman. Darrow's eyes, with the "wounded look of the child, [grew] moist." The group reveled until after midnight, and as they went their various ways in the quiet, empty streets, Tveitmoe's last words—"Fighting the fight is all"—sounded in Mary's ears.[7]

A few days later, with the acquittal in hand and the trial finally over, Mary joined Darrow, Ruby, and other celebrants at a café down the street from the courthouse. A photograph of the victory party showed Darrow and his wife sitting at a table with supporters crowded around. A smiling Mary stood in the center, between the Darrows.[8]

His star among labor again on the ascent, Darrow appeared at the head of San Francisco's 1912 Labor Day parade. He presented a soaring speech about the necessity of redistribution of wealth, before moving on to Portland, where Mary and Sara worked the newspaper offices to provide flattering coverage of his tour and lecture on "Industrial Conspiracies." Sara momentarily put aside her suffrage work to help Mary. How she wished Wood could join them for dinner and afterward retire to 419 and "sleep together—all three—*Why not?*—Does that shock you, To tell the *honest* truth at the sleeping point I'd rather darling Mary withdrew."[9] Such a suggestion from the wife of a Baptist minister indicated Sara's sensual imagination had expanded considerably.

Sara closely observed Mary's role as Darrow's advance agent—"her wonderful love at work for the man she has given her soul to." Mary so believed in Darrow's virtues, Sara dared not express her misgivings about him. "What is truth," Sara wrote Wood, "our illusions or our cold and careful speculation and analysis? . . . I would scald my throat rather than . . . take away the mantel [*sic*] of the Ideal with which [Mary] has gently and lovingly covered the naked soul with its ugly sores and empty hollows."[10] One wonders if Mary harbored similar sentiments regarding Sara's devotion to Wood.

Darrow had been acquitted, but his legal nightmare had not yet ended. The state had charged him with *two* counts of bribery, intending, from the start, to try them separately.[11] In the months before that second trial, Mary traveled east to tour steel mills for an exposé she was writing on their treatment of workers. As she put it to Wood, she was there to observe "the wonderful process of making steel and killing men." While in Chicago she dined with friend and former lover Charlie Hallinan, the first radical man she had ever known, who was himself now married. After dinner he came to Mary's hotel room in free-love style. It surprised her to find "how different was this more equal love, this youth love, from the love for Darrow, which, too[,] will never, never die—only this was of a fresher, younger character." Mary admitted that while time had soothed the blow of Charlie's marriage to another, she still searched for his qualities in every man she met. Her new friend

Lemuel Parton, a fellow journalist in San Francisco, came close. In fact, she once mistakenly called him "Charlie." Now, the real Charlie wanted to join her in Pittsburgh while she researched her steelworkers piece. Mary turned him down. Instead, she concentrated on her work and wrote letters to Lem.[12]

In Pennsylvania during November 1912, Mary squirreled her way into the American Steel Corporation by claiming to be a schoolteacher named Edna Todd, interested in learning about the process of making steel. She was admitted entrance and soon became overwhelmed by the liquid iron, ladles of metal, and ingot ironed out into long red sticks that then folded over as if paper. Tiny steel and graphite particles penetrated her clothes and skin like stilettos. She visited the dismal, smoky shacks that housed men who labored twelve to fifteen hours a day. Their wooden-faced, shoeless children whispered among themselves that Mary must be rich because she offered them candy and cookies.[13]

From Pittsburgh, she moved on to Gary, Indiana, where she witnessed the horrors of child labor. Ten-, eleven-, twelve-, and thirteen-year-old immigrant children trudged off to work with their dinner pails in hand. No one protected them—not their parents, not the Catholic Church, and not the parochial schools that instead essentially served as recruiting stations for workers. Dark circles under the children's eyes disturbed her. She wanted to write something powerful and important about them and on behalf of all workers. Her prospects looked bright, having three orders from *The American* for essays and an additional assignment from *The Masses*. In addition, Theodore Dreiser had asked Mary to collaborate with him on a labor novel. Her career seemed in ascendancy.[14]

By December of 1912, she returned to sun-drenched California. The East seemed gray in comparison. True, New York sparkled, but there "the power of money and the powerlessness of need" prevailed. Only progressives and radicals such as Frederic Howe, Ida Rauh, and Dreiser made the place worthwhile. She also came back because she had promised Erskine to help Sara wrest her freedom from Ehrgott. She told her "Big Brother," as Mary began calling Erskine, that she would help care for Sara and Katherine in Southern California and did not require pay, as she earned her own income from writing. She also intended to be around to help Darrow manage his second bribery trial.[15]

Mary, then, stepped in to care for Katherine when Emma Wold returned to Portland while Sara remained in the Pasadena sanitarium. This was no small thing. A working woman, Mary had no children and little experience with them, yet she accepted the responsibility. Further, Mary became a sounding board for, and advisor to, Sara as she contemplated the next step on her road to freedom. In this role, however, she aroused Ehrgott's righteous anger. He held Mary nearly as culpable as Erskine for his wife's desertion.

For the sisters, 1913 became a year of transition, new challenges, and dramatic personal changes. At the start, Mary's intellectual and emotional life angled outward, while Sara's tacked inward. Partly this reflected Sara's illness, partly it reflected her personality, and partly it reflected Ehrgott's and Erskine's domineering characters and shared determination to force Sara to make a final choice between them. By year's end, Mary, who had always been the braver and more audacious—the first in the family to push for independence and autonomy—had reversed her course and chosen a more conventional path. Sara then became the rebel, willing to gamble all.

That the sisters had such options at all is significant, not to mention indicative of the remarkable changes that women (or at least middle- and upper-class American white women) were now experiencing; it was an exhilarating moment in time for those willing and able to reconsider, recalibrate, and take risks. Ten years earlier Mary and Sara, standing on the brink of adulthood, had selected distinctive courses—Mary pursuing not just professional opportunities as a journalist but love outside of marriage, while Sara chose her role as a helpmeet to her husband and a mother to their children in a Christian household. Now, the sisters both reassessed those choices, having discovered that their youthful decisions left them feeling unfulfilled. They reached for alternative lives, ones that better fit their current needs, desires, and talents. To do so required heart and more than a little courage.

That both wanted more of what the other already had, however, revealed the limitations society still placed on women. To "have it all"—family and career, love and liberty—came much more easily to men than women. And men exercised considerable power over women, especially their wives, perhaps especially rebellious wives. Sara's most immediate obstacle to crafting a new life remained Albert Ehrgott's fierce determination to thwart her ambitions with respect to having both her free-love relationship and custody of their children. Beyond his religious convictions, his arsenal included social norms and legal practices that greatly favored men and conventional notions of marriage. If his powers of persuasion failed him, he could always turn to the courts for the power to, if not bend Sara's will and bring her back, at least prevent her from achieving all she hoped to gain (meaning both Erskine and the children) by leaving him. He tried both.

———————

Not long after he settled into his new position with the San Francisco YMCA, Ehrgott began a new offensive: waging a war of words to regain his wife and to point out to those he believed most responsible for her desertion that their sins were against the sanctity of marriage and against God. He focused on Erskine and Mary, the latter having bluntly told him Sara no longer loved him. Albert swiftly and scorchingly replied, "A bat cannot see clearly in the light of the sun. So divergent are your ethical and moral standards from mine, that I will not try the hopeless task of getting you to see this tragedy, at least from my point of view." Mary was "unfit to measure" or understand his kind of love, he said, blinded as she was by her tragic relationship with Darrow. He also resented his sister-in-law's claim that he had been standing still while the world went on. How dare she presume that just because he did not agree with her, he remained mired in the past.

Albert believed that Sara had been true to him until she "became inoculated with the insidious poison of what you and others call advanced freedom!" His wife had not outgrown him; "the fact is that she will need to grow up to me." Ehrgott retained faith in "the resurrection of Sara's love" and believed that at Christ's feet was the "trysting place and the only one, where her soul and mine can be united in harmony." As for Erskine's loans to Ehrgott (which Mary apparently mentioned), he took the money because Erskine offered it and Ehrgott viewed the sums as "paltry compensation for the inexpressible agony endured." He hinted he did not intend to repay the loans. Finally, he asked that while Mary took care of Katherine, she shield the child from things that would shock the girl's "tender sensibilities," such as cigarette smoking.[16]

Ehrgott next set his sights on Erskine. Unvarnished anger and hostility replaced the veneer of gratefulness and friendship Ehrgott had maintained while living in Portland. Now, both men shed their masks. They believed deeply in their own philosophical positions and shared a penchant for self-righteousness. Both revealed a similar inability or unwillingness to allow the other's position any credence. If ever there was a case of people "speaking past each other," surely this was it. Ehrgott understood it as a debate between righteousness and sin, God's word and man's blasphemy. Erskine saw it as the relic of religion versus the vitality of nature, the past versus the future, and repression versus liberation. The debate centered on adultery, or free love—whatever one decided to call it. Each was determined to win ... not only Sara but the philosophical argument behind the struggle for the woman.

The debate quickly devolved into threats of legal action. Ehrgott charged Erskine with alienation of Sara's affection and insisted any court would hold him accountable. The new tone and the new threat surprised Erskine, who told the minister, in words designed to rankle, "[You] have some need of me as a preacher." His lengthy letter, however, read more like a lawyer's brief than a sermon. It was a letter of "truths," but not complete truth. It was more the kind of truth an attorney might make in court—encouraging his client to be honest, but maybe not completely honest.

Erskine argued that Christian philosophy was not the sole source of Truth regarding love. Free speech, free thought, and the recognition that love can die offered compelling counterpoints to Ehrgott's orthodoxy. Mutual love of spouses is the lone foundation upon which homes and child rearing should rest. Marriage without love is prostitution and should be severed. Time would tell whose view, his or Ehrgott's, came closer to "the truth," but, Erskine believed, the current age seemed to be "settling it in my favor."[17]

The minister responded, although it took him three days to control his anger over Wood's "egotism and selfishness." "Yes, love is free, and in such freedom do I love her whom God has bound to me in a deathless bond." Believing in his prerogatives and powers as a man and husband, Ehrgott pointed out that he *gave* Sara the freedom to leave their home, just not to pursue legal separation. He intended to save her from the "wrong use of freedom" and trampling on *his* rights. He would never agree to divorce. Then the threats returned. If

Sara applied for legal separation or an annulment of their marriage, he would sue for alienation of affection. If Erskine would not recognize Christ's "superior claims," Ehrgott would drag him into court, force him to testify, and reveal himself as a sinner having engaged in "spiritual seduction."[18] Ehrgott next enlisted Sara's parents on his side. George Field called Erskine "the vilest of the vile," though the two men had never met. In reply, Erskine composed "a confession of [his] faith" regarding free love and an individual's right to live outside of interference from church or state. He disputed George's claim that he had converted Sara and Mary. The sisters had embraced free love long before they met him, being "unusually intellectual and by nature progressive if not revolutionary." "Free love, my dear Sir, means purity," he wrote. "Forced love . . . means impurity and lies." At the bottom of the letter, Wood indicated he was sending the original as well as a copy to Mary, and she would decide whether or not to forward the letter to her father. There is no evidence that she did. But she might have.[19]

Erskine and Ergott did not correspond again until 1918. As they each backed off into their own corners, it would be difficult to judge which man's ego was more robust. Perhaps on this score their duel ended in a draw. Neither refrained, however, from pressuring Sara to follow *their* wishes.

Through the early months of 1913, Erskine pressed Sara to pursue a divorce. So obsessed did he become about the topic that, at one point, he stopped short to say, "Confound it. I am getting to be as bad as he—I can't drop the subject." He railed against Ehrgott's bigotry, bullying, egotism, and fanaticism. The man was "tenacious, relentless, selfish." Erskine determined to "obliterate him . . . . He must pay the penalty of the unfit, of those who seek to obstruct true development . . . . Nature . . . must kill him in love and firmness that there may be no more idiots." Moreover, Ehrgott's threat to sue Erskine worried him. In court, the "venomous" Reverend Ehrgott could muster conventional public opinion to his side and cause Erskine and Sara great harm. So, Sara must push back. "Never let Mr. E feel you are receding one inch."

Even as he was pushing for Sara's divorce, however, Wood also counseled they remain apart. A clandestine meeting would be fodder for Ehrgott—evidence he could use against them. Meanwhile, Sara needed to establish residency in California for one year or Nevada for six months in order to file for divorce. With a sympathetic judge, she could not only prevail but possibly gain custody of Katherine and Albert. As for the cost of the divorce, Erskine would funnel money to her through Mary or friends. Sara would have to admit to some loans from him to appear credible to the judge or jury, but they could also make a strong case for her ability to support herself and her children through journalism and suffrage work.[20]

Sara responded to both men with timidity. She preferred to drop the divorce and preserve Erskine's money and reputation. Rather than stoking her anger, Ehrgott's ferocity encouraged surrender. Besides, she retained some sympathy for her husband, and she knew she could not deprive Ehrgott of both children.[21] Her willingness to surrender may have stemmed from her weakened physical condition, but it also reflected the very different advice Mary and Darrow gave her about divorce. And the question of Erskine's commitment remained a factor. She had no guarantee he would join her after she paid the emotional and psychic costs of divorce and the possible loss of her children. What seemed preeminently a philosophical matter of principle to Erskine was a matter of real pain and loss for Sara.

Mary and Sara had not lived in close proximity for many years, except for the brief interlude of the McNamara trial in fall 1911. Now, winter 1913 found their lives closely intertwined once again, in sometimes uncomfortable ways.

Down-to-earth Mary fought authority her whole life through wit, ridicule, and, if those did not work, diffidence. She smoked cigarettes held between thumb and forefinger, and she found suffragists and feminists boring. Ethereal Sara, on the other hand, relied on "cajoling sweetness rather than wit, often to the point of hypocrisy." She abhorred cigarettes, dedicated much of her time to women's suffrage, and embraced feminism. The sibling bond, however, forged by the shared childhood traumas induced by their father's harshness, proved strong. When Sara needed her, Mary came through.

Of course, Mary had her own motives in coming to Los Angeles: she wanted to be on hand for Darrow's second jury-tampering trial. She did not attend every day but showed up on the two days when Lincoln Steffens testified on Darrow's behalf and saw firsthand that "law is the process by which the truth is excluded." Mary marveled at Steffens's masterful performance on the stand as he adroitly turned the prosecutors' questions into opportunities to broaden the conversation to philosophical matters. Privilege, he argued, was the source of evil, capital the aggressor, and labor merely sought to gain for itself a little privilege.[22] She did not comment, however, on one of Steffens's more famous moments in the trial. The prosecuting attorney asked if Steffens was an anarchist, to which Steffens replied, "Oh, I am worse than that . . . I believe in Christianity." Anarchists, socialists, and labor men believed in justice, but Steffens thought justice alone would never fix the world's problems. "Nothing but love will do the job. That's Christianity. That's the teaching that we must love our neighbors."[23]

The bonds of friendship among the radical labor leaders remained steadfast through this second trial. They stood together in solidarity, or so it seemed to Mary. At 5:00 p.m., after his first day of testimony, Steffens telephoned her to invite himself, Darrow, Fremont Older, and Anton Johannsen for dinner at her small apartment. She quickly assembled a meal, simply piling everything she had onto the table—an acceptable move "since they were all men"—and hosted a delightful evening. While Katherine fell asleep on her cot in the kitchen, the adults enjoyed red wine, cigarettes, and true friendship. One can only imagine Albert Ehrgott's horror had he witnessed the scene.

To Mary these men seemed like "fine violins." Older talked with deep empathy for prisoners. Darrow was his usual brilliant self "with his Mephistophelian wit." The "dramatic" Johanssen and the "mercurial" Steffens stayed the longest into the night, debating the use of force as a political tool. Mary loved the company of men, and they appreciated her. In fact, Johannsen and others made her a lifetime member of the Building Trades Council, the first woman to receive the honor.[24]

Unfortunately for this group, Darrow's 1913 bribery trial did not end as happily as had its 1912 predecessor. Perhaps emboldened by the first acquittal and assuming it would be followed by a second, Darrow started his closing argument by restating his earlier claim that he was on trial not for bribery but for daring to oppose the strong and mighty and to defend the poor and weak. Then he demonized the prosecution in personal, nasty terms, while claiming the McNamaras' "crime" was no crime at all. The brothers did not commit murder. The Rockefellers, Morgans, and Goulds were the true destroyers of the poor, the people most responsible for industrial violence.

The jury began deliberations on a Thursday night. By Saturday noon they had hopelessly deadlocked. The judge declared a mistrial, and so ended the case, falling far short of the vindication Darrow and his allies wanted.[25] The outcome did not surprise Mary, who heard the jurors singing the hymn "Nearer My God to Thee" during deliberations. More troubling to her than the legal outcome, however, was labor's apathy over the mistrial. Darrow's thirty-five years of service to workers had not produced a single resolution or telegram of support from unions or labor leaders. Mary believed him "absolutely guiltless" and prepared to help raise money for the next trial, but as it turned out, the state declined to try him a third time and Darrow's nightmare finally ended.[26] In early April, Clarence, Ruby, and their entourage headed back to Chicago, where they remained for the remainder of Darrow's life.[27]

Mary, meanwhile, began recreating her life, too. She delighted in Katherine and began considering starting a family. Finding the little girl "arch" and "sweet," Mary marveled at the questions the girl asked: "Where does electricity come from?" "Is a person a tourist when he goes home?" "What makes roses pink?" "Why do I have toes?" She thought her niece a "rare child, uncanny in understanding." When Lincoln Steffens said of Katherine, "Who can say which is the greater creation, a beautiful, sensitive child like that or a poem like Shelley's?," Mary voted for the child. One evening she took Katherine to the movies. Three of the four films were about love triangles. Katherine wanted to know why two men could not both love the same girl, and why the girl chose the captain over the man she truly loved. Mary had no response, not wanting to disturb "the little Eden where she walks and talks" with commentary about grown-up jealousy or the coarse but real attractions of money.[28]

If she loved Katherine, Mary absolutely adored Albert Field. She had become better acquainted with him the previous September while passing through Portland. She had stayed with the Ehrgotts for a few days, and her visit coincided with Sara's thirtieth birthday. Eleven-year-old Albert Field worked feverishly to decorate the table with garlands of nasturtiums (their yellow symbolizing suffrage, he told his aunt) and to place "cunning little notes" under each plate. Mary found him handsome, imaginative, sensitive, noble, and gifted. He was a new child of the new home that "throbs with suffrage, socialism, anarchism, free love, trade unions . . . with the spirit of inquiry, of quickened interest, of restless direction toward something, a veiled God, a mystery." As she observed the children, she thought that families and homes remained "wonderful institutions" and doubted that they would ever disappear.[29]

Mary wrote this not to Sara but to Lemuel Parton, the fellow journalist she had met in a San Francisco boardinghouse earlier that year. She had noticed him reading Algernon Swinburne poetry, which impressed her. Friendship and love grew. Parton, a talented journalist and a graduate of his home state's University of Colorado, lacked Darrow's flair but offered other attributes, not the least being that he loved Mary and was single. By the time she headed to Los Angeles to help Sara with Katherine, they had begun talking about marriage.

Parton wrote lovely letters to Mary while she was away, promising her, "We are going to take hold of life together and find beauty and power and wisdom in it." He worried about her "down there among the Philistines," in the midst of "this whole business [that] seems sinister and hopeless." Not that Lem did not support Mary's writing career. He did. Nor did he want to make her economically dependent upon him, although he longed to take some of the load off her shoulders, to protect her. Lem believed it was "a man's business to protect and care for the woman he loves." Being together would also mean peace, freedom, and the opportunity to grow together.[30]

At age thirty-two, Mary was finally ready for someone like Lem. The challenges of making a living as a writer—not to mention as a woman writer—had begun to take their toll. She lived on the economic edge. A few days in bed sick would wipe out her meager savings. Editors proved unreliable in making timely payments. She considered going into advertising or real estate to assure steady income. She loved to write and had always assumed writing would come first, making a living would be second, but now she rethought that priority as financial anxieties pressed.

Darrow offered no future. Mary would always love him, but the time had come to move on. She wanted to live in California to be near Sara and her children. Lem became one more West Coast attraction and a potential father to her future children. Not that she had completely overcome all doubt about becoming a mother. Life, she thought, was full of disillusionment, pain, and suffering. "I doubt *my* right to bring forth a child. But ah! precious little Katherine and beautiful Albert!"[31] In fact, Mary's experiences with Katherine combined with Parton's visits to Los Angeles helped settle her doubts.

She and Lem shared much, including a love of walking. In San Francisco they hiked eighteen miles from the Embarcadero to the Cliff House and back; in Pasadena they went up and down 5,710-foot-high Mount Wilson in a day, quite a physical feat. For many years, her daughter later hypothesized, Mary had operated along the "hard, brilliant and masculine side of her nature," the part formed through battle with her father, George Field. Lem's love awakened another side of Mary, the "wistful, feminine, and yearning" side. The "deep unconscious, operating wisely within her body," told her the time had come to commit.[32]

When Mary revealed her plan to wed, Sara expressed happiness over the news, though privately it worried her. She doubted Mary felt the deep love for Lem she had for Darrow and feared an unhappy outcome. In the midst of Sara's own messy, traumatic effort to disentangle herself from marriage, these feelings were unsurprising. Mary, however, assured her that she and Lem would willingly dissolve the tie should either desire it. Sara also admitted one more concern: when Mary and Lem married, she would be bereft of the only other person, besides Erskine, she wanted as a companion. She might be left alone.[33]

Mary admitted she did not love Lem with the same intensity she loved Darrow. She did not "give him the great wonder song of songs, yet I do give him a quiet, steady deep affection which will make a peaceful loving home atmosphere. I seem capable of only one masterpiece," she explained to Erskine. "I cannot sing it again and the score is lost." To Sara, this seemed tragic. She had only one love—"a Sun whose radiance swallows up all other shining bodies." Mary's great luminary, on the other hand, did not put out the light of other stars.[34] Sara's misgivings aside, outsiders might actually see Mary's choice not as tragic but as mature and altogether appropriate.

By 1913 the two sisters stood at a crossroads, both on the brink of exchanging their respective marital statuses and career paths. Many years before, Sara had disappointed Mary when she married Ehrgott, especially at a time when newly opened opportunities for college and career beckoned to women. Mary herself had raced down that path. Sara selected traditional marriage and Mary watched her treasured sister slip away into the world of domesticity, forfeiting the chance to realize her full potential. Certain that there existed outside the "four narrow walls of marriage" a brilliant alternative, Mary had determined to reach for it. For her, "first, must come the independent life."[35]

Fifteen years later, Mary had fully experienced that wider world. She lived independently, loved several men, had an established writing career, and was hobnobbing with some of the most interesting and important intellectuals, labor leaders, and literary figures of her time. She also experienced loneliness, financial insecurity, and the ache for her own child. Marriage looked different now. Sara, on the other hand, had come to the conclusion after a dozen years of marriage to the wrong man that her soul had been stifled, her potential unrealized. She was miserable. She wanted out. It remained to be seen if she had the strength and courage to break for divorce.

Nine

DIVORCE

Divore in America, like so many other things in the 1910s, was an evolving proposition, yet it still carried stigmas, particularly for women. In this, Erskine thought the country far behind many Native American cultures that provided fluid, socially acceptable ways to separate.[1] Most western cultures only slowly loosened marital ties, grudgingly acknowledging vows as contracts that could, and sometimes should, be broken. Divorce consequently remained extremely uncommon in the United States until the 1880s, when one out of about fifteen marriages ended in divorce.

In some ways, though, divorce cohered with American ideas and behaviors regarding freedom and mobility. Several centuries of continental expansion encouraged willingness to break bonds and relocate. Even after the Census Bureau no longer identified a discernible "frontier," Americans kept moving. This commonly accepted cultural practice of separation and loosening of family connections (not as viable or available in other parts of the world) made divorce seem less threatening to the social fabric. Other values—individualism, independence, pursuit of happiness—seemed compatible with divorce as well. Yet opponents of divorce worried about its destabilizing effects on children, family, and the nation. Many raised religious objections. Even as divorce rates rose, marriage and commitment to family remained robust.[2]

The first breakthroughs in easing barriers to divorce came in the West. Between 1867 and 1886, western states and territories granted the highest number of divorces—twice the rate of the North Atlantic states and seven times that of the South Atlantic. Officials established legal codes that reduced the residency requirements of those seeking divorces, and they increased the variety of grounds for separation. Some states, including Utah and Nevada, became known as divorce mills in which women and men could establish temporary residency for the purpose of achieving speedy split-ups. People cited desertion as the most common basis for divorce (nearly 50 percent nationally), followed by adultery (28.7 percent) and cruelty (10.5 percent). Drunkenness was cited in 1.1 percent of divorces between 1887 and 1906.[3] By 1913, Nevada emerged as the best-known destination for divorce migrants, with its six-month residency requirement and an expansive menu of possible justifications. Lawyers geared practices specifically to the divorce trade, promising quick and reliable outcomes.[4]

Identifying appropriate grounds for Sara's divorce proved challenging, however. Desertion, cruelty, or failure to provide financial support did not fit her case, and claiming incompatibility was also not an option. Ehrgott, of course, could press on the basis of adultery, but he did not want the divorce. Aside from the legal complications she was up against, Sara faced additional concerns as well. Divorce not only carried social costs, it often meant exchanging economic security for possible penury in a world where work opportunities for women proved scarce and poorly paid. It could also end in terrible scandal. Ehrgott might try to destroy both her and Erskine's reputations in court.

As Sara weighed the options, Mary and Darrow discouraged divorce. Darrow's argument rested on professional opinion and personal hunch about Erskine. While in Los Angeles for his second bribery trial, Darrow visited Sara several times at the sanitarium. When the issue arose, he asked about Erskine's long-term plans. Sara replied that they both intended to join a writers' colony with Fremont Older and other radicals not far from San Francisco. Darrow warned her not to count on it.[5]

Actually, the plan had some foundation. In 1912, Erskine, Helen Todd, Lincoln Steffens, Fremont Older, his wife Cora, and Darrow began pulling together just such a colony when Older found a 160-acre farm for sale in the Saratoga foothills, west of San Jose. Erskine eventually contributed $5,750 of the $11,000 price, seeing the venture as a post-Portland poetry haven. Otherwise, he left decisions concerning property management and improvements to the Olders, although they did consult Erskine about the colony's organization, membership, and dues.[6] Anarchist Erskine advised: the less government, the better. Every participant should own his or her tract in fee simple, but all should share possession of and expenses for the clubhouse, vegetable garden, and orchard. As for new members, the Olders thought it best to invite only those "we all agree on."

Erskine anticipated potential conflicts within the group's charter members over that last issue. For instance, he knew that Steffens found Ruby Darrow objectionable, as did Helen Todd and the Olders. They worried she might poison the place and unsettle an otherwise congenial, sympathetic, and tolerant community. The definition of "freedom" could also spark disagreement. As a true believer in and practitioner of free love, Erskine made clear he intended to bring any woman he wanted into his home, whether as a literary companion, secretary, mistress, or all combined in one person. He assumed Ruby Darrow would object.[7]

As it turned out, the Darrows quickly peeled off from the plan, as did Todd and Steffens. When a young anarchist from Seattle paid $100 down on a ten-acre site and indicated he intended to bring his girlfriend to live with him, the Olders turned him away. Local papers had begun attacking the place as a "free love colony," a label the owners wanted to avoid. The residents also began to have problems with access to water and the need for costly repairs on the property. Erskine paid one-half of the bills, even though only the Olders enjoyed the benefits of any permanent improvements. He never objected to the growing expenses, but he did eventually decide to sell his interest to the Olders, ending his experiment in communal living. The Olders, however, spent the rest of their lives on the property.[8]

Issues concerning the colony possibly informed Darrow's gut feeling that Erskine would never break from Portland. Or maybe he just spoke from his own position as a free lover who never intended to leave his wife. Whatever the reason, Darrow's caution that Sara not pin her faith on a "chimera" sent a chill through her. So too did his overall pessimism about her divorce prospects. She could not obtain one in California on the grounds of incompatibility. Wherever she went, Darrow believed, Ehrgott would probably file a countersuit against Erskine, and most judges or juries would see the reverend as a pillar of society with faultless morals and unassailable behavior. Sara's only possible argument—her youth at the time of her marriage, and the inevitable changes she had since undergone—would not prevail.

Darrow also believed Ehrgott would insist on custody of both children, and since Sara could not show means of support beyond Erskine, Albert would win them. She and Erskine deluded themselves if they thought Ehrgott would not use their "friendship" against them in court. Even with no absolute proof of their relationship's sexual side, any judge or jury would make their own inferences, particularly since Sara readily admitted her love for Erskine. In the end, Darrow cautioned, she would risk health, children, and Wood's reputation "for nothing."[9]

When Darrow visited Sara one last time before leaving Los Angeles, however, his mood and attitude had changed. That day he did not see her situation as hopeless. On the spot, Darrow wrote a letter to Ehrgott, asking to meet with him in San Francisco. He intended to tell Albert that further resistance to Sara's freedom would lead to exposure of his wife, possible loss of his job, and "unwelcome notoriety to him and the children." Darrow then penned another letter to a judge in Nevada, asking for a recommendation for a good divorce lawyer. Darrow knew this judge would do anything he could to help any friend of Darrow's, and that he had a reputation as "lenient" when it came to divorce.[10]

Mary more consistently discouraged divorce. She believed Sara should live as she pleased and not worry about legalities; she should take her freedom and not depend on the state to grant it. She also opposed the divorce because it would damage others, particularly Katherine and Albert Field. When Mary asked Sara how she could possibly consider giving up her children, a sacrifice Mary herself would never make, Sara made a swift and emphatic reply: "Because I love Erskine beyond all human computation or even the terms to attempt it." To that, Mary said nothing, though her silence meant neither acquiescence nor agreement.[11]

Mary proved even more forthright with Erskine. She doubted he would leave his home for Sara, nor did she think he should. Erskine had a large life of civic, social, and family relationships that he should sustain. Then, asking him not to repeat this information, Mary went on to say her sister was incredibly selfish, putting her desires before the best interests of him and, more importantly, her children. Sara's neglect of Albert Field's care—he was wearing worn-out clothes, for instance—shocked Mary. "I'd make those little children that I had called into being *my* concern and not my life with some man who is already obligated."[12]

Mary did not blame Erskine for her sister's predicament. She completely understood married men in love—or at least involved with—other women.

Although she did not know Erskine well, she thought him "a wonderful, big refuge in this storm" and regretted he had been drawn into this sordid family conflict in which Ehrgott made him the target of his vengeance.[13] Not that she was indifferent to her brother-in-law's feelings. She acknowledged that it is "hell" to experience unrequited love. The problem was Albert was "no sport!" He once tracked down Mary in a train station and, with arms crossed and mustache bristling, regaled her for encouraging Sara's desertion. Not intimidated, Mary scolded him for trying to hold Sara to her marriage. Yet she also promised Ehrgott she would keep Katherine's love for her father "warm and hold it sacred," believing love between parent and child sacrosanct.[14] Mary kept returning to the point that the most important and vulnerable people in this tangle were the children. Their happiness, their well-being, mattered most. Yet none of the adults—Sara, Albert, or Erskine—seemed particularly focused on or concerned about them.

What those children, ages twelve and seven in 1913, thought at the time about the issues tearing their family apart is not easy to discern. Occasionally the adults talked *about* Albert Field and Katherine, but rarely did they talk directly *to* them about the situation. They certainly did not solicit their opinions. Still, some clues can be found. Sara emphasized Katherine's solicitous, tender, and loving qualities. Sara herself was, of course, the primary beneficiary of those traits. Katherine seemed willing, Sara observed in her diary, to sacrifice her own happiness for her mother, holding back her questions, impulsiveness, and simple childhood energies to save Sara's patience and serenity. "My problem with my child," Sara wrote, "will be to teach her where unselfishness ends (for this is good for character) and where self-sacrifice begins (for this is suicidal to personality)[;] to live largely and simply one's own life without killing the lovely buds of thoughtfulness for others is a delicate task." This, of course, defined the crux of the issue for Sara. To what degree would she sacrifice herself for her children? Where would she draw the line between her needs and theirs? Between her love for Erskine and her love for them? Mary concluded Sara had drawn that line in error, already sacrificing the children in favor of self.[15]

Both children, while fully aware of the disintegrating family situation, seemed remarkably generous to the adults who had created it. Katherine, unusually self-aware and sensitive, confided to Sara that God had given her two things she did not like: a crooked lower front tooth and a "sad heart." Sara assured her the first could be fixed and the latter was not true, for Katherine happily played and laughed. Katherine replied, "You don't understand, Mother, the sadness is *underneath* my play and happiness. I'm worried all the time about you." That Sara's illness or the drama playing out between her parents contributed to the child's "sad heart" had not occurred to Sara. That such a young child expressed this level of insight indicated she had already experienced considerable unhappiness and trauma. Later, Katherine would remember her childhood as deeply sad and her mother as mostly absent. She claimed her parents made her choose between them at age six. Although that was not literally true, it is telling that she opened her memoir with this scenario, an indication of how deeply she felt caught "in between" during her parents' breakup.[16]

Albert Field, twelve years old when he visited his mother in the sanitarium, was better able to understand the situation and to tender sympathies to his sickly mother while living loyally with his father. He seemed, in other words, more adult than the adults.[17] During a visit to Pasadena, the boy became sick, so he stayed with Sara, sharing her bed and bringing his mother "unspeakable comfort." At one point he broke down and sobbed, "I want to live with you. I want a mother." Believing he could understand, she explained "some of the basic principles of my life's actions." Receptive, Albert concluded he would not accept his father's views regarding Erskine or the larger issue of his mother's freedom. Still, the boy expressed empathy for his father. He cried when he talked about Ehrgott's grief and loneliness and how he, the son, had tried to cheer his father up. "I'll have to stay by him, Mother," he said. "He's a good fellow, awfully kind and I'm so sorry for him."[18]

But the children could not always sustain their ability to put their parents' well-being ahead of their own. A few weeks later, when Mary went to pick up Katherine at her father's home after a short visit, Katherine exhibited behavior that most would not only expect but completely understand. She did not want to leave him or, more precisely, as Katherine herself put it, she "wanted the family to be together." Mary did not report this to Sara, but she did tell Erskine, with the added admonition that he also not share the heartbreaking scene with Sara.[19] Yet Katherine's distress, however heartrending, would not have altered Sara's growing determination to end her marriage. She marveled at her children, who were "precious . . . sweet wondrous blossoms" and hated the thought of giving them up. She simultaneously assured Wood, "Never mind—it's all right, dear—Your love is my supreme compensation."[20]

Sara meant every word, but she also meant to remind Erskine, who unswervingly pushed for divorce, of her sacrifices. He had consistently ignored or underplayed the child custody issue, telling Sara both that Albert Field would soon be old enough to choose which parent he preferred to live with and that the love she shared with Katherine trumped any court decree. He firmly believed parents should not sacrifice themselves for their children.[21] For much of his adult life, he had done exactly that, to his great regret, putting law before poetry because he had to provide for his family.

The analogy between his parental situation and Sara's, however, was faulty. Erskine's children were now adults and parents themselves; his child-rearing days were well behind him. Sara's young children needed her in the most intimate, everyday aspects of their lives. Interestingly, Erskine emphasized his yet unfulfilled parental duty—to provide trusts for his adult children once he received the significant payout from the land grant sale. He would not leave Portland until he had assured their economic futures. Neither literature nor liberation would eclipse this nonnegotiable commitment to his children.[22]

———————

After Sara left Portland in November 1912, she did not see Erskine for several months. She kept up a persistent campaign to lure him to California, but for all his bravado and bluster when it came to Ehrgott, Erskine proved exceedingly cautious. He told Sara he preferred to wait and win rather than be impatient and lose.[23] Mary, a braver soul, encouraged him to visit Sara in Pasadena. It was complete nonsense to allow Ehrgott to "stand like a turkey in the middle of the road and say that vehicles shall not pass." Finally, in February 1913, Wood traveled to the sanitarium, where the couple spent the afternoon walking the lovely grounds and talking about poetry and, undoubtedly, divorce.

Three days later they reunited at San Francisco's Union Square Hotel, Sara taking a brief respite from the hospital. While Erskine attended to business, Sara met Mary's fiancé, Lemuel Parton, for the first time. She liked him and knew they would become warm friends. The following day Sara, Mary, and Erskine took the Sausalito ferry to Marin County, on the other side of the Golden Gate. As they floated away from the city, Erskine marveled at the San Francisco skyscrapers reaching forty stories high, the array of electric lights reflecting red and green from the docks upon the rippled water, and the white ones lining the streets "like diamond necklaces for the Titans."[24]

At the Manzanita Inn Sara enjoyed the first night of deep, "natural sleep" she had had in months. The next morning, fog enshrouded the silent, ghostly eucalyptus trees outside their window, but the sun eventually made an appearance and the little group, joined by Lem, spent the day in the Marin Headlands. Erskine sketched, Sara read aloud, and they settled on one thing: Sara would move forward on divorce.

A few days later, she took the train to Reno, Nevada, to begin establishing state residency. She dreaded the trip and its implications. "Nothing is beautiful in our struggles," she wrote in her diary, "till they are past." Certainly Reno was not beautiful. Her sensitive soul loathed the divorce colony. It made her feel dirty. She found it coarse, even if her purpose was "righteous." She resented the process, too. Why did she have to go through this legal farce? Who gave anyone the right to determine another's freedom? Still, she followed procedures and hastily returned to San Francisco the next day.[25]

After slipping off for a few more quiet days with Erskine, Sara took one more overnight train trip to Reno as part of the process to secure residency, and then the time came to return to the sanitarium—"a sad day, a sad life," Erskine declared.[26] As Sara turned south, traveling in an expensive railroad berth courtesy of her lover, she fretted about her dependency on Erskine and its cost to him of both time and labor. Sara wanted and needed little in material terms—their accommodation in the Marin Headlands, a rough miner's cabin, had sufficed—and while Erskine agreed that the only things that really mattered were things they already had, he still could not—or would not—tear himself away from Oregon.[27] For his return to Portland, Kitty decorated the office at 419 with violets and daffodils. Nanny met him at the train station and they went home together.

Over the next several months, Sara vacillated about the divorce. Finally, in exasperation, Erskine demanded she decide if she wanted a relationship of "intellectual and soul companionship" conducted through correspondence or a full life together. In the end, the anarchist told her, "Do as you feel freely called to do in your own heart . . . . In the name of all the future, Sara, *Be Free.*"[28] That seemed to do the trick. In May she informed Ehrgott she had begun divorce proceedings. Before he could swoop down and grab Katherine, Sara and her daughter hurriedly departed for Nevada to begin the six-month residency. Leaving the sanitarium for good (something she could have done at any time, as she did not require a doctor's release), she recalled feeling like a "convict who walks with heavy chains on his feet," inwardly rebelling at the necessity of going to a strange land to ask a strange man for freedom. She also made one more appeal: "Come to me Erskine in the fullness of time. I will make your life sweet."[29]

———————

Goldfield, Nevada, was hard duty. Sara had never lived in such an isolated, godforsaken location. She described it as a "town of the living dead" and "a place of abounding ugliness and glaring desolation." Treeless and windswept, it offered only volcanic and barren Columbia Mountain in the distance for scenic variety. After prospectors had found gold nearby in 1902, Goldfield popped up the following year. The railroad arrived in 1907 and, for a time, the town had the largest population of any in Nevada Territory, reaching a peak of 15,000 to 20,000. Initially Sara took up residence in the Goldfield Hotel, the biggest and finest building in a substantive business district. As county seat, the city boasted several churches and a high school. Yet by 1910, as the gold played out and the boom busted, the population dropped to 4,838. By the 1920 census, only 1,558 inhabitants remained.[30]

Sara chose Goldfield on Darrow's advice. His friend, Judge Peter Sommers, lived there, and Darrow surmised Sommers would rule in Sara's favor should Albert contest the divorce. She hired Bird Wilson as her lawyer. As her six-months-long residency requirement stretched ahead, Sara fell into depression and self-pity. Erskine encouraged her to write him honestly. Not one to hold back, she filled her letters with news about her physical ailments, loneliness, spiritual dissatisfactions, and overall unhappiness.

Making matters worse, Ehrgott shifted tactics, now writing heartrending letters in which he humbled and humiliated himself before her. Dropping the angry, threatening postings of earlier missives, his words now conveyed a pitiful tone. His life had become flat, stale, desolate, and unbearable. If she would only tell him what he had done wrong, he would remedy it. Ehrgott even enlisted Sara's mother, who pleaded with her daughter to cease and desist from pursuing the divorce.[31]

Mary, ever generous, accompanied Sara and Katherine to Goldfield and stayed two weeks, providing moral support and help with settling in. In doing so, she postponed her own wedding. Lem's adoration of Mary endeared him to Sara, and his emotional, intellectual, and economic support, Sara believed, would assure Mary's flourishing literary career. Lem talked about "vital things" and, as a journalist, valued literature and good writing, although he himself would "never set the world on fire," particularly compared to the great Darrow. On the other hand, Sara continued to worry that Mary's feelings for Lem were "maternal," lacking the passion she had for Darrow. That Mary openly admitted she gave Parton only "moonlight—a reflection of another love" underscored Sara's concern, as did Mary's comment that under her home near the Golden Gate was a "deep crypt . . . dark with memories—it holds my beloved dead." Sometimes Mary would steal down to place a flower there and remember "how love really felt." It is a strange allusion, and one wonders if it refers to a buried fetus.

Sara described Mary's June 19 wedding, however, as "delightfully erotic and romantic." The couple married in Calistoga and honeymooned at an old inn where Robert Louis Stevenson used to live. If she had hesitations about the wisdom of this marriage, Sara now insisted it was the institution of marriage itself—the "ignominy and wretchedness of the marriage bond to which they have had to bow because they are poor"—that worried her. When Mary wrote, after the honeymoon, affirming her happiness, Sara could only think to herself, "Poor girl."[32]

Mary, on the other hand, concluded she had done well. She understood that if Lem did not have Darrow's mind, Darrow did not have Lem's heart. Parton did not reach out to help the "weary and heavy laden" as Darrow had, but "for daily living, for home consumption, for the daily wear and tear of common existence," Mary thought him a wonderful man. She grew to "almost" fall in love with her husband day by day. In fact, she wished that someone like him had been Sara's fate. Only one year before, Sara sat entrenched in conventional, domestic life while Mary sailed "out on a storm tossed sea, driven hither and thither without harbor or haven." Now, Sara's future seemed nothing but a question mark while Mary's was settled and secure.[33]

To pass the time in Goldfield and to justify Erskine's outlay of funds for her divorce, Sara continued to edit his poetry. Erskine had begun a philosophical poem called *Civilization* during his annual sojourn at his real-estate partner William Hanley's ranch in late summer 1912. Sara believed it would become his masterpiece. It exposed injustice and, as he put it, expressed his "soul." Inspired by his youthful experiences in eastern Oregon's Harney Desert, the lengthy verse addressed mankind's—or civilization's—capacity to generate poverty, crime, degradation, and ugliness. Artistry mattered less to him than the message. He announced at the poem's outset:

> I will lie like a mourner
>
> Upon a bare and barren bosom of the great Mother
>
> And I will chant a dirge unto Civilization.

The Poet (an anarchist) and Truth then discuss—for over one hundred pages—society's corruption as revealed in politics, economics, and marriage. One version included the following:

> This is the pedigree of Degradation:
>
> Authority, father of Laws;
>
> Laws, father of Privilege;
>
> Privilege, father of Poverty;
>
> Poverty, father of Degradation.
>
> I am a reaper of disordered fields,
>
> And the sheaves which I gather are
>
> Despair, drunkenness, crime, hate, ugliness,

Churches, jails, palaces of the idle rich,

And filthy nests of the debased poor;

Tormenting pain, unsatisfied longings,

A killer of the body;

The hunger of the soul denied.[34]

By June 1913 Erskine had completed a draft, admitting it not "worthwhile" but jokingly hoping Sara would declare him "a great man" anyway. He knew it did not read "as big as I thought it would" and that she would have serious criticisms. Erskine welcomed them even as he warned he would not necessarily accept them. Anticipating she would object to repetition, for example, he explained he used it because it echoed Nature's rhythms and assured his central message would not be missed. As music repeats themes, Erskine wanted to do the same "with slightly changing cadences." Another problem: the poem lacked an ending of "beauty and fire." It just petered out.[35]

Sara agreed with Erskine's self-criticism. His determination to preach dominated, making the poem more sermon than art. It was too long and repetitious. He never rose above man's failures. For an ending, she suggested he provide hope, "a picture of the soul's possibilities." The best parts came in the nature passages; he should emphasize those. Most importantly, he needed to devote time and effort to revision. Poets spent years creating great poetry. She understood that *Civilization*, which he would later rename *The Poet in the Desert*, reflected years of thought and meditation, but he had written it in a feverish fashion. He needed to slow down and reconsider it in a workmanlike way.[36] Erskine resisted. The poem *was* a sermon, and to drop the fire of its message would leave only a "colorless insipid lot of Nature thoughts." In the end, he preferred being an agitator to a poet.

If they did not see eye to eye on his poetry, they did agree on another issue: Sara's literary potential needed to be developed. For the first time in their two-year relationship, in fact, Erskine acknowledged her poetic ambitions. He believed she had talent. She, too, should have her say. As the glimmerings of reciprocity began to appear, they switched roles. Sara now shared her sonnets and Erskine offered criticism, praising her verses' "growing quality and imaginative power."[37]

He also encouraged her to produce newspaper and periodical essays. Her story on Goldfield's Fourth of July celebration, published in Portland's *Oregonian*, became her first paid piece from Nevada. A compelling portrayal of the town, the article noted that Goldfield's inhabitants, accustomed to mining's booms and busts, found "the sky-rocket characteristics of Independence Day" especially appealing. Sara described the various floats in the parade, paying special attention to the "Votes for Women" entry, festooned with masses of yellow chrysanthemums and young girls with yellow bows in their hair. It heartened her that, in Nevada's "sand of desolation," that float had won first prize. At the end of the celebration, which lasted deep into the night, some people were poorer in pocketbook than the day before, but they had enjoyed themselves. If they had to "walk soberly for awhile to make up, what of that? It's all a part of life's uncertain game."[38]

Her other offerings, however, proved less commercially appealing. *The American* turned down one essay, *The Century* another. The rejections reinforced Sara's sense of failure and inability to support herself. Erskine cautioned her not to fret, as even he had received many rejections.[39] The most important "return" of these forays into publication, as it turned out, was Erskine's clear support of her aspirations. He saw her as an equal—if not in experience and publication record then in ability and untapped potential.

Sara's lawyer, Bird Wilson (one of few women in the profession), did not impress Mary, who dismissed her as "the lawyerette." Mary also worried about Sara's stamina and commitment to see the process through. She was "such a *female* after all," completely devoted to Erskine rather than to freedom or any other principle. Mary ridiculed women whose sole purpose in life was "*Man.*" She doubted Sara's capacity to manage on her own. Notably, Katherine told her mother not to cry when Mary departed, for she would become the caretaker in Aunt Mary's absence.[40]

Sara was not, however, incapable of looking after herself. For all her physical complaints and mental distresses, she demonstrated a steel-willed resolve to get what she wanted. First, she quickly sought out Judge Sommers. Although he held many progressive political views, his Roman Catholicism concerned her.[41] She also agreed with Mary that her lawyer seemed a bit narrow-minded on the matter of sex, attributing it to a presumed lack of sexual experience. Wilson, though, strongly supported Sara's case, grasping Ehrgott's character and also understanding that two people, once congenial, could grow apart to the point that it was "immoral" for them to continue living together. Client and lawyer differed on one thing, however: Wilson attributed to human nature the trickery and deceit that sometimes came with marriage, while Sara believed the fault lay with the "wicked institution" itself.

In Goldfield, Sara distanced herself from other divorce seekers. Their stories sickened her. These women, accompanied by the men they intended to marry next (and who paid the bills), lived together "in the most unrefined promiscuity." Sara saw their cases as completely distinctive from hers, partly because she and Erskine did not intend to marry. More importantly, these other affairs lacked the "sublimely rare" aspect of her own—a love not merely about sex but about souls who met on many levels: physical, mental, intellectual, and spiritual.[42] She found equally distasteful the realization that predatory men treated all women awaiting divorce as fair game. Having Katherine with her provided some protection from their unwelcome advances. The little girl also offered occasional diversion from Sara's self-absorption.

Yet, she did not protect Katherine from her mother's depression and mood swings. One evening Katherine asked if Sara regretted marrying Ehrgott. When Sara said yes, the little girl cried, noting that without that relationship neither she nor Albert Field would exist. Sara insisted she wanted *them*, but the marriage itself had caused her to hurt Ehrgott. She said she never wanted to live with any man again. Silent for a moment, Katherine then gravely replied, "I am perfectly certain that you would be happy if you could live with Mr. Wood because you both write such beautiful poetry." The daughter saw through her mother's deception and called her on it. She completely understood Sara's determination, even obsession, to live with Erskine.[43]

In September, Katherine became seriously ill with typhoid and Sara rushed her back to California. After nursing her at Mary's for a few days, Sara met her husband and son in Oakland, where they took Katherine to the hospital. Panicky with fear, Sara knew that if Katherine died Albert would never forgive her for taking the child to Goldfield. Happily, Katherine recovered.

Meanwhile, Albert Field was deliriously happy to see his mother and sister, and Ehrgott hoped that the crisis would change Sara's mind, that she would agree to reconcile and reunite. He apologized for past threats and confessed he never intended to fight her in court. Ehrgott also revealed that he had borrowed money to stay afloat and could not afford a lawyer. Sympathizing with his economic woes, Sara gave him $50—money that, of course, came from Erskine—but she would not desist from pursuing the divorce.[44]

Sara did, however, consider handing over Katherine. In June Ehrgott had requested she do so in order that he might enroll her in school later that summer. Further, he and Albert missed the little girl. Sara had made her choices, but she had "no moral right" to determine the actions of the rest of the family, particularly when it came to depriving them of one another's company. Sara considered his arguments. She had chosen to leave and ought to accept the consequent sacrifices. Yet, when she thought about being utterly alone, without any child at all to cuddle up to at night, she hesitated. She was willing to live without a home to call her own, but to know motherhood and then give it up was a far worse fate. Notably, her concerns focused on *her* needs, not her daughter's. Of course, if Erskine joined her, that would go a long way toward soothing her loss. Bird Wilson, meanwhile, counseled against voluntarily giving up Katherine. She should avoid antagonizing Ehrgott in the hope he would not contest the divorce, but handing over their daughter could ruin all chance of ever getting her back.[45]

Sara and Wilson drew up the divorce papers in November. Initially the lawyer considered arguing for legal separation on the basis of nonsupport. Of course, such grounds lacked credence. Ehrgott could have, and would have, supported Sara had she not left their home.[46] Uncertain about alternative options, Wilson consulted with Judge Sommers about her client's case. All three met. First, Sommers reassured Sara she would get the divorce, even if Ehrgott contested. So much for judicial impartiality. Darrow's friendship with the judge, along with Sara's own charms, seemed to be working. The trio then agreed to change the justification to cruelty, arguing Ehrgott's resistance to her wishes had caused her physical and mental suffering. Sommers would require Ehrgott to show cause why he should not pay $500 in attorney's fees (equivalent to $13,000 today), knowing he could not afford it. Finally, the judge told Sara, he hoped she would remarry for he "hated the thought that some worthy man would not be thus blessed." Erskine, meanwhile, disagreed with the plan, certain they would be unable to prove their case, and equally certain Ehrgott would never consent to the divorce.[47]

Several nights later, Wilson, Judge Sommers, and Sara convened so Sara could read some of Erskine's poetry. She chose a section of *The Poet in the Desert* that related to free love—a choice that turned out to be a miscalculation. The alarmed judge took exception to its assault on marriage and its repudiation of the Church and of the State's role in intimate relationships. Sommers admitted marriage's imperfections but feared free love a worse alternative. He asked Sara if she would live with a man she loved without marriage. Before she could consider the politics or sensitivity of the moment, Sara answered she would not live with a man any other way. She scorned a system that caused so much misery. Bird Wilson gasped. The judge stood up and walked away. Sara immediately feared that in speaking honestly she had done damage to her divorce, but, to everyone's surprise, the judge soon reappeared with a bottle of whiskey in one hand and ginger ale in the other and mixed her a drink. He told her she had the stuff of martyrs and that he respected her and her convictions.[48]

That very day, the divorce papers reached Ehrgott. For weeks Sara and Wilson had debated his possible reaction. He had forty days to respond. Within twenty-four hours, she had her answer. Ehrgott would contest. It devastated him that she had charged him with cruelty. Sara's reply that "cruelty" was merely a "technical term" did nothing to ease his pain. Both his Christian principles and the necessity of maintaining a home for their children obliged him to refuse a divorce based on such humiliating and false terms. He knew the lawsuit would impoverish him and bring shame on all the family, but that was Sara's fault, not his. That Sara demanded alimony, attorney's fees, and support money during the duration of the case, when she knew he did not have the means to pay, absolutely stunned him. He intended, nevertheless, to meet it all.[49]

Bird Wilson and Judge Sommers advised Erskine to prepare to testify. He resisted, imagining that his presence and physical appearance—"not so decrepit as 62 would seem—attractive perhaps"—would do more harm than good. "I think if it to be a prejudice of the court that an old anarchist should break up a home . . . we will have lost ground . . . tho I have been frank and brilliant in it myself," he told Sara. His hesitation derived from a combination of legal experience and spinelessness regarding the consequences a public role in the divorce trial could have for him. He admitted as such. Mary's independent assessment, though, got him off the hook when she agreed Erskine should stay well in the background as a man with a busy life and thousands of more important things to do.[50]

Erskine undoubtedly breathed a sigh of relief when, in mid-March 1914, Ehrgott suddenly appeared ready to settle out of court. What turned his mind is not clear. One possible explanation was the intervention of an attorney from the respected Nevada law firm of Hoyt and Gibbons, who had apparently been alerted to Sara's case by suffragist Anne Martin. Hoyt offered to help at no charge. Ehrgott's meager resources matched against this high-powered addition to Sara's legal team might have finally weakened his resolve. Money matters most likely played a big role in his surrender. No trial, no testimony from Erskine would be necessary. Only details about custody of the children remained. Erskine rejoiced. Sara felt little happiness or exhilaration.

In September Sara and Ehrgott finalized the divorce but at a fierce price. Ehrgott received sole custody of Katherine and Albert Field, the sacrifice Sara hoped she would not have to make. She thought her husband might allow her, at least, to keep Katherine. He would not. She fought for liberal visitation rights but otherwise accepted the ruling. Of her children's needs for their mother or the price they would pay, she remained largely silent. Instead, she asked Erskine if he would now provide her with a child. His response to the custody decision seemed flippant: "If throwing poor darling little Kay into her father's bigoted arms" meant divorce would be a certainty, he favored it. He also mistakenly referred to Albert Field as "Alfred," although several days later he offered a more sensitive response, acknowledging the heavy price she had paid.[51]

The divorce ended one long-simmering problem but created another: What happened next? Where would Sara go and what would she do? She wanted a place of her own where Erskine would join her in "tiny home-comings." If that was not possible, Sara intended to find a job in the suffrage

movement to "drown the bitterness of disappointment." She wearied of waiting for him. Time and distance had provided a clarifying vision. In the early
part of their relationship, in a period Sara now understood as one of "ecstatic
egotism," she had assumed they loved one another equally. Now she understood this was not the case. She figured as merely one factor among many in
his life. She had given up everything for him, while Erskine had sacrificed
nothing. In spite of his age and great mind, Sara now realized, during the
spring of 1914, as their affair reached its third year, "I am bigger than you." It
was a stunning statement of self-realization and an equally devastating critique
of Erskine. She did not, however, want to end things. Instead, she urged him,
yet again, to acknowledge the swift passage of time and lost opportunities and
to embrace immediately their true destiny with one another.[52]

Erskine agreed with much of this, although if he also believed she was
"bigger" than him, he did not say. He suggested she return to Portland, live with
Kitty, who was divorcing Dr. Irvine, and come to work for him in 419. Eventually, he promised, they would leave Oregon together . . . just not quite yet.[53]

Ten

SHIFTS

To many Americans it must have seemed the whole world splintered apart in 1914. A war erupted in Europe, leading to horrific battlefield mortality rates. At home, deep divisions between capital and labor took another violent turn, leading to the deaths of women and children trapped in the crossfire at Ludlow, Colorado. Radicals who had recently enjoyed some electoral victories, particularly in 1912, unknowingly sat on the cusp of a fierce reaction that eventually led to repression of free speech, deportation of noncitizens on the basis of their ideology, and imprisonment of homegrown socialists and antiwar activists such as Eugene V. Debs. Militancy increasingly characterized elements of the women's suffrage movement. Some suffragists protested in the streets as they aggressively pushed for a federal constitutional amendment that assured votes for all women, and suffrage groups vigorously lobbied President Woodrow Wilson, who resented the increased pressure.

Erskine and Sara engaged in all of it. They opposed the war and advocated for labor, free speech, and women's suffrage. Even as they seemed preoccupied with self, their connections to these larger issues drew them in and simultaneously shaped their prospects for a future together.

———————

On August 3, 1914, Germany declared war on France and invaded neutral Belgium. The next day, Great Britain waged war against Germany while the United States claimed neutrality. Erskine thought the brewing conflict a "great horror," but he also believed the Germans stood at the apex of "their good fortune" and that England, with its "dogged resourcefulness" and in alliance with Russia, would mobilize and successfully invade Berlin. Even if Paris fell, the vitality of France assured a quick reversal. The Germans would realize their weakness, declare themselves the victors, offer peace, and end the violence. The war would plant "the seeds for many future wars" unless disarmament and the minimizing of state power followed peace.

No better evidence of anarchism's attractions existed, Erskine thought, than the current mess in Europe. This war derived from rulers' wishes, not those of the people. He did argue, however, that the conflict would have some value if it crushed German militarism, crippled the Russian autocracy, and catapulted the Hague Tribunal into status as an international court with significant influence.[1] Erskine's powers of prophecy proved faulty. The war raged on for four more years and the United States eventually joined in.

From the beginning Erskine understood the far-off conflict had serious implications for his economic future. In spring 1913 he prepared to receive the first of two $100,000 payments—part of his eastern Oregon land commission—but by summer those funds suddenly appeared in jeopardy. W. P. Davidson and a syndicate of interested buyers from Minnesota threatened to pull out unless Lazard Frères postponed final payment until 1921. The banking firm balked. This threat to his compensation, totaling $750,000, sent Erskine scurrying east. It took months of negotiations between, on the one side, Davidson and the Minnesotans and, on the other, Lazard Frères to resolve the dilemma. In addition Erskine lobbied Wilson administration officials to back irrigation projects in Oregon. The latter would soothe Davidson's fears about the land grant's prospects for profit and enhance Wood's as well.

Finally, in August, all parties settled on an agreement and Erskine's commission appeared safe, although presumably delayed for eight more years. He would be nearly seventy years old when he received his windfall. Erskine accepted that late was better than never, plus, he assured Sara, he could use other investments to buy his freedom before then. Now, however, the European conflict intervened and put these plans at risk. "O this damned war," he wrote. "If it were not for that I could see railroads and sales of my land next summer. How long I have waited."[2]

Meanwhile, he integrated his feelings about war into his revisions of *The Poet in the Desert*. Wood knew its antiwar passages sounded too much like a lawyer arguing a case. Ideas overwhelmed imagination. So too did personal memory: "You see I've been there. Seen the wounds and smelled the stench." He wanted to convey the literal cost of war to individual human beings and their bodies. Subtlety and aesthetics mattered less than getting that message across.[3]

Sara's reaction to the war was less political and economic, more emotional and xenophobic. Germany's invasion of France, she believed, would be a return to savagery, distinctive only in the "more artful way of brutality" that modern warfare allowed: killing from a greater distance. Her fear morphed into racism as she worried that the rise of industrialism had also infected Asian countries and soon the "yellow race by sheer force of numbers will swarm us out of existence until they, too, becoming devotees of this same life-destroying industrialism[,] are overrun by—whom? Will it be the black race?" The only hopeful possibility she foresaw was that the war might accelerate a workers' revolution, apparently meaning *white* workers. That result would make the war "almost holy—I mean it would be terrible teaching but it would justify itself in its outcome for its horrid cost."[4]

Sara and Erskine's greatest political concerns, however, focused primarily on the American side of the Atlantic Ocean. As radicals, they continued to support leftists. The war might threaten progressive or radical change, but at this stage optimism about significant, structural change still remained robust. Erskine publicly championed Emma Goldman when she returned to Portland in July 1914 to speak on "Intellectual Proletarians." He paid the rental fee and the advertising costs for her talk at the Central Library, packed to overflowing with listeners. Proletarians, she explained, included not only people who worked with their hands but anyone who depended on another for salary or wages, including teachers, nurses, doctors, librarians, and lawyers. All should join the revolution.

Goldman went on to satirize wealthy people who sympathized with and financially supported labor. Socialite Alva Vanderbilt Belmont, for instance, furnished bail to striking women in New York, and novelist Jack London stood in a breadline to get "copy" for stories. But they were dilettantes who, at the end of the day, drove back to their comfortable, often luxurious, homes. As he listened, Erskine suddenly felt himself under attack, particularly when Goldman mentioned him as an only occasional contributor to her anarchist periodical *Mother Earth*. She wanted more from him, but Erskine was "too busy." That remark, coming on the heels of her indictment of Intellectual Proletarians who were "too busy with their money making . . . respectability . . . comforts and the friendship of their swell friends," elicited some tittering from the audience.

Mother Earth, which Goldman had founded in 1906, was a natural outlet for Erskine. Its pages advocated all the things he supported: workers' rights, women's emancipation, sexual freedom, birth control, literature and the arts. Its contributor list was a virtual who's who of American radicals. The journal's open opposition to the United States' entry into war and its encouragement of draft resistance also appealed to Erskine, even as it attracted the federal government's hostility. Later, under the auspices of the Espionage Act of 1917, officials searched its offices, confiscated past issues, and arrested Goldman and her lover and fellow editor, Alexander Berkman. As noncitizens, Goldman and Berkman proved more vulnerable to having their right to free speech suppressed, and the courts found both guilty under the wartime measure. After serving several years in prison, they were deported to Russia. The magazine ceased publication. Erskine was distressed at this turn of events, but his status and profession protected him from prosecution.

Goldman's remarks during her 1914 Portland speech about rich people's dilettantism annoyed Erskine, even as he admitted some truth to her charge. If intellectuals gave up all for the revolution, it might come more quickly. Erskine felt, however, that Goldman undervalued the good done by those she labeled "cowards and prostitutes." To Erskine's mind, they actually lent respectability to revolution. Their writings attracted middle- and upper-class readers, encouraged tolerance of revolutionary thought, and gave "the truth a hearing." As for himself, Erskine happily embraced the role of Intellectual Proletarian. He joined fashionable clubs and counted wealthy men and corporations among his clients, but he never concealed his revolutionary philosophy or politics from them. He used his involvement in these clubs and with these clients as an opportunity to share radical ideas.

Even Emma Goldman would have agreed, Erskine mused, that his numerous articles in regional periodicals and his public speeches had done something "to promote the idea of anarchy as a blessed ideal of great economic and soul freedom." Most people who came to hear Goldman already shared her views, whereas the thirty thousand readers of the *Pacific Monthly* represented the middle-class bourgeoisie who only learned, albeit perhaps reluctantly and from the comfort of their armchairs, about anarchism from Erskine's contributions. They would never go to hear Emma Goldman speak, but they would read his essays. He spoke in churches and colleges, and to "the prosperous indifferent and ignorant contented class." In showing them the sins of the current system, Erskine maintained, he had encouraged tolerance for anarchism and even won some converts.

Finally, through the thousands of dollars he donated to causes and the time he donated to publications, speeches, and pro bono defenses, Erskine protected radicals' free speech and saved them from jail—something he could not have accomplished had he been incarcerated. Every movement needed its "wily supporters . . . [as] no rebellion has been able to do without its 'respectable' and 'wealthy' sympathizers." No one could ever claim he kept silent when he should have spoken or that he ever denied the fundamental truth and value of anarchism.[5]

Following her swipe at Erskine, Goldman redeemed him to an extent when she went on to tell her Portland audience that, four years earlier, when she could not find a hall to speak in, just one man had stood by her: C. E. S. Wood. He had found a venue and presided at the lecture. Pleased that Goldman was reminding the audience of his radical credentials and commitment, Erskine concluded that Goldman was essentially "tolerant" of wealthy intellectual radicals—only momentarily did her satirical nature get the better of her. "No one can really find fault with this woman who has entered upon martyrdom for the sake of humanity," he wrote. "Her faults are petty—her virtues great." Several days later, while adding up his financial support for this visit, he noted with just a bit of a bite that he had "demonstrated some use of the intellectual dilettante proletarians."[6]

Sara found Emma Goldman more off-putting. In spring 1914, while staying with Mary and Lem in San Francisco, she attended a birthday party for Goldman. Mary's radical friends and contacts had welcomed Sara into the thick of their social and political life and included her in this celebration, but she felt out of place, as she had with Mary's friends during the Los Angeles McNamara trial. "Such a weird[-]looking group. Such talk! Such smoke! Such drinking!" Although Sara was every bit as committed to radical change as women who smoked six cigarettes an hour or men who drank nearly as many beers, she felt like an outsider.

This particular evening, she concluded, was a wasted one. Guests talked of "isms[,] with rancor for all that was not anarchism and praise for all that was." She thought it tiring and futile to emphasize differences rather than similarities that could strengthen radicals through solidarity. Sara shared Erskine's distaste for the unaesthetic elements, the rough edges of the radical crowd. Admitting that revolution would eventually come only through bloodshed, she saw her role and Erskine's as leaders who articulated its purpose: "We must teach them for what they are fighting and what they must hope to attain," while they kept their own hands clean of the radical movement's coarser elements. As for Emma, Sara found her intellectually superficial, her greatest value being to "those in the first primer of radicalism." That said, she did admire Emma's spirit.[7]

———————

By spring 1914, Sara resided in vibrant San Francisco with Mary and Lem—not a perfect arrangement. The always generous and supportive Mary could be difficult to live with because of her strong personality and inclination to dominate Sara. One particular issue weighed upon Sara: Mary's pregnancy. Sara feared the child was Darrow's and that Mary was engaged in deception, even betrayal, of Lem. She had no substantive reason to believe this, but she passed her concerns on to Erskine, who encouraged Sara to keep quiet. Sara's apprehensions possibly derived from the curious ways Mary talked about her pregnancy. "Lem will have a baby," Mary said, suggesting the conception was her husband's idea, not hers. Sara's leap to Darrow as the father, however, put the worst possible spin on the situation.[8]

Sara's dark view arose from jealousy; she admitted as much. "I envy her," Sara wrote Erskine. "I wish my great love had fallen into the heart of one I, too, could reproduce—I feel so life-cheated and denied." The likelihood of ever having Erskine's child seemed dim, plus Sara had lost her own children and family just at the moment Mary created both.[9] When Mary gave birth to daughter Margaret Parton, Sara did not mention it to Erskine. Nor did she sympathize with what was likely Mary's postpartum depression. Sara could not refuse to help Mary, who had done so much for her, but she privately complained about the added workload. Sara acknowledged the new mother's insomnia and her difficulty in adjusting to her new role—one that kept her from her work, her writing, and her public life—but Sara attributed the trouble to the vague issue of "repressions of [Mary's] soul." Before motherhood, Mary had been strong, independent, and self-reliant. Now she clung to Sara—"amazing and pathetic," the younger sister coldly concluded.[10]

Mary, however, also made their lives hum with excitement and energy. She loved socializing, thinking nothing of hosting a dinner for fifteen Industrial Commission people and asking Sara to help out. Mary wanted to distract Sara from her obsession with self and from brooding over Erskine. Bringing her sister into the company of people dedicated to big issues, reminding her of the needs of the poor and the oppressed, was Mary's way of kicking Sara out of her self-absorption and irritating narcissism.[11]

Hesitating to accept Erskine's suggestion that she return to Portland, meanwhile, Sara instead considered rejoining the suffrage fight. She knew her constant focus on Erskine had left her alone, dissatisfied, and unhealthy, plus her economic dependency continued to demoralize her. Suffrage work could solve some of those problems. Job offers came from as far away as Alice Paul's Congressional Union for Woman Suffrage in Delaware; the Congressional Commission on Women's Suffrage in Washington, D.C.; the New Jersey suffrage movement; and the New York State suffrage campaign. The last of these, offered by Carrie Chapman Catt, included a salary of $150 per month (about $3,800 today) plus expenses. Sara wanted to take it, if Erskine would join her, leaving Portland and devoting himself solely to writing. Sara could earn enough for both of them to live on. He scoffed at the idea.[12]

Opportunities closer to home proved more compelling. Anne Martin, state president of the Suffrage Society in Nevada, had pleaded with Sara for months to help that state's effort. Finally, as the fall campaign ratcheted up and Nevada's citizens prepared to vote on state suffrage, Sara decided to pitch in. It was a short-term commitment, and closer to Wood than New Jersey, Delaware, New York, or Washington, D.C. Little by little, she allowed herself to be pulled back into what Sara called the "vortex of the struggle of men."

Martin, who had trained with the English suffragists, impressed Sara. In fact, all these women thrilled her with their bravery, solidarity, and willingness to endure great indignities (such as soldiers thrusting their "dirty hands up [their] skirts" or abandoning them to ruffians who violated them) for the cause of freedom. Martin wanted Sara to write about the movement for periodicals such as *Out West* and to stump in Nevada as she had in Oregon.[13] Although uncertain about the new push for a federal suffrage amendment and the consequent rising criticism of President Wilson, who would not back it, Sara thoroughly supported state suffrage movements. Sounding a note that would appeal to Erskine, she thought it dangerous to extend the powers of the central government. At this point, Sara believed it best to leave suffrage decisions to the states, the cities, and even the wards.

As election day neared, Sara joined the Nevada campaign. She gave two speeches a day, linking up with nationally known suffrage activists Jane Addams and Dr. Anna Shaw in the particularly challenging battle. Nevada newspapers opposed votes for women. Stumping could be difficult and even boring, and certainly little honor or glory came of it. Still, Sara's enthusiasm for the fight picked up. Suffrage meant much more than mere votes, it meant the end of "sex monopoly."

The satisfaction of once again bringing an audience to rapt attention invigorated her. Anne Martin declared Sara the best speaker she had ever heard on either side of the Atlantic. Enthusiastic press reviews of her speeches in Fallon and Reno convinced Sara she was a better orator than poet. Sara rediscovered the happiness that came with "tumbl[ing] into the distraction of activity—to feel [herself] earning a new dollar in a righteous cause—to once again have men and women . . . say 'You spoke to our hearts tonight—You must know life, to talk about it this way.'" The greatest satisfaction of all, however, came on November 3, 1914, when the voters of Nevada endorsed women's suffrage by a sizeable majority.[14]

Erskine paid little attention. Only in the wake of the Nevada victory did he even mention her work there in his correspondence, acknowledging her superb speaking skills along with her charm, sincerity, earnestness, intelligence, and imagination. Though pleased with the victory, he worried about the toll on her health and wanted her to put his literary work first. A social cause should not supersede her dedication to *him*.[15] He suggested, again, that Sara return to Portland to work as his editor.

Mary advised against it. Sara and Erskine would have to meet in secret or she would risk becoming a "social leper." Stay in San Francisco, near your children, Mary advised, especially with the holidays coming up. Sara shrugged off her arguments, insisting her sister did not understand Sara and Erskine's kind of love. Erskine had saved her—"bought [her] life with his own sacrificial endeavor." She owed it to him to go. Thus began the "Portland experiment," as Sara called it.[16] Wood booked a room for her in the Multnomah Hotel, as she had refused his suggestion to live with Kitty.

For years Erskine controlled almost every aspect of their affair. By the winter of 1915, however, discernable shifts emerged. Up to this point, Erskine had always had the money, experience, and supposed greater wisdom. Now Sara, by virtue of her divorce and the loss of her children, had the moral upper hand. She used it for leverage, insisting she would not move to Portland until he told both his wife and Frances Burke, a newer companion and possible lover, about the depth of his commitment to and love for Sara. Erskine acquiesced to this demand, adding that if anyone ever published their love letters, as had happened with those of Elizabeth Barrett and Robert Browning, he would come across as either "the most extensive polygamist or the damnedest liar of the poet tribe."[17] Sara did not disagree.

Confessing to Burke that Sara was his "all in all" was easy. An honest conversation with Nanny was not. Claiming that he had asked Sara to return to Portland to help with his literary work and that she was a friend, not a lover, did not fool his wife. Instead, Nanny accused him of deserting his family in favor of a woman who flattered him.[18] Nevertheless, just having this conversation proved enough for Sara. She came to Portland in early 1915 and stayed for two months. The record is silent on what took place, but by early April they had given up the "Portland experiment" and Sara returned to San Francisco.

There, Wood agreed, she needed a home of her own, and so he paid the rent for an apartment near the crest of Russian Hill. The flat took up the second story of a rambling gray-shingled house, parts of which had been brought "around the Horn" in the early days of the Gold Rush. It was one of the few structures that survived the ravages of the San Francisco earthquake and fire of 1906. The entrance led up a steep stairway to a long hallway. A bedroom at one end opened to a large living room with a white marble fireplace. The apartment contained a sizeable but dark dining room and a kitchen with a cheerier breakfast room. Most importantly, the front rooms offered sweeping bay views and abundant sunlight. Sara replaced the awful wallpaper, patterned with magenta, pink, and green cabbage shapes overlaid on "jaundiced yellows and brick reds and diarrhea shades—Terrible," with an inexpensive gray one. In the bedroom she hung light-blue wallpaper. Erskine funded new linoleum, a gas stove, a water heater, curtains, linens, cooking utensils, and a bed. With breathless anticipation akin to that of a newlywed, Sara admitted feeling "bride-like" as she selected this last piece.[19]

Initially feigning indifference to the furnishings, Erskine claimed he only cared about having a place to live with Sara: "Camp. Barn—shack— anything—the shell is immaterial." But in the next breath it became clear Erskine's aesthetic tastes and demands would prevail. He advised her to hire a carpenter to make a large table of oak or cherry. He wanted heavy, coarse table linens rather than loose and cheap ones. Erskine liked the "medieval" look, along with Russian brass and Italian pewter dishes. Then he began shipping pieces down to her, including a desk. He intended to send an antique chair and settee, until Kitty expressed dismay he was breaking up *their* house, so those pieces stayed at 419. He also sent two cases of old Chinese jars, worth about $1,000, and another bale of items worth a total of $3,000. Suggesting Sara might consider buying insurance in case of fire, he still insisted he did not care about material things.[20]

Sara moved into the house at 1607 Taylor Street happier and more hopeful than she had been in a long time. She spent the first night "in *our home, our bed*," dreaming of Erskine. She looked out upon the city, "a mass of looming shapes and shadows sprinkled with lights brilliant and wan like diamonds and pearls [that] lie at our feet." The illuminated tower of the Ferry Building shot up into the darkness, and far in the distance Oakland's lights gleamed while moving illuminations—ships—traveled in between. Sara mused about future mornings when she and Erskine would wake up to sunrise on the bay and write all day long. The sunshine pouring into the apartment was a "prophecy of the soul's light that we shall find therein." The place tangibly symbolized their love, a material reality that took their relationship out of the realm of test or trial and into "settled surety." Sara christened the apartment "The Eyrie." Only the precipitous hill and steps worried her, for they would be hard on Erskine's "rheumatic" knee and ankles.[21]

Then, just as her hopes lifted in anticipation of their reunion, Erskine reported that when he next came to San Francisco his wife would accompany him. He would have to stay in a hotel. Shattered, Sara angrily replied that if he came with Nanny, she herself would not be available. "I sometimes wonder if you have ever grasped the emptiness of my life . . . the constant separation from the children in order that you and I may have a few weeks together?" She went on: "[The] lot of a mistress is hard. The man may love her best; find in her his solace and life but the center of his universe and the basis from which he starts and to which he returns will ever be the wife." Chastened, Erskine scrapped the plan. But the damage was already done. That he had floated it at all revealed that things had not changed nearly as dramatically as Sara had hoped. The old pattern of promises followed by disappointments reemerged.[22]

Eleven
SALVATION IN SUFFRAGE

SAN FRANCISCO HAD ITS UNDENIABLE CHARMS, EVEN FOR A LONELY DIVORCED woman. On winter days Sara could saunter down to Fisherman's Wharf, sit on a pile of lumber, and take in the sun-washed bay. The soft Marin hills and the white and gray boats that gently rocked against the long wooden wharves soothed her. She delighted in the contrast between the browns and blues of the fishermen's clothes and their ruddy red faces, as well as the huge crab baskets and the multitude of nets.

On summer evenings, Sara could look out the Eyrie's windows as fog rolled in and covered nearby rooftops "like thick tufted branches of trees." Occasionally lights gleamed through the mist. The Ferry Building seemed to float above it all, as if resting on a foundation of cloud. The view resembled a J. Alden Weir painting. Its "enfolding mystery and the thick, rich silence" brought her to tears.[1]

Beyond natural beauties, the city offered energy and excitement. Only nine years earlier, an earthquake and fire had nearly devastated San Francisco. Now it rose again. To celebrate that rebirth and the city's robust future, as well as the completion of the Panama Canal, business leaders, boosters, and the Bohemian Club (made up of wealthy white men, most decidedly not cultural radicals) began planning a world's fair. They needed public support to carry it off and turned to Congress, who voted in favor of San Francisco over New Orleans for the 1915 Panama-Pacific International Exposition (PPIE). The California city prevailed, in part, because it promised not to seek federal funds.

The exposition opened to great fanfare in late February. Constructed on 635 acres of San Francisco Bay land near the Presidio and Fort Mason, it boasted a wonderland of buildings, exhibits, artwork and sculptures, and carnival-like attractions, including "villages" featuring peoples of the Pacific in an area called "The Zone." The fair unambiguously celebrated the city's recovery from devastation and asserted San Francisco's emerging place in international trade. It boasted the "manly triumph" of the nation's past expansions as well as its prospects for further empire building overseas. Messages regarding the intersection of nationalism and race appeared throughout, with exhibits openly promoting the supposed superiority of whiteness—an ummistakable reflection of the nation's endemic racism. But the subjects of this bigotry and xenophobia pushed back. At the fair, African Americans reiterated their rights as citizens, especially as related to the Fifteenth Amendment, which asserted that the right to vote could not be denied on the basis of race, color, or previous servitude. China and Japan used their own presence at the fair to negotiate better treatment for Asian people in the United States. Suffragists, too, turned the celebration into an opportunity to challenge the patriarchy.[2]

More than just a place of entertainment and boosterism, for Sara the exposition became a venue for political action, employment, and, more importantly, personal fulfillment. Here she rejoined the women's suffrage movement. In fact, her work during the PPIE launched her into the national limelight as she joined forces with the Congressional Union, which in 1916 became the National Woman's Party. This organization transformed the fight for women's voting rights from piecemeal, state-by-state referenda to a movement focused on adding an amendment to the United States Constitution that would, in one fell swoop, enfranchise all citizens. Determined to use direct action to achieve this ambitious goal, Sara, a new convert to the amendment strategy, joined with other women ready to grab and utilize raw political power.[3]

No one better embodied this new militancy than Alice Paul, a slightly built Quaker and a graduate of Swarthmore and of the University of Pennsylvania, where she had earned a Ph.D. Paul, who unequivocally believed in the equality of women, began her career as a fearless suffrage leader when she joined Emmeline Pankhurst's Women's Social and Political Union (WSPU). The English group's hallmark strategy focused on opposition to any political party in power that failed to support suffrage. The WSPU's tactics included taking their campaign to the streets by organizing processions, parades, and picket lines. Some members resorted to window smashing, often punishable with imprisonment. When the incarcerated women went on hunger strikes, prison officials sometimes subjected them to forced feedings, as Paul herself was. Her forced feeding during one prison term proved so brutal it took her months to recover from its most debilitating and immediate consequences.[4]

Nevertheless, the WSPU's actions were making a difference, and so Paul brought their tactics home, where an American cohort adopted them.

Paul initially worked for the National American Woman Suffrage Association (NAWSA), planning outdoor rallies and automobile speaking tours. NAWSA, however, focused mostly on a state-by-state approach, not pushing for a federal amendment. So, Paul planned a grand procession in Washington, D.C., timed to coincide with festivities related to President Woodrow Wilson's first inauguration. She did not want to be part of Wilson's inaugural parade, for that could be construed as support for his administration—not to mention it would elicit little publicity. Instead, Paul organized a separate spectacle, scheduled for the day of Wilson's arrival in the city. Her event would publicize suffrage as a national cause and hold the new president accountable for advancing an amendment in its favor.

This bold plan worked. On March 3, 1913, media focused not on Wilson's arrival but on the suffragists' massive procession, which "wed beauty to spectacle." The huge, unprecedented event garnered the enormous national publicity Paul intended. The only significant march to take place in Washington before this one dated back to 1894, when five hundred men known as "Coxey's Army" walked four hundred miles to the Capitol to protest unemployment. By contrast, the women's suffrage parade, though shorter in distance, attracted many more participants—between five and eight thousand. Inez Milholland, seated on a white horse and dressed in white with a blue cape, led the parade's marshals. A wagon bedecked with a sign reading "WE DEMAND AN AMENDMENT ENFRANCHISING THE WOMEN OF THE COUNTRY" followed her. College women in academic gowns, including African American students from Howard University, joined in. To placate the racist suffragists who objected to the presence of these women of color, however, Paul separated the Howard University contingent from the other college women. Representatives from the Men's Equal Suffrage League also took part. At least 250,000 (though some sources estimate 500,000) spectators lined the route, most watching respectfully, although some men harassed the marchers. An army cavalry unit (today's National Guard) intervened and provided minimal protection.[5] The hugely successful parade demonstrated that "respectable" women intended to push for power by making a spectacle of themselves.

Paul next fixed her sights more directly on Wilson, who agreed to a ten-minute meeting. She told him he had a "national mandate" and urged him to use that power to support a federal suffrage amendment. Wilson denied such a mandate and added that Congress had more important issues to address, such as currency and trade reform. Meanwhile, the NAWSA leadership had grown to find Paul's means and ends alarming, unseemly, and radical, and so Paul peeled off from NAWSA, created the Congressional Union for Woman Suffrage (CU), and began to woo wealthy supporters. She found a particularly useful donor in Alva Vanderbilt Belmont, whose social status and financial resources provided the CU both the autonomy and money it needed to pursue its goals. Following Paul from NAWSA to the CU were mostly younger suffragists who shared Paul's appetite for direct and dramatic action.[6]

Sara became acquainted with the CU while working with the Nevada suffrage campaign. The CU's straightforward strategy to punish federal legislators who opposed a suffrage amendment and reward those who supported it, regardless of political party, proved controversial. Paul had assigned two organizers to each of the nine suffrage states to explain this form of "oppositional politics" to voters. Sara hesitated to endorse the campaign until Mabel Vernon, the organization's Nevada representative, convinced Sara an amendment would best assure universal women's suffrage. It would be a challenge to achieve, but ultimately more speedy and effective than the slower state-by-state strategy.[7] Once converted, Sara jumped in full bore.

A few months after Nevada endorsed women's suffrage, Alice Paul found a job for Sara at San Francisco's Panama-Pacific International Exposition. Determined to put suffrage on the national agenda, the CU organized a booth at the fair under the direction of Doris Stevens. Paul and Stevens then hired Sara to oversee it. Oberlin graduate Stevens had nearly married a minister, but when her fiancé discouraged participation in the suffrage movement, she chose the Congressional Union over matrimony. Sara thought Doris beautiful, brave, militant, and thoroughly radical, with a mind so "rich and deep and lighted in all its depths with a fire-fly flash of humor."[8]

The CU exhibit was located in the Education Building, beneath a banner declaring: "The world has progressed in most ways, but not yet in its recognition of women." The long, narrow space was decorated with hanging

Lieutenant Charles Erskine Scott Wood, Twenty-first Infantry, U.S. Army, ca. 1877. All photos are courtesy of the Huntington Library, Art Collections and Botanical Gardens, San Marino, California.

Nanny Moale Smith Wood as a young woman in the 1870s.

Charles Erskine Scott Wood, in the 1890s, when he was an attorney in Portland, Oregon.

Nanny Wood, in the 1890s.

Sara Bard Field (standing left) with her mother, Annie Field (seated center), and siblings: brother Eliot (standing right) and sisters Alice (seated left), Marion (center), and Mary (seated right), in Detroit in the late 1890s.

Sara Bard Field's wedding portrait, September 1900.

Sara Bard Field Ehrgott (seated) with daughter Katherine, son Albert Field, and husband Albert Ehrgott, in 1906 or 1907. The woman standing behind Sara is most likely her sister Mary.

Charles Erskine Scott Wood, ca. 1910, as he looked when he and Sara first met in Portland.

Sara Bard Field Ehrgott, ca. 1910. This is the first portrait of herself she gave to Wood.

Left to right: Sara Bard Field, Maria Kindberg, and Ingeborg Kindstedt standing before the automobile they drove across the continent from San Francisco to Washington, D.C., in 1915. Their goal was to present to President Wilson and the U.S. Congress a petition signed by thousands of western women (and men) in support of a federal amendment to the Constitution to give women the vote.

Katherine Ehrgott, Sara and Albert's daughter, ca. 1912.

Albert Field Ehrgott, Sara and Albert's son, ca. 1917.

Sara Bard Field, ca. 1916.

Charles Erskine Scott Wood, ca. 1918.

Sara Bard Field, in the mid- to late 1920s.

C. E. S. Wood at The Cats, in the late 1920s or early 1930

C. E. S. Wood, Sara Bard Field, Katherine Ehrgott, and Jim Caldwell at Katherine and Jim's wedding at The Cats, 1929. Photograph taken by Ansel Adams, who photographed the wedding for his friends, Erskine and Sara.

The famous stone cats at the entrance to The Cats, in 1955.

The patio at The Cats, with the "Maia" sculpture in the background, 1955.

Interior of The Cats in 1955.

Sara Bard Field and C. E. S. Wood at
The Cats, in the late 1930s or early
1940s.

Sara Bard Field and her granddaughter, Sara Caldwell, in the early 1950s.

baskets teeming with flowers, a portrait of Susan B. Anthony, a map of the United States showing the status of suffrage in every state, and an enormous chart revealing the votes of every House of Representative member on the matter of a proposed suffrage federal amendment. Most importantly, it showcased a parchment petition in support of the amendment. The huge document hung over and onto a table, welcoming all visitors to sign it. As more signatures accumulated, booth workers rolled the petition into a scroll that remained in full view to demonstrate the enormous enthusiasm for women's suffrage. The CU hoped to garner millions of signatures, particularly from women who already had the vote in their states or countries, and then present the scroll to Congress.[9]

Sara's responsibilities included publicizing and working the booth. She engaged prominent people to speak there and occasionally sought out well-known figures that visited the fair, but not the booth, to debate suffrage. When William Jennings Bryan visited the exposition, Doris and Sara knew he would avoid their exhibit, so Sara tracked him down. Bryan, an unsuccessful Democratic candidate for the presidency in 1896, 1900, and 1908, had just resigned from his position as President Wilson's secretary of state, fearing Wilson's policies with Germany would lead the nation into war. Bryan opposed eastern moneyed interests, American imperialism overseas, and Darwin's theory of evolution. He favored prohibition of alcohol. At the exposition, he pronounced support of women's suffrage because he believed women would vote for peace and prohibition. Sara invited him, in front of several reporters, to visit the CU booth as a sign of his solidarity with suffragists. Bryan refused because the CU currently opposed the Democratic Party.

There was truth to Bryan's claim, but that wasn't the whole story. The organization did oppose the Democratic Party, Sara explained, but only because it failed to back the federal amendment and was therefore, as the party in power, damaging the effort. This was not a partisan position but one of principle. Had Republicans held the White House and controlled Congress, the CU would have opposed *them*. Bryan blithely ignored Sara's clarification of the CU strategy and instead charged her with being paid by the Republicans to attack the Democrats. To this, she reminded Bryan that he believed suffrage would bring peace. The CU was simply trying to find a shortcut to justice for women, bypassing the much slower state-centered effort, while also ending war. After a mutually rude exchange, Bryan gave Sara a steady look, grabbed his hat and coat, and repeated that he would not support an organization that fought the Democratic Party. That evening, news of the encounter between the diminutive suffragist and the political giant went out over the Associated Press wire. Sara's emergence on the national stage had begun.[10]

Sara also took the campaign off exposition grounds. She led a delegation of four hundred women, for instance, to meet with newly elected California senator James D. Phelan, a Democrat. The son of an Irish immigrant who became wealthy in Gold Rush years through trade, banking, and real estate investments, Phelan served as mayor of San Francisco from 1897 to 1902, with a record notable for its fervent opposition to Japanese and Chinese immigration and his support of exclusion laws.

On the issue of women's suffrage, Phelan expressed ambivalence, though not opposition. Sara impressed him with her oratorical skills. He called her speech "the most compact and beautiful appeal" for suffrage he had ever heard and then invited her to visit his library, perceiving her as "a woman of letters." Upon hearing this, Mary laughed and told Sara that he was California's most eligible bachelor and "greatest catch," suggesting there might be ulterior motives behind the invitation. Although he did not currently favor a constitutional suffrage amendment, Phelan promised he would do nothing to stop it and suggested he might, in time, even be persuaded to support it.

The night after meeting Phelan, Sara could not sleep, she told Erskine, "because of life's terrible sadness."[11] For all the excitement of the suffrage fight, her personal loneliness offset the brilliance of her professional activities. She was referring not only to Erskine's absence but also to the swirl of letters they had been exchanging about Erskine's growing involvement with a new woman friend, Janina Klecan, a medical doctor Erskine had consulted with on some of his minor ailments. Now in early 1915, Sara once again found politics to be a welcome distraction from such personal melodramas. Suffrage brought her satisfying, meaningful work in the company of other talented and bright women.

That said, the suffrage cause did not represent her highest aim or ambition in life. Living with Erskine remained preeminent, and she turned to the movement only when things with Erskine seemed at a standstill or worse. As he consistently put off her entreaties to leave Portland and, now, pursued a new lover, she looked for something else to fill the void. In this Sara perhaps was an unusual suffragist, motivated to action more by thwarted love than political belief.

It did not make her any less committed to the goal or effective in her work, however. Attention and acclaim came her way, particularly for her oratory. The venerable Oregon suffrage pioneer Abigail Scott Duniway described one of Sara's speeches as "the most brilliant . . . she ever heard from the lips of a woman" and pronounced that her own forty years of [suffrage] work had been well spent "if only to have produced a woman like [Sara]." Although embarrassed by the praise, Sara appreciated the tribute. It underscored her determination to support the movement that needed, and valued, her help.[12]

Erskine had always urged her to create a life apart from him, but finally Sara herself understood that it was her duty, to both of them, to follow this advice. Suffrage would be the portal to the broader existence she wished for herself and Erskine. Suffrage would also be the arena in which Sara gained greater clarity about her values, views, and capabilities. Time away and distance from Erskine brought his weaknesses and hypocrisy into greater relief. These realizations did not erode her love, but they did make her more confident in challenging him and pushing for greater equality within their relationship. Personal issues drove her into the political arena, and in turn that political experience transformed her personal life.

Initially, though, Sara told Erskine little about the work. She knew that his anarchist beliefs and preference for local and state action over federal law would raise his ample eyebrows. She shared his concern about the evils of government but also thought women's suffrage consistent with radical beliefs. Anarchists applauded human liberty and equality; women, then, should wield every instrument of power, including the vote, available to men. Not until women obtained equality under the organized state could they achieve it under an anarchistic one. In her speeches, Sara encouraged women who had the vote to use their power, and not to advance "quixotic moral reforms" but to go deep by striking at monopolies and the poverty they created. This would lead to revolutionary change in the entire economic system. And rather than stew about prostitution and red-light districts, women should combat the greater wrongs of marriage itself. In other words, suffrage could be a tool to realize radical ends. As for seeking a federal amendment, Sara believed a national solution made the greatest sense and hoped Erskine would see the wisdom of it.[13]

As it turned out, while Erskine encouraged Sara to create a life apart from him, the suffrage movement was not what he had in mind. He discouraged "platform work," preferring she focus on his literary endeavors (for which he was paying her) and spare her health. As it became clear she was becoming more involved in the movement anyway, Erskine acknowledged she needed to "express herself," though he added, "It would revolutionize the world for me far more than any of your speeches if you lay on the divan in this cool and Sunday quiet hour." Her remarkable and newsworthy encounter with William Jennings Bryan warranted barely a mention from Erskine. Only in late July, as Sara began to share more information about her triumphs, did he concede that others' appreciation of her—"my pet, my sweet woman," as Erskine now referred to her—thrilled him. Otherwise, tied up with a lawsuit and his affair with Janina Klecan, he did not seem particularly interested.[14]

When Bryan came to speak in Portland, however, Erskine's attention perked up. He believed Bryan belonged to the "great average middle class mind" and stood "just a little above the millions of mutt minds but not so far above as to lose contact with them." Nevertheless, Erskine met and talked with him. Eventually, the encounter with Sara at the exposition came up. Bryan remembered her as "the little woman who wanted [him] to speak for the Congressional Union." He also remembered telling Sara she was the mother of only one child (suffrage) while he had many children. Erskine set him straight: Sara had many interests, commitments, and causes. He also promised Bryan, however, that she was not technically a member of the CU, which apparently pleased both men.[15]

Sara remained steadfastly supportive of CU strategy. State campaigns had been waged fairly autonomously, with women in the West paying little attention to eastern women's needs. The PPIE booth, the speeches, and the petition all helped educate people about the larger picture and provided a vision of what could be done beyond their individual states' borders. Women (and some men) signed the petition in droves, with no urging or exhortation from the CU representatives. They simply wanted to demonstrate the power of their vote to change men's minds in Washington and elsewhere.[16]

CU efforts at the Panama-Pacific Exposition climaxed in the fall of 1915, when, from September 14 to 16, it assembled the first convention of women voters in the nation. The party's purple, gold, and white banners hung from all the buildings on the exposition grounds and along the main Avenue of Palms, so that all fair attendees would know about the conference, even if they did not attend. The event sparkled with pageantry and speeches from prominent suffragists. Alice Paul supervised, and Alva Vanderbilt Belmont poured a great deal of money into the event. Delegates from "free and unfree" states gathered together, and a spirit of possibility and optimism pervaded the conference. Sara's speech emphasized the distinctive atmosphere that existed in the West, where people remembered the pioneer women's spirit and knew they, too, had shared in the hardships of developing the region—a factor that Sara said made western men more willing to extend the ballot to women. In the East, however, the Puritan mothers' part in establishing "a new land" had been forgotten, and now western women were coming to the aid of their eastern sisters, using their vote to exercise power on behalf of the disenfranchised.

Erskine came down in the midst of what Sara described as the "glittering . . . wonderful . . . wildly enthusiastic" conference. Nanny accompanied him to San Francisco to attend the exposition, although it is highly unlikely she visited the CU booth or attended the convention. Erskine, however, slipped away to spend time with Sara and observe the festivities. And he came for one other reason: to say goodbye as Sara embarked on a cross-country automobile trip on behalf of the Congressional Union.[17]

In early September, Alice Paul asked Sara to drive across the continent, to publicize the federal amendment campaign. Sara would gather additional signatures on the petition along the way and then deliver the huge document to Congress once in Washington. She would also meet President Wilson and participate in a congressional hearing. The CU's periodical, *The Suffragist*, described Sara and her drivers as "envoys," underscoring their role as diplomats carrying an important message. The trip was breathtaking in ambition and the challenges it put forth. When Sara reminded Paul that few service stations existed along the proposed route, she replied, "Oh well, if that happens, I'm sure some good men will come along" to help.[18]

Sara's first line of support, however, came from women. Ingeborg Kindstedt and Maria Kindberg, two Swedes and ardent suffragists who lived in Providence, Rhode Island, had purchased an Oldsmobile in California and offered to drive Sara and another suffragist, Frances Jolliffe, as passengers. Rumors circulated that Senator Phelan was in love with Jolliffe, a bright, attractive "society girl" from a wealthy family. She had just returned to California from Europe "with her heart full of sympathy for the dying proletaire," Sara acidly wrote Erskine, "and her trunk full of wonderful clothes for the living Frances." Still, Sara thought Jolliffe demonstrated good organizing skills and depended on her company for the long road trip. The Swedes, however, made Sara a little uneasy; she thought them "strange." Plus, the venture seemed poorly financed. The CU paid Sara's expenses going east, but not coming back home. Paul promised Sara she could write and sell newspaper accounts of the adventure and thus cover her return fare. Or, she might find other work in the East and decide to stay.[19]

As Sara laid out the plan to Erskine, she estimated it would require about three months time, including the days spent in Washington. After that, she might remain in the East until he committed to a long visit with her in California. In the meantime, the adventure offered several benefits: She could gain publicity for the cause, acquire more public service experience, and seek eastern publishers for Erskine's poetry. On the downside, it meant prolonged absence and greater physical distance from him. "Half mad" for him now, how would she feel to have an entire continent between them? If they lived together, she would never consider going, but they did not and her life was empty. This opportunity offered a compelling alternative, although, she assured him, "I am absolutely yours for any service by way of this trip or by staying at home."

All of her friends encouraged her to go except Mary, who, Sara thought, suddenly envied Sara's freedom and "wider life circle." Mary accused her sister of doing it for personal glory. Sara dismissed the charge, insisting she took up the challenge to further the suffrage cause and "for [her] own soul's sake."

She apparently did not consider the impact of a long absence on her children, both now living with their father across the bay from San Francisco.[20]

To his credit, Erskine unambiguously encouraged her to go: "Every wise thought calls go[,] and only love cries no." He knew that it could mean national celebrity for Sara and the chance to meet influential people. The trip offered the possibility of great returns for both of them if she made connections with publishers for his poetry. He added somewhat wistfully, "Now it is you who play the part of the active adventuress. I sit at home and gnaw my fingers." Indeed, positions were shifting, with Sara launching off into the public world while Erskine stayed behind. Still, he urged her to go, for "it means lifting you to recognition and influence."[21] Erskine's encouragement was likely also based, at least in part, on knowing this chance for Sara to have an adventure would relieve him of her constant pleas for time and attention. In the excitement of travel and in the thick of national politics and notoriety once in Washington, Sara would not have time to dwell on Kitty, Nanny, Janina, or her own loneliness.

Erskine seemed to literally feel the burden lift, remarking on the "fresh communion" between them. Of course, the venture carried some risk that she might not return, particularly if she found a well-paying position that eliminated her financial dependence on him. To this possibility, Erskine implored, "In the name of God consider my years—give up your feeling for independence to my happiness and believe me your support is not a burden."[22] Most likely, he did not seriously worry. Between her love for her children and, even more, for him, she would not likely forsake her California home.

So, Sara grabbed the opportunity. True to his word, Erskine visited her before she departed. When he stepped onto the Great Northern Pacific Steamship to return to Portland on September 26, however, it was Nanny who kissed *him* goodbye, as she stayed behind for a longer visit to California. (Sara and the small suffrage entourage had left several days before.) Nanny, Erskine reported to Sara, thanked him for "giving me last night," a possible reference to intimacy. Wishing he could make mincemeat of himself and throw chunks to Nanny, Janina, Kitty, and Sara, he knew it would not solve the problem. None of them wanted a piece of him; they each wanted all of him. His dilemma was trying to satisfy four women—one wife and three mistresses—simultaneously. As for Sara, he had last spent time with her in a booth at the Cat 'n Fiddle with Albert Field and Katherine; he called her a "sad woman tangled in complexities." One of these complexities included another possible pregnancy. He urged her to seek medical advice, put her health before all else, and consider an abortion. As much as the thought of their child thrilled him, he said, he could not bear to risk her.[23] Sara, as it turned out, was not pregnant.

The early days of the trip invigorated Sara, starting with a highly theatrical send-off the last night of the CU convention. Ten thousand people gathered in the Court of Abundance, a magical section of the fairgrounds lit with orange-colored lanterns. Under a gorgeous night sky, a large women's chorus sang the "Woman's Hymn," written by Sara. After the small traveling party climbed into the decorated car at midnight, the crowd followed them to the fairground gates and cheered them on their way.[24] Maria Kindberg, whom Sara described as a "gentle and rather self-effacing soul," did most of the driving, while Ingeborg Kindstedt, who knew more about automobile mechanics, took care of the car during the long and rugged journey ahead.

A cross-country car trip in 1915 was an incredibly ambitious undertaking for anyone. Decades before the interstate highway system traversed the nation, and long before paved stretches of roadways marked the way for motorists, these women faced a daunting physical challenge. A group of men had carried off the first transcontinental trip in 1903, yet even well into the twentieth century nearly everyone presumed that such a feat remained a test of "masculine strength and endurance." For a woman with children to launch off on such a venture was remarkable and unprecedented. (Automobile companies, however, wanted to sell cars to everyone, and in 1909 the Maxwell-Briscoe Company sponsored Alice Huyler Ramsey, a twenty-one-year-old Vassar graduate, to become the first women to drive from coast to coast. The trip from New York to San Francisco, along with her three women passengers, took forty-one days. This commercial venture attracted much attention, but it did not start a wellspring of women cross-country drivers.)[25]

Actually, it was a relatively new phenomenon to see women driving cars *anywhere*. Automobiles had become available to consumers, at least affluent ones, around 1904, and ten years later only 15 percent of registered cars in Los Angeles County belonged to women. Some believed women too emotionally unstable, intellectually deficient, or physically weak to drive. Others had political concerns, finding the idea of women drivers "fundamentally disruptive" to an orderly society. "Taking the wheel," as historian Virginia Scharff put it, was a perfect way to challenge such sentiments. Autos quickly became emblems of emancipation. For a woman to drive *and* use the act to promote suffrage proved an especially provocative way to attract media attention. Carrying their message to far-flung places by driving themselves there neatly demonstrated and encapsulated women's equality. Doing so at a time when women also demanded access to education and a place in the public arena further underscored the potency of the act.[26] In 1910 the Illinois Equal Suffrage Association sponsored a series of tours using cars as transportation but also as literal public platforms. Suffragists in New York City featured motorcars in their parades and spectacles, and Sara spoke from open cars on the streets of Oregon in 1912. The CU's transcontinental road trip was part of this greater effort to capitalize on the novelty and effect.

That Sara, Frances Jolliffe, and the Swedes were not the first to undertake such a venture did not mean it would be easy. Mechanical issues arose over the course of the trip, and interpersonal problems emerged almost immediately. Neither driver spoke particularly good English, which sometimes made communication within the car challenging. Ingeborg in particular chafed at her role as driver and mechanic rather than as an equal spokeswoman for the cause. The assignment to make speeches along the route (often to audiences set up by Mabel Vernon, who, traveling by train, preceded them as advance agent) went to Sara and Frances, but when the car reached Sacramento, the location for their first public event, Sara learned Jolliffe had decided to quit the trip altogether. The news stunned her. She concluded Frances was a "traitor" who lacked the spirit to carry on, and she theorized Jolliffe was abandoning the journey because the Swedish women bored her, she missed her accustomed luxuries, and she simply did not want to endure the expedition's inevitable hardships. Only several years later, when Frances died from cancer, did Sara regret her resentment and realize the woman probably lacked the stamina for the adventure. Meanwhile, organizers worked hard to keep

Frances's exit secret, leaving Sara responsible for explaining her absence when-ever it was noted.[27]

Alone with Kindberg and Kindstedt, Sara found things went fairly well, at least initially. She and her mostly "trustworthy and agreeable" companions enjoyed a wonderful ride across the Sierra, helped by the decision to hire (and pay out of their own pockets) a male chauffeur to drive the steepest parts of the mountain road. If they felt any remorse in relying upon a man at this juncture, Sara did not say. Instead, she raved about the moonlit drive through the wooded roads, occasionally sighting a crystal-clear mountain lake "lying face to face with the moon." Only Kindstedt's constant chatter detracted from the beauty, as she talked nonstop during the ten-hour journey to Reno. Still, Sara declared the woman a "full-fledged radical, a Syndaclist [sic] (first cousin to an anarchist) and a friend of any movement that will bring greater freedom to mankind." In Reno, citizens and the press welcomed them enthusiastically and supported their cause.[28]

So far, so good. The trio next faced the "most perilous part of the trip," across the Nevada and Utah deserts to Salt Lake City. No towns existed between Ely and Salt Lake, a three-hundred-mile stretch, so they stocked the car with food, water, and medicine. Sara assured Erskine her companions demonstrated "caution personified," and Kindberg, who as a midwife had delivered two thousand babies in her life, would certainly be able to deliver Sara safely to their next destination. They left Reno on a cold, late September morning and before long had lost their way, traveling through the night with-out sleep and searching for any signs or guidance. In the early-morning light they finally came upon a ranch, whose occupants gave them hot coffee and breakfast (for a fee) and, most importantly, a map—a crucial tool neither Alice Paul nor anyone else had thought to provide.[29]

Bitter cold, desolate countryside and fear of running out of gas overshad-owed this part of the journey. The women felt constant anxiety and experi-enced a good deal of physical distress. The car, for one thing, could not be completely closed to the elements. When they tried to shut themselves in, fumes overcame them. Erskine had provided a fur-lined bag for Sara to keep her legs warm, so that helped, and she had a warm overcoat and gloves. Even so, they stopped periodically, stamped their feet, and moved about to warm up.

Otherwise, Sara explained, they would "freeze into icycls [*sic*]."

They finally made it to Salt Lake City, where local suffragists whisked them off to the State Capitol Building. Ten automobiles decked out with banners of purple, white, and gold escorted the CU car up to the statehouse. There, Utah governor William Spry, Salt Lake City mayor Samuel C. Park, congressman Joseph Howell, and other officials greeted them. Sara climbed to the top of the capitol steps to address the crowd. The scene, flooded with afternoon sunlight, offered a dazzling panoramic view of the city and the Great Salt Lake in the distance. Sara took it all in and then began: Susan B. Anthony had been told to wait until African American and Filipino men (the latter recently liberated from Spanish colonialism) became enfranchised. Then it would be women's turn. Anthony died before that day had come, but in the years since, women had been pleading for their rights. Now, with eleven states passing suffrage laws and four million women voters exercising the franchise, they no longer begged for universal suffrage. They demanded it.

Sara described the petition she lugged with her: "I'm a small person to carry such a volume but it is the most precious part of my baggage." She wanted as many signatures as she could get from already enfranchised women and male public figures such as governors, senators, mayors, and congressmen. During her speech, Sara also acknowledged Kindberg's and Kindstedt's part in the journey. When they had reached the Utah border, she admitted, they were tired and so hired "a 'mere' man" to drive the car. Alas, he got lost and took them forty-five miles out of the way. Sara promised hereafter they would rely only on women.[30]

The hearty welcome the three travelers received, especially from Mormon women, intrigued Sara. They assured her all Mormon women supported the federal amendment. When Sara warned it might mean voting against their political party and thus creating conflict with their fathers, husbands, and sons, the women seemed undaunted. One of her hostesses, from a distinguished and historically important Mormon family, took her on a moonlight walk around the Salt Lake City temple. As they walked the grounds, the women talked Mormon theology and sociology, emphasizing their extraordinary community organizations dedicated to providing relief for the aged, sick, and poor. Sara secretly wondered if their dedication to women's suffrage derived from their sense of powerlessness within the family structure, which, although it was no longer officially sanctioned, had grown from a tradition of polygamy. Or maybe the idea of sharing and cooperating among polygamous wives actually made them more amenable to cooperating and working together now for universal suffrage. Either way, the women supported Sara's message.[31]

Back in the car, disgruntlement arose among the three occupants. Kindberg remained happy enough, as a rather retiring soul, to stay out of the limelight, but Kindstedt felt overlooked and underappreciated. Photographs of the traveling party always featured all three women, but Sara, as the spokeswoman, attracted more copy. Kindstedt, "stout and very Nordic," became increasingly belligerent, complaining Sara presented her companions merely as drivers, as menials. They never spoke. Sara replied that the division of duties was due only to her better English skills and knowledge of the West and suffrage. Not mollified, Kindstedt ended the conversation by fiercely saying, "I'm going to kill you before we get to the end of this journey." Feeling a bit terrified, Sara later learned that Kindstedt had been released from a mental institution just before the car trip commenced.[32]

The Swedish women's commitment to suffrage and perhaps their Scandinavian physical constitutions, however, proved critical to the venture's fate, particularly when they encountered their first snowstorm of the trip, near Cheyenne, Wyoming. Early October snows in Wyoming are not uncommon and did not faze the Scandinavians. They never considered waiting for the storm to pass. By this time, Sara, too, had become fairly oblivious to the hardships and shared a dedication to moving along without hesitation. If this meant getting out of the car to push it out of snowbanks, they did it. In addition, Kindstedt's knowledge of the car's mechanical workings meant she could take it apart, grease it, and put it back together. When something went wrong and no service station was within sight, she usually solved the problem. When they did visit service stations to purchase gasoline, the two women thought Sara much too friendly to attendants, who, they believed, overcharged them. People had warned them to bring red pepper along on the trip to protect themselves from dangerous men. But, Kinstedt told a newspaper reporter, the only protection they actually needed was from service station attendants who jacked up prices and stole tools from their car.

Sara, on the other hand, found most attendants helpful and believed they had the women's welfare in mind. Time and again their friendliness amazed her. The more remote the place, the kindlier the people. Service station employees offered hot coffee and begged the women to stay and talk awhile. After Sara explained their schedule and the need to keep going, they sent the party on their way "with God speed."[33]

Politicians offered a different kind of support. After Sara's speech on the Wyoming capitol steps before a small Cheyenne audience, Democratic governor John B. Kendrick signed the petition and the mayor read senator F. E. Warren's endorsement of the amendment. Sara and her companions then motored down to Denver, where a brass band, Colorado governor George Carlson, and congressman Bill Hilliard received them on that state's capitol building steps. The Colorado Springs mayor credited women's suffrage with cleaning up election day, saying it used to be a day of disorder, drunkenness, and debauchery, a time when political bosses bought votes with liquor. Now, candidates realized they risked sure defeat if they did anything that offended the refined women of the community.

All seemed to be going amazingly well. And then the convoy hit Kansas. It was not the "enemy country" Sara had been warned about, and in general people seemed willing to listen, especially about the daring adventure of the automobile trip, but the trio's enthusiasm for their cause diminished in relation to the quality of the roads and the car's stamina. The roads between Hutchinson and Emporia, poor to begin with, turned impassible after a heavy rain. The car stalled and sank deep into mud at two o'clock in the morning. Kindberg and Kindstedt refused to budge. So, Sara walked two or three miles back to a farmhouse they had passed. Without boots, and sinking to her knees in muck, she managed to slog through by crisscrossing the road to spots that offered more secure footing. By the time she reached the farm, her traveling suit was caked in mud. What worried her more than her appearance, however, was the prospect of waking the inhabitants in the middle of the night.

Sara's predicament, not to mention the distance she had walked, astonished the farmer. Without hesitation he brought out two heavy workhorses and a wagon and drove her back to the car. Along the way he asked what brought her to Kansas. She explained, though he seemed to have little awareness of suffrage or any other kind of social movement. Several times he said, "You girls have guts." The friendly farmer pulled the car out of the mud, refusing any compensation. "You have paid me," Sara later remembered him saying, "by letting me see what some women can undertake." Not all men proved supportive, however. Another farmer charged them $5 for helping extract the car from a ditch. When his mule then slipped into a gully and he needed *their* help, they charged him $5 in return. In another case, a man at a garage sneered at them, "If you want votes, why can't you take care of yourselves when you get into trouble?"[34]

In Emporia, Kansas, Sara found one especially important champion. William Allen White tracked her down as soon as he learned of her arrival in town. A Kansas-born journalist and leader of progressive reform, White's common-sense approach to politics won many readers across the nation. A friendly article from White about Sara's mission would be worthwhile. Having sent off her only suit of clothes to the cleaners, however, she received him "in bed" with "enough proper covering" but no appropriate "outside clothes." Nevertheless, he was simultaneously amused and impressed with the women and their project, and White in turn impressed Sara as a warm, sincere, delightful "dear old grandfather." He published a positive editorial in his famous *Emporia Gazette* and continued to support suffrage long after Sara's entourage departed.[35]

They encountered their first real political resistance in Missouri. Democratic senator James A. Reed told Sara he voted against suffrage and would continue to do so, based on his constituents' wishes. Sara replied, "Do you have to follow your constituency all the time? Can't you lead them once in a while?" To that, the senator only laughed. The same issue came up in Lincoln, Nebraska. Governor John H. Morehead, another Democrat, declined to sign the Congressional Union petition because, in his words, "the majority of Nebraska people had voted against an equal suffrage amendment." According to the news account, a Mrs. F. M. Hal interrupted him—"You say the majority of the people?"—to which Governor Morehead hastily amended, "I meant to say voters."

Perhaps the lowest point came in Omaha, where the transcontinental travelers received an especially bleak reception. Only five women showed up to welcome them. Apparently a large segment of the Omaha suffragists did not support the Congressional Union and its strategies. To this snub, Sara told the *Omaha Bee* reporter, "Women need this organization more than the organization needs the women." That remark probably did little to win converts.[36]

Everyone, however, seemed impressed with the journey itself. As they traveled farther east the mystique only increased. One Kansas City reporter explained to readers these "young women . . . have been lost in the desert and have had to follow mountain trails in blinding snowstorms in order to keep their appointments." Yet, he added, "attractive," "vivacious" Sara maintained her femininity while Kindberg's and Kindstedt's faces appeared "tanned and weather-beaten."[37]

Enthusiasm picked up when they reached Chicago. There, on the steps of the Art Institute, mayor William "Big Bill" Thompson greeted them before an enormous crowd. The Hearst-Selig Company filmed the intrepid trio reenacting tire trouble on the road. The newsreel, to be shown in theaters across the nation, featured Sara jacking up the car and waving farewell.[38]

While in Chicago, Sara took time for other things. She lunched with staff of the *Little Review*, a literary magazine founded in 1914, hoping to interest them in Erskine's poetry. One person, Margaret Anderson, proved quite unpleasant, according to Sara, having the arrogance of youth and "a certain impish intolerance." She swept the suffrage movement away with the wave of her hand, describing it as "bourgeous [*sic*], respectable, inadequate, the acquisition of a decaying social system." Sara, understandably offended, found this judgment reflective of the "Emma Goldman school," believing it possible to remake mankind over in less time than it took God to create the world.

Sara also visited Clarence Darrow, who, at the time, was involved in a "horrible case," a trial dealing with the Mann Act, which Congress passed in 1910 to criminalize sex trafficking. The Hearst papers had published "the most beautiful and sacred love letters of the fine woman who was this man's mistress—spreading them with salacious mouth-smacking before a filthy-minded public." This aspect of the case naturally seemed particularly horrific to Sara, the author of more than one sacred love letter herself. She and Darrow talked, inevitably, about her relationship with Erskine. Darrow told her he wished she had found a younger man, to which she replied that Erskine was her life and "the day he goes, I go, too." "Dear Sara," Darrow answered, "such a love comes only once in a million years." Within the hour, however, he suggested the two of them have an intimate rendezvous in New York. He also provided her with a fistful of letters of introduction to use there.[39]

The pace and demands of the trip had been so hectic that Sara had little time to write her customary long letters to Erskine. But from Chicago on, when Sara was able to take a train, or even a steamer on Lake Erie, she could write. These letters teemed with excitement and energy. Occasionally she returned to old themes—urging Erskine to do "the big, brave heroic thing" and join her—but she also described her successes on the journey, taking pride in her role as the voice of the movement and in the publicity she received. "But you don't want to hear about that, do you, darling," she wrote, and quickly added that all she truly wanted was to be with him. He was all—"husband, children, home, society, intellectual food and spiritual powers"—to her. None of the public acclaim or excitement compensated for his absence.[40]

Erskine followed Sara's progress as best he could, urging her to send newspaper clippings regarding the trip so he could paste them in a scrapbook. Sara managed to forward some, suggesting Kitty might compile them. Either Kitty declined or Erskine wanted to do it himself because he, at least, began the process though never finished it. (Her children later did.) Erskine also tried to line up the *Oregonian* as an outlet for Sara's dispatches from the road. So preoccupied with getting across the country and presiding over public events, however, Sara did not have time to write for newspapers.[41]

Erskine's own days seemed comparatively subdued. He worked on his law cases and his poetry. He dashed off some short stories for a contest (which he did not win) and began writing satirical essays, which he called "Heavenly Discourses," for Max Eastman's Greenwich Village–based leftist periodical, *The Masses*. Eastman asked Erskine to help raise $1,000 ($25,000 in today's money) in Portland for the magazine, though he doubted he could raise $20, let alone $100 in excess of whatever he personally contributed. Overall, compared to Sara's dazzling new life—meeting mayors, governors, congressmen, and eventually the president—Erskine's suddenly seemed dim and small. Not that he resented her new experiences and successes; he was proud of her.[42] Yet he also began to understand, perhaps for the first time in his life, how it felt to be the less-sparkling figure in a couple, to be the one who stayed behind, the one who might be deserted in favor of another lover. His protestations of love and commitment grew stronger. Sara's active life elsewhere made her infinitely more attractive.

By writing to him less often and backing off on her pleas for time together, in fact, Sara became Erskine's ideal free lover. "Here is Sara claiming nothing," he wrote, "loving me absolutely free. Here she is far away turning to new scenes—meeting attractive men and I lay on her not so much as a cob-web of claim nor she on me. But we are bound by the only bond which can bind. The great craving to be together for our own pleasure. Love." He had to admit that never before had she been so compelling. In this moment they had achieved the finest kind of free-love compact, with no pressure from either side. Interestingly, neither Sara nor Erskine noted his marked enthusiasm for a relationship in which they not only lived physically very far apart but did not see one another at all.

The irony of this, in fact, did not even cross Erskine's mind. Instead, he soldiered on. Acknowledging the lies and deceit with which he had "weakly deluded other women," he now understood Sara was his one and only mate. Then he added, thinking he had gone a bit overboard on the self-criticism, that perhaps it was not *all* lies to these other women. "I would like to think I was myself deluded"—though not about Sara. Such sentiments, in turn, renewed Sara's faith in Erskine. She was grateful for "the perfect understand-ing at which we have arrived over a blood-marked trail" and for "the holy purity of our un-bonded love . . . no chains, no vows, no outward symbols of rings and licenses—all proofs *within* ourselves; within our every breath of longing for each other."[43]

When Sara reached Detroit, though, her relationship with Erskine threat-ened to derail the transcontinental suffrage project. An anonymous person from Portland mailed letters to several people in that city describing Sara as a bad woman who had deserted her husband and children and carried on ques-tionable relations with men. One of the letters found its way to a Detroit-based pro-suffrage Episcopal priest. He requested a meeting and asked about the let-ter's accuracy. Sara explained she and *one* man had discovered they belonged together, yet his wife, a Roman Catholic, would not agree to divorce. They intended to take up a life together sometime in the future, for they loved one another very much. Convinced of her earnestness and integrity, the pastor put the letter aside and from then on publicly supported the suffrage travelers.[44] Sara also received support from family, including her mother and brother, who now lived in Detroit.

The nonstop pace of the trip continued. Cleveland offered a cold reception, while in Albany, New York, the governor's ardent suffragist wife insured a warmer welcome and her husband's support. Reporters arrived from New York City for advance interviews with these valiant travelers who had "aroused the country."[45] In Boston, Kindberg and Kindstedt put the car on a steamer and shipped it down to New York, where sight of the vehicle thrilled even "sophisticated old New York." Frances Jolliffe, who rejoined them in Albany, gave a "wretched" speech, according to Sara, while she herself had held the audience "spellbound as [she] blazed before them the newer, more militant aspect of suffrage" and asked "a solid East of women to meet a solid West." Reporters loved Sara. One newspaper called her "a dot of a woman with a giant's power"; another, "a born orator."[46]

Washington, D.C., the final destination, produced the high adventure's climax. On a bitterly cold December day, Sara and the Swedes climbed into the famous automobile for one last trip, this time to the United States Capitol Building. Jolliffe met them on the outskirts of town and, "having done *none* of the hard work, rode groomed and serene, into the glory of Washington limelight," Sara grumbled. The parade included marching bands, "a cavalry division" of women in long purple capes with yellow lining, and girls decked out in the suffrage colors of purple, white, and gold. Then came the battered and worn-looking car bulging with the adventurists' luggage. Behind the car rode twelve women on twelve horses, representing the enfranchised states, and behind them trailed an assortment of other decorated cars and groups of people marching on foot.

When the entourage arrived at the Capitol Building, the marchers divided into two columns and ascended the long staircase, with Frances and Sara in the center. Wyoming congressman Frank Mondell welcomed them from the House, and Utah senator George Sutherland from the Senate. Per instructions, the women requested a hearing on the floor of Congress while others unrolled a section of the petition. Sara pointed out that the document's full length exceeded four miles.[47]

The suffragists moved on to the White House. Three hundred women crowded into the East Room to meet President Wilson. He looked, Sara thought, "nervous and a bit abashed." Frances spoke on behalf of working women whose enfranchisement would help improve labor conditions. Sara, feeling some "maternal concern" for the president, who seemed both "humble and apologetic," focused on Wilson's states' rights argument. She encouraged him to forsake that position and show he was big enough to change his mind, as he had done on other issues. Wilson should openly support suffrage, now a national issue. One million men and four million women endorsed it. Now, it was Wilson's turn.

The president appreciated her acknowledgment of his ability to change his mind. He might do that on this issue, he said, but first he needed to consult with his colleagues in Congress. He then shook hands with Frances and Sara. Before he slipped away, Sara kept her promise to Erskine. She told the president she brought him greetings from C. E. S. Wood and offered to provide him a book of Erskine's recent verse. Wilson replied, "I would like to see anything Mr. Wood writes." She promised to post a copy, and then he was gone.[48]

Sara's encounters with powerful people continued. Over the next ten days she spoke before the Democratic National Committee, the Republican National Committee, the Senate Suffrage Committee, and the House Judiciary Committee. The last of these turned out to be a particularly grueling experience. Some members grilled her for two hours. She returned their rudeness with sassiness. "I simply detested the rotten bunch," Sara reported. She delighted, however, in remembering when Democratic Colorado senator Charles S. Thomas had refused to meet her in Denver: "'No I will not meet this woman who is here to intimidate me' (wonderful word)." Now in Washington he consented to give the Congressional Union a hearing.

The more resistant her audience, the better Sara's speeches. The Republican National Committee particularly angered Sara, since she held it responsible for keeping the suffrage "envoy" off the House floor, by one vote. "Fired by this rebuff . . . I tore up the former records for any good speaking. It was wonderful to feel my self gripping that audience and then lifting them to my own desire by the very strength of spirit which came to me." Her sister Alice, in the audience, overhead some of the men admiring her, or at least her appearance.[49]

In Washington, D.C., as she had all along the journey, Sara addressed people outside of government as well. One speech at a Congressional Union event helped raise $45,000 in fifteen minutes. People from all over the nation clamored to book her for speaking engagements. Seemingly overnight she became a sensation, a "semi-national figure." "Truly it reads like a fairy tale," she told Erskine. "Out of obscurity, sorrow, divorce, disapproval and a bohemian existence—in three short months," she had transformed her life. One year ago she lived "submerged in the unknown! A little stranger in Goldfield—a town so small and insignificant that millions never heard of it!" Now newspapers across the country reported on her interview with the president. Senator Phelan grumbled that people associated her with Oregon, when she rightly belonged to California. Whenever she appeared on a platform to speak, prolonged applause greeted her. Sara's fame even reached New York City.

Then Sara stopped herself short, fearing she might sound overly boastful to Erskine. Rushing to reassure him of her commitment to their relationship and his poetic ambitions, she quickly added that personal fame would vanish "like a bubble" once she returned to her normal life. In the meantime, she would use it to promote Erskine's work with publishers. Her limelight was "grist for [his] mill." True to her word, when Sara spoke as guest of honor at a New York theater club luncheon, she regaled the group with praise for Erskine's *Poet in the Desert* before turning to the suffrage movement and her "gasoline adventure." She intended to do the same with all the other speaking and dinner invitations she received in "this cauldron of a town."[50]

Twelve

FREE LOVE

CHRISTMAS 1915 FOUND ERSKINE, AS ALWAYS, IN THE WARM EMBRACE OF LOVING family and friends. He showered gifts upon all. Grandson Davy Honeyman requested a drum. Everyone else opposed the idea, but Erskine determined the boy would have his wish. He purchased the smallest tin drum he could find and adorned it with the words "1915 David Erskine Honeyman." In this, the indulgent grandfather made everyone, except Davy, unhappy. Twenty people attended Christmas dinner at the Wood home while Erskine's thoughts, he claimed, remained with Sara "in bitter loneliness." After dinner, friends came to call and the merry revelry lasted until midnight.[1]

Sara spent her quieter Christmas with her sister Alice and brother-in-law in Radnor, Pennsylvania—a "childless home" where Sara felt like an "alien." Alice's husband was a businessman who smoked cigars, opposed unions, supported preparedness for war, and expected to purchase an automobile soon. He found Sara amusing and a "little dangerous." Alice, otherwise completely conventional, dabbled locally in the suffrage movement. She most enjoyed, according to Sara, mahogany furniture and socializing with the upper class. Sara heard nothing from Mary, her mother, or her children. Only Erskine remembered her at Christmas. "You are the triumph of evolution and of hope," she told him.[2]

Beyond its holiday gaiety, Erskine's life paled in comparison to Sara's, however. While she addressed the president and Congress, he spoke to the Portland Rotary Club. He interacted mostly with Kitty, his new love interest Dr. Janina Klecan, and the uninteresting people he encountered in the "orgie [sic] of social engagements" to which Nanny dragged him. One rare exception to this pallid fare came in a conversation with young journalist and radical Jack Reed, who was visiting his Portland family. Having just returned from Russia, Reed reported an absence of revolutionary spirit there. The Russians wanted to fight only if someone invaded their country. If revolution emerged out of the current war, Reed predicted, it would be from seeds not yet apparent.[3] During this same visit, Reed met Louise Bryant, who, several weeks later, abandoned her husband to live with Reed in Greenwich Village.

Back in New York Sara spent her free time with *Masses* editor Max Eastman and a cluster of other "splendid young radicals" and free lovers. On New Year's Eve she joined this Greenwich Village crowd for dinner at a café. They moved on to an artist's studio, sipped punch before a fire, heatedly debated the war in Europe, and danced into the wee morning hours. George West, a writer for the Commission on Industrial Relations, escorted Sara home and, on the spot, confessed his love and desire to marry her. A Californian, West had worked for Fremont Older on the *San Francisco Bulletin*. Now, he lived with his mother in Washington, D.C. West eagerly pursued Sara. His letters, reminiscent of Sara's early letters to Erskine, overflowed with desire and devotion. "I love you, dearest, and want you terribly." "I'm hungry for the sight of you." A life without her loomed barren and bleak.[4]

Apparently Sara returned some affection, because he called her love "the realest, finest thing in my life," though he also recognized it as less intense than his, more "maternal." That she found him "melancholy, and heavy in spirit" suggested problems, too. Still, they shared a passion for poetry, art, and social justice, and West's appreciation of Sara's intellect and spiritual depth boosted his prospects. Interestingly, she did not tell West about her commitment to Erskine, although Sara kept Erskine fully informed about West's attentions.[5]

The Greenwich Village bohemians decidedly suited her more than Erskine's New York upper-crust friends Corinne Roosevelt Robinson and her husband, Douglas. Erskine had long known Corinne, Theodore Roosevelt's sister, and insisted that the two women meet. The Robinsons invited Sara to their home. She thought Corinne was warm and sympathetic but her husband offensive. When Sara, running late, entered the dining room and discovered the other guests already seated, Douglas boomed out, "Here's the Anarchist and free lover!" Sara thought the comment overly familiar and, coming from a stranger, unforgiveable. Worse, it shocked some guests and made her the object of prying curiosity. The Robinsons' son, Monroe, proved especially annoying, feeling free to "open all gentleman's promiscuous attentions." He described a play he had seen as indecent and "most immoral" and asked Sara if she thought suggestive things immoral. She tartly responded,

"Why ask me? Am I an arbiter of immorality?" The young man howled, "Oh I forgot . . . you don't suggest naughty things. You just do them." Humiliated, Sara vowed never to return to the Robinson home.[6]

As for Sara's new suitor and dazzling East Coast experiences, Erskine neither wallowed in self-pity or jealousy nor resented Sara's expanding life. He enjoyed her successes and even claimed a little personal credit for having taught her how to dress appropriately and captivate a crowd with oratory. Her frequent mention of other men's attention did not cause him great alarm. He knew she might meet someone else but (somewhat) jokingly noted, "There is no one to compare to me—never was and never will be." Still, he admitted that losing her would devastate him. Things continued to shift between them, subtly but undeniably. Now, Erskine fretted when no love letter appeared. Sara might land stimulating suffrage or writing work and never return. Or she might take another lover, find a better mate. If that happened, Erskine hoped he would be "lover enough" to let her go.[7]

More realistically, of course, Erskine would be the one to wander. In fact, he already had. Less than one week after Sara gave up the "Portland experiment" and returned to California, he had begun his relationship with Janina Klecan. This young, intellectual, emotional, attractive, and mysterious Polish immigrant and immunologist offered an irresistible combination to Erskine. He sought her help for his rheumatic knee, but their conversations quickly evolved from the medical to the metaphysical. Janina revealed she had sacrificed all—including her daughter, who remained in Europe—for her personal freedom. She shared Erskine's anarchistic values and found Portland "a miserable mediocre village" with very few interesting people except for Erskine. That hooked him.[8]

He informed Sara that Janina was developing a romantic interest in him, although this was "ridiculous—a man of my age." Yet, what could he do? He had already committed to a regular regimen of shots and appointments (to which he brought books and flowers for her). She insisted she loved another man and thought of Erskine only as a kind, considerate friend, but then she put her arms around Wood's neck, her head on his chest, and sobbed.[9]

One can imagine Sara's reaction: Not again! Still, she controlled her response. She presumed Janina loved him and asked only that Erskine be honest. She promised in return "a perfect Joan d'Arc heroism," suppressing jealousy and accepting the affair with the equanimity of a committed free lover. To this he replied with pique: "Thanks awfully for permission to love Dr. Klecan. It makes things easier." Sara must understand he had the freedom to develop relationships with other women without her consent, even as Sara remained first in his heart.[10]

One wonders why Erskine found himself attracted to women given to overwrought, emotional outbursts and melodrama; why he found the soap opera aspects of their lives compelling. Certainly, these entanglements satisfied his longstanding appetite for the admiration and adoration of women other than his wife. Perhaps the drama and pathos made him feel more alive as, at age sixty-three, mortality loomed closer. Although he insisted he did not think of himself as old, his constant worry that Janina saw him as a white-haired father figure suggests otherwise. Sara understood "the new voice will always be an attraction" to Erskine; a new woman would always tempt him. She warned that he was "playing with fire" by allowing himself to be drawn into Klecan's complicated life, but otherwise she, like Nanny, hoped the Janina complication would just fade away.[11]

Free love, then, continued to be a personal, political, and philosophical issue for Sara and Erskine. There was probably no better place in the nation than Greenwich Village, with its growing cluster of young radicals and "new women," to observe how others negotiated free love. Sara was in the right place at the right time to witness and analyze these new "arrangements." She took great interest in her friends' experiences and shared what she learned with Erskine.

Free love, a cornerstone of many radicals' lives at the time, raised an important question: Did it demonstrate growing equality and mutual freedom between the sexes or was it a portent of growing tension? Historian Christine Stansell concluded in her study of Greenwich Village bohemians that free love did *not* successfully recalibrate equality and power between men and women, and it rarely lasted the test of time. Although increased opportunities for women's employment in cities, the growing poularity of anarchistic faith in the ability of individuals to sculpt their own lives, and more frequent discussion of New Womanhood in American culture inspired experiments in love, these innovative practices could not eliminate timeworn sexual hierarchies overnight. Male privilege persisted even in the context of attempted egalitarianism. Men benefitted more than women. Patriarchy, as it turned out, could not be easily overthrown.[12]

A close look at individual cases reveals more variety than Stansell suggests, though. Men alone did not determine the long-term outcome of these affairs. Women, too, exercised power and made decisions that advanced their goals and self-interests. They, too, pursued professional opportunities that weakened relationships, they engaged in sexual affairs with various partners, and they initiated breakups. Further, the dynamic within a couple could change over time. Stability, security, and predictability did not characterize free love. That, in fact, was often the point . . . for both men and women. If it did not completely overthrow patriarchy, however, free love dealt it a blow, and women's actions and choices moved the needle toward greater equality and mutual freedom. These experiments were not painless, but both men and women experienced the pain.

The affair between Sara's close suffragist friend Doris Stevens and her lover Frank Walsh, a progressive lawyer and head of the Commission on Industrial Relations, provided one example of how women exercised power. In its early months this relationship had been in the "spiritual" but not yet physical phase. If Walsh, a married man, wanted more, Stevens told Sara, she would demand to know what sacrifice he would make for her (although it is not clear what Doris wanted). Assessing the Erskine/Sara relationship as dramatically uneven, Doris determined to not make the same mistake. She would not risk all while her lover risked nothing.[13]

Sara shared Doris's view with Erskine, who ignored the woman's declaration of authority and choice. He also evaded its personal implications, worrying instead that Doris might get her "wings broken" and find herself "ruffled and crumpled in the gutter" at the hands of "Lothario Walsh." Embracing free love dignified Doris, but attaching herself to a man who only wanted to play with her body and then discard her without demonstrating any responsibility was another matter. Erskine, of course, assumed Walsh held most of the cards. He ignored Doris's assertion that she herself had initiative and options, although he agreed she should make demands upon Walsh regarding economic matters—the kind of provision Wood had made for his lovers, even after love faded.[14] Patriarchal in its assumptions, this constituted responsible behavior to Erskine. He admitted he caused women misery but never intended to be fickle, reckless, or selfish. Over time he had learned that any worthwhile man must be completely honest and forthright and that secrecy demeaned love. Sara must have smiled wryly at this.

The relationships between Greenwich Villagers Jack Reed and Louise Bryant, and between Max Eastman and his wife, Ida Rauh, offered additional opportunities for Sara and Erskine to contemplate the perils and practices of free love. Bryant had fallen instantly in love with Reed, left her husband, dashed off to New York, shed her married name, and moved in with the writer. Sara knew Reed had "smashed a hundred hearts a week," abandoning a string of women from Manhattan to the Brooklyn Bridge. Louise's euphoria, she believed, would be short-lived, then replaced with inevitable sorrow. Erskine, too, thought Reed would abandon Louise. The young man serially seduced and ruthlessly abandoned women. It was not Reed's fickleness that bothered Erskine, though, but, as with Walsh, it was his lack of economic responsibility. Nevertheless, Louise should not be denied the "present high ecstasy" and chance to *live*.

Ida Rauh dismissed Sara's concerns and agreed with Erskine that Louise wanted life experience. Bryant had left stagnant Portland willing to accept the risk and possible pain that accompanied her gamble. Perhaps sensing that Louise's situation—abandoning a loyal husband for a man with an equally robust record of breaking hearts—resembled her own, Sara capitulated, even as she wrote Erskine saying, "God you men are made to give us exquisite bliss and fearful agony! Why, must it be?" A month later, Sara reevaluated Jack's devotion and Louise's acumen. She had underestimated both. Louise blossomed in the relationship.[15] Further, against the odds Sara and Erskine placed on this relationship's lasting power, Bryant and Reed remained together until Reed's death in 1920, weathering mutual sexual affairs outside their own and even marrying.

The ruin of Max Eastman and Ida Rauh's marriage on the rocks of free love elicited much more commentary. Sara possessed an intimate view of its dissolution, having lived at Ida's flat in Greenwich Village when the drama began to unfold. Again, this situation presented issues familiar to Sara and Erskine. Both couples shared long-term attachments that stumbled on the thorny issue of monogamy. Eastman, like Erskine, was indisputably handsome and tall, with a great shock of hair, yet the men differed in other ways. When Max married Ida in 1911, he was probably a virgin and was not yet radicalized. Rauh, six years older than Max and a trained lawyer, secretary of the Women's Trade Union League, and a feminist, was more sophisticated and better traveled in revolutionary circles. Ida introduced Max to Marx and Engels. She, along with his sister Crystal Eastman, led him into radical politics.

The couple wed quietly and set sail for Europe. Only when they reached Tangiers did Eastman write his father the news, noting, "I straight out disbelieve in and dislike marriage," hardly a propitious start. Ida saw the marriage casually, too, choosing to keep her own name, an avant-garde thing to do in 1911. She told a newspaper reporter they married only to placate convention and that Eastman did not wish to besmirch either the suffrage movement, in which he was a prominent figure, or his father, who was a minister.[16]

For a time the couple seemed happy, and in 1912 they welcomed a son. Ida loved Max; his commitment to her was tepid. He felt increasingly trapped and concluded that in marrying he had betrayed his ideals regarding freedom. Having discovered the pleasures of sex, Max wanted intimacy with other women. He neither offered nor asked for monogamy. Ida wanted only Max. His wife, Eastman later rather sourly wrote, was "violently monogamous," and when he revealed his affairs she "transformed into a vengeful animal." For a time, Ida reluctantly agreed to his affairs, but that became a position she could not sustain.[17]

The final break came in December 1916, when Max met a beautiful twenty-one-year-old movie and stage actress, Florence Deshon, at a *Masses* fundraising gala. Max moved out of the home he shared with Ida and began a passionate affair with the woman, thirteen years his junior. Eastman informed Ida he intended to marry Deshon (so much for his antipathy toward marriage). Sara, staying with Ida at the time, ungraciously described Deshon as "a bit shop-worn sexually speaking, having been handed about among a number of men in and about Washington Square." Actually, Deshon, a daughter of unmarried musicians, had greater claim to bohemianism than most of the

Greenwich Villagers. She made truly liberated choices in matters of sex, pursuing relationships freely and of her own volition. Professionally ambitious, she had no interest in marrying Max or anyone else.[18]

Sara mostly heard Ida's side. After Ida agreed to give Max freedom within their marriage, Ida claimed, he humiliated her. For his part, Max believed his wife had tarnished his reputation by telling others he was selfish and egotistical. Not even intervention by "warm-hearted poet Sara Bard Field," Eastman later wrote, helped the couple, for "nothing helps when love turns to rage." Sara's sympathies rested with Ida, although her friend's obsessiveness over abandonment wore thin. Rauh, meanwhile, complained that every other word Sara spoke was "Erskine."[19]

Women such as Rauh accepted sexual freedom theoretically, but it proved a difficult way to live and potentially more costly to women when the experiment failed. Certainly in the Eastman example, the aftermath proved easier for Max. He had Florence Deshon, whereas Ida was alone and became the single parent to their son. In their situation, the theory of "an enlightened amity between the sexes and women's right to the world's bounty" seemed impossible to realize.[20]

In analyzing Eastman's case, though, Sara drew distinctions and thought it offered little insight into her own free-love life. Her relationship with Erskine, she insisted, was healthier, as the "cool, sweet meadows" of their love helped them avoid the bitterness of the Eastman/Rauh relationship. She and Erskine were also not married. Still, Sara wondered why there were so many more bright women "of evolved personality" than men. Max's behavior particularly baffled Sara. He left an intelligent, creative woman, "pure and lofty in her ideals, able to grow with a man and lead and follow by turns," for an actress. Why did men refuse to fight their destructive tendencies just to grasp a temporary pleasure? Why risk losing the woman they truly love? What did they gain from deceit and infidelity that could possibly compensate for the loss of a "fine, noble soul and a flashing intellect"?[21]

Wood, characteristically, turned to Nature for answers. Sex, he explained, is much more "controlling" for men than women. Animal appetite and "aesthetic thrill" can simply win out over mental companionship. A man ranges about "like a plundering bumble bee," looking for both beauty and variety. Such behavior falls short of the philosophical ideal, but it is biologically driven. Even Wood still felt that "old promiscuous, general[,] and fearfully dominant instinct." Women did not struggle with the same natural drives. Their "blood inheritance is exclusiveness—reclusiveness." Sex to them meant not momentary pleasure but motherhood.

Erskine went on: Men, particularly handsome ones who crave all beauty they see (which included Eastman and himself), experience greater difficulties remaining faithful. Willing women partners continually tempt them. At the same time, no single woman can be all things to him: blonde and brunette, tall and short, "spirited and dreamy. She cannot be poet—artist—sculptor—critic—wit—athlete all things." Not that Erskine excused or promoted mindless promiscuity. Given Max's relative youth, Erskine assumed Eastman, who was just a few months younger than Sara, was still "in the animal stage." If Max sought multiple partners simultaneously, he loved only himself and simply enjoyed the "lure of conquest and variety." Then, Erskine pivoted away from male responsibility. Maybe Ida's unhappiness and jealousy had forced Max to be untruthful and hypocritical. Did she nag him? Perhaps he preferred peace and enjoyment elsewhere to life with his wife.

As for the idea that Ida's life was in ruins or that, under similar circumstances, Sara's would be, Erskine scoffed. Only death meant final destruction. Life meant growth. He had seen Japanese cherry trees broken, split, and heavy with ice and snow that then grew new shoots even more beautiful than the originals because of the "struggle and endeavor." Ida should be thankful for all her experiences with Max, including the most painful ones, for they all added to her larger growth.

Finally, Erskine thought Ida and Sara shared unrealistic expectations about men. No man could live up to their expectations. If their lovers inevitably revealed shortcomings, they should reconsider their impracticable standards rather than despair over the failures of the men. The problem was not that they dreamed of an ideal man but that they allowed themselves to become disenchanted when they "returned to earth." "Instead of whining about their wounded souls or blighted hopes, they should shoot up new leaves. Stop all the introspection." As for himself, Erskine claimed, he was "no longer of the promiscuous herd." What would have tempted him in the past no longer appealed. He now shared Sara's ideal of monogamy and complete honesty. She had awakened him to the spirit and beauty of those practices.[22]

By this time, Erskine and Sara, for all their theoretical talk, had become embroiled in their own free-love crisis. Sara's disingenuous claim that she was not talking about Erskine "under the guise of talking of Max" belied the facts. Their relationship had been sorely tested, yet again. This time they nearly ended their relationship over Janina and, more importantly, Erskine's deceit.[23] For five months—between September 1915, when Sara departed on her cross-continental automobile trip, and February 1916, when she came back west—the couple had been apart.[24] Only upon her return from New York did Sara learn with absolute certainty that Erskine and Janina had become lovers. Erskine admitted his lies, hypocrisies, and romantic failures and promised not to repeat them.[25] Janina, meanwhile, pleaded to retain a corner of his life and, emotionally distraught, spent one night in the hospital. When women ended affairs with men, Erskine complained to Sara, the latter accepted it and moved on. When men ended relationships, women made scenes. Janina's tears, wailing, and despair nearly did him in. Although he intended to end their sexual relationship, he agreed she would remain his doctor.[26]

Sara's trust in Erskine was in tatters. Her loneliness, illnesses, and pain resumed, as did recriminations, although with a qualitatively different tone. Her patience had run its course. His devoted attention for a few weeks per year followed by months of separation would no longer satisfy. She now realized that over the last five chaotic years, her happiest times came during the transcontinental trip and suffrage campaign. That work, with its larger social purpose, rich social life, and the attention she received from many attractive, appreciative men, buoyed her. When engaged with others, she stopped brooding over Erskine. She must recapture that. She would go east for the summer, perhaps take up work with the Congressional Union, make a life apart from Erskine, earn her own money, and "find my equilibrium in order not to annoy you with my idle wailing."[27] Making that decision calmed her down and lifted her spirits.

Erskine responded with a fit of pique. He tired of her suspicions and the impossibility of pleasing her. He stopped going to his office at 419 to avoid her letters, dreading even the sight of the envelopes with their depressing contents. As for Sara's threat to return east, Erskine testily told her: go. He had too many other things to worry about—his debts, the "crushing cruel law business," Kitty, Janina, Nanny, and his children. He would not wrangle with her anymore.[28]

Sara did not go east, at least not right away. Several times during these tempestuous weeks, she hinted to Wood about a secret. Finally, in May 1916, she realized she was pregnant again. Remarkably, given how open the couple was about most things, they never discussed birth control in their letters. They knew about the options available, but Sara's pregnancies suggest they either did not use them or they did not work. As in the past, Wood offered a measured, but mixed, response to the news. Insisting that the possibility thrilled him, he quickly added that he feared for her health—his perpetual position. Giving birth might risk her life, and thus the pregnancy should be ended. What for many would have been unthinkable came easily to Erskine. His response would not have surprised Sara, although it probably devastated her.

She boarded the *Shasta* for Portland in mid-May. Given the turmoil in their relationship, not to mention the pain and humiliation a baby would bring to their families, Sara and Erskine decided on abortion. Most astonishingly, they asked Janina to perform the procedure.[29] Why select Wood's lover and Sara's nemesis? Abortions, of course, were illegal and the options limited. Portland was a small town, Erskine well known, and confidentiality and discretion of utmost importance. Janina, perhaps, was the person they could most trust with their secret. Still, it was a strange, disturbing, truly terrible choice.

Two weeks later, Sara returned to San Francisco a physical and emotional wreck. She understood she had loved "a phantom of [her] own idealism" rather than the actual man. Yet, remarkably, she was not ready to give up on Erskine. She clung to their literary partnership as reason to continue the relationship. "And while a cynical world might smile at my faith-revivals," she told him, "yet I must let 'hope create out of its own wreck the thing it contemplates' or else lose my soul." Their artistic achievements would make it all worthwhile.[30]

Albert Field and Katherine met Sara's train when it pulled into Oakland. Her son, exuberant with news of his high school graduation ceremony, scheduled for the very next day, was relieved to see her. As class president, he would be giving a speech. Albert admitted it would have been "funny" if all the other boys' mothers came but his did not. Worried that his father might create a scene with Sara, though, Albert relaxed only when he learned Mary would join his mother, for she could, and would, protect Sara from his father's seething resentment and wrath. Albert Field's speech was a huge success—composed, clear, and frank, lacking only his humor, which the school principal had insisted on eliminating. Afterward, Albert Field rushed about introducing Sara and Mary to all his friends while his father sat alone in a far corner of the room. What a shame, Sara thought, that they could not sit together, hold hands, and enjoy their son's triumph. What a shame they could not celebrate the present rather than let past bitterness keep them apart. Then Sara hurried back to San Francisco to catch a train going east.[31]

––––––––––––

True to her word, once again Sara threw herself into suffrage work. She felt older, wiser, and sadder, but upon arriving in Chicago the excitement of transforming the Congressional Union into the new National Woman's Party swept her up. The Republicans convened there to select their presidential candidate, and Theodore Roosevelt had come on board for suffrage. These factors partly explained the CU's decision to hold their convention there as well.

Composed solely of voting women, most from the West, the NWP elected Nevada's Anne Martin as chair and California's Phoebe Hearst, widow of Senator George Hearst and mother of newspaperman William Randolph Hearst, as vice chair of their new organization. Representatives of five political parties—Prohibition, Progressive, Socialist, Republican, and Democrat—addressed the suffragists' convention. Woodrow Wilson's pro-suffrage aide, Dudley Malone, faced heckling when he urged the audience to stop impugning the president's motives. Wilson had kept the nation out of war and could eventually shift on suffrage, he said. The argument did not impress his audience, however.

Harriot Stanton Blanch, daughter of the late suffrage pioneer Elizabeth Cady Stanton, followed Malone to the podium. Women had gained nothing by being polite in the past, she pointed out, and now they would stop at nothing short of victory. She promised to deliver 500,000 women voters against the president's Democratic Party. Alva Belmont announced her donation of $500,000 to NWP campaign coffers. Achievement of a federal suffrage amendment remained the party's goal, and if the Democrats refused to support it, the NWP would continue its strategy of punishing the party in power.

The Republican Party did not sufficiently appreciate this potential electoral help, however. When Anne Martin urged them to endorse the amendment, they chose only vague support for suffrage as they selected Charles Evans Hughes as their candidate. The Progressive Party supported the amendment, but Theodore Roosevelt's return to the Republican Party this time around destroyed any ability the Progressives had to shape the electoral outcome.[32]

Next, attention turned to the Democratic Convention in St. Louis. Sara joined the equally futile attempt to convince that party's Resolutions Committee that the NWP would champion Wilson if the Democrats gave them something "big to take to voting women." Sara wrote a letter to Wilson, which Malone hand-delivered, urging him to court the women's vote as urgently as he courted the Progressives'. Sara, Alice Paul, and Anne Martin even convinced one delegate to draft a federal amendment plank. Wilson would have none of it, however, continuing to hew to his states' rights position while publicly acknowledging his personal support for suffrage. Even that small admission displeased the Southern wing of Wilson's party, which wanted no mention of suffrage whatsoever. From the NWP's box on the convention floor, Sara and others watched anxiously as the Southern delegates lost that battle. The suffragists preferred at least a states' rights plank to absolute silence. In the end, neither of the major parties committed to a federal amendment, though both formally acknowledged the suffrage campaign's importance—a first in the nation's history.[33]

Sara found convention work difficult and distasteful with its nonstop lobbying, speeches, meetings, and half-eaten meals. "What a terrible revelation of the heavy mediocrity in humanity these conventions are," she reported to Erskine. "Hundreds upon hundreds of heavy-jowled, red-nosed, thick-necked, pudgy-fingered men—crushes and crowds of them! By day filling the lobby of the hotels with tobacco fumes and spit. By night adding whiskey fumes

. . . . I believe more than ever in birth control." The experience reinforced her anarchism, reminding her that only particular individuals were worthwhile. In fact, the whole purpose of the human race, she now understood, was the exceedingly rare prospect of producing an occasional Shakespeare, Shelley, or Charles Erskine Scott Wood.[34]

––––––––––––

In the thick of national political campaigns and a movement she passionately believed in, Sara ended up neither satisfied nor happy. All she wanted was a "husband." By that, she did not mean someone to protect or provide for her, or a state- or church-sanctioned spouse. She wanted someone to share love and day-to-day life. In this time of "ripening womanhood," Sara believed, the idea of true partnership between men and women was possible.[35] Several men, in fact, offered her that very thing. She had options beyond Erskine. Returning east renewed the possibility of a relationship with George West, for instance. Thrilled at another shot, West promised to "blow all [her] troubles away . . . . We'll be happy for ever and ever." At one point they shared a hotel room in Brooklyn and possibly consummated the affair. The latest crisis with Erskine had predisposed Sara to at least consider a fresh start with someone else.

Yet obstacles quickly popped up. West smoked, had a history of alcohol problems, lacked Wood's fulsome confidence—in fact, seemed plagued with self-doubt—and was particularly close to his mother. Sara sensed West's mother discouraged his relationship with Sara. West disagreed, insisting his mother liked and respected Sara, although when George told his mother Sara would never marry again because of her free-love philosophy, Mrs. West replied she could not save him from his mistakes, implying Sara was one of them. The difficulties of living with an antagonistic mother-in-law and an overly dutiful, loving son must have been supremely evident to Sara.[36]

When Sara finally dashed his hopes for love or marriage, West took it hard. "Never before has any girl or woman engaged my slightest personal interest in a sex relationship that I . . . fell short." Even though she spurned him as a lover, however, West continued to encourage her writing prospects. She had a bright future in New York, he insisted, if she broke away from "a situation that is impossible and quit living as a shadow and sacrifice." Sara had finally revealed her commitment to Erskine. West believed it an unwise choice. Sara could "grasp life, and make of it something complete and beautiful," or she could surrender herself to someone who would not make "an equal sacrifice." Erskine did not deserve Sara. Knowing this would wound her and she would probably not forgive his candor, West claimed self-interest did not motivate him. He simply pointed out what she could become if she left Erskine.[37] This was a remarkable assessment—one others may have shared, but only West articulated and recorded in a letter that Sara saved. It did not, however, change her mind about either man.

Another suitor emerged that summer. In August, Gilson Gardner, a journalist who worked for E. W. Scripps's syndicate, sent Sara a postcard from Indianapolis. It pictured a small cottage. Scribbled on the back, Gardner wrote, "The little cottage that the moon won't stay over," possibly referring to a place where they had rendezvoused. Gardner declared his love for Sara even though she had apparently discouraged him. He continued to pursue her for a few more weeks. She forwarded one of these letters to Erskine.[38]

In the context of their shredded relationship, Erskine encouraged her to explore the bright prospects of New York over the loneliness of their San Francisco Eyrie. He again acknowledged the considerable age difference between them, and told Sara that if she found the right man, she should not consider herself disloyal. "Now Sara dearest it will not be worthy of you and of that holy deal between us of my child you bore in your body if you seek to distort my words beyond the solemn meaning I give them out of my love which seeks self sacrifice as its expression." Perhaps he was being manipulative. Perhaps he was living up to his free-love creed. Whatever his motives, Sara did not seriously intend to leave him even though it meant the "sad emptiness of our enforced duality of life."[39]

Once back in San Francisco in mid-July, Sara needed medical attention. Ever since the May abortion, she had been bleeding almost continually, and finally, in mid-July, the flow became a hemorrhage. Alarmed, the doctor told her to go directly to the hospital. As it turned out, Janina had insufficiently curetted Sara's uterus during the abortion, leaving it infected and acutely inflamed. Worst-case scenario: her entire uterus might be removed. More likely, it just needed to be thoroughly cleaned. Her son, Albert Field, came to stay with her, providing great comfort. The evening before she entered the hospital, she gave a speech at an antiwar preparedness meeting of four thousand people. She was the only woman speaker. With "shameless immodesty" Sara decided she gave "the only real speech of the evening."[40]

After the procedure, Sara learned she had experienced a "narrow escape" on the operating table due to heart problems. Her uterus had not been removed, but she still awaited word about whether that dreaded outcome might be in her future. Sara hoped Erskine would come to San Francisco. He did not. That he deprived her of a visit, "especially just now," was nearly more than she could bear. To make matters worse, Albert Field, who had been "so wholly golden and songful of soul," had to return to his father's home. She would be totally alone—something Erskine never experienced, she bitterly noted.[41]

Erskine seemed remarkably unconcerned about Sara's physical or emotional health, blithely wishing he could be there and making vague promises to get away, but always putting it off. Perhaps her matter-of-fact tone in the earliest letters about the medical emergency—excusing Janina's mistake and expressing gratitude Erskine had not been there to witness her agony—explained his absence. She probably hoped he would see through her false flippancy, drop everything, and rush down to comfort her. Surely she wanted her needs to come before all else, at least in this particular case in which Wood shared responsibility for the problem. Apparently, they did not. Legal work, he explained, kept him in Portland.

Besides, he had health problems of his own: inflammation of the prostate, which Janina was treating. She cautioned him "against undue sexual excitement." Another doctor urged him to postpone train travel, advising Wood that "any disturbance down there at your age should be very carefully considered." To this, Sara reminded him that when it came to her, "sex has certainly been a remote temptation for you." They had not been together for more than 60 or 70 days out of the last 365. Moreover, Janina had advised Sara to remain near Erskine precisely because he was a man who, given nature's urges, would seek another lover in Sara's absence. How inconsistent Janina's guidance now seemed. Sara assured Erskine he need have no fear any physical harm would come to him should he visit her in Russian Hill.[42]

To this Erskine angrily threatened, again, to end their relationship. He would set her free; perhaps more honestly, though, he would set himself free. Although Erskine acknowledged some legitimacy to her complaints of loneliness and the constant deferment of a life together, he also believed Sara's love had changed. Ever since her last trip east, her personal ambition had grown. She wanted to reach out for her own "place in the sun." Erskine wanted to help put her there. So he let go.

After this initial show of what he intended as generosity, he then took the offensive—a Max Eastman tactic—and became the aggrieved one. He said Sara had nagged him about his shortcomings and failures, and blamed him for all her sorrows. She needled *him*, "the already suffering victim." Moreover, Sara had more options than he did. She was free while he was "helpless and bound." He could not leave Portland, but she refused to live there. If he killed her ideal love, she killed his belief they were soul mates. "I shall always love you but you are not for me . . . . So here is the end." He would continue to pay her $150 per month for her literary work, and she could keep everything in the San Francisco home except for the J. Alden Weir paintings, valuable assets he needed to pay off his debts. As he wrote this, he claimed to be heartbroken and not "playing cheap hysterics."[43]

By the time she received these messages, Sara was on her way to Colorado Springs, where she rejoined the NWP's campaign against President Wilson. Her own spirits revitalized, she telegraphed Erskine of her continued devotion to him and followed up with letters addressing his complaints. She did not take his threat to end their affair seriously. In the presence of "the big men and women in big movements," she brooded less about smaller things. She wanted to put her arms around him, feel their hearts beat close together.[44]

Wood calmed down. Sara's reassurances helped, and so did his willingness to acknowledge his own "unworthiness," his miserable faithlessness, and the less-than-fulfilling life he offered her. He had violated his own ideals. Having discussed this latest dust-up with Kitty, his loyal secretary pointed out to him the great risk involved in Sara's abortion and its aftermath. He now felt "aghast and ashamed." If Sara wanted to go on, so would he. Wood promised a honeymoon. Moreover, Janina planned to leave Portland for good. He thought that outcome best, as she seemed on the verge of insanity. Erskine said, however, that he would not visit Sara in California until Janina left Portland, and before long, excuses, delays, and self-pity returned to Wood's letters. Anger, mistrust, and demands for honesty resumed in Sara's.[45]

Once again, discussing another couple's love affair provided an outlet to address, although indirectly, their problems. This time it was Doris Stevens's affair with Dudley Malone. Convinced Frank Walsh would not leave his wife, Doris had moved on to Malone, another married man. Although sexually active outside of marriage, Doris apparently did not reject the idea of marriage itself, and in fact, Malone intended to secure a divorce, in spite of the pain that it would inflict upon his wife and his career. Sara wrote to Wood that Malone had said he wanted to marry Doris with "a kind of indomitable desire that one thinks has died in the course of the materialistic ages." Malone appreciated Doris's beautiful body, fine soul, and acute mind. For her sake, he was willing to risk his position as the highest paid appointee in the Wilson administration and to break with convention, public opinion, and his powerful father-in-law (a United States senator who believed he "made" Dudley's political career). While in California, Sara helped the couple escape to Monterey for a few days by taking on Doris's campaign duties. Doris and Dudley relished the lovers' tramp "off in the wide freedom while the world stood at the telephone and tried to get them."[46]

Their affair, however, hit at a snag. One month after their California tryst, Doris secured an abortion with the help of Erskine and Kitty, turning to the latter's now ex-husband, Dr. Lloyd Irvine, for the procedure. Sara empathized with Doris. No man could understand the agony of illegal abortion, Sara told Erskine, and added, "I hate trying to live the ideals of free love under this hellish system. Poor darling Doris—and the first time is so terrifying—such an unknown inferno into which to plunge."[47]

A few weeks later Doris required hospitalization. Irvine had apparently performed the abortion while drunk, and so, not unlike Janina, had bungled it. Infection set in, Doris's fever ran up, and she became delirious from the pain. The incompetent Irvine disappeared, off on another alcoholic spree, so they called upon Sara's doctor, Millicent Cosgrave, to help. Cosgrave, furious at their delay in seeking help, brought Doris through the crisis. In the meantime,

Dudley arrived at her bedside, tearing back to the coast in spite of the major commitments his role in the Democratic Party demanded. Malone was "absolutely indifferent, almost reckless of public opinion," Sara told Erskine. Deeply concerned about his lover's suffering, he wanted to hold her in his arms.

Malone was, Sara thought, just the kind of husband Doris needed. He was also just the kind of partner Sara wanted. Doris, on the other hand, seemed "dazed and uncertain and questioning the future."[48] The difference between, on the one hand, Dudley's devotion and insistence upon being there during Doris's post-abortion health scare and, on the other, Erskine's absence in Sara's case could not have escaped either of them. Erskine's constant postponement in leaving Nanny contrasted sharply with Dudley's determination to leave his wife as quickly as possible. Adding to the friction, Sara and Erskine were now political adversaries. As Sara traveled the country on a National Woman's Party campaign to knock Wilson out of office, Wood supported the president. Protestations of renewed love aside, Sara and Erskine seemed to be spiraling further and further apart.

Thirteen
POLITICS

THE EARLY NOVEMBER WIND AND RAIN STRIPPED PORTLAND OF ITS AUTUMN reds and golds, leaving only a few remnants of an exuberant October. More subtle colors dominated now, with dogwoods glowing rather than burning, maples shedding mere flakes of gold rather than masses of it, harmony in the carpet of fallen leaves, and hazel bushes fringing the fir forests with a warm, yellowish gray.[1]

Among the human residents, harmony was less evident. The 1916 presidential election roiled the Pacific Northwest and the rest of the nation, along with other contentious issues. People disagreed fiercely on access to birth control, the right of the "Wobblies" (Industrial Workers of the World) to form a union, and, of course, the drafting of a federal amendment to enfranchise all women. Erskine and Sara took their places in these fights—not always on the same side. In some respect, the contests for power in the public world mirrored the contest for power in their personal relationship. To complicate things further, Erskine's support of "radicals"—whether that meant birth control advocate Margaret Sanger's right to speak publicly or the Wobblies' right to exist as a labor organization—suddenly threatened his position in the law firm he had founded. Sara's suffrage work, on the other hand, positioned her for career advancement. It was a trying time, with much at stake for both of them.

Erskine supported Wilson's reelection. He favored anarchists but voted for progressives. Erskine feared a Republican victory would return plutocrats to power and end meaningful reform. Wilson would, at least, salt the Supreme Court with people somewhat sympathetic to radical ideas, and that would provide a foundation for future liberal transformation. True, Wilson did not currently support a suffrage amendment, but that would change.[2] Erskine decided, however, to abstain from actively campaigning for Wilson this time.

Sara, on the other hand, campaigned hard against him. For her, suffrage took precedence over all other issues. Since Wilson would not support the amendment, he had to go. Erskine tried to dissuade her. If Charles Evans Hughes won the presidency, he would not push for suffrage either, nor would the suffragists have any leverage over him. If Wilson won, the radical suffragists would have destroyed, through their miscalculation, any political influence they might have had. Further, Wood doubted women spoke with one voice. Those who favored child labor legislation or wanted to remain out of war would not desert Wilson. Too many other "really great issues" mattered more than suffrage. The wiser move: wait four more years and pressure Wilson's successor instead.[3]

Erskine also thought the suffragists' anti-Wilson campaign, which had emerged from the East, smacked of regional arrogance. Western women, he said, resented eastern women telling them how to vote. When the NWP's Inez Milholland spoke in Portland, Erskine thought she had made two mistakes. She was too stridently anti-Wilson and anti-Democratic Party. Then, by berating women who did not share her position, she incited resentment toward "eastern dictation." Sara should not make the same errors in her speeches.[4] He heard one pro-Wilson woman skillfully skewer the anti-Wilson suffragists, labeling the NWP as the "Hughes Alliance," funded by rich women such as Alva Vanderbilt Belmont and Anne Morgan, financier J. P. Morgan's daughter. The audience went wild in resentful agreement with her. Erskine understood women's suffrage was vital, and he agreed a federal amendment would be a legitimate tool and that Wilson and the Democrats erred in failing to support it, *yet*, he repeated, it was not the most important issue of the day. Women would support Wilson because he kept the United States out of war.[5]

Indeed, the war, with its slaughter of people and waste of billions for no substantive purpose, was what mattered most to Erskine. It proffered no revolution. Rather, it represented a conflict among the ruling classes over access to resources; it was a fight for the privileged few and their corrupt social order. He opposed sending Americans off to die and paying taxes to fund a war that only protected "a few plutocratic masters under a capitalist system." He certainly opposed any movement toward preparedness. To prepare only encouraged militarism and aggression. It would accelerate American involvement in the conflict.[6]

On this Sara agreed. Preparedness taxed the poor to provide "protection to the property of the 2% land-owners of America." Citing the *New York Times*, which described the army and navy as insurance policies for American capital invested overseas, she believed workers received meager dividends from such expenditures. It was a "wicked scheme" generated by the munitions industry, but Wilson and the Democratic Party shared responsibility by pushing preparedness. It was one thing when greedy people duped the ignorant, but quite another when an educated, informed, and powerful person such as Wilson served the bidding of wealthy people and corporations. He might oppose the war, but he simultaneously worked on behalf of the moneyed interests, and that was "a blow to our hope of the evolution of mankind into something worthy of soul," she told Erskine.[7]

Sara's involvement in the anti-Wilson campaign further damaged their already tattered relationship. Characterizing her political activities as youthful antics, Erskine claimed she mostly sought personal attention and admiration—the same criticism Mary had once lodged against Sara's involvement in suffrage. Such condescension infuriated Sara, even as it revealed her growing self-confidence and willingness to push back. "To aid in gaining political freedom for half a nation which is struggling toward 'democracy' does not seem to me an amusing spectacle," she told Erskine. Moreover, suffragists did not receive public applause but rather attacks, affronts, and the necessity of working with "filthy-minded, tobacco-soaked men."[8] She demanded he acknowledge her commitment as serious and worthy of respect.

Of course, she also vehemently disagreed with Erskine's claim that other issues were more important. Men would always find things to put before votes for women. They would always find reasons why women must wait. But women would wait no more. If they did not put enfranchisement first, no one else would do it for them: "If the situation were reversed you'd be fighting for manhood suffrage first, I know, as the great issue against the menace of a privileged sex." She and her cohorts, however, did not "expect men to get our psychology. Once in a while one does, and a few men had pledged to make the issue their priority," but they were rare.[9] If she fought to enfranchise black citizens or laborers, he would think that honorable, but because it was women, and antithetical to his political goals, Erskine demeaned it. "You men are right to stand pat for your interests. We women are right in standing pat for ours." It gave her a "queer and unpleasant sensation to be advocating an opposite cause" to him. It was the first time this had happened in their "combined lives."[10]

The disagreement proved unsettling to both. Trying to dial the discord back, Erskine declared political parties "paltry" and wished he and Sara could just "get away in silence to poetry." Sara, too, preferred to talk about their reunion and coquettishly claimed that once she was in his arms she was "liable to be as meek as Petruc[h]io's Kate after her submissive era began." But neither backed down.[11] Sara, in particular, continued to press her cause's righteousness.

Wood's continual postponement of a reunion only steeled her resolve to stay the course of her campaign work. An early September telegram mentioning that he would soon come to San Francisco momentarily thrilled Sara. Yet, Mary's cynical comment—"Don't get excited. Some clients from Afghanistan will probably turn up on the day he is to leave and you will have had all your expectant joy for nothing"—tempered her optimism. As it turned out, Mary was right—not about the origins of the clients but about his postponement.[12] So Sara threw herself into the campaign, writing pieces on the National Woman's Party for *The Masses*, arguing women's suffrage was "the greatest advance in human freedom since the slaves were set free." For the first time in their relationship, she told Wood, "I am doing a bigger thing than you."[13]

In October 1916 she undertook an exhausting campaign trip to Nevada, Utah, Idaho, and Wyoming. Newspapers branded her "the silver-tongued orator of the Woman's Party" and the "second great emancipator." She found the chance to reach people, particularly women, to be "the thrilling part of a social movement." A poet could find beauty everywhere, even in Golconda, Nevada, where the poplar trees flamed "candle-like to the blue skies, golden in their autumn-dress." The pungent smell of the sagebrush encouraged her to believe she could still create in her relationship with Erskine "a strong unbreakable fibre." Sara thought the sturdy sage better represented her new-found determination than the more delicate scent of violets or lilies they had exchanged in the past.[14]

Her moods proved changeable, though. In late October, while campaigning in Casper, Wyoming, Sara experienced a "new desolation." A snowstorm that lasted all day had replaced the "happy hearted October of yesterday lying with wide-blue eyes and golden hair in a cradle of haze." Only a fireplace could offer cheer against the bitter cold and a "melancholy gray" sky. Sara began to doubt the NWP's efforts would alter many votes, yet the effort had been worthwhile. They had worried some politicians and, in that, they could see the stirrings of substantive change. The NWP had created political organizations at the county and congressional district levels, which would provide a future base for political influence and potential power. As for this election, she admitted to Erskine, she hoped Wilson would lose the suffrage states (which would signify the power of women's votes) but win the East and South and so remain in office.[15]

The last days of the campaign brought Sara to Oregon and closer to Erskine. That in turn sparked a competition over which of them would attract the bigger Portland audience when they appeared on separate stages on the same night. Many years later Sara claimed she won that contest. But as for the bigger contest, the presidency itself, Wood's candidate prevailed.[16]

Sara claimed indifference. She did not believe Wilson would be motivated to support a federal amendment, in part because some women voters had helped him win a second term. In truth, Sara argued, it was the women who had *fought* him who caught his attention. Their rebuke stung. The NWP, meanwhile, felt energized by its "magnificent campaign" and was already mobilizing for the next congressional election in two years. "I am so proud of women," Sara wrote to Erskine, "and I shall never desert the cause—I mean in my allegiance and sympathy if not in actual service . . . . It was a fine, brave dash for liberty these women made and I shall always be proud to cast my lot with them."[17]

If Erskine thought that "most of the brilliant women" did not join the NWP, California senator James D. Phelan disagreed. As Sara explained to Erskine, "It took vision, mentality and political sagacity of an unusual kind to see our principles and to fight for them—a new sort of woman . . . a militant type, unemotional and logical and yet fired by a desire for justice." Phelan, a Democrat, understood the suffragists' talents and value, telling Sara, "We've got to have you with us not against us in our next fight and we will have to make it possible for you to be with us."[18]

Although Sara's dedication to the labor movement paled in comparison to her sister Mary's, her sympathies remained firmly with the cause, and she understood why workers and organizers sometimes turned to violence. So, in 1916, she pressured Wood to take up the legal defense of Mathew Schmidt and David Caplan, who were being belatedly prosecuted for their part in the McNamara bombing of the *Los Angeles Times* Building five years before. The duo had accompanied James McNamara to the Hercules Powder Plant in San Francisco, where they had purchased the nitrogelatin used in the explosion. When the McNamaras went to trial, Schmidt and Caplan fled underground, becoming, in the process, heroes of the radical bohemian crowd.[19]

They evaded prosecution until 1915, when authorities captured and charged them. At that point, Anton Johannsen and Olaf Tveitmoe asked Wood to help defend Schmidt and Caplan. More was at stake than just the fate of Caplan and Schmidt, however. If the prosecution proved a conspiracy (which they were not able to do in the earlier case because the McNamaras pleaded guilty and cut the case short), the defendants might implicate others, including Johannsen and Tveitmoe, and further damage labor's cause. Wood agreed to take the case, but only under certain conditions. He wanted to be designated chief counsel, as a way to assure the defense met his standards of integrity and to avoid the tawdriness of the Darrow experience. Wood also needed to be paid, although he left the fee up to Schmidt and Caplan's defense committee.[20]

In truth, Wood was deeply ambivalent about the case. Sara, however, pressed him to take it, sparking another lively and sometimes angry debate between them. The primary point of contention focused on fees. Sara emphasized the damage to his reputation should Wood refuse the case because of money. Schmidt and Caplan saw themselves as fighting for a "great abstract principle" and would ridicule Wood's focus on compensation. Sara believed the two men virtuous—even if somewhat "wayward"—a lesson she had learned from *The Poet in the Desert*, she said. Schmidt and Caplan's example "made [her] want to use [her] voice always and forever in a song of rebellion."[21]

Erskine did not take the bait, sloughing off labor's judgment that he only cared about the money—something "so untrue it does not bother me." Then, he characteristically contradicted himself, explaining that compensation was, in fact, the crux of the issue. He hated the money angle, but "it happens to be with me the one important thing." Labor should not expect free services from him when everyone else would be paid. Plus, his law partners needed him to focus on William Hanley's lawsuit regarding water rights for their eastern Oregon land. True, the latter focused on property rather than "human freedom," but Hanley believed *his* freedom was in jeopardy since he was trying to bring water to desert homes (and profit to Hanley and Wood if they won and could consequently sell their holdings). Wood's firm needed money or else it would dissolve, a disaster for his son Erskine. In short, the Schmidt and Caplan case required the kind of self-sacrifice he was no longer willing to make. "I want to express myself—to be myself," he told Sara, surely a winning argument to a woman who had been urging him to do just that for years. Although he had never taken a cent from labor, socialists, anarchists, or any poor clients, he now believed he had done all he could for them. They should seek help elsewhere. He regretted Sara's disapproval but made his decision "according to my self desire and self approval. I am also a wage slave. That is the whole root of the matter."[22]

None of these arguments satisfied Sara. For several more weeks she continued pressing him to take the case, arguing there was no better use of his talent than on behalf of "the finest flower of Labor." She and Anton Johannsen's wife, Margaret, would raise funds to pay Wood's fee. He must assume his place "at the head of the army and win the land for Truth." If he refused, she would forge ahead in support of Schmidt and Caplan anyway. This cause inspired her even more than suffrage, she claimed, because "lives are at stake." Letter after letter she poured it on.[23]

At the end of July, Erskine reconsidered. He told his law firm colleagues—with the exception of his son Erskine, who was away in eastern Oregon—of his inclination to defend the two men after all. He doubted he would ever receive pay or that the effort would help labor's cause. Our vanity, he wrote Sara, has us believe we make a difference, but really things move on "like a slow glacial flow" regardless of anyone's personal effort. What worried him most was that he would lose his health and postpone "our day of freedom," by which he meant their life together.[24]

Just at this moment, Sara began backing off. She had learned that labor leaders were hesitant to give Wood the power he demanded. This outraged her. They clearly did not appreciate him. She also found her own talents undervalued by radical labor men. Quite confident in her growing skills as an orator, Sara gave a speech to help raise funds for the case in San Francisco, but the outcome disappointed on several levels. First, the event raised very little money, perhaps $100 total. Most of the audience consisted of "poor radicals" or unemployed union men who had little cash to donate. Second, after her hour-long speech, a militant labor organizer from Ireland named Larkin spoke. He was a working-class man who shared laborers' suffering, bitterness, and determination. Sara thought his eloquence and wit powerful, indeed irresistible.

She realized, however, that Larkin resented sharing the stage with her. He dismissively told the audience he had enjoyed watching her and listening to the "poetry of her words" but, he added, "she is a flower, a dream, a painter of pictures . . . . She is not one of us." The working class should fight its own battles, and not through court proceedings but by general strikes that would cripple capital until it surrendered. In this, he completely discounted her bourgeois argument for legal defense. Aware this might wound Sara, Olaf Tveitmoe immediately reassured her of her talent as a spokesperson for labor—telling her she was as good as Darrow. Others told her she gave the finest labor speech ever presented by a woman. Such comments, however, did little to soothe the insults Larkin inflicted when, at the end of the evening, he told her, "Go home and stay in your own place," invoking not only class but gender prejudice.[25]

Gradually, she realized that Tveitmoe and others feared that Erskine's determination to try the case "only on the facts" could open them up to prosecution. She learned Schmidt and Caplan had meanwhile succumbed to a "less noble influence," striving for acquittal and freedom from jail rather than martyrdom on behalf of the labor cause. She doubted they would be hanged. She now knew Erskine could not have worked with these people after all.

Erskine's insistence that he maintain complete authority over the legal effort ultimately gave him his out. In August the defense committee requested Wood come to San Francisco to discuss the matter. He refused. Hearing nothing more, a few days later Erskine withdrew from the case and chastised Sara for having pressured him: "Now no more explanations. My time is too precious."[26] Her tenacity on the matter was new, as was her increasing willingness to challenge Erskine on matters beyond their personal affairs. Not accustomed to it, Erskine did not like it. She tired of his evasions and inconsistencies. He tired of offering explanations that she no longer accepted. To help repair the breach, though, Sara agreed the Schmidt and Caplan case's particular sacrifices would have been in vain. They decided to put it aside. Erskine turned to his Oregon land concerns. At least he would be paid for that effort, and so, Sara admitted, would she as "I too get a parasitic living off it."[27]

In November 1916, one more opportunity arose for Wood to defend labor. Police officers and vigilantes fired on two boatloads of IWW members as they disembarked in Everett, Washington. They had come to support a strike of American Federation of Labor shingle weavers. Not averse to using violence themselves, the Wobblies had not, however, expected lethal resistance to their mere arrival. The "welcoming party" killed five Wobblies and wounded many others. Two lawmen died in the melee. Authorities then arrested seventy-four Wobblies, charging them with murder, although they found no guns on them.

This injustice appalled Wood, who believed the Everett business interests had "arbitrarily and anarchistically" aided the police. He also thought the Wobblies had stupidly traveled to Everett expecting their right to protest would be protected when "such rights exist only when the public concedes them." Public sympathies for the IWW were rare. Portland medical doctor and radical Marie Equi urged Wood to get involved. He hesitated, but when IWW people invited him to advise them on selecting local attorneys, he capitulated.

Once in Everett, he found the cause compelling, certainly more so than the McNamara-related cases, because in this instance truth and justice rested firmly on labor's side. Big business had initiated the attack with their henchmen hiding in a warehouse, armed with, among other weapons, a machine gun. It was deliberate murder, the kind that reminded him of the Nez Perce War of 1877–78. The mayor of Seattle agreed, calling the Everett businessmen "cowards and anarchists" responsible for the bloodbath.

Wood did not fully commit, however, helping only to organize the systematic collection of evidence for a trial. He visited the IWW men and women in jail and those in the hospital. He saw the bodies of the dead "riddled with bullets." When they offered him $25,000 to formally defend the Wobblies, however, he turned it down. "I want my time for poetry," he explained to Sara, plus he doubted they could actually raise that amount. One other factor was also in play: he needed to go back to Washington, D.C., to lobby for irrigation projects in eastern Oregon that would exponentially increase the value of his real estate.[28] Perhaps exhausted by her earlier unsuccessful efforts to move him, or perhaps wearying of their disagreements, Sara did not argue with his decision to refuse the case.

Fortunately, they found accord on other issues, including birth control and Margaret Sanger's fight for the freedom to disseminate information about it. Sanger, a national figure who defended women's rights to control their bodies and procreation, came to speak in Portland in June 1916. Wood introduced her. When several people distributed her pamphlet *Family Limitation* to the audience, police arrested them. Wood quickly stepped up to defend them in court. Ten days later, Sanger returned to Portland to attend the trial of those who had been arrested for handing out the booklet, and she discovered the Portland city council had passed a law in the interim forbidding distribution of "obscene literature." In response, Sanger and Marie Equi quickly organized a rally, distributed more copies of *Family Limitation*, and found themselves also under arrest. Erskine denounced the ordinance and arrests, and he defended Sanger and Equi pro bono. Their municipal court trial attracted great local interest. Women in particular filled the seats to witness the outcome. Although Erskine spoke eloquently about the folly of censorship, the judge ruled *Family Limitation* obscene, fined the workers $10, and suspended Sanger's and Equi's sentences, since they were first-time offenders.[29]

Nothing closed ranks between Sara and Erskine more, however, than an attack on Erskine himself. This time it came from within his law firm. In September 1916, his son Erskine, who worked at the firm, alerted his father that several attorneys wanted Wood to retire. Their clients no longer appreciated paying him to "attack their system." Distressed, young Erskine suggested he and his father create a new firm and tell the others to go to hell. Less upset than his son, the father thought if he could arrange a financial deal that would provide sufficient support for Nanny and freedom for himself, he would gladly leave.

Sara, too, saw in this turn of events Erskine's possible release from Portland.

The impetus to expel Erskine came from a young lawyer, Isaac Hunt, a recent addition to the partnership. Believing he did not receive a fair share of the firm's profits, and himself in personal disagreement with Wood's radical politics, Hunt hoped for a coup. The two Erskines fought back. Wood thought his son heroic when he informed Hunt he would not work with people who "demanded his father's head for opinion sake." Instead, the younger Erskine would leave the firm. Once his son understood the situation, Wood told Sara, he became "in his hard iron[,] Indian way—furious—outwardly calm—but cruelly determined." Wood, on the other hand, found it comical that a young man in Wood's own business thought he could dictate the rules.[30]

The affront angered Sara. That someone would punish Erskine for his brave beliefs was outrageous. His political and social activism had never caused him to shirk his duties or harm his clients' interests. Hunt's brain, of a size that made "a mustard seed loom cosmic," seemed ridiculously inadequate compared to Erskine's "colossal intellectual height." The experience also demonstrated how difficult it would be for Erskine to ever leave Portland. He might never cut the tie. Such thoughts led to sleepless nights shadowed with visions of "a dark cloud about the future." Not long after, Erskine visited Sara at the Eyrie, and his stay, as his visits always did, at least temporarily, put such fears to rest.[31]

Erskine's defense of his father was impressive. Caught between parents whose marriage had been unraveling for some time, the son sympathized with his mother yet retained a fierce loyalty to his father. In this way, both Sara and Erskine proved that, for all their narcissistic obsessions about their own problems, they were occasionally moved by the perspectives of family members who loved them and demanded their attention. Sara and Erskine were not the only ones whose happiness, growth, and self-realization mattered; their children, sisters and brothers, fathers and mothers, and, yes, even spouses mattered, too—at least some of the time.

Fourteen

FAMILY AFFAIRS

Five years into their love affair, Sara and Erskine had spent considerably more time with their respective families than with one another. Day to day, month by month Erskine continued to share a home with his wife, while his children and grandchildren lived nearby. Sara had lost custody of her son and daughter, but they resided across San Francisco Bay in Berkeley, and she saw them regularly when not traveling for suffrage.

That said, the turmoil of Sara and Erskine's relationship ensnared both families. Erskine's love for Sara left his children torn between a charismatic and generous father and a gentle, loving mother. Sara's children, who were much younger, dependent, and impressionable, experienced even more acutely the wreckage of their parents' marital conflict, their bitter divorce, and the brooding anger that followed in its wake. The continuing tensions left them caught in the crossfire.

At some level Erskine and Sara understood this, but they did not muse upon it at length. Instead they focused, and continually insisted upon, the morality, legitimacy, and righteousness of their love and determination to be free. Acknowledging others paid a price for their desires did not cause them to waver. They did, however, feel the need to justify their choices to family members, although they could not always choose when to make their defense. Wood, for instance, was forced to address these issues in summer 1915 when his son Max received an anonymous letter regarding his father and Sara. It characterized their relationship as "white slavery," based on information provided by a private detective who had tracked the couple in San Francisco. Malice generated the letter, Wood told Max. He then presented his usual philosophical justifications for the affair: life is too short and valuable not to be free. He would not succumb to the dictates of smaller minds. His relationships with women concerned no one else, and neither marriage certificates nor ceremonies defined love. When love ends, be honest. Lying generates hypocrisy and greater unhappiness.

Then Erskine turned more personal. "Mrs. Field" helped him with his poetry and they held common radical views. She is "the most stimulating, understanding friend I ever had." Nanny did not provide those things for him. He knew this hurt his wife, "but there are bigger things even than sparing another's sorrow." A person should never stop growing, changing, and developing new relationships with people who understood and appreciated you. Wood concluded with his habitual lament: before he died, he wanted to achieve some measure of personal happiness. He avoided commenting on sex.[1]

The heartbreak that Erskine's free-love ideas and practices caused Nanny most concerned their children, especially firstborn son Erskine, who engaged most pointedly with his father over the affair. The two shared not only a name but an especially close relationship. The son had followed his father into Nez Perce country (though as an adopted son of Chief Joseph rather than a soldier seeking his surrender), and when tuberculosis struck the younger Erskine, his panicky father did everything he could, at great expense, to save him. Both Erskines practiced law, and they worked as business partners. They both loved open spaces, western skies, and fresh air. Erskine lived with his own family in a house right next door to his parents, on the heights above Portland. Father and son had deep confidence in their own opinions and shared a self-righteous streak. When they took a stand, they dug in their heels. On the issue of Sara and the agony Wood caused Nanny, however, they disagreed. The younger Erskine unambiguously stood with his mother.

Perhaps prodded by Max's anonymous letter, Erskine chose the 1915 publication of *The Poet in the Desert*, his lengthy poem now printed in book form, to make a more formal case about his relationship with Sara to the family. He gave each child an autographed copy of what he called his "creed." He then composed a letter to Erskine and asked him to share it with his siblings and mother. It presented a statement of, and justification for, his intentions to eventually leave Portland, the law, his wife, and his family. He made Sara's role as literary editor central to that decision. *The Poet in the Desert*, he explained, was his most serious work. Without her encouragement and editorial skills, it never would have appeared. Further, this was not his last work. He had much more to say. To accomplish that cherished goal, he must have solitude, the company of likeminded souls, and the support and help of Sara. "It would be . . . life-defying and wicked to expect me not to grow in her direction." He would not lie, cover up, or be hypocritical about that.

The family needed to see him clearly—as the man he was. Only Sara and a few mutual friends understood him, he said; his narrow, barren Portland life was no life at all. It impeded his true expression. To date, he had not abandoned family, as other writers, such as Goethe, Ibsen, and Shakespeare, had. And although perhaps he did not share their literary talent, he wanted to try for transcendent poetry. Once he could provide Nanny with financial independence and the rest of them with trusts, he would leave. He also preferred not to sever relations, hoping to return periodically and enjoy his family, although he feared Nanny would not allow that. She believed he "chose" to be a cold, heartless deserter. Erskine insisted he did not push her aside. "I have simply walked further into a country where she cannot follow . . . and where I have found true understanding and beauty." Nor would he ever forsake his children. Who could question his love for them? Yet they must understand that "poetic imagination" meant life to him. He offered *The Poet in the Desert* as assurance of his love of his family. He hoped they would read and understand it.[2]

In emphasizing Sara's literary and spiritual affinities, Wood was honest. He valued those attributes far more than her youth or sexual attraction. Initially, Erskine did not press his father on that point, possibly assuming his sixty-four-year-old father too old to be sexually active, or perhaps preferring not to think of his father as a sexual being at any age. The following March, Erskine even offered to write a letter to Nanny supporting his father's work with Sara. But before he sent it, Erskine needed to know if the two were lovers. His father's explanation had left that issue ambiguous, and so the son now demanded more forthright information. If Erskine and Sara were lovers as well as literary partners, he could not endorse their relationship.

Replying that sex was irrelevant, Wood then added, "Certainly there is sex[,] for she is a woman." Embarrassed, Erskine explained that he meant to ask if his father *loved* Sara. Wood answered "yes" but quickly added, "She displaces no atom of love for your mother." That did not satisfy Erskine, who then refused to write the letter endorsing his father's relationship with Sara.

Sex made all the difference. The younger Erskine went on to say that if he felt a woman coming between him and his wife he would turn away from temptation: "I know I would." His father acknowledged that might be true but then added, "You are you—I am I . . . and, my son, do not boast till your life is over. Love is a life force and does not come with drums and banners but as sleep comes. It is a growth."[3] The son did not give his father the blessing Wood had hoped to receive, and never again did Erskine offer to smooth the way for what he saw as his father's grave transgression. It remained a source of hurt, anger, and alienation for years to come.[4]

Only Wood's daughter Lisa offered a more sympathetic, though anguished, response to her father's plea for freedom. She understood him yet could not openly support him, for that would "make deeper the wounds of my little mother who adoring you now as from the very first, can never understand or reconcile herself to the change in your philosophy of life." To support him would devastate her mother, whereas to withhold open approval would not hurt Wood. Her father was mentally and physically stronger and his social life richer, as he had a loving companion and a lively cohort of friends who appreciated and supported him. Nanny would never find another husband, for, although Lisa did not explicitly make this point, older men had many more options than older women to find friends and lovers. Further, Wood's ideals would live on in the pages of *The Poet in the Desert*, its philosophy becoming "life long food for thought for me and your grandchildren and all who read it."

As for her father's plan to eventually leave Portland—most likely years from then—Lisa and her family now lived in the San Francisco area. Erskine's move to California might mean Lisa would actually see her father more often. Meanwhile, Erskine appreciated his daughter's sympathy, just as he understood her position to keep it secret.[5] All of Wood's children felt drawn to his appealing personality, bound by their love for him, and persuaded by some elements of his philosophical position, but the everyday reality of witnessing their mother's pain and her fear of abandonment late in life meant that, if forced to choose, they would choose her.

Sara did not compose elaborate philosophical explanations for her children. Instead, Katherine and Albert took cues about her choices from her behavior. The boy sympathized with his mother's bid for freedom and only rarely revealed the difficulties he experienced because of her choice. Younger, more vulnerable Katherine shrank from alienating either parent. She remained largely silent but perhaps suffered most of all. She believed neither would tolerate her love for the other. Even as she could not possibly understand the circumstances that created the break, she witnessed their anger, feelings of betrayal, and resentment. To choose one would be to lose the other. She had already lost a great deal.

Sara's physical and emotional distance, compounded by frequent absences from San Francisco, also took their toll. During 1917, for instance, Sara did not see her children for nearly seven months. January through February she traveled east on suffrage business. Afterward, she hurried to Portland for six weeks, stretching her absence to over three months. What pulled her away from Erskine at all was acknowledgment that she had some responsibility for Katherine and Albert. Admittedly, she told Erskine, she had "no right to indulge in the luxury of motherhood when it is easy and convenient and demands no sacrifice . . . and then deny these children a mother's presence . . . when it becomes hard and sacrificial . . . when my lover is one place and my children in another." Yet, that is exactly what she often did. Self-awareness did little to alter her behavior.

In fact, after six weeks in San Francisco, she returned to Portland for another month, came back for a month at the Eyrie, and then headed east in July for three months on a writing project. At the end of that sojourn, she wanted to go back to Oregon. Wood discouraged her. "For what am I crossing the continent?" she asked. "How absurd to end my journey anywhere but in your arms." She reluctantly returned to California, scurried to Portland two weeks later, came back to California mid-November, hosted Erskine for a mid-December visit, and remained home for the holidays.[6]

After long months apart, reunions led to "clinging caresses" from Katherine. That annoyed as much as touched her mother. One night Sara awoke to hear Katherine crying. The reason? "I love to be near you so much and the days are so lonesome without you." Sara admitted she had not given Katherine enough credit for her sweet, sympathetic soul and tender nature, "standing as she does in the blaze of [her brother] Albert's larger light." Yet Sara seemed unable to truly comprehend her daughter's needs. Many of her rare comments about Katherine presented the child as loving and longing *for Sara*. Few other elements of her personality or character merited much attention.[7] That Katherine more closely resembled her father physically and that her relationship with Ehrgott seemed less troubled than her brother's were strikes against her. That she responded to her mother's frequent absences by sometimes revealing understandable resentment toward Erskine created friction between mother and daughter.

Occasionally, though, Katherine bested Albert Field when the seemingly inevitable comparisons between siblings arose. Sara thought her daughter the more intellectual and the more "dependable radical," even as she attracted less attention than her brother, "with his hummingbird flash of wings." Katherine, or Kay, as she was sometimes called, took things in quietly; only after careful consideration would she state her views. It especially pleased Sara when those views coincided with her own. And the girl grew more beautiful, Sara assured Erskine, to whom such things especially mattered. The girl's face glowed rich in color and expression. Her beautiful fingers and hands suggested an artistic temperament.[8]

Erskine, for his part, urged Sara to address Kay's shortcomings—to tell her to "think less of herself by thinking more of others." Sara obliged, sending her daughter a six-page letter about her faults, a style that had shades of Wood family missives. Sara thanked Erskine for opening her eyes to "so much that is basically and dangerously wrong" with Kay, much of it inherited or learned from her mother, who had a duty to repair it. It is impossible to know the full impact of this letter, so full of her mother's disapproval, but it must have been intensely hurtful to receive from a much-absent parent.[9]

A few months later, Sara reported that Katherine was working on her faults. The girl acknowledged she had not been nice to Erskine during a recent visit, particularly in contrast to Albert Field, who so clearly worshipped him. Kay understood Erskine loved her brother more because Albert had a sweet nature. She pleaded, "Please tell Pops," as Sara's children affectionately referred to Erskine, "in your next letter that I love him so and I will be better to him the next time he comes down." Sara rewarded Katherine for such sentiments, telling her their shared love for Erskine brought them closer together. The episode most clearly revealed that Kay had learned that to keep her mother's love, secondary as it was, she must accept her mother's lover.[10]

Albert Field, a teenager growing into a man, displayed the full trappings of adolescence: a changing voice, long legs ensconced in long pants, huge feet, and huge hands emerging from too-short coat sleeves. He sought his mother's favor by showering her with admiration. Not that he was manipulative or deceitful. He understood and loved her. He also marveled at Erskine, yearning to achieve the masculine ideal "Pops" embodied. Even his poetry, with its manly verses, particularly those regarding war, meant he was no "sissy poet." Sara thought this last comment reflected "adolescent bravado and provincial ignorance," but she otherwise believed her son had rare insight into Erskine's greatness.[11]

His father paled in comparison. Ehrgott had the thankless responsibility of raising Albert during adolescence, and friction developed between the teenage boy and the custodial parent responsible for enforcing rules and discipline. That Ehrgott was conservative, strict, and still licking the deep wounds inflicted by Sara's desertion only made the relationship thornier. Sometimes they fought over Sara. Once, when Ehrgott raged that she had deserted the family, Albert replied she had done more for him than anyone else, including his father, having experienced enormous pain in childbirth, cared for him as a boy, and tried to do the best for him and Katherine. This must have devastated Ehrgott. (Sara's unwillingness to rush back to California in 1916 when she learned Albert Field had been hospitalized for an appendectomy might have given her son doubts about his mother's true commitment, but on this occasion he overlooked it.) Another time, young Albert accidentally mentioned Erskine's name, and his father subsequently lectured him for an hour. "If a man stabbed me you would not be his friend, and this man has stabbed me to the soul," Ehrgott fumed, "taking from me that which was more than my life—your Mother." Albert recognized his father's pain but refused to abandon his allegiance to his mother.

Sara delighted in the support. Straightforward, sensitive, vibrant, and loyal, Albert made his mother feel "as though I am a better person. He teaches me so much." When he fell ill, Sara realized "what a terrible price of freedom would fate exact of me, if . . . that child of promise" should die. Nothing produced greater dread except, of course, Erskine's possible demise. In the wake of her 1916 abortion and its consequences, Sara knew she would probably never have Erskine's child. That heightened Albert Field's value even more. She turned to him "with a more passionate hope [that he would become] something greater, finer, nobler than even my dream for myself. Had we had a child," she told Erskine, "I would have had a certain, serene surety of something akin to the superman." Albert might not be a superman, but he was her best prospect.[12]

The boy and Erskine shared a warm, affectionate relationship. "I do love that boy," Erskine told Sara, "because he loves me so." When Erskine gave each of his sons and sons-in-law one of his own rings for Christmas in 1917, he presented one to Albert, too. Erskine found him nothing short of "bottled sunshine" and "dynamic joy." Sara believed the two had a spiritual bond or affinity. When a waiter at a San Francisco restaurant called her "Mrs. Wood," Albert seemed pleased; Kay was less certain.[13]

Sara, too, emphasized what Albert gave *her*, how he loved and understood her. The emotional energy of this little family remained firmly focused on the mother's needs. The children implicitly understood that, and at times they each literally took care of her. Sara's abandonment through divorce, frequent absences from California, and above all obvious preference for Erskine hurt. They gratefully accepted what they could get from frail, poetic Sara. She believed she gave them all she could.

In fact, what neither Erskine nor Sara acknowledged or admitted was that both Albert's and Katherine's love were given and received totally on the adults' terms, requiring the children's devotion to both Erskine and their mother. Sara pointed out to Erskine that the children's affection for him was "surely . . . a great tribute to you who see them so comparatively little." Perhaps it was. More likely, they understood their mother required it. Without Erskine, their mother was miserable, and they could never fill the void of his absence. If they wanted Sara to be happy, they had to welcome Erskine.[14]

Kitty Beck was not a family member, yet her close, intense, long relationship with Erskine, which he sometimes likened to that of a father and daughter, meant the Sara/Erksine relationship deeply affected her world, too. In 1911 she had married Dr. Lloyd Irvine on the rebound, having learned Erskine preferred Sara. Kitty, however, continued spending much more time with Erskine than Sara did, monitored the ebbs and flows of his various love affairs, and had probably hoped—much like Nanny—that he would never leave Portland or her.

If he did, Erskine believed, she would commit suicide. And she provided fodder for such a concern, as she was emotionally unstable and periodically spoke of suicide. On an April day not long after one of Sara's visits to Portland, Erskine and Kitty took a walk in the terraced heights above Portland. They held hands and talked of Sara. Kitty insisted she wanted Erskine to be happy and understood that meant living with Sara. When that happened, all she wanted was to "lie down and go to sleep." A few months later, she returned to this theme. She had hoped to live near the couple and occasionally spend nights in Erskine's arms—not in a sexual way but simply in the warm embrace of an old friend, she said—but Kitty knew Sara would never allow it. When Erskine no longer needed her, Kitty wanted to die.[15]

Sara gave Kitty's suicidal thoughts little consideration, often letting reports of these conversations go unanswered, but one time, fed up with the refrain, Sara claimed *she* longed for "sleep" even more than Kitty. Her life too was "a vale of tears." For Kitty to call her selfish was outrageous. Kitty had months with him; Sara only the few days or weeks they patched together. "[N]o woman has tried more than I to harmonize her ideals and dreams with the fact of your life and nature than have I." Kitty and Erskine might think she failed in that endeavor. Sara did not agree.[16]

She did, however, empathize with Kitty's unhappy, tragic marriage to the wrong man. Irvine's alcoholism and Kitty's love for Erskine doomed the relationship from the start. By November 1916 they had been separated for some time. Then Irvine became mortally ill while in San Francisco, not long after he performed the bungled abortion on Doris Stevens. Sara despised the man yet visited him in the hospital. When Irvine surprisingly appeared to be recovering, Sara talked with his nurse about "disposing" of him through a lethal dose of morphine. Sara argued it would relieve him, "and a dozen others who are worth while," from misery. Shockingly, she even offered to administer the drug herself. The nurse refused and Irvine lingered for a few more weeks. Kitty came down to say goodbye. When he died on December 4, only Irvine's mother mourned his death.[17]

Erskine was in Washington, D.C., when he received Kitty's wire that Irvine had died. He was grateful Lloyd's suffering had ended and relieved "the fearful load, the ever present menace is taken from darling sweet Kitty." She had paid all his medical bills . . . with money Erskine provided. He looked forward to coming home and seeing "darling" Kitty, "the most unselfish soul that ever lived," as well as his children and grandchildren, and even "Dear brave Sippie [Nanny] who bears her sorrow proudly."[18]

Whether she bore sorrow proudly or not, Nanny certainly bore it silently. Or at least she did not articulate the agony she experienced over Sara and Erskine on paper. Only through the words of others, particularly Wood, does one get a glimmer of her perspective, which apparently remained consistent year after year. She believed her husband was vain, needy (particularly for the attentions of younger women), deceptive, and disloyal. She also, in spite of all, loved him and wanted to live with him for the rest of her life. Nanny rejected free love. Her philosophy about marriage was rooted in her religious beliefs and her loyalty to the lifelong commitment she had made. Like Albert Ehrgott and her son Erskine, she believed people exercised free will and could suppress temptation. Her husband, however, willingly and willfully embraced illicit desire. She also placed much blame in this particular case on Sara, who, Nanny believed, aggressively pursued Erskine, a man who could not, or more precisely *would* not, resist the attentions and advances of attractive, brainy women.

More than anyone else in the family, Nanny paid the heaviest price for Erskine's behavior, but she did find a way to exercise power. It was not clear when, or if, Erskine would ever leave Portland, and for all the pain and humiliation Mrs. Wood endured, she still had a husband with whom she continued to share a home, a growing family, and a social life. She made it abundantly clear she would never agree to a divorce.

For Albert Ehrgott, divorce ended all hope of reconciliation with Sara and prospects for a family life with her. Or at least it should have. On several occasions he made overtures to win her back. He once asked a mutual friend to broach the possibility of reconciliation. Sara quickly dismissed the idea, finding it "pitiful." Still, not indifferent to his loneliness, she hoped he would find a new companion. A year later she interpreted his efforts in a blacker light. Ehrgott sent her a bouquet of pink roses for her birthday and their anniversary, which she saw as a gesture designed to "rub in his sanctified patience and unfailing love." Why did he do these things? Did he really love her or did he intend to "sting me with my own unfaithfulness?" It amazed her how easily he could bring misery by reminding her how she had wounded him.[19]

In truth, Ehrgott continued to harbor rage toward Sara and Erskine, although he tried to conceal it. Albert Field's reports, however, made clear his father did not always control his anger. The custody agreement mostly held up, but strains inevitably arose over visitation issues. Like Nanny, Ehrgott held his spouse's paramour primarily responsible for his marriage's demise and could not abide this man having access to, and influence over, his children, poisoning their lives with his disgusting ideas. Ehrgott had insisted Sara never allow Erskine to be in the same room with the children, and he was infuriated to learn she was not adhering to his wishes.

By the end of 1916 everybody was unhappy. A pall hung over the Wood and the Ehrgott households. All the philosophical justifications Erskine and Sara generated did nothing to alleviate the pain they were causing others. Nor had the year been kind to the central figures in the drama. Sara and Erskine fought over politics, monogamy, and each other's true character. They nearly broke apart permanently, then reconciled through letters and short visits, only to approach the brink of ending the relationship yet again. Such turmoil took its toll on the thinning threads of connection. By December, Sara's health plummeted, as it so often did during emotionally difficult times. She checked herself into the El Reposo Sanitarium and then, three days later, checked herself out and agreed to head to the East Coast for suffragist Inez Milholland's memorial service.

Milholland, a beautiful young woman and star of the suffrage movement, had died unexpectedly of pernicious anemia in Los Angeles after fainting on the stage of an anti-Wilson rally. Milholland had dramatically asked, "Mr. President, how long must women wait for liberty?" before crumbling to the ground. She immediately became a martyr for the women's suffrage cause. Alice Paul and the National Woman's Party seized upon the occasion of mourning her death as an opportunity to mobilize support for suffrage by organizing memorial events nationwide.[20] Paul wired Sara to come immediately to New York City, at NWP's expense, and speak at a service on Christmas Day. Sara hesitated, having promised her children they would spend the holiday together. But if Erskine, still in the East at this time, gave the word, she told him, she would race across the continent to join him and they could have their first Christmas together, the childrens' Christmas be damned. Erskine said no. He intended to spend the holiday in Portland.

Meanwhile, Paul offered to postpone the Milholland memorial service until New Year's Day so Sara could be with her children on Christmas. Sara agreed, even though her doctor discouraged travel altogether. Anticipating Erskine's negative reaction, she disingenuously hoped he would support the trip (knowing he would not) and explained it would allow her to make some literary contacts for him and visit her mother.[21]

Furious with her decision, Erskine replied he was tired of her crying wolf about her health. He had been "demanding and dictatorial" in the past because he feared for her well-being. Now, he no longer worried about it. Convinced she was selfish and dishonest, that she persistently prioritized her wishes over those of others, he was, yet again, falling out of love with her. Sara tried to cover up her self-centeredness with insincerity and hypocrisy, pretending the motive was duty rather than egotism. He no longer fell for it.

Of course, as an anarchist, he admitted it was her right to be selfish. He simply had to learn to stop caring. Their dream of a life together was "vain" and the time had come to give up hopes of "a false experiment." "I am not as important in your life as we both have assumed," he wrote. He was not "all [that] your dear extravagant phrases led my egoism to believe." He was no longer "necessary" to her. Yet, he wanted her to live life "in crystal truth." She should boldly be herself, listen to her own instincts, express herself no matter the cost to others, and be honest, frank, and open.[22]

The irony of this letter evaded Erskine. For years, Sara, Nanny, and Kitty— all the women in his life—had charged him with the very sins he now lay at Sara's feet: selfishness, hypocrisy, deceit, and self-righteousness. Sara's quick reply, via a telegram sent on Christmas Day, did not make any of these points, however. Instead, she typically backed down, admitting the "cold white light of truth" of his assessments of her. She would not go east. She would wait for word from him to come to Portland. Erskine remained her great love.[23]

He immediately turned remorseful about the incendiary letter. Not that he renounced everything—she had faults, but not fundamental ones. He had simply exaggerated them in the heat of the moment. Perhaps he had been spoiled by other, submissive women. Perhaps he was self-centered. He asked Sara to "pardon . . . my sins." He loved her with a love that "seems too big for my body. Too big for the stars themselves."[24]

In the end, Sara went to New York after spending Christmas with her children. She did not take a direct route east, however. Instead, she traveled via Portland, a northern detour that took additional time but allowed a brief meeting with Erskine. It jeopardized the likelihood of her arriving on time to the Milholland memorial service, but she did it anyway. Erskine always came first, even before the opportunity to play a major role in an important national suffrage event. A more politically ambitious woman would have chosen other-wise, but Sara determined to see Erskine and so she took the risk.

They met for one hour in a "strange . . . sort of snapshot" encounter at the train station. She came prepared that Erskine might end the relationship. Instead, they fell into one another's arms in an "unbelievable cosmicaly [*sic*] big moment of wild, holy delirium." He still loved her, in spite of her faults. Erskine agreed that one hour together did wonders. He regretted making her Christmas so grim. How could he be so cruel? They must forgive the other's weaknesses and strive to be better people.[25]

Most likely any who knew the couple well would have agreed with Erskine's assessment. They did share many faults . . . selfishness perhaps pre-eminently. This particular time, though, it was not family members who suf-fered the consequences but the suffrage movement. Only as she left Portland and the train charged across the continent did Sara begin to fret that she might not make the memorial service in time. What would her suffrage colleagues think after they had paid her fare and delayed the event just for her? On December 29, a porter in Helena, Montana, assured her she would still make it. Her anxiety growing, Sara sent a continual stream of wires to New York, urging organizers to begin the service later in the day, start without her, and place her last on the roster of speakers. By the time the train reached Mandan, North Dakota, five hours behind schedule, she knew an on-time arrival in New York would be impossible. Yet, she convinced herself that she had done all in her power to get there. Of course, that was not the case. Instead of taking the fastest, most expeditious route, she had chosen a significant detour so that she might spend one hour with Erskine.

She did not arrive in time to speak. In fact, she missed the entire memorial service.[26]

Fifteen
WAR

If President Woodrow Wilson's supporters greeted the dawn of 1917 with expectations that he would keep the nation out of war, by Easter he dashed those hopes. If anti-suffragists assumed Wilson's election would slow demand for a federal amendment to enfranchise women, the National Woman's Party proved them wrong. If Americans believed a war to make the world safe for democracy meant their own civil liberties would be sacrosanct, reactionary forces obliterated such expectations. It was going to be a strife-ridden, devastating year in both Europe and the United States. Radicals—whether within the women's suffrage, labor, free speech, or antiwar movements—particularly faced violent repercussions for their stands. Warfare, it seemed, was beginning to penetrate all aspects of American political life.

As Sara traveled eastward in late December 1916, however, she had no sense of foreboding. Rather, she felt lighthearted. She and Erskine had survived yet another rough patch. True, she now set her course away from him, answering the call of the suffrage movement once again, but the separation would be temporary. And who knew? Maybe this would be the year he would receive his land grant commission, make his break for freedom, and join her in California.

Meanwhile, other matters required Sara's more immediate attention. The NWP had not removed President Wilson from power, but it continued pressing him on a suffrage amendment. Inez Milholland's martyrdom provided the latest opportunity to do that. At least, that was Alice Paul's plan as she organized memorial services nationwide to honor Milholland and simultaneously rally the troops. The most impressive of these services occurred on Christmas Day in the U.S. Capitol Building's National Statuary Hall. Maud Younger, an NWP delegate from California, presented the memorial address, followed by Elizabeth Thacher Kent, wife of a California congressman, who demanded Wilson support the amendment. The audience unanimously approved the resolution as strains of *La Marseillaise* filled the grand space. Although Sara missed the New York City memorial, she took consolation in having read a selection from *The Poet in the Desert* at the San Francisco service on Christmas morning.[1] And she did arrive in Washington in time to meet with President Wilson.

Milholland's death had attracted such widespread attention that the president felt compelled to accept a deputation of mourning suffragists. Expecting a brief meeting, Wilson discovered the three hundred women in attendance had other intentions, as they renewed their pressure on him to support the amendment. The president's face darkened. Sara, who thought he remembered her, spoke last. It was like speaking to a "very black thundercloud." Surely, she told Wilson, he could see that the spirit of the suffrage movement fit perfectly with his own ideals. Doris Stevens thought Sara's speech the high point of the meeting. Yet, Wilson did not soften. Instead, he angrily told the women he would not have agreed to the meeting had he realized they intended to lobby him. Then, in an "obdurate mood," he dismissed them. Wilson, Sara concluded, was cold, petty, and "a master of artifice." Doris Stevens found him patronizing. "We feel so superior to him," she wrote.[2]

Actually, the NWP leadership had anticipated Wilson's response and crafted a contingency plan should he reject their plea. It kicked in the very next morning, when "silent sentinels" for suffrage picketed the White House, intending to sustain their vigil through Wilson's second inauguration ceremony in March. As it turned out, the picketing lasted much longer than that. It was a radical tactic, another import from Britain's more militant suffrage campaign, and the technique elicited debate and criticism from both inside and outside the suffrage movement, although a majority of NWP members supported it.

Picketing, though a lawful and nonviolent form of protest, still carried risk, particularly in a climate of increased militarism, for it gave anti-suffragists an opportunity to paint protestors as unpatriotic. It also transgressed commonly accepted behavior for women; "respectable" women did not demonstrate in the streets. As a result, the picketing aroused violent responses from those who wanted to punish them for breaching prescribed gender boundaries. Alice Paul, however, smartly exploited the attacks, which, it turned out, mostly led to greater sympathy for the demonstrators.[3]

Certainly initially the picketers attracted curious attention and general support. President Wilson even invited them into the White House for coffee. They declined. The number of protestors grew. On March 4, 1917, hundreds of marchers walked around the White House, in the wind and rain, while thousands of onlookers cheered them. Then, as the president moved the nation toward war, attitudes shifted. Some decided a suffrage amendment was expendable in the new context. Paul and the NWP disagreed. In April, when Wilson called for a war to make the world safe for democracy, the NWP jumped on the contradiction between that goal and the presence of unenfranchised women left at home while their men went off to fight for others' rights. Picketing continued.

The first arrests came in June. As protestors stood vigil at the White House gates while a Russian delegation from the postrevolution provisional government passed through, some women held up signs that read "AMERICA IS NOT A DEMOCRACY" and "TELL OUR GOVERNMENT THAT IT MUST LIBERATE ITS PEOPLE." An angry crowd destroyed one of the signs and accused the picketers of disloyalty, while municipal police officers arrested picketers for blocking traffic. These women subsequently used their court appearances as a public forum for advocating suffrage—a move that was part of the larger strategy all along. An unsympathetic judge found the women guilty and sentenced them to either a fine or three days in jail. They chose jail.[4]

During the summer, picketing continued to heat up, as did police response. On July 14, sixteen protestors, including Doris Stevens and Alice Paul, were arrested. This time the court sentenced them to sixty days in jail, and not at the district prison but at the Occoquan Workhouse in Virginia, where incarceration would be particularly unpleasant. It was an unduly harsh punishment for the crime of "obstructing traffic." The jailers forced the women to strip in front of other prisoners and denied them toothbrushes, combs, and writing implements. They brought African American prostitutes, normally segregated, into the suffragists' dorm to sleep. "Not that we shrank from these women on account of their color," Stevens wrote, "but how terrible to know that the institution had gone out of its way to bring these prisoners from their own wing to the white wing in an attempt to humiliate us." The jailers intended this gesture as further punishment to the "respectable" suffragists. Stevens tried to deflect their goal, but her words reveal the difficulty of shrugging off the deeply ingrained racism and condescension toward African Americans, as well as toward sex workers, that most white Americans, including some militant suffragists, openly shared at the time.

Meanwhile, the NWP prisoners had some powerful people watching their every move. Among those in the courtroom when the judge pronounced his sentence for the women were Doris's lover, Dudley Malone, who was serving as Wilson's Commissioner of the Port of New York, and other prominent progressive men such as Frederic C. Howe, Amos Pinchot, and Clarence Darrow. Although the "benighted" Darrow told the defendants they deserved punishment for "helping the Germans to get us," Malone felt differently. Outraged at the sentence's excessiveness, he immediately visited Wilson to object. He demanded the president stop fighting the suffragists and join them in their drive for democracy at home. If Wilson did not alter his stance, Malone threatened, he would resign. He infuriated Wilson by claiming the president was responsible for the worsening situation. The two men parted in anger. At the same time, telegrams opposing the conviction and punishment poured in across the country, and within several days Wilson issued a pardon to all the suffragists. According to Stevens, they did not have the option of refusing the pardon. So they went home.[5]

While this summertime drama unfolded, Sara was in transit east to take up a special writing assignment. Inching closer to the vortex of radical suffrage resistance, she closely followed news regarding the persecution and prosecution of the picketers, her friends. She heard Wilson was considering a suffrage amendment as a "war measure" and hoped that was true, especially since she wanted Alice Paul, ill with Bright's disease, to live long enough to see this outcome.[6] Once in Washington, Sara learned more about the suffragists' "brave stand, their unjust trials." She reported to Erskine that prison officials made these "refined, lovely women" sleep with "syphilitic negres [sic] prostitutes and eat awful food." She did not add Doris's caveat that the problem was not the color of their cellmates but the jailers' intention to humiliate the suffragists through integration.

In August Paul asked Sara to join the picket line. She had not made the request earlier because she believed Sara's value as speaker and fundraiser took precedence. Now, however, they needed bodies. Sara turned her down, although she felt like a "wretched deserter" for doing so. Her excuse, she told Erskine, was she could not risk a prison sentence of sixty days or possibly six months without his consent, a remarkable comment for a feminist New Woman to make. If he was willing to give her up, she would enlist. Sara knew, of course, he would not. She left Erskine out of her explanation to Paul, however, when she declined picket duty, emphasizing instead that, given her frail health, a jail sentence meant possible death. Paul agreed. In acknowledging that Sara might die, she added, "That would be very good for the cause." Paul expected everyone to devote their life to suffrage, as she had—a sacrifice easier for a single woman with no children to make, Sara thought. But she herself did not aspire to martyrdom, nor would she be shamed into picketing.[7]

Of course, Erskine supported Sara's decision. He would have preferred, in fact, that she back off from the suffrage fight altogether, repeating his longstanding fear that her colleagues would work her too hard. Plus, he emphatically disagreed with the strategic turn toward what he called "hostile militancy." It was one thing to carry a banner quietly appealing for rights, but quite another to use inflammatory language. By August picketers had indeed ratcheted up the rhetoric. One banner called the president "Kaiser Wilson" and asked, "Have you forgotten how you sympathized with the poor Germans because they were not self governed?" They chose incendiary words deliberately, understanding their effect.

Erskine continued to advise a more moderate approach, in which western women voters who supported Wilson would peacefully work with the president toward an *eventual* federal amendment. If that failed, then, in a year or so, they could resort to more militant tactics. In other words, he continued to counsel, work through the system . . . and wait. Erskine agreed that Wilson was a cold man, but he was not a "small politician" who made political calculations simply for immediate gain. Wilson pondered the long-term, larger good. In this, he "leaned toward humanity not property."[8]

Meanwhile, men continued to attack the picketers while police provided no protection. Instead, they arrested the women protestors. On one occasion the police even led a mob in the attack. Erskine continued to be more bothered by the supposedly unfair charge against Wilson than by the treatment of the women exercising their right to free speech. Further, the protestors had invaded the White House grounds, and while he admitted that they had a constitutional right to do this, he preferred more prudent tactics. Radical, anarchistic Wood turned out to be conservative and pallid when it came to suffrage.

Most ironically, Erskine refused to support the picketers because of America's involvement in World War I. He opposed the war, yet this was not the right time—in "the hour of national crisis"—to harass the president about suffrage. Germany threatened the democracies of England, France, and the United States; for the president to promote a federal suffrage amendment now meant risking the loss of support for the war. Southern Democrats in particular backed his international policies but abhorred women's suffrage. Wilson would not alienate them. "You women must put yourselves in Wilson's shoes—realize what he is up against." The time simply is not right for suffrage. Wait, Erskine again urged.[9]

This advice Sara could not abide. Waiting was not an option. For years (white) women had waited for the right opportunity, which never seemed to come. Now the NWP's more aggressive strategy was proving effective, sometimes in unexpected ways. The racist jailers' tactics proved to be getting under white people's skin. Sara told Erskine that being forced to live among black women "eaten up with disease, placed in solitary confinement for the least offense, [and] rendered weak from wretched food" actually encouraged public support for the suffragists. Such comments, of course, demonstrated Sara's own racism, disparaging the black women rather than sympathizing or expressing solidarity with them. She abhorred such tactics but also concluded they ultimately served the suffragists' cause. The government's attempt to humiliate the suffragists backfired, especially among outside observers, who shared such appalling attitudes about race and therefore concluded that even militant suffragists should not be subjected to such supposed degradation. It transformed the protestors into victims.

Rather than entertain Erskine's advice to desist, Sara instead pressured him to send a letter of protest to the White House about the latest arrests. Only after learning Dudley Malone had resigned his post, and after reading Malone's letter to the *Oregonian* on suffrage, did Wood reluctantly write to

Wilson. Otherwise, the whole suffrage thing made him tired. "O dear Sara .... It is not my mission nor I venture to think yours. Haven't you had enough of it?" His only obligation to humanity was poetry, not politics. He longed to leave the world and its problems behind, to escape it altogether.[10]

Although for years they had shared this dream, in summer 1917 Sara did not agree the moment had come to withdraw. If not for the pickets, Sara believed, Malone would never have resigned his post, and if Malone had not resigned, Wilson's close advisor Colonel Edward House would never have told the president his attitude on suffrage was "the unforgiveable mistake of his present administration." Still, from his great physical distance in the West, Erskine could not understand either the need for, or the result of, the picketing. Sara told him that, if Erskine was her age, she knew he would do all he could to help, implying that a younger man would push more aggressively for radical change. Once more Americans became aware of Wilson's indifference to democracy at home, Sara was certain they would force him to support the amendment.[11]

Then the stakes grew even more desperate. The women demanded to be treated as political prisoners, and when they were refused that status, they engaged in hunger strikes—a strategy used by British suffragists. Again, Alice Paul led the way. From there, things turned increasingly more violent. Authorities force-fed the hunger strikers, holding them down while feeding them through the nose. Jailers threw them about, handcuffed them, and, in Paul's case, placed her in a psychopathic ward. Such repression of the radicals did not work. Rather, such heavy-handed treatment finally and decidedly turned the tide of public opinion toward the militant suffragists. A judge released all suffrage prisoners, and four months later the District Court of Appeals reversed all guilty verdicts. It was complete vindication for the NWP and Alice Paul, who pronounced the picketing campaign a success.

As 1917 ended, President Wilson too succumbed, endorsing the so-called Anthony Amendment as "vitally essential" to the war effort, even while insisting the "foolish and intemperate agitators" had not influenced him. Not until a new Republican-controlled Congress took power in early 1919, however, did congressional approval seem imminent. In May, the House approved the amendment, and the Senate followed suit in June. As Alice Paul headed out to inaugurate the ratification campaign, she noted, "Freedom has come not as a gift but as a triumph." In August 1920 Tennessee became the thirty-sixth state to ratify the Nineteenth Amendment—tipping the scales to the required two-thirds majority. The seventy-two-year-old struggle for women's suffrage in the United States was finally over—for white women. Black, Hispanic, Native American, and other nonwhite women in some states would have to wait much longer.[12]

───────────

For all her fervor, it was not the suffrage movement that had brought Sara east in summer 1917. She came to ghostwrite Alva Vanderbilt Belmont's autobiography, earn money, and promote Erskine's poetry among New York publishing houses. Belmont originally wanted to hire someone to write speeches, look after her affairs, and otherwise "be [the] brains for her," as Sara once put it. The idea of working on her memoir, however, appealed more to Sara. It took some time to work out the details, but by summer 1917, Alva and Sara agreed on the project's terms.

Alabama-born Alva Smith had moved to New York City with her family at age six. She married Cornelius Vanderbilt's grandson William. After twenty years and three children, Alva divorced him and then married another millionaire, Oliver Belmont. The second marriage ended when Oliver died in 1908, after the couple had been married for just over a decade. At that point Alva embarked on a new stage of life, using her wealth and status for social reform. In particular, she joined the militant NWP, becoming its major underwriter and donor. Earlier in her life, Alva, "strong-willed, domineering, and determined to be the center of attention," had attracted journalists' attention as a "social celebrity," but she learned she could not control what they wrote. When she moved into labor and suffrage issues, she decided to tell her own story.[13]

She then asked Doris Stevens to recommend a woman to help her write that book. Doris immediately thought of Sara. Alva and Sara first met at the 1915 Panama-Pacific International Exposition. Alva considered Sara a likely prospect for the job. Sara, however, harbored doubts about Alva's suitability as an employer. Rumors circulated that she could be quite "a jealous old dame" and wanted no one near who threatened to outshine her. She had the "usual lack of brains and culture," Sara told Erskine, like most "rich people who have depended on their looks and their money to win them place and applause." Even Doris agreed Alva demonstrated the psychology of a plutocrat. Also, the job would mean moving to Newport, Rhode Island, at least temporarily.

On the other hand, Alva's devotion to suffrage and support for labor appealed to Sara. The paycheck would relieve her dependence on Erskine, even though it meant moving to Newport.[14] All of these details took time to work out, but by December 1916 Belmont had settled on Sara and offered $300 (about $6,000 today) per month plus a percent of the book's royalties. The rest of the profits would go to the suffrage campaign. For several weeks Sara equivocated. Convinced that the heiress was "gluttonous to get at [Sara's] spirit[,] . . . to have it . . . just as she buys gowns and jewels," Sara hesitated to sell her soul. She resented the idea of handing over her intellect, talent, and time to this woman. Alva could be affectionate, but mostly she seemed "flinty" and "brutal to her inferiors." Such a character would be challenging to mold into an attractive figure on the page.[15]

Erskine, too, was ambivalent about the project. Not surprisingly, he dismissed the issue of Sara's economic dependence upon him and scoffed at Sara's idea that the salary would do anything to hasten their life together. Plus, no amount of money could compensate for their separation from one another, he said, conveniently ignoring that money had been his primary reason for putting off a life with Sara. He also worried this project would hinder and delay Sara's own writing career. He once again mentioned his fear that time apart might mean she would find a better mate, since Wood would not be able to join her unless he was willing to walk "Ibsenly off[,] leaving my children to pay my debts and care for their mother." In the end, though, he encouraged Sara to take the job. It had potential to open doors in literary circles that would help them both. Stay "in the limelight," he advised, while looking for publishers. Give this no more than six months and ask for $400 or even $500 a month. If Belmont refused, then Sara would be saved the work. If she agreed, Sara would be well compensated.[16]

Not until summer 1917 did things finally fall into place. Sara accepted the job and took up residence at Belmont's Marble House in late July. She did not bring her children, although Alva offered to pay their expenses. Sara's misgivings about Alva and the rich, of course, had not subsided, and she believed Newport to be a "breeding place of evil," where "lawmakers and lawbreakers . . . war lords and their ladies luxuriate." Initially, Alva set Sara up in a suite of rooms in her mansion with a private maid. It embarrassed Sara to be bathed by someone else, however, and she desperately wanted to live on her own. Finally, Alva agreed to let her settle into a boardinghouse not far from Alva's palatial residence.

Although Sara found the mansion's excesses deeply off-putting, she knew Erskine would be hungry for details of the beautiful objects with which Alva surrounded herself. Construction on the home had begun when Alva was still married to William Vanderbilt. Made of warm brown- and gold-toned Sienna marble, the house took three years to complete. Its Gothic Room featured walls, ceilings, windows, and a fireplace that evoked fifteenth-century workmanship. The Great Hall opened out onto the ocean. On the edge of the sea stood a Chinese temple filled with rare Chinese vases, prints, rugs, and various pieces of furniture—the sorts of things Erskine loved. Sara and Alva often sat on the temple's balcony for lunch, working into the afternoon on the autobiography. As for the mansion, even Sara could not deny its beauty, finding it more breathtaking "in its splendor and stately massiveness than [Alva's] New York residence—and the grounds! Well, you know," she wrote Erskine, "how the rich live."[17]

Sara's job consisted of interviewing Alva, taking extensive notes, and occasionally socializing with her employer's friends. Sara then wrote up the notes every evening, intending to compose the narrative upon her return to California. It helped that she found Alva's story interesting. Alva Smith had spent her early childhood in a slave-owning culture in Mobile, Alabama. When she was six, the family moved to New York and settled into the city's wealthy social circle. Alva claimed that, even as a child, she understood girls' and women's subordinate position, resented it, and rebelled. Her feminist impulse ran deep, although it did not keep her from forcing her own daughter, Consuelo, to marry Charles Richard John Spencer-Churchill, the 9th Duke of Marlborough, when the young woman loved someone else.

Alva would not tolerate her husband's sexual escapades outside their marriage, and when she learned he was having an affair with a woman in Paris, she filed for divorce. Her lawyer attempted to talk her out of it because of the negative publicity it would attract, but Alva insisted on going forward. In 1895, on the grounds of adultery, she received the divorce, custody of their children, the right to remarry, and a generous financial settlement. She also endured some ostracism from her social cohort for her actions.[18]

Less than a year after the divorce was finalized, Alva married Oliver Belmont. The son of August Belmont, a Jewish banker from Germany who had originally come to the United States in 1837 as a representative of the Rothschild family, Oliver was something of an aging playboy. He and Alva, though, enjoyed a happy partnership until his death. Meanwhile, Consuelo's marriage collapsed in 1906. She subsequently committed herself to women's suffrage and to social welfare campaigns regarding women laborers. Three years later Alva turned in the same direction, devoting her considerable energy, wealth, administrative ability, and celebrity to the "sex battle." Alva found Alice Paul's assertive approach particularly suitable to her own temperament. By the end of 1914, Alva sat on the Congressional Union's executive committee and provided about one-half of all the money the organization raised that year. She remained very active through 1916 and 1917, publicly supporting and funding the picketing campaign, although, at age sixty, she declined to take to the streets herself.[19]

This was the context in which Sara arrived to work on Alva's memoir. The daily routine began when Alva sent a car with chauffeur to pick her up. Sometimes Sara accompanied Alva on shopping errands. After lunch at the "palace," waited upon by butlers and maids, they retreated to the Chinese temple. Alva kept nothing back, though some stories were off the record, particularly regarding her first marriage. Alva shared "the sacred confidence of a woman's inner heart" with Sara, bringing "tears from her hard heart to her eyes—and to mine." That her first husband had brought his mistresses into their home and deliberately humiliated Alva in other ways underscored her painful story.[20]

Alva's divorce from Vanderbilt had caused a storm of controversy and made her a pariah among the very rich for what Sara saw as the "merest first threads in the fabric of Liberty." This made her a sympathetic figure. It also explained Alva's strong advocacy for women's rights, divorce, and suffrage. According to Sara, she entered the women's rights movement primarily because of personal experience and her particular personality, not out of ideological or philosophical inclinations. Alva loved power and so resented and resisted efforts to curb her exercise of it. Her ability to empathize and support women proved limited, however. Her treatment of Consuelo, for instance, struck Sara as a terrible violation of another individual's rights. Moreover, Sara believed the women servants in the household hated Alva. She sometimes physically abused them, but they stayed because she paid good wages.[21]

What particularly bothered Sara was Alva's indifference toward working-class women. She did aid the women shirtwaist workers' strike of 1909, soliciting a strikers' fund from dinner guests and then sitting all night in police court bailing out the women, one by one, yet Sara believed Alva's primary motivation was a desire to "get even" with men. In this particular case, she exhibited "no sense of spiritual values other than the extension of her rage against men." Alva felt no warmth for individual women, and she certainly did not weigh in on the side of labor over capital.[22]

She did, however, respect Sara and took an interest in her personal life. Knowing Sara was divorced and a mother, Alva urged her to remarry for the sake of the children. She even offered to find a rich husband for her. How could Alva consider such a thing, Sara asked, after her experience with Vanderbilt? First, Alva replied, not all men were "weak nonentities." More importantly, Sara needed to "bury Romance for the cold Facts of life." She must bring advantages to her children that only money, not "sentimental romance," could provide. Sara disagreed. The best thing she could do for her children was live as closely as possible to her own ideals. A "deliberate, cold-blooded, premeditated sale" of herself would "slaughter [her] soul." No advantage of money could atone for that. Alva listened and then asked if Sara loved a married man. Yes. Was he young? No. Was he rich? No. Then what did she expect to get out of the relationship? Love and companionship "from one of the choice souls of all time." When he died, where would that leave Sara and her children? Sara responded that, as for herself, she did not care. And her children would have to make their own way in the world.

Now that the door had been opened, Sara eagerly revealed more about Erskine, including his many talents, genius, knowledge of art, and collections of beautiful objects. Alva thought she would like to meet him, even as she insisted that if he truly loved Sara he would marry her. "You are too big to take a lower place," Belmont announced. "And I am surprised that he with a man's knowledge of the world lets you. It is all well to talk about the beauty of free love but you pay too heavy a penalty for it—the woman, I mean." Sara explained that she and Erskine did not share the world's standards or cares. Their kind of relationship occurred once in ten thousand years, and if the world denied them, they did not care, for they had "such a completeness of joy as made up for the loss—or nearly so." What Alva made of that pronouncement, Sara did not say. It is, however, noteworthy Sara shared this conversation with Erskine.[23]

Alva, meanwhile, encouraged Sara to join her in social engagements, another indication that Alva held her ghostwriter a cut or two above her other employees. Sara believed she wanted to show her off. After all, she was a writer, an intellectual, and a political activist helping record Alva's impressive life. Sara dreaded these events, yet felt she could not refuse. Among this social set, she found no one who shared her views and values. Sara judged them as almost universally insipid—"mindless creatures of inherited wealth or of piratic riches [who] live . . . lives of selfish indulgence and unvirtuous sloath [sic]." Quite simply, she hated them. She reported to Erskine that in the wake of one afternoon tea, she had decided that Newport, more than any other place she had ever been, needed the kind of revolution he called for in *The Poet in the Desert*. These "smug robbers" produced nothing, had "casterated [sic] spirits," and "babbled and murmured and thought only of themselves." They were completely indifferent to the poverty and sorrow found not only in Chicago or New York but in nearby Newport neighborhoods. By contrast, she and Erskine understood that when one person or group suffered, all people suffered. Erskine's "church and hers [was] Humanity."[24]

The vapid conversation among the rich exasperated Sara. Even Alva sometimes found it infuriating. Once, upon returning from a bridge party, she threw her gloves on the table and told Sara, "I *loathe* these people!" All they cared and talked about was money. She socialized with them solely to keep her social position. When Sara noted it was a bit odd that their focus on money put off Alva, given she had a great deal of it herself, her employer fiercely replied: "Money is power." Alva cared about money and the many benefits it brought, she just did not like to talk about it.[25]

The men could be particularly boorish, especially the ones who drank heavily. When one offered to escort her home one evening, she had a "most revolting contact" with him. To make matters worse, he later told others about Sara's rebuffs of his advances. Yet, not all the men were unpleasant. She talked at length with Alva's son Harold Vanderbilt, boldly pronouncing her antiwar position. He surprised her when he agreed that peace would be best—not the response she expected from a "plutocrat." Later Alva invited Sara to join them for dinner, at Harold's request. Sara declined, to the annoyance of her employer. Sara reported the event to Erskine with sarcasm: "What! I refuse the invitation of a Vanderbilt . . . the heir to untold millions. Everyone does as he asks." But Sara held firm as she privately delighted in the man's interest and, of course, told Erskine about it. "Here I am a gray-haired, crooked toothed, pale faced person approaching middle age—tho I am only a year older than Harold; and yet her son liked me," she reported, "so it could not be looks."

Sara's assessment of Alva waxed and waned. They shared moments of genuine admiration and affection, and their conversations proved lively. One month into the project, Sara found that Alva wore well. At times in her life, Alva had been quite brave, and her part in the shirtwaist strike, motives aside, were admirable. She had character. What she lacked in "gentleness" she made up in "justice"; what she did not understand intellectually, she often grasped "through a fierce maternal passion." It did not hurt that when Sara read aloud one of Erskine's letters about free love, Alva declared it beautiful and moving. Yet, she did not waver from her conviction that women should not accept the economic consequences of free love. Sara, she continued to believe, should go for an "advantageous marriage."[26]

Other times, Sara felt aversion toward her employer. She found Alva "selfish to the core . . . weighted down . . . with the heaviness of too much possession." Alva's appetite for material things seemed insatiable, as Sara saw firsthand while accompanying her on shopping trips during which she would purchase exquisite expensive garments. Never once did Alva offer to buy anything for Sara—not that she wanted anything, but her employer's insensitivity to those of lesser means and limited consumer capabilities, Sara thought, revealed something about the woman's character. The beauty of her home could not mask the unlovely aspects of its occupant, who lived in "selfish ease in the presence of Want" and, again, treated her servants harshly.[27]

The memoir manuscript itself became a source of disagreement between the women. Sara had understood she would receive a share of the book's profits upon its publication and understandably became distressed when she learned, in late July, that Alva did not intend to publish the book until after her death. That meant not only a postponement of proceeds but a hindrance to using the book as a springboard to publishers for Sara's other work, not to mention Wood's. In addition, Alva drew up legal papers providing herself and her heirs all the legal rights to Sara's notes on the project. Frustrated by these maneuvers, Sara intended to be more "foxy," pushing for a higher percentage of the book's royalties, regardless of its publication date. She believed Alva had obtained her services "dirt cheap" and that the "old woman," as she sometimes called her, rejoiced in the bargain. Alva tried to hide her delight in the work for fear Sara might angle for better pay. Sara now wished she had charged $1,000 per month (equivalent to $20,000 today). She intended, whatever the outcome of this project, to use Alva as a model for a character in a novel and include details about her life that would never appear in the official autobiography.[28]

Once Sara began turning notes into chapter drafts, the differences between the two women became more pronounced. Alva found Sara's chapters too ethereal, spiritual, and intellectual. They lacked her own voice and style and, she told Doris Stevens, they bored her. Only intellectuals would find them interesting. Sara complained that Alva didn't understand what sort of information would make a good book, believing the world cared about, for instance, the number of bridesmaids Consuelo had at her wedding and what they all wore. The problem was not Sara's but Alva's. Her thin, meager life lacked substance. Sara emphasized ideas, rather than actions, to give the manuscript lasting worth. Two hundred years from now, Sara thought, the book's significance would be "as a voice from an exterminated class . . . as an indictment of a monstrosity—for that is what this over-rich element are. I hate them—their ideas, their psychology." That, perhaps, explains the most profound reason the project ran into problems: Sara lacked empathy and respect for her subject.[29]

She also pushed her own political views into the manuscript under the guise of Alva's supposed voice. Sara took liberties with the manuscript, turning three pages of notes about Consuelo's wedding, for example, into a fourteen-page wide-ranging feminist critique of marriage. In another example, Alva presented herself as devoted to her children, although she mused about whether she might have been a greater and wiser person had she developed her own talents while raising them. As she took notes on this particular conversation, Sara wrote in the margin the word "extrapolate." And extrapolate she did. Beginning with a Bertrand Russell quote stating that not all women were maternal, Sara expounded on this idea for nine pages. Devoting one's self solely to children was "a crime." "I deplore the eternal sacrifice of women for another or others," Sara wrote, declaring that there should be no conflict between motherhood and individualism, between duty to self and to family. Children do not need constant care. They benefit more if their mother develops her own intellect and personality, and if she fails to do this, she will end up like "a diamond already cut and ready to sparkle" but "lost for the sake of children who may be only limitations." These were not Alva's words or sentiments. One can see, instead, Erskine's influence and Sara's rationalizations for her own life choices.[30] Surely, Alva balked.

The project ultimately came down to a quarrel about money. After Sara sent Belmont the revised and polished chapters from California, Alva refused to pay for the additional work, stiffing Sara $500. Sara decided not to fight it but nevertheless grumbled that "Old Lady Belmont" should be ashamed of herself. When Doris told Sara that Alva still wanted to hire Sara as her permanent literary secretary for $500 a month, Sara retorted she would never take the job, not even for $5,000 a month.[31]

Erskine, meanwhile, read some of the chapters and agreed with Alva's assessment—not that he put it so bluntly to Sara. He gently urged her to give the manuscript more "color." Every life, he advised, gets its interest from incidents, adventures, and details that become "bits of crystallized human nature." What gave Boswell's biography of Samuel Johnson its greatness was the particulars: how he drank his tea, how he touched posts with his fingers as he walked by them, as well as his larger views on philosophy. The Belmont manuscript was, so far, both fascinating and disappointing. It hurried toward the suffrage story and skipped too many other areas of Belmont's life. Erskine wanted more anecdotes from her childhood, life in France, and divorce. Alva needed to take a braver stance, abandon a sketchy resume in favor of "a work of art—a carefully detailed drawing of her life." If she provided the facts, Sara could add the "color and poetic quality." As for her refusal to pay Sara for her editing, it did not surprise him. He had known many millionaires who were "meaner than dirt." In fact, that was how they became rich. That said, Alva had "fallen into two great fortunes" and cared for things other than money; why she would not be generous to a needy artist baffled him.[32]

As it turned out, neither Alva's autobiography nor Sara's idea of a fictional treatment of her life ever materialized. When Sara's time in Newport ended in late August 1917, both women had every expectation they would meet again and continue the project. It never happened. Sara later blamed it on Alva's capriciousness. Initially the book excited Alva, but then she began to lose interest, particularly as her health deteriorated. It is also clear Sara's manuscript did not satisfy Alva. Finally, according to Sara, Alva's ex-husband, William K. Vanderbilt, had learned of the project and opposed its publication. Even after Alva's death in 1933, he made sure the manuscript remained buried. So ended Sara's firsthand experience with the very, very rich. She was happy enough to escape it altogether.[33]

In the larger scope of this tumultuous year, Sara and Alva's problems regarding the book project paled. Consequences of the raging war in Europe reached deep into the United States—even Newport, where Sara occasionally walked among young sailors stationed nearby, on the verge of deployment to war, for the United States had officially entered the conflict. She wanted to shout, "Why will you die for these rich fools upon the cliffs and Belleview Avenue?" Sara saw the military draft as little more than a "lottery for death," which sickened her. When she returned to New York in late August, the city teemed with war energy. Thirty thousand soldiers paraded down Fifth Avenue. Some people wept as the young men passed by, others cheered, and Sara became distraught. She saw the soldiers as "men picked before ripeness for death's table."[34] Her resistance to the war was visceral, emotional, and uncomplicated.

Erskine's more circumspect, rational, and restrained reaction ended in the same place, however. He, too, opposed America's involvement in the war. The April day after Wilson presented his decision to go to war to Congress and the nation, Erskine had ambled over to the Arlington Club. As he took his place among other members in their plush leather chairs, he wanted to have his say about the war "in three words." It took him, not surprisingly, quite a few more. War was a stupid way to resolve differences, he explained. It meant abandonment of reason in exchange for brute force and a waste of enormous material resources. This corrupt war pitted one nation's privileged ruling class against another's while "shrieks of Patriotism—Loyalty" masked that reality, luring people in to die for interests not their own. When another club member raised the example of Russia, where the people had expelled the ruling class, Erskine replied that this was an example of revolution—a fight between the disinherited and their overlords. The European conflict, by contrast, set overlords of rival nations against one another while forcing the disinherited to engage in the actual combat.[35]

Nor could Erskine ignore the rich irony of declaring war on the eve of Easter Sunday. How could a nation claim to be Christian while preparing for battle, rather than turning the other cheek? To call this war righteous and solely defensive, he believed, was completely hypocritical. On Easter Day Erskine listened to a uniformed man exhort the crowd to demonstrate their patriotism through military service. Soon after, *Oregonian* cartoonists lampooned the young men who would not enlist, hinting at their cowardice and degeneracy compared to the Civil War generation. How could they print such cartoons, Erskine wondered, while refraining from enlisting themselves? Meanwhile, the newspaper's editors threw into their wastebaskets letters of "satirical inquiry" about the war, some penned by C. E. S. Wood.[36]

By summer Erskine had become even more outspoken about the war effort and its frightening erosion of civil liberties. First among these abuses was President Wilson's appointment of progressive journalist George Creel to develop a national pro-war propaganda campaign. Then, Congress passed and the president signed the Espionage Act, which defined as criminal any action that encouraged "insubordination, disloyalty, mutiny, or refusal of duty."

Broadly interpreting the legislation, the government began to prosecute widely, with special focus on leftists. Eugene V. Debs, Emma Goldman, and IWW founder Bill Haywood, among others, were arrested for their anti-war speeches. A Max Eastman *Masses* editorial challenging the government's power to draft war objectors led the federal government to forbid the periodical from sending future issues through the United States mail—the death knell for the radical magazine, which stopped publication in November. Eastman and several others also faced indictment for obstructing the recruitment of soldiers. That trial, however, ended in a hung jury.[37]

Erskine stepped up. When asked to support legal efforts to counter government repression, he joined the Civil Liberties Bureau of the American Union Against Militarism (predecessor to the American Civil Liberties Union). Addressing an audience of four thousand at a Los Angles radical labor conference, he attacked the draft, militarism, and the war itself. Erskine's message encapsulated much of his basic philosophy about the problem with America's "Industrial Democracy": the rich ruled and the people served as industrial slaves. Private banking and industrial interests either ignored the peoples' interests or used their power to shape public opinion (a nod perhaps to Creel's efforts) to serve themselves. The belief that in going to war America was helping England fight for democracy was a sham. Imperial England subjugated people all over the world to advance its economic interests. The United States did the same in the Caribbean and Central America. At the conclusion of this rousing speech, audience members rose to their feet in boisterous support for his position. Mary Field Parton, whom Erskine had invited to join him on the trip to Los Angeles, enthusiastically joined in the ovation.[38]

A few weeks later Erskine presented a speech in Seattle before six thousand people rallying against the Espionage Act. Even though the police swarmed around him, he showed no fear. He exhorted the audience to exercise their rights, as citizens, to free speech. And no time better tested that constitutional prerogative than wartime. What better demonstration of American democracy could be had? How could anyone consider such ideas seditious? It was a masterful performance.[39]

Paradoxically, Wood's investments meant he, too, benefitted economically from the war. He did not, however, openly acknowledge the pesky contradiction that, as always, dogged him when it came to the gap between his rhetoric and his actions. Rather, he quietly celebrated the good news that war demand raised food prices and, consequently, increased demand for those eastern Oregon lands that he and Willliam Hanley had held on to for so long. The prospect of finally unloading them at a handsome profit had arrived. So, he railed against the war profiteers in the forest industry who supplied Pacific Northwest spruce for Allied airplanes at boosted prices, yet he did not see himself in the same category. Neither he nor Hanley believed the war was a blessing, and they knew they would pay high "war taxes" on their profits. But they also could not help quietly exulting in the likelihood that they would, at long last, cash in on that property. The hour had come.[40]

Erskine also held out the possibility that the war might transform into a "peoples' war." He believed Wilson intended to support weaker nations, insist on their right to self-determination, and protect them from annexation. The president's "encouragement of Russia" heartened him, as did his movement toward support of women's suffrage, even as he wondered at the Wilson administration's silence about the abuses of individual liberty, free speech, and a free press.[41]

When it came to the growing assault on civil liberties, Erskine, interestingly, expressed considerably more anger toward the rank-and-file labor movement than he did Woodrow Wilson. He particularly criticized Samuel Gompers, president of the conservative American Federation of Labor, for his willingness to head the American Alliance for Labor and Democracy, a Wilson initiative to assure worker support for the war. Where was the AFL on the issue of free speech? Why did it fail to defend radical newspapers, or IWW members, or Emma Goldman and Alexander Berkman? Why did the union, in fact, forsake anything revolutionary? Gompers, Erskine charged, had no vision beyond wages and his own job.[42]

Where Wood sometimes equivocated, Sara threw herself wholeheartedly and unambiguously into efforts to stop the president's war. As early as January 1917, she began speaking on behalf of a group that demanded a cabinet-level Department of Peace with its own secretary. In April she delivered a speech declaring the current war "the most sordid in the history of this country" and received long, loud applause.[43] When she learned her son's employer compelled all employees to buy Liberty bonds at a cost of $5 per month—automatically deducted from their paychecks—she called the boss, told him Albert could not afford the deduction, and announced she opposed the war. The man explained that the chamber of commerce had forced his hand on this and then, to appease Sara, he agreed to pay Albert's portion.[44]

Although she hated to distract attention and time from women's suffrage, Sara joined the People's Council of America for Democracy and the Terms of Peace, a coalition of antiwar people who "tilted toward the radical wing" of the pacifist movement. Crystal and Max Eastman, suffrage colleague Fola La Follette, Presbyterian minister and six-time Socialist Party nominee for president Norman Thomas, anthropologist and folklorist Elsie Clews Parsons, and Stanford University president David Starr Jordan were among the People's Council organizers. The group advocated a speedy peace, supported the principles associated with revolutionary Russia, opposed the draft, and insisted on free speech and assembly during wartime.[45]

In the company of other People's Council members, Sara traveled to Chicago to speak out against the war over Labor Day. The trainload of participants from New York was a "motley assembly," she told Erskine, including many Jewish delegates with "high browed, unusual faces" and "idealized determination to stand against this tidal wave of oppression." The forces against them, including the governor of Illinois, made it nearly impossible to obtain the necessary permits to assemble, and once in Chicago with speeches under way, the authorities threatened to arrest them. Sara prepared to go to jail, but police detained no one in the end, and, in fact, that evening some officers provided protection for secret People's Council assemblies.

The situation in Chicago remained chaotic nevertheless. Even old friends crossed words, if not literal swords over the war. "The truth is we have no democracy and I am more a rebel than before," Sara told Erskine, having just had a heated exchange with Clarence Darrow, who charged pacifists, as well as militant suffragists, with aiding the Kaiser. When one man told Darrow he had "sold out again" (referring to the McNamara trial), Darrow flushed and furiously replied, "Well, I haven't sold out to the Kaiser."[46]

Meanwhile, wartime measures to suppress dissent made radical resistance dangerous everywhere in the nation. Even simply defending those who dissented carried new risks. Undaunted, Sara worked to raise bail money for persecuted friends, including Goldman, Berkman, and various IWW figures. A *New York Tribune* article claimed that anyone who furnished bail for these people would be considered accessories to their supposed crimes. That prospect frightened many donors away, and others donated only if promised anonymity. Sara refused to be intimidated. She used her name when covering the full price of bail for one radical and $8,000 of another's. Sara encouraged friends to overcome their fear and cowardice as well.

Finally, in early October, Sara returned to the West. She wanted to visit Portland, but Erskine discouraged it. "I wish we could end our days respectably married," she wrote, "so we wouldn't have to . . . falsify everything so much . . . . We are only free to separate so far as people go."[47] Of course, she did not mean a legal or church-sanctioned marriage, for that would be a denial of all their deepest principles. Sara simply yearned for the stability and security normally associated with marriage. Yet Erskine had growing concerns about the legal implications of their relationship as an unmarried couple. As the prospect of receiving his land grant commission finally brightened, the lawyer in him wanted to ensure her right to some of that property, apart from those of his legal wife and his children. He also wanted to carefully—and finally—plan a beautiful home they would share.[48] Their attentions once again turned inward to their personal affairs.

Sixteen

INTO THE ABYSS

IN SPRING 1918, ERSKINE'S PROSPECT OF RECEIVING HIS COMMISSION AND SELLING off the eastern Oregon lands firmly and finally materialized. The time to join Sara in California had come. They both loved the state. Sara reveled in spring's sunlight, the slightly medicinal smell of the eucalyptus, and the meadows' brilliant greens. On equally enchanting autumn days, she kept the Eyrie's windows open all day, with just a hint of soft breeze stirring the curtains. This was San Francisco at its finest—"one long, golden joy."[1] For Erskine, it was less about California sun and more about freedom. He could, at long last, realize his dream of a home away from people, politics, and other distractions. Surprisingly, to these plans and Erskine's sudden urgency to move forward, Sara offered a tepid response. Too often Erskine had disappointed her, building up hopes with promises then followed inevitably by procrastination and delay.

Erskine faced the daunting task of shutting down three decades of Portland life. That meant retiring from the law firm, cleaning out his private office's trove of poetry and art treasures, securing the family's financial future, and coping with the emotional pain of separation. His son Erskine, distressed about the changes but wanting to be generous, told his father that although the time would never come when he could be spared, his father had earned his retirement. It is not clear that any of the Woods realized at this juncture, however, that the patriarch intended this as a permanent move away from them and out of Oregon.[2]

Establishing a trust for Nanny became the first priority. In May 1918 Erskine learned the land grant money would arrive in installments rather than one huge sum. He intended to divide the first payment into thirds, one-third for Nanny and two-thirds for himself. He needed the greater share to liquidate his debts, continue to support his son Berwick in the farming operation, and address his own needs. Nanny would eventually receive about $6,800 (about $116,000 today) in annual income, along with $5,000 yearly from the law firm. Erskine recommended she use the latter to run her household and pay taxes and bills before drawing on the trust funds. Upon her death, proceeds from the trust would be distributed among their children or their heirs, although not in equal shares. Erskine thought they should be divided according to need. Max, Lisa, and Berwick would need more; Erskine and Nan less. He wanted Nanny to understand the terms of the trust, but she would not control it. Their sons Erskine and Max would serve as trustees to spare her the burden of business matters, plus splitting the trust would reduce taxes. The younger Erskine worried about the legality of this maneuver but eventually succumbed to his father's wishes. Finally, Nanny would retain the Portland house and its contents. Erskine wanted only the Albert Pinkham Ryder painting *Jonah*, which he sold for $20,000 (over $340,000 today). He then distributed the proceeds in equal shares among his five children.[3]

Disentangling from the law firm proved trickier. Delays in the settlement of deeds related to the land grant, for instance, slowed things down. Only Erskine could do the work, and the contract made clear his client held him alone responsible. While waiting impatiently for the deeds, Erskine spent time gathering his literary papers for shipment to California, where Sara would organize them. He remained uncharacteristically silent about Kitty's reaction to all these changes. As for his family, Erskine expected them to understand (although he did not make it explicit) that clearing out his literary materials from 419 signaled his intention to live with Sara and return to Oregon only occasionally.[4]

Nanny most likely did not realize this, although she asked for a few days of his time before he departed, as she had much to say to him. Erskine agreed, but the conversation never took place, to his relief, as he preferred no more talks with his wife about their irreconcilable differences. He found Nanny's "fine restraint" heartbreaking, but he less charitably commented that she did not suffer over his departure, and any wounds she might incur would heal once she realized the size of the endowment Erskine was leaving her.[5]

Sara encouraged Erskine to be completely satisfied with how he left his Portland family, but she expressed no sympathy for Nanny. She believed the woman's loss was of pride, not "one of the spirit—of love—deep love as we know it but of the more superficial emotions connected with ego." She wished Nanny would agree to divorce, which would make their California future more secure and serene. Instead, Sara believed Erskine's wife demonstrated "hardness, an unyielding quality that is always more or less present in selfish people and which indicates a lack of heart-sympathy."

In mid-August Erskine departed his home of many years, leaving behind its "spiritual soddeness," a quietly heartbroken wife, and a bereft mistress. Portland would never again be his home, for "home is where the soul lights": with Sara. The long-awaited moment of living together openly and permanently—one that had taken over seven years to achieve—had finally arrived.[6]

Erskine next turned to purchasing an automobile. His son-in-law David Honeyman had recently acquired one, and Erkine thought it just the thing for his new life. Sara, however, would have to drive it. At age sixty-seven, he considered himself too old to learn. The idea did not thrill Sara. Cars offered all the disadvantages of being outside—dust, noise—and none of its advantages, such as fresh air and a sense of oneness with Nature. Although she had once crossed the continent in a car, she had never taken the wheel herself. To her, automobiles were tools to get you from one place to another—an object of service, not pleasure.[7] As in most matters regarding money, however, Wood prevailed.

On the other hand, news of a car—a Chandler that Pops bought in September—thrilled Albert Field, who hoped he would be able to borrow it. It would be "swell to take the dames out for a ride," he wrote his friend Homer Johannsen. It would also offer freedom from his father. Ehrgott loved his children—providing affection, security, religious training, camping and bicycling trips, and even, for Albert, an Indian-brand motorcycle that could reach fifty-two miles per hour, on the proviso that Albert always put safety first. And yet a deep-seeded rage toward Sara and Erskine continued to roil the man's soul. Sometimes he struck out at others, including his son.[8]

Father and child, in fact, seemed in constant conflict by the time Albert turned sixteen. Once, an argument escalated into fisticuffs. As Ehrgott raised a hand to strike his son, Albert put up his fist to fend off the blow and pulled his father's tie. Ehrgott hit his son in the face, Albert punched him back, and then, as Albert told his mother, "We had an awful time." Katherine witnessed it all.

Afterward, all three cried and, at their father's insistence, prayed. The appeal of the open road, then, proved strong for Albert. He promised Sara and Erskine that wherever they moved, he would find his way there, too—far away from Ehrgott.[9]

In July Albert turned seventeen. What would he become? his mother wondered. She hoped he would leave the world something worthy of his character and intellect. He was her pride, her joy. The admiration was mutual. On her birthday in September, Albert applauded the noble things Sara had done over her thirty-six years of life: suffragist, antiwar orator who did not fear arrest, poet, socialist, lover of nature, and, like Erskine, a person ahead of her time. He felt certain he would live to see people "talk of Sara Bard Field as one of the most wonderful characturs [sic] the world has ever known . . . . And won't [I] be proud to say, 'why that's *my* mother.'" As "best chums," they could talk about anything. Albert even, to his own surprise, appreciated her literary talents, and literature in general. "I wonder what has gotten into me," he wrote Erskine. "I have read seven books in the last three weeks and before I did not read books at all." Most amazingly, he especially loved poetry, poring over his mother's work, which he found he could understand![10]

As for his own future, Albert remained uncertain. One teacher encouraged him to think about the law, but he rejected that option, having heard Erskine describe the occupation as little better than "a scavenger wagon driver." Lawyers saw the worst in humans and dealt in the wreckage of peoples' lives. Another teacher suggested medicine because he excelled in chemistry and worked well with people. Of one thing Albert was certain: he did not want to be a soldier. He had learned from the "GREATEST Mother in the world" to hate war and killing, to look out for the welfare of others, and to do something to make the world a better place. These ideals, he would never abandon.[11]

Erskine, still in Portland at the time, could not attend Albert's birthday celebration that summer of 1918 but sent the young man an opal and a pair of cufflinks he had first worn when he graduated from the United States Military Academy. Albert loved the gifts. He also loved Pops's birthday letter, full of advice on entering adulthood, similar to the long letters Erskine had sent his own sons. "It woke me up, Pops dear," he said, particularly because it contained no preaching. Instead, Erskine addressed the boy as an "old pal would do," appealing to reason on such practical matters as the harm cigarettes and coffee caused the body. In contrast, Ehrgott had insisted his son ask for God's help in avoiding these things, to which Albert's reaction was, "Oh hell." Albert feared his friends would consider him a sissy if he turned down a cigarette, but Erskine's admonition that only the weak succumbed to public opinion struck him as just right, so "good by [sic] smoking."[12]

Wood's precautions about sexuality and prostitutes also made sense to the boy. That streetwalkers carried diseases dissuaded Albert from "seducing" one. But sex outside marriage did not disturb him. In fact, he hoped the day would come when people who loved one another would "not have to have a few silly damn words said over them by a parson to make them a so called husband and wife." He thought the love between his mother and Erskine beautiful, adding "if any one could be happier by a few words said over them by a parson you gotta show me." Surely this touched Erskine. None of his own biological children had ever expressed such a sentiment. It also, of course, repudiated Ehrgott's creed.[13]

Young, earnest Albert deeply wanted Erskine's approval. He also knew this would hurt his father, so he tried to keep his relationship with Pops a secret. To his credit, Erskine told the boy that Ehrgott was "a truly good man" who "loves all of you dearly." Albert Field should do all he could to lessen his father's loneliness and make his life brighter. He tried. It required deception, however. He lied to his father about seeing Erskine. He asked his mother to send him two letters every time she wrote: one he could read aloud to his father, who always demanded it, the other a "secret" letter, just between mother and son, that he could spirit into his pocket and read only to himself.

For all Ehrgott's efforts to win the battle between what he saw as good and evil, for Albert Field, when it came to choosing between the strict Baptist minister and the likes of Sara, Erskine, and his Aunt Mary, the bohemians emerged victorious every time . . . even when they entangled him in dishonesty.[14] Outside his father's home, Albert expressed especially enormous pride in his relationship with Erskine. He told all his friends about Pops, identifying Erskine as his grandfather, and urging Erskine to call him grandson in return. He asked Erskine to inscribe a copy of *The Poet in the Desert* but to address it to "Albert Field" and leave off the "Ehrgott." As Erskine's move to California neared, Albert could hardly contain his enthusiasm. Unlike his father's cold home, "every nook & craney [sic]" at Erskine and Sara's place would be "oozing over with love." "I am aching to see you," he wrote Erskine. "Someday soon it will be OK and we will all be together."[15] And so it was intended.

Wood eased into San Francisco life with caution, however. He took seriously Ehrgott's threats to withhold the children from Sara should she live openly with her lover. No doubt news about Erskine's retirement from his law practice and his plans to move to California upset Ehrgott. His old rival would now live much nearer to Sara, Albert Field, and Katherine, and so Ehrgott wrote Erskine a letter, the first in several years. It was a desperate effort to thwart Sara's longtime plans for a life with her lover. In it, the spurned Ehrgott, still smarting from the pain and humiliation of rejection, urged Erskine to repent for breaking up a home and to "devote all your powers to the Service of God." Ehrgott found that faith in God provided consolation, comfort, and peace, saving him from hatred and inspiring forgiveness. He wanted Erskine to share the same vital faith in "the Unseen One." Indeed, he prayed for that outcome.[16]

Erskine could have ignored the letter, but that was not his nature. So, after "prayerfully" wrestling with its message, he fired off a long response, offering not repentance but his own now-familiar creed. Ehrgott believed the laws of Christ and man to be right; anarchist, agnostic Wood believed many of them wrong. The world's salvation lay in freedom of thought and action, as long as it does no violence to another. As for Sara, she would not suppress her own deep feelings and convictions. She grieved over the hurt she had inflicted upon Ehrgott and the children, but she also understood it was better for them to experience "this schooling in freedom and honesty of living than a false harmony easily seen through."[17]

Ehrgott waited nearly three months to respond, but "duty" and "honor" compelled him to answer Erskine's "insolent and blasphemous letter," which represented "a vain attempt to justify" guilt. Unleashing the anger he claimed to have conquered, and dropping the pose of forgiveness he professed to extend, he was adding Erskine's latest letter to the growing collection of correspondence Ehrgott had kept regarding the affair since 1912. These letters and Erskine's conduct would condemn him in any court. So far, Erskine had not appreciated the gentleness with which Ehrgott had handled him—a gentleness that could change at any moment. Erskine understood this as a thinly veiled threat of possible legal action against him.

Ehrgott's views toward Sara also hardened. She had nullified any achievement in career or "self expression" by her abandonment of husband and children, he told her. Only sincere repentance, renunciation of Erskine, and submission to Christ would restore her former husband's respect and affection. Their children, as adults, would condemn her, and God would punish Erskine, and presumably Sara, too. In the meantime, Ehrgott repeated his "injunction" that Erskine have no interaction whatsoever with the children. There were to be no gifts, no meetings. "Patience," he warned, "has ceased to be a virtue," meaning he would no longer be so complacent on the issue. Up to that point, Ehrgott had attempted to keep Erskine away from his children, and while he hadn't been especially successful, nor was he especially aggressive about it.[18] But now that Erskine was moving to California, the likelihood of more frequent communication and connection deeply disturbed him. So Ehrgott threatened Sara: if she ignored his demand that she keep her lover away from Albert Field and Katherine, he would withhold the children from her and pursue legal action.

Sara worried about Ehrgott's renewed threats, even as she was determined he would not dictate the terms of her life. She went on the counteroffensive—for the first time, actually—unloading her own basketful of fury upon him. Albert could see the breakdown of their marriage only through the prism of his own pain, Sara told him. She no longer loved him, and their natures and faiths differed so greatly that it made their separation morally imperative. She had begged him to work toward a solution that would cause the least harm, but he had refused. Instead, he fought her every step of the way. Rather than follow Jesus's teachings to judge not, he declared the people who hurt him to be "evil," and followed up with a course of revenge and hatred. In response, she had battled for "clean, righteous freedom" in the face of the many obstacles Ehrgott put in her way.

Meanwhile he had poisoned Sara's parents, friends, and relatives against her. Her own father died estranged from her, having listened only to Ehrgott's perspective. Sara also accused Ehrgott of having polluted their children's minds with insinuations about things they should never have heard. He "paraded" his "grief and suspicions" before the detectives he had hired to spy on Sara. He even wrote a letter to Nanny Wood that so enraged her son Erskine that he wanted to visit Ehrgott and give him a piece of his mind. His father had talked him out of it. The Wood family experienced sorrow, too, but they did not condemn Erskine or Sara with the kind of "vindictive rage" Ehrgott demonstrated. He lacked "natural delicacy or reserve." Their children shrunk from him. He "staged" his grief and wrath before others. This did not reflect sincere sorrow; it reflected supreme egotism.

His letters, with their usual threats of exposure, she went on, no longer frightened her. In fact, the correspondence that, he claimed, would condemn Erskine and Sara, would actually do just the opposite, for it revealed the honesty with which they had explained themselves. While she preferred to spare their children a public baring of their private lives, Sara welcomed a "dispassionate judgment of a court." Nor would she let Ehrgott take the children out of her life because of his own jealousies and desire for revenge. Erskine's relationship with the children did not hurt them; it was Ehrgott's "evil suspicions" and demands for obedience that damaged them. He must understand that many people no longer supported his doctrines and dogmas. The time had come for him to realize others had faiths different from his that they believed pure, holy, honest, and righteous. Sara's views of morality derived from her experience, reflection, and prayer. She intended to push back against those who tried to silence her. She would not tolerate his efforts to interfere in her relationship with the children. She intended to defend her rights . . . and theirs.[19] This—the strongest, clearest letter Sara had ever written Ehrgott—revealed the same self-confidence and command found in her more recent letters to Erskine. She knew her mind. She had found her voice. She fearlessly deflected Ehrgott's threats. Most decidedly, she would not allow him to interfere in her long-awaited life with Erskine.

This was the last time the three debated these issues. Not one had moved an inch from their original stance. Not one acknowledged their own failures, responsibility, or fault for the pain they had created.

Nevertheless, Erskine did not immediately move into the Russian Hill apartment. Instead, he rented a place in Marin County, where he could write and wait for things to calm down. The children lived in Berkeley and continued their weekend visits to Sara. She determined to bring them all together. On the lovely Saturday of October 12, 1918, she piled Albert and Katherine into the Chandler and surprised Erskine at his home. Delighted to see them, he packed a picnic lunch and off they drove to explore the golden Marin Headlands. Albert knew these hills well, having frequented them with his pals. He found his mother's reluctance to drive on the inevitable grades annoying, however. Several times she refused to go forward when the roads ascended, turning around because elevation made her nervous.

After their picnic, Sara wanted to return to the ferry for the trip back home across the bay. Albert gave directions but became confused, and before long they found themselves on another hillside. To the right was a precipitous water-washed embankment dropping down to a dry, rocky creek bed thirty feet below. Feeling dizzy, Sara would go no farther. But neither was there sufficient space to turn around on the narrow lane. Erskine suggested she back up. Unbeknownst to them, a bad jolt caused by hitting a rut earlier in the day had weakened a spring shackle, and now, when Sara backed up, the shackle broke. The rear axle swung directly toward the bank. The brakes failed. Sara whirled the steering wheel in the correct direction to avoid the bank, but nothing worked. Slowly the car sank over the road's edge, followed by a "blinding crash" as the car toppled off the roadway, rolling over before it came to rest at the bottom of the embankment.

Thrown from the car, Wood struggled to get up. He then realized the car had landed upside down and the other three remained pinned under the wreckage. Sara was on one side, and Katherine, on the other, was crying for help and wanting to know if her mother was hurt. From Albert came only low groans. He was unconscious and his whole body was badly crushed. Wood, in a foolish impulse, tried to lift the car but could not. He succeeded in opening one door and pulling Katherine partially out, at which point he realized he had himself sustained serious injury and was covered in blood. Knowing he must find help, Erskine scrambled up the steep bank and staggered down the road until he found two men with an automobile. While racing to the accident site, they came upon several other travelers, whom they asked to hop onto the running board and help as needed. The men lifted the car off Sara and her children while Wood lay down by the roadside.

During the interval between the crash and the rescuers' arrival, Sara noticed Albert's moans had ceased, and she thought him dead. Katherine begged her mother to continue talking, so she would know Sara was still alive. Powerless to help her son, she tried her best to calm her twelve-year-old daughter. Eventually, ambulances arrived, delivering all four to the hospital. There, attendants told Sara and Erskine that Albert was seriously injured but would recover. At this news, Sara thought perhaps she had been mistaken about the severity of Albert's injuries, but later that night she began to suspect she had been lied to, and she insisted on knowing the truth. Only then did she learn that her son was dead.

Katherine suffered bruises and, of course, emotional trauma. Wood sustained a scalp wound, a huge lump on the back of his head, cut lips, a badly sprained knee, and gashes on his elbow and the small of his back. Sara broke one of her legs and received a deep gash in the calf five inches long. The lower part of her leg and foot were temporarily paralyzed, but the doctor promised nerve sensation would eventually be restored. Beyond the physical pain, however, Sara was overcome by the inexpressible agony, the absolute devastation, of Albert's death and her responsibility for it.[20]

Sara and Erskine remained hospitalized, but Katherine was treated and released. Ehrgott, who at the time of the accident was speaking at a YMCA in Sutter, about sixty miles north of Sacramento, could not fetch her for several hours. The girl sought solace and reassurance from her distraught mother, but Sara rebuffed her with the words "Don't speak to me." Lost in her own anguish over Albert, she could offer no comfort to Katherine.

Over fifty years later, the daughter still felt the profound pain of that cold rejection. It amazed her that Sara later claimed Albert's death had little effect upon Katherine. How could her mother think such a thing? "My God! . . . the hardest thing that happened to me in my childhood was losing my brother. I relied on him. He just meant everything to me. And we both were, had to be, mature beyond our years."[21]

When Ehrgott received word of the accident, he rushed to the hospital, driving two hundred miles overnight to reclaim his daughter. He arrived at eight in the morning. To cope with his son's death was difficult enough, but to discover he had died in the company of much-hated archrival Wood made the situation beyond unbearable. Remarkably, he kept his anger in check. The next day, after Sara's surgery on her leg, he attempted to comfort her, but Sara pushed aside his attempt to connect in their shared shock and sorrow, as she had with their daughter. The day after that, when he attempted to discuss funeral arrangements with her, she asked him to leave her room.

On Wednesday, Reverend Ehrgott conducted Albert's funeral. Sara, still hospitalized, could not attend. But Mary did. Ehrgott told the congregation he found some peace in knowing the boy had died before influences around him robbed him of his Christian faith. Sara went unmentioned until near the end of the service, when a friend of Mary's and Sara's indicated she wanted to say a word about Albert's "stricken mother now in the hospital." Every beautiful aspect of Albert's gentle, loving, sweet character came from his mother, she said. He had been forced to live between two opposing ideals but had escaped intolerance and found a way to bridge the chasm. He was like the one great Christ, who neither judged nor condemned others. Furious, Ehrgott chided the woman for her remarks, for creating a note of discord at an already difficult, heartbreaking service. He later characterized the woman's comments as cruel, brutal, hateful, and false, but he blamed Mary, his old nemesis, rather than the woman for the outburst.[22]

The following day, Ehrgott took Katherine to see her mother, but upon arrival he learned that Sara had moved from the hospital to Erskine's rented bungalow in San Anselmo. Father and daughter trudged about trying to find the place before finally stumbling upon it, only to find seated beside Sara's bedside "that incarnation of subtle selfishness, that base scoundrel C.E.S. Wood," as Ehrgott put it. The toxic combination of shock, sorrow, and rage finally overwhelmed poor Ehrgott. He could no longer contain it. How could his beautiful son be dead? How could his former wife have continued to ignore his demand that their children never be in Wood's presence? How could Sara offer excuses for the accident and refuse to acknowledge her responsibility? How could she claim "no one is to blame" when she was so clearly to blame?[23]

Standing over Sara's bed, he told her Katherine would never be allowed to visit again as long as Wood was present. She had murdered Albert Field and now she wanted to rob him of Katherine. Sara had had her way for eight years; now it was her turn to suffer. As he pulled Katherine away, the girl sobbed to her mother, "I will always love you dear mother," while Ehrgott shouted over his shoulder, "You killed your son! You killed your son!" It was a horrible, poisonous scene, with neither parent able to put the emotional and psychological needs of their daughter before their own. Their agony consumed them. In this, at least, they still had something in common.[24]

For at least seven weeks, mother and daughter remained apart. Finally, Katherine disobeyed Ehrgott's edict that she stay away from Sara. When her father was out of town on church business, she made her way to San Anselmo alone. Concerned someone might see her and report the visit to her father, Kay disguised herself by wearing a raincoat with a hood, and she plastered around her face some yellow hair extracted from a doll. She carried a cane and pretended to limp.

San Anselmo—twenty miles north and across the bay from Berkeley— was not an easy place to get to, but Katherine determined to do it. She took a train down to the water, a ferry to San Francisco, another ferry to Sausalito, and another train to her final destination . . . all in the pouring rain. She found the house, opened the door, and surprised Wood, who greeted her with, "Kay, darling!" She burst into tears, distraught he had recognized her in spite of the disguise. Otherwise, it was a triumph that she had made her way on her own, and she had a comforting reunion with her mother.[25]

Sara attempted to soften Ehrgott's grief-lacerated heart on the matter of her future visits with Kay. She appealed to her rights as a mother and asked him to cease acting out of revenge and vindictiveness. Albert was not moved. How could she claim a "mother's right," he charged, when she had so clearly and recklessly defied his wishes regarding Wood and consequently caused their splendid son's violent death? Katherine had barely escaped alive herself. He returned to old ground: Sara was totally insensitive to the humiliation and agony he had suffered, for years, over her selfish conduct. She had abandoned their home to seek a career and freedom and had, in the process, forfeited any maternal claims. As long as Sara shared a home with "scoundrel" Wood,

Katherine would not be allowed to visit. The mother clearly chose her lover over her own child. She had no one to blame but herself.[26]

Stung by Sara's claim that their friends and family saw him as hardhearted for keeping Katherine from her mother, Albert composed a Wood-length ten-page letter addressed to Sara, but apparently meant for others, too. It detailed the history of their marital discord and ultimate divorce. He wrote it for two reasons: to justify keeping Katherine from Sara and Erskine, and to expose Sara's "destructive philosophy." He pitched it as a struggle between Christian home and marriage, on the one hand, and atheism, anarchy, and free love on the other. As if preparing for a day in court (which he possibly never truly intended to have), he rehashed the long record of Sara's transgressions and the role Mary and Erskine had played in wrecking his marriage. Blow by blow, he went way back. He remembered the day in March 1910 when Clarence Darrow came to visit. He said a "shadow fell over us" when the lawyer found the couple in their garden and invited them to the fateful dinner where they met Wood. He recalled the first meal Erskine ever had at their home: Ehrgott had no sooner finished grace than Wood launched into a denial of God.

Ehrgott said that when he realized Erskine was insinuating himself into Sara's heart and she was throwing herself at him, he, the ever-faithful husband, had tried to save her, but she scorned his pleas. Then, in July 1912, she wrote "that fatal letter" in which she admitted the love she had given Ehrgott had now passed on to Wood. It was clear that Sara abandoned her husband and children not for freedom but for Erskine. After the divorce, he had generously allowed Albert and Katherine to visit her, although he had custody of them. Only very recently had he restricted Sara's access to the children.

Over the years of separation, he was the one who had encouraged Albert Field and Katherine to write letters to their mother when otherwise, out of childish negligence, they would have forgotten. He did this even when she was across the continent on suffrage "agitation" or in Portland collaborating with her lover, which in both cases meant *she* often forgot or failed to write to *them*. Ehrgott recalled Albert Field's appendicitis operation in 1916. Sara was in New York and they had no way of immediately contacting her, but once they found an address and notified her of her son's condition, several days passed before she answered. She did not come rushing home to be with her son. Albert, meanwhile, never mentioned her throughout the ordeal of his operation and recovery. He had "learned philosophically to endure his mother's silence."

To punctuate his case against his ex-wife, Ehrgott threw out one more thing: Sara had planned and executed the "snuffing out of the life of an unborn baby." How he learned about one of her abortions is unclear, but he also somehow discovered which doctor had performed the procedure, and when he confronted the doctor to ask how he could do such a thing, the man answered, "She wanted it so." Sara had done it, Ehrgott assumed, for the sake of her career, with the consequence that a "helpless innocent child was sacrificed" before that child's career could ever begin. "Somehow you have managed always to have your own way." This subjugation of motherhood to selfish purposes had also eventually "opened the way later to the untimely and unnecessary killing of our noble son." Two innocent lives had been lost. She and Erskine, who shared responsibility for Albert's death, had "sacrificed [his life] on the altar of Anarchy, Atheism and Free love."

In the wake of Albert's death, Ehrgott decided to show Katherine, still just twelve years old, all the correspondence he had kept related to her mother's affair. He wanted her to know the true story of Sara's course. After reading it, Kay turned to her father in tears and asked if he had ever shown the letters to Albert. "Would that I had," Ehrgott told Sara, "and then his innocent, impressionable soul would not so easily have fallen prey to [his mother's] misguided philosophy." Now Albert Field was beyond her influence and had entered a life of "love fitting his great soul." Ehrgott, hearing that Sara was searching for truth about life after death, reminded his former wife that no better answer, no better solace existed than that offered by Christ's resurrection. He commended Sara to "Him the Lord and Savior of your childhood, and young womanhood, to Him who is undying Love."[27]

Neither Wood nor Sara replied to this epistle. They had nothing more to say to Albert Ehrgott. As for Ehrgott, perhaps in writing down the whole saga in one place he found therapeutic relief from his anger and agony. He did not pursue legal action, and he gradually realized he could not keep mother and daughter apart. By December, Katherine was visiting her mother again, even as Sara shared a roof with Wood. Kay was relieved to have access to her mother once again, but the tragedy of her brother's death and her parents' bitter acrimony had left her deeply wounded. Without Albert, she was alone in that impossible place, caught between a feuding mother and father. To Ehrgott, Katherine's visits were yet one more bitter instance in which Sara managed to get her way.

Sara, meanwhile, fell into an abyss of grief, which was compounded by medical complications related to her injured leg. She wore a cast for three months, after which doctors found the break had not healed. She underwent another operation to remove bone splinters and remained incapacitated for another three months. Through it all, Wood stayed by her side, walking several miles every day to visit her at the hospital. He brought special food to encourage her appetite and spent hours at her bedside, silently holding her hand.[28]

Letters of condolence poured in from across the country. It is difficult to know if Sara found consolation in them. Greenwich Village friend Ida Rauh wished she could hold Sara like a child to comfort her and told her, "Life is like a great wave breaking over us. We either bend to it or are broken ourselves." Ida urged Sara not to grieve: "We know too little of the beyond to believe that the pains of this life are a loss for any soul." Clarence Darrow offered a darker prospect, saying death is better than life for it is "peace—it is nothing." He said some might have foolish illusions about an afterlife and if she could believe in such a thing she should grasp it, but he fancied "you are so made that you can't." Alva Belmont promised Sara that out of her physical and mental pain would come an even stronger woman who would commit further to the suffrage movement. Sara had lost her son, but now the whole world was her child. "You will come unto yourself! And we shall know our leader. You have given much, but Oh! How much greater now the gift you bring."[29] Such letters provided more insight into their writers than probable solace to Sara.

Those who were closer to her attempted more personal support. Sara's mother, Annie, expressed the most loving, gentle concern. Having buried a child of her own, she deeply empathized. She testified to her grandson Albert's loveliness and kept his portrait on her dresser, where she could talk to him daily. Annie also wrote Mary that the whole family now found Ehrgott's behavior contemptible and concluded he had never truly loved Sara.[30]

Albert's best friend, Homer Johannsen, living in Chicago with his parents, Anton and Margaret Johannsen, apologized for the delay in writing to Sara, explaining that he did not know what to say. As it turned out, he said the most wonderful, loving things. Homer testified to the "deep love" that existed between Albert and his friends. To know him was to be convinced that a soul such as Albert's could not vanish. Although Homer was not a "spiritualist," he often felt his friend's presence near and sensed that Albert longed to communicate. Once, the boys had read Alfred Lord Tennyson's "Crossing the Bar" together. At the time, Albert told Homer that was how he wanted his friends to remember him when he died:

> Twilight and evening bell
> And after that the dark!
> And may there be no sadness or farewell
> When I embark.
>
> For tho' from out our bourne of Time and Place
> The flood may bear me far,
> I hope to see my Pilot face to face
> When I have crost the bar.

Homer ended by urging Sara not to blame herself for Albert's death. "I know how you are Sara. You carried more of other peoples' burdens and sorrows than I know anybody else has." She must spare herself that pain. What a remarkable message from a teenage boy.[31]

Sara longed for affirmation that Albert's soul was still alive. She told Emma Wold, her close friend from the Oregon suffrage campaign days, about moments when "whisperings, faint gleams of light" came to her, but nothing absolute and convincing. Most of the time she sat in "great darkness" and silence. The crushing pain from her leg kept her awake at night, and the "inevitable accompaniment of agonized thoughts" left her unfit for the day that followed. Since Albert's death, all she wanted was release. The world had lost its grip on her. Only "an old man and a little girl ask me to stay and suffer here for their sakes."[32]

Erskine and Sara now lived together at the Eyrie, but Erskine was looking for a larger home and, in late spring 1919, he purchased a house several doors down, at the corner of Taylor and Broadway. Perched nearly at the crest of Russian Hill, they called it the "Flowering Wall" for the large wall covered with trailing vines that surrounded the property. Its garden ran wild. Although a lovely place, and theirs to share, Sara's poor physical and mental health inexorably overshadowed what they had hoped would be a time of joy. The fragility of life, the way her son's brilliant personality had ended in an instant, her role in his death—all of this weighed heavily on her. How could it be otherwise?

Wood was just emerging from "the Valley of the Shadow of Death" himself when business and family concerns required his temporary return to Portland. Nanny and son Erskine knew about the automobile accident and had expressed concern about Wood's well-being but said nothing of Albert's death or Sara's loss. His absence meanwhile added to Sara's despair.[33]

When, the following summer, he traveled to Portland for a more prolonged stay, Sara's fears and insecurities became more pronounced. That Erskine stayed in the home he had shared with Nanny was galling. That Dr. Janina Klecan was back in Portland administering vaccines to Erskine and, from afar, diagnosing Sara as "hysterical" infuriated her. How could anyone trust her medical expertise after she had so badly bungled Sara's abortion? Kitty Beck's new love interest only added to Sara's concerns. Kitty knew that Erskine's move to California meant he was abandoning his Portland life, including her, and on the rebound she began a relationship with George W. Vanderveer, a lawyer for the IWW with an alcohol problem. Sara understood that Kitty choosing yet another alcoholic, repeating her self-destructive patterns, would upset Erskine, who still felt some responsibility for his former employee and lover.

During this separation, which lasted two and a half months, Sara openly and repeatedly expressed her anxieties to Erskine, and he, losing patience, finally wrote in a fit of pique, "My instinct is that all is over between us." He said that never again would he come to the Flowering Wall as her lover. As usual, however, the crisis passed, and by mid–October 1919, just over one year since Albert Field's death, Wood returned to Russian Hill. By this time his Portland family now completely understood he intended to make San Francisco his primary residence. Sara's mood lifted considerably.[34] Permanently reunited, their disagreements evaporated. The stormy waters calmed.

And then Sara became pregnant. In January 1920, her California doctor recommended an abortion, believing her physically unable to survive a pregnancy. She followed his advice. Later, Wood asked his Portland doctor if Sara could "experiment with pregnancy" in the future. That doctor thought it might soothe her nerves and provide a new hold on life. Then he asked her age. She was thirty-eight and Erskine was sixty-nine. The doctor would not forbid a pregnancy if Sara "deliberately and sanely not just emotionally" yearned for a child. Yet, it carried risk. Hearing this, Erskine concluded he would never jeopardize Sara's life for a pregnancy. The likelihood of their ever having a child together—something Erskine probably never really wanted anyway—now ended once and for all.[35]

Seventeen

ON AND OFF RUSSIAN HILL

A FEW WEEKS AFTER ALBERT FIELD'S DEATH, THE BUTCHERY BETWEEN ALLIED and Axis powers in Europe ended, although the armistice did not resolve all conflict. Woodrow Wilson's idealistic plans for a new world order quickly fell apart. Proposals to assure colonial people self-determination, to level no punitive indemnities against Germany, and to leave the Russians alone to work out their own destiny disintegrated at the postwar treaty conference in Versailles. France, Great Britain, Italy, and Japan spurned Wilson's high-minded goals regarding colonial expansion, "peace without victory," and revolutionary Russia. Only his much weakened idea for a League of Nations survived. The Unites States Senate, however, refused to ratify the Treaty of Versailles and so did not join the League.[1]

Nor did the end of war lighten restrictions on free speech. Actually, the opposite happened, and radicals suffered the most. The 1917 Russian Revolution, which instilled even greater fear of radicals and leftists, set off the "Red Scare" in the United States. The government stepped up its attacks, particularly targeting Communists, Socialists, anarchists, leftist labor organizations such as the IWW, and just about anyone else who dared criticize the American government, flag, or Constitution. War powers codified in both the Espionage Act and the follow-up Sedition Act of 1918 provided the legal foundation that led to the arrest of William "Big Bill" Haywood, Emma Goldman, Eugene V. Debs, and general secretary of the Socialist Party Charles Schenck. Some went to jail, some fled to Russia, and the government deported others.[2]

In the midst of such dispiriting developments, Sara and Erskine lived on a hilltop in vibrant San Francisco, not the best place to escape the problems that plagued postwar America. If they did not seek out the world and its troubles, however, the world and its troubles came to them, sometimes to their very doorstep. In spite of their determination to devote themselves to poetry, they could not—at least not yet—turn their back on political affairs that mattered to them.

The Russian Revolution, for instance, sparked their interest and support. In April 1919, Louise Bryant presented a lecture on it in San Francisco. She hailed the revolution, in spite of U.S. government efforts to suppress favorable reports. Sara and Erskine sat in the front row and listened raptly. Erskine especially believed the Russian Revolution represented the greatest step toward democracy since the French Revolution. True, it had its drawbacks, particularly the repression of individualism, but what revolution was perfect?[3]

Of all the current issues, the one that most distressed Erskine was government assault on free speech. American men had not been slaughtered and national debt had not been incurred so free speech and a free press could be silenced. He railed against Attorney General A. Mitchell Palmer, whom he held primarily responsible. Erskine feared that, short of another revolution, the nation would never regain the freedoms it had lost during the war. He had devoted too much of his life to free speech to stay silent now. Less than one month after Albert's death, Erskine marshaled enough vigor to write President Wilson's secretary of labor, Louis Post, a pointed letter regarding the administration's assault on free speech and, in particular, its persecution of the IWW. "This administration," he warned, "has sown the wind and it's going to reap the whirlwind . . . . No war for *real* democracy needs such despotic methods . . . . You can't sow tyranny and expect to reap democracy."[4]

When the problem struck even closer to home in 1919, Erskine emerged from retirement to litigate a free-speech case. Marie Equi, a Portland medical doctor and fierce advocate for workers' rights, women's suffrage, and civil liberties, had outspokenly opposed World War I, and her passion, fearlessness, and temper sometimes exploded into violent confrontations, particularly with men. Once, she drove her automobile into the midst of a 1916 Portland Preparedness Day parade sporting a banner that read "PREPARE TO DIE, WORKINGMAN—J.P. MORGAN & CO. WANT PREPAREDNESS FOR PROFIT." An angry mob surrounded the car, ripped up the banner, forced an American flag into her hands, and dared her to deface it. She defiantly tore two strips from it. On another occasion the stocky middle-aged woman climbed a telephone pole to unfurl a sign that read "DOWN WITH THE IMPERIALIST WAR." Police asked firemen to remove her from the pole, but they refused. She descended only after she had finished her speech.

Equi lived openly as a lesbian and provided abortion services to women who requested them. She was blunt, abrasive, and unafraid to buck convention. Those qualities affected her personal relationships, too. She lacked what today we call "filters," sometimes deeply offending people, including Erskine and Sara, with her candor. Nevertheless, her activism was inspiring, and when the Department of Justice mounted a nationwide assault on leftists, including Equi, Erskine rushed over (at her request) to observe as federal agents raided her office in search of evidence of treason. A few weeks later, a Chicago grand jury indicted 166 Wobblies, and the atmosphere grew increasingly ominous. Equi remained free for the time being, but as arrests began to focus on small-town, relatively unknown people, she knew she was at risk. She continued to denounce the war.[5]

Then, on June 27, 1918, agents from the U.S. Army's Military Intelligence Division attended one of her speeches and concluded she had displayed disloyalty. Two days later a grand jury indicted her on eight charges under the Sedition Act. Eight agents worked the case, zealously determined to convict Equi, and labeling her "the very worst agitator we have in town." They installed wiretaps, spied on her medical practice from adjoining rooms, and hired a Radcliffe College graduate as an undercover agent to infiltrate Equi's inner circle. The combination of Marie's political views and sexual orientation—which one agent characterized as "perverted" and "degenerate"—made her extremely dangerous in their eyes. That they could neither cow nor silence her underscored their determination.[6]

When her trial began on November 8, 1918, Equi harbored some hope the war's near end would work in her favor. That was not to be. First, the jury consisted of twelve men, mostly undereducated and from small towns. Women could vote in Oregon, but they could not yet serve on juries. Second, the prosecution ranged widely in its accusations, focusing on her speeches and her longstanding support of labor organizations and strikes. Prosecuting attorney Bert Haney referred to her "kind" as "long-haired men and short-haired women," a less-than-subtle homophobic reference. He also "red-baited," warning the jury that unless they convicted people such as Equi, communists would soon rule the United States.

One of her lawyers, IWW attorney George Vanderveer (Kitty's new beau) focused on Equi's dedication to improving workers' lives by advocating the eight-hour workday, better working conditions, and free medical care for the poor. To attest to her integrity and loyalty, Vanderveer brought in an impressive stream of character witnesses, including former governor of Oregon Oswald West and a former president of the University of Oregon. Equi took the stand. She denied the label "anarchist," identifying herself instead as a progressive who voted Democratic—a patriot loyal to the country she criticized. The jury found her guilty. The judge sentenced her to three years in jail and a $500 fine. Equi was, as her biographer put it, "convicted for conscience."[7]

Hoping for justice from the Ninth Circuit Court of Appeals in San Francisco, Equi added Erskine to her legal team. First, he wrote to Attorney General Palmer and explained Equi was of "Latin temperament," which supposedly accounted for her admittedly volatile temper. She belonged to neither the IWW nor the Socialist Party. The wealthy, privileged people of Portland despised her and pressured federal authorities to shut her up, and that, he believed, partially explained why she was pointed out for persecution. Finally, Erskine pronounced the wartime Espionage and Sedition Acts unconstitutional and urged Palmer to overturn her conviction. There is no evidence Palmer responded to Wood's letter.[8]

Next, Erskine represented Equi in appeals court, eloquently defending her freedom of speech. Every citizen has an absolute right to criticize government policy at any time, including wartime, without fear of consequences, he argued. Free speech is not conditional, available only when the nation feels secure. In fact, Erskine told the justices, "if ever individuals need protection for free speech, free press, and free conscience, it is in time of war." Whether people liked Equi or her ideas did not matter. To speak, even if listeners found her words objectionable, was not treasonous. The Constitution clearly protected minority views from the tyranny of the majority. He cited the recent Supreme Court decision *Schenck v. United States*, an espionage case in which the majority opinion compared the defendant's speech to a person falsely crying "Fire!" in a theater and causing great harm. In contrast, Erskine, maintained that Equi's complaints about the government had posed no threat. If anyone inflicted harm, it was the rich, the powerful, and the U.S. government when it violated citizens' First Amendment rights. In this, Erskine took a gutsy position that attacked not only the current political culture but the current judiciary. His masterful statement of principle, though, fell on deaf ears. The Ninth Circuit Court affirmed the lower court's conviction.[9]

Equi's next hope for reversal of the conviction rested with the Supreme Court. It was a long shot, but she gave it a try, retaining Erskine as counsel once again. The court refused to hear her case. She tried one last option: clemency granted by President Wilson. In her plea to the president, Equi attested that the lumber industry, which resented her work with the IWW, had worked behind the scenes to silence her through this legal prosecution. She believed her "private moral character"—an oblique reference to her unapologetic and open relationship with another woman—also played a role in her trial and conviction. Friends sent letters and telegrams in support of clemency, including some who opposed her political positions but believed in free speech. Erskine did not join them. It was not that he deserted her but that he simply felt, as an "anarchist" openly hostile to the Wilson administration, his letter would hurt rather than help her chances. This gambit for freedom also failed. The U.S. pardon attorney and the assistant attorney general supported clemency. Attorney General Palmer did not.[10]

On October 16, 1919, carrying a dozen red roses and accompanied by her adopted daughter and two dozen other friends, Marie turned herself in. Only then did she learn she would be incarcerated at San Quentin. Several days later a deputy marshal and a police matron escorted her via train to the grim prison on the San Francisco Bay. Sara and Erskine did what they could for Equi during her imprisonment not far from their home on Russian Hill. They sent books, including *The Poet in the Desert*, which Marie shared with other inmates, and the couple visited her at least once. "It was bread and wine to see you," Equi told Sara, calling her "the breath of out of doors and all the beauties of early springtime. You little fluttering brown bird held for a moment in my hand and then away on brown wings flecked with gold." The women prisoners thought Sara and Erskine "Romance personified." One person wondered if Erskine was Marie's father. Marie loved the mistaken identity but doubted Erskine would be pleased.[11]

Equi's supporters continued to lobby for a pardon, and the mood of the nation seemed to favor general amnesty. Neither happened. That left parole, which her enemies worked to prevent. Finally, in August 1921, the warden released her after nearly two years in prison. Equi returned to her medical practice in Portland, continuing to provide abortion services and living a quieter, and frankly sadder, life. The Equi case deeply disturbed Erskine, causing him to lose hope in "common sense and justice." He determined, once again, to withdraw from the world. "I have made up my mind that I am in a mad-house, from which there is no escape, and to prevent going mad myself I am going to get off in a corner and write poetry, or what I think is poetry." As it turned out, the Equi case was his last significant courtroom appearance.[12]

Not all political developments proved disheartening, however. At least one very significant progressive victory materialized during this period. In August 1920, after years of hard campaigning by various groups and individuals, a sufficient number of states at last ratified federal women's suffrage, adding the Nineteenth Amendment to the United States Constitution. Sara's personal tragedies and poor health, as well as Erskine's move to California, kept her out of the final push for the suffrage amendment, and in fact her involvement in the movement had essentially ended in 1918, but in their moment of triumph her suffragist colleagues did not forget her contributions. Alice Paul invited Sara to Washington to celebrate the victory at the National Woman's Party Convention in February 1921. Plans included a ceremonial farewell to the suffrage movement, with attendees singing Woman's Party songs and picketers receiving special recognition. It was also going to be the moment to decide the future of the NWP. Paul asked Sara to give a speech, but then she changed her mind and asked Sara to help dedicate a suffrage memorial in the Capitol rotunda rather than address the convention.[13]

In spite of her infirmities, Sara agreed and took Kay along. Sara had not been east in three years. Barely under way, she already missed Erskine, and by the time she reached the Great Salt Lake she was asking herself, "Why did you leave him?" Once in Washington, however, she mustered enthusiasm for the February 15 Capitol Building pageant. Women dressed in the National Woman's Party's colors of blue and gold filled the rotunda for the presentation of the suffrage statue to the Speaker of the House. The unattractive monument consisted of a block of marble carved with the heads of Lucretia Mott, Elizabeth Cady Stanton, and Susan B. Anthony. One commentator thought it looked like the three women had sat up quickly after being startled in bed, or in a bathtub.[14]

The National Woman's Party Convention troubled her more. Sara pushed the party to support the postwar disarmament movement, and while Helen Todd, Belle Case La Follette, Crystal Eastman, Anne Martin, and others agreed, Alice Paul and her followers "steam rollered the convention like any old Republican machine," Sara told Erskine.[15] Paul, it seemed, wanted to take a rest. The suffrage victory had exhausted her. With that goal achieved, she preferred to focus on "some non-vital, bourgeois measure that will offend nobody and . . . keep wealth at its command," such as lifting all legal impediments to women's equal rights (hardly a small thing, Sara's criticism notwithstanding, and an effort that led to the NWP's creation of, and push for, the Equal Rights Amendment) or establishing a National Women's Party clubhouse. In the face of global issues such as starvation, cruelty, and murder, it disgusted Sara that Paul shrunk from them. Expecting an open convention, at which any issues might be addressed, Sara found instead that the only matters up for consideration were those that had been agreed upon ahead of time by the inner circle. It bitterly disappointed Sara to learn that these women, like so many men in so many contexts, never intended open, free discussion. They had already decided on a more restrained, restricted political agenda.

Sara concluded that the National Woman's Party had failed her and, more importantly, had failed the cause of women's suffrage. She decided to end her relationship with the NWP by refusing to pay the organization's $10 annual dues, which would have entitled her to use their proposed clubhouse when in Washington. "God, it makes me ill," she told Erskine, "the Woman's Party—a club house!!" Alva Belmont eventually provided $146,000 for the purchase of a mansion, and the NWP, in turn, had elected Belmont president. Paralleling Erskine's disillusionment over the Equi case, now Sara, too, decided to turn from politics to poetry, helping Wood while also writing her own verse.[16]

———————

In June 1921 Erskine left Russian Hill for a six-week sojourn in Oregon to visit family, attend to business affairs, and continue his vaccine regimen with Janina Klecan. Interestingly, as Sara's drama with her family calmed, Erskine's quickened, as Nanny and the children were now fully understanding, and experiencing, the implications of his absence. That he would never make Portland his home had finally and truly sunk in, and so the relationships between Erskine and his children, and certainly his wife, became increasingly tense.

That Erskine chose to renew talks about divorce only made matters worse. Nanny responded with anger over Erskine's "selfish willful indulgence" and repeated she would not be a divorced woman. He expected everyone to put aside their values and beliefs in favor of his, Nanny complained. She wondered why an anarchist, claiming to be indifferent to law, societal norms, and customs, wanted a legal divorce anyway. Did he not see the inconsistency between his purported free-love philosophy and his request for legal acknowledgment of divorce? Then she turned to more personal wounds: Sara was not the pure, innocent woman of high character Erskine claimed she was. She was a liar, an adulterer. To this, Erskine simply shrugged and dismissed Nanny's charges as "self-righteous."[17]

Their son Erskine had already expressed sharp disapproval regarding the Sara affair, and it caused an undeniable rift with his father.[18] Nan, whose children had not been allowed to visit their grandfather in the home he shared with Sara, insisted it was her husband, David Honeyman, who so totally sympathized with Nanny that he would never allow their children to visit Sara and Erskine. Nan and Dave, he reported to Sara, were sadly conventional, superficial people who lacked spiritual or intellectual character. Their lives consisted of card parties, suppers, golf tournaments, cigarettes, and cars. Only his son Max, the middle child, was warm, sympathetic, easygoing, and non-judgmental. Max had three young sons of his own, including "a merry blue-eyed baby just walking" and "not a bit afraid of whiskers or long hair." Named John Gibbon Wood, the little boy would toddle over to his grandfather with a sunny smile and arms lifted in anticipation of being picked up. Wood concluded this grandchild was "probably a Radical in embryo."

Max was friendly, but even he, like all Wood's offspring, preferred to avoid discussion of Sara. If Erskine mentioned her, they remained silent—fearing a response might hurt their mother, or seem disloyal to her. Everyone seemed to worry only about sparing Nanny's feelings, Erskine grumbled. No one cared about his. Miserable, he longed to break free from the repressive, unfriendly atmosphere. At one point he claimed he would never visit Portland again.[19]

A camping trip with the family on the Metolius River, however, lifted Erskine's spirits. Siblings Erskine and Nan had purchased land on both sides of the river as a trout fishing location and family gathering place. In this atmosphere of gorgeous mountains, clear alpine streams, and fir-scented air, Erskine the grandfather found the rest and pleasure he sought. He purchased a new fishing rod for grandson "Erskineson" (the third Erskine in the family, so nicknamed to distinguish him from his father and grandfather). Erskineson and his father set out to christen the rod and provide trout for dinner. The boy tossed his line into a dark pool overhung with bushes, "just the place where a robber baron trout would set up his feudal castle." An enormous trout took the fly and Erskineson's reel sang as the wily fish shot toward the mid-river rapids, no doubt hoping to break free in the turbulent water.

The boy's father quickly realized Erskineson could never land the trout from the bank, and so he shouted for the boy to play the fish while he grabbed the youngster around his thighs and jumped into the river, holding him up. Erskineson remained focused on the trout, feeding and then reeling back the line while his father leaned into the swift current and gingerly found his way between the slippery boulders. Then, just as they neared a grassy island in the middle of the river, Erskine slipped and fell. He had managed to set Erskineson down on his feet, however, and without a glance back toward his father, the boy waded to the shore, continuing to work the trout until he finally landed the exhausted fish—"a whale of a trout." Erskine made much of his son's triumph. Erskineson, inwardly proud, smiled as he looked up at his father.

The episode set Wood musing on fathers and sons. "How these two do love each other," he thought. "Erskine *idolizes* the boy—the boy knows no god but his father. Always it will be so yet not always as now." The inexorable law of change meant Erskineson would eventually grow into his own life, personality, and passions. If his father learned the wisdom of change, he would not be disappointed but rather thankful for the memories they made together "and for the love a splendid son will always give him—as I am." Wood and his son Erskine had their fierce disagreements, yet "all that little Erskine is now to his father—Erskine was to me and I feel the best of it, the deepest is still there and we could not be to each other what we now are were we not also what we once were when he was a boy."[20]

As he lazed along a shady stretch of the Metolius, Erskine also reflected on his past as a young man, father, husband, and lover. He felt shame at the occasional moments of crudeness and cruelty he had shown as a soldier. He regretted the one time he had spanked his son. As for his marriage and his treatment of Nanny, he felt sorrow and pity but no remorse.

Regarding Sara, though, he did have regrets. He had bound her "to my wheel and made [her] my victim and victim to all the falsities, until within me grew the larger knowledge and courage." He wished his children could know how she had suffered for him and how she made his life worthwhile. It pained him that Sara could not know, and influence, his grandchildren. Erskine and Nan withheld their children from Sara because of a "false view of life and love which is sure to pass. I doubt if it exists among intelligent people for 3 more generations."[21] Only he and Sara, "disciples of Truth," understood the stream of life and its harmony of forces. He wanted his family to know and love her, and he wanted them to validate his choice. What he did not acknowledge was that Nanny was right: Wood really *did* want everything.

———

Sara spent the weeks apart from Erskine learning how to drive a new Buick coupe Wood had purchased. It terrified her because the emotional fallout from the accident two years earlier remained raw, yet she determined to master driving. She had not recovered psychologically or emotionally from Albert's death, and Wood's absence left more opportunities to brood. She longed to reunite with her son and tried to communicate with him through mediums, a ouija board, and other spiritual vehicles.

American Spiritualism—the belief that spirits communicated with living people—first emerged in the antebellum period. Believers used various methods, including mesmerism and channeling, to reach the spirit world, mostly for the purpose of finding consolation in loss and reassurance that their deceased loved ones still "lived." There seemed to be a connection between spiritualism and some reform movements, including the women's rights movement. "Not all members of the women's right movement were Spiritualists," one historian explained, "but women's rights were inseparable from Spiritualism."[22]

Certainly some suffrage friends and women family members supported

Sara's attempt to connect with Albert Field. In winter 1920, when Mary had the flu, she said she saw the boy standing in her room, silent and calm, with arms folded. He looked older and wanted to tell her not to fear death. The ever rational, cynical Mary was not prone to spiritualism, but she shared this experience with Sara, who was eager to believe.[23]

During Sara's 1921 visit to Washington for the National Woman's Party Convention, she reconnected with her old friend Emma Wold, now working for the NWP, and met Emma's roommate Julia Emory. Julia, a spiritualist, offered to reach out to Albert on Sara's behalf. Not long after, messages began arriving. Sometimes they came though a medium named Teresa; other times, through Julia herself. Once, a message from Albert burst upon Julia while she was in the bathtub. On another occasion, Albert was in the company of suffrage movement martyr Inez Milholland, who compared the boy to "sunshine."[24] Julia advised Sara to "take a walk" with Albert and invite him to communicate with her. Julia said the boy's message for his mother was, "Love the wind and the sky and sun because I am in them all."[25]

Sara experienced at least one instance of what spiritualists call automatic writing, or the practice of spirits using a medium to communicate through writing. The longhand message, produced by Sara but ostensibly from Albert, was written in pencil and had no breaks between words or lines but was instead a continuous flowing script. "Mother dearest," the message read, "the immense love over here is the key to everything. Its power and possibilities are absolutely unlimited and are a continual joy and revelation." Albert wanted her to join him but understood the "importance of growing to the full on your own plane." She still had things to learn but would be "well prepared" when she did "come over." Only her material body held her back from closer communication with him now. Albert also spoke to Erskine: "You are big. You are picturesque. Please wear a jaunty tie for me." And to Kay: "Learn to call on us." If Sara found solace in such messages, they also held the darker prospect of encouraging her to commit suicide as a way to hasten a reunion with her son.[26]

Erskine remained completely skeptical about it all. He went easy on Sara, though, fearing his honest opinion might undermine her fragile health. When she showed him the "Albert letter," he told her he wanted to believe it came from the boy but admitted he could not. Only scientific exclusion of every other possibility would convince him. He wished, however, scientists would study the phenomenon.[27]

It is not surprising that Sara also turned to letters and poetry to express her grief and find consolation. She compiled all of Albert's letters into "Albert Field Ehrgott's Memory Book" to preserve his "beautiful and rare personality." She intended it primarily for Kay and anyone else whose love of beauty led them to seek its "supreme manifestation in character."[28]

And, of course, she poured her heartbreak into poetry.

Oh, Grave, Where Is Thy Victory?

No longer I fear you, little grave;

Once I shrank from your sinister cold.

Now I think of the pain you save

And the infinite riches that you hold.

For you have become my treasure cave

Though Youth made horrible all you had.

No, it is not that I've grown more brave

But one I love lies still in your bed,

And I would fall deeper and yet more deep

Into the nothingness of his sleep.[29]

Nothing helped. In fact, she swirled deeper into depression. Sara could not shake off the trauma of Albert's death and her role in it.

By 1922, Erskine had purchased land near Los Gatos, California, as a retreat from San Francisco. The couple often motored there with Kay to enjoy the beautiful oak-strewn hillside spot overlooking the Santa Clara Valley. A small shack on the property offered rustic lodging. Erskine also scattered cement tables and benches around the place so everyone could have solitude to write poetry and enjoy the quiet beauty of the natural surroundings. Kay and Erskine learned, however, that Sara had secretly taken a ouija board to her bench and, day in and day out, did nothing but attempt communication with her dead son. One night she went outside in her nightgown and stared at the moon as if in a trance.

Erskine and Kay finally admitted Sara desperately needed professional help. On the way back to the city after one stay in Los Gatos, she tried to hurl herself out of the car. Only Kay's quick effort of throwing her body across her mother thwarted the suicide attempt. In San Francisco, Erskine institutionalized Sara, and when he brought her back to their home, she found he had installed bars on the bedroom windows. He hired a nurse to stay with her round the clock. The few visitors who came by had to be scrutinized for any item that might be turned into a tool for suicide. Sara's pen went silent.

Sara's black period lasted nearly two years. And then, after passage of time and with tender care from Erskine and Kay, she emerged from the darkness of guilt, anguish, and remorse. Almost like waking from a trance, she seemed herself again, her recovery apparently complete.[30]

———————

Sara's breakdown was not Erskine's only tragedy at this point in his life.

Of Erskine's three sons, Maxwell was purportedly his favorite. Max seemed trouble-free, responsible, loving, and—especially important to Wood—accepting of his father's life choices. The affection was clearly mutual. Well into adulthood Max referred to Wood as "Daddy," and Wood referred to him as "Maxie." Through the years of Erskine's increasing distance from Nanny, father and *this* son steered clear of conflict. They exchanged affectionate, mostly sunny letters regarding career, health, family news, and financial advice regarding investments for the family trusts.[31]

It was Max who, with Kitty, had accompanied his father to the train station when Erskine left Portland in August 1918. Max understood something of the departure's implications, noting he felt "kind of gloomy . . . but there was consolation in the thought that you were doing just what you wanted to do . . . . I wish to h____ everybody would let everybody else do just what they want to," he went on, "without each trying to force the other into his way of thinking."[32] A man after his father's heart.

It was a devastating blow, then, when in November 1921 Max died suddenly and unexpectedly. His doctors discovered a ruptured internal abscess, probably in his kidney. They could do nothing for him except prescribe morphine to dull the excruciating pain of his inevitable death.[33] Erskine rushed to his son's bedside. Max greeted him, "Hello, Gaga," the grandchildren's name for him. Erskine promised Max he would recover, to which Max replied, "I hope so." Within an hour of Erskine's arrival, forty-year-old Max slipped into delirium "and that's all I had of my boy but I would not have missed that for worlds." Wood stayed by his side through the night, tending to the young man burning with fever and suffering great pain from every movement of his body. He died two days later, on November 4, 1921, at two o'clock in the afternoon. "Life is a gift of mixed proportion," Erskine wrote Sara. "If Love—Why Death?"[34] He and other family members wrapped Max's body in unbleached sheets; they could not stand the thought of an undertaker and his hirelings handling him.

Nanny wanted a burial, with a clergyman, rather than cremation. The next day, Max's brothers and several friends placed his body in a plain pine box covered with black cloth and carried it to the cemetery in an informal procession. The day was perfect, not foggy but misty with autumn haze. The maples and poplars shimmered with gold; the dogwoods pink. A huge bank of flowers from friends and family rested at the gravesite. After a minister offered a reading from Psalms and a prayer, Erskine tried to speak but broke down. But he could not leave his dear son without a few words. Regaining momentary composure, he told those gathered there that "from the day of his birth till now [Max] had never caused his mother or me anxiety—never made us worry not for one hour—not for a moment. He had brought us nothing but joy—tender sweet affection and thoughtfulness." Erskine then began weeping. "Everybody loved him."[35]

Erskine now joined Sara in that sad fraternity of parents who bury their children. He did not know if Max's spirit survived, but he did know it was not in the grave. "What loved us and we loved," he wrote his daughter Lisa, "what spoke to us and we spoke to cannot be buried. It either does survive or has escaped back into the general cosmic whole as part of the eternal and indestructible force of the universe. I would give my soul to believe in survival but I am not convinced."[36]

Sara wrote condolences to both Myrtle, Max's wife, and Berwick, who was particularly devastated by his brother's death and grasping for some hope that their separation was not final. Sara encouraged them to try psychic communication. Actually, Max had expressed interest in psychic phenomenon, telling his father that anyone who "doubts the existence of such forces brands himself a fool." Sara's friend Julia Emory had promised to add Max to the list of souls with whom she sought communion. Apparently, Max did not respond. Sara also penned a letter to Nanny, leaving to Erskine whether or not to pass it along. He offered it, explaining Sara wrote "as a mother who has lost a son." In the context of Max's death, Erskine refused to withhold any expression of love, including this one from Sara to Nanny. Nanny accepted the letter, but she never spoke of it.[37]

Erskine's last responsibility before returning to San Francisco was to address the financial needs of Max's widow and three children. Wood remained the head of the family, and he felt responsibility for each member and would not forsake his beloved son's heirs. Max, a young family man, had received a relatively small income from his job, but he had scrupulously saved $15,000 in securities. These investments plus his life insurance would provide Myrtle and the children some income. Erskine and Nanny agreed to provide additional monthly support and to augment Max's nest egg as a college fund for his sons. Wood asked son-in-law David Honeyman, Nan's husband, to succeed his "dear, dear Maxie" in overseeing the family trusts Wood had set up before departing Portland. Max's childrens' financial future rested, in part, on those trusts.

After getting these affairs in order, Erskine left Portland for San Francisco. It was a few days before Thanksgiving. Myrtle wanted him to stay longer—as, no doubt, did the rest of the family—but he believed he had the right to his own consolation, which he would find only with Sara. He felt "amputated" in Portland, where it was all "spiritual clouds." On Russian Hill he found "spiritual sunshine." He "craved the warmth of [Sara's] soul."[38]

Unfortunately, being back with Sara could not prevent tragedy from once more casting its shadow on Erskine's life. Not long after Max's death, Janina Klecan, Wood's doctor and former lover, and Sara's former rival and arbortionist, committed suicide in Portland. A talented physician, Klecan was also a deeply troubled soul. During summer 1921 Wood experienced a particularly peculiar evening with her. When Janina's latest married lover was on his deathbed, his wife would not allow her to visit, and so, after the man died, Janina went to the undertaker's on a "stealthy visit" to view the body. She took Erskine along. As she stood before the body, she began to plead with the deceased man to give her just one last look, one last word. She kissed his face. Wood left the room but could still hear her keening cries, "like an insane mother to her child." Wood thought this especially bizarre behavior coming from a scientist.[39]

By October 1922, Janina could no longer bear living. As she explained to Marie Equi in a suicide note, she took her life because she was "worn out" and had prescribed for herself "a long, long rest." Wood heard about Janina's death from his son Berwick, who, blithely unaware of his father's intimate relationship with the doctor, wrote to him about the suicide in a letter filled with miscellaneous news. Berwick mused that she must have been terribly unhappy and lonely and thought perhaps she believed she would find contentment in the next life.[40]

Wood's thoughts on Janina's end went unrecorded.

Eighteen
ON TO THE CATS

IF DARKNESS SEEMED TO PREDOMINATE DURING THE FIRST YEARS OF SARA AND Erskine's life together in California, sunnier days eventually prevailed. Old issues that often threatened to end their relationship now faded. Sorrow, sickness, and loss did not disappear, but living together day to day brought greater joy, serenity, and security. The transformation proved piecemeal but permanent.

In San Francisco, during times of health and equilibrium, Sara and Erskine welcomed a rich assortment of friends and acquaintances to their home. Pivoting from politics to poetry, their guest lists were more likely to be dominated by literary figures than labor leaders. A "glittering array" of theater people, musicians, painters, poets, and sculptors came through their door. Just as Erskine always surrounded himself with beautiful objects, he and Sara now surrounded themselves with the people who created such things. Erskine's wit and generosity combined with Sara's warmth and intellect to generate evenings of lively discussion, debate, and dramatic presentations. They loved people, and people loved them.[1]

California writers including George Sterling, Genevieve Taggard, and Lincoln Steffens joined literary guests from elsewhere, including Edgar Lee Masters, Mabel Dodge Luhan, and the Welsh brothers Llewelyn and John Cowper Powys. Bay Area sculptors Beniamino Bufano and Ralph Stackpole visited, as did art patron Albert Bender, internationally known printer of fine books Edwin Grabhorn, photographer Ansel Adams, and musicians Helen and Ansley Salz and Yehudi Menuhin.[2]

"Evenings" on Russian Hill could be unpredictable. Once, German actress Hedwiga Reicher mounted a step between the living and dining rooms and began reciting—yelling, actually—from an English ballad: "I have killed my father, my mother." One of the servants rushed out of the kitchen, certain something terrible had happened. Everyone had a good laugh.[3]

Erskine usually presided. Most of the guests enjoyed his company and conversation, but not always. Mary's husband, Lem Parton, recounted an incident at one of these evenings that suggested some people found Erskine boring. It all began when poet Genevieve Taggard's husband, Bob Wolf, paid no attention to Lem. Lem saw that as indicative of Wolf's "boorishness"—a quality supposedly derived from his "Jewish lack of subtlety" and a kind of New York snobbery that made him uninterested in anyone who could not be of personal use. Meanwhile, Wolf fawned over Erskine, who read "interminable poetry." While outwardly effusive in his praise, Wolf gave Genevieve furtive looks, which Lem believed signaled his true attitude: that he thought Erskine was a "poor old simp." Although offended by Wolf's behavior, Lem agreed that Erskine did go on too long when reading his own poetry.[4]

Erskine and Sara enjoyed the parties but understood that entertaining distracted from writing. Balancing social life with creative work proved nearly impossible. They began to consider an escape. The Los Gatos property offered one prospect; Europe, another. Lem encouraged an overseas adventure. A visit to "the shrine of the poets" (presumably Europe in general) would be the best possible thing, especially for Sara. She needed to resurrect her own literary gifts and personality.[5]

Lincoln Steffens also encouraged a trip abroad. In the depths of Sara's breakdown, he had promised that life remained "very rich" but the couple needed to understand that "there is a time in life when we should cease to carry the burdens of this world, withdraw from the fighting and the working, and become spectators." All three of them had tried for years to make the world a better place; they had earned the right to now stand aside. "You are ripe enough in understanding and humor," he went on, "to appreciate [that life] is a play." When they had taken their places on the stage, they acted upon their convictions and thought they were right, even though deep down knew they were not—no one is. Steffens had come to understand, through revolutions and world wars, that he had often been wrong. "So I say, let the new generation take up the play . . . [and] they will lay it . . . probably nearer right than we would." Come abroad, Steffens urged in 1922 from his own sanctuary in Italy. Visiting Europe would be "as right as the flow of a river. You must do it."[6]

Erskine, who loved everything Greek, had never been to Greece. In fact, although he had visited Canada and Mexico, he had not traveled off the continent. Kay graduated from Berkeley High School in 1923, and Sara and

Erskine thought a year's adventure overseas before college seemed perfect. Surprisingly, Ehrgott made no objection. It was probably easier to let her go given that she had been, at her own insistence, living with her mother in the aftermath of a fire that had destroyed Ehrgott's house that summer. Sara and Erskine's search for solitude and a place to write poetry, however, remained the primary motive for going abroad.[7]

In December 1923, the trio set off, although leaving California and the Las Gatos property provoked ambivalent feelings. Erskine lamented forsaking the sunshine and peacefulness, and Sara wondered if they would find any more beauty on the Rhine or the Nile than in the Santa Cruz hills with their "copper red earth—where spring and autumn are meeting in an ecstasy that crowds out winter during the golden days" and where the nights are cold but cozy thanks to fireplaces and electric blankets. Why leave this "enchanted" place?[8] The property had begun to soak into their souls. Before departing, Sara scribbled one last entry in the oversized leather-bound diary they kept as a record of "The Cats" (the English translation of "Los Gatos"), which was the name they had chosen for the home:

> It is here I have spent the most growthful years of my life— meditating on death, learning thru painful experience that I will come closest to my dear dead son living as he would live—in the sunshine—joyously . . . . And here it is that my love for my poet has grown until we feel death itself can never sever us, one from the other. And here I have grown closer to my reserved little daughter with her grave, difficult nature yet so loyal, so loving, so brave . . . . And so long as my lover-husband and I go forth together, all life is ours for life is love.[9]

Then they were off. In Chicago they visited Clarence Darrow, who "still strides a thunder cloud of gloom yet is getting rich and prosperous," and Harriet Monroe, the founder and editor of the magazine *Poetry*, who promised to publish a cluster of Wood's work in the next issue. In New York they dropped in on Doris Stevens and Dudley Malone, who had married in 1921. Sara thought Doris looked older and sad. Doris no doubt silently returned the assessment, as Sara had unquestionably aged visibly in the years following Albert's death.[10]

The Partons now lived in New York, too. The family had toured Europe that year, and Mary and Margaret were still in Switzerland when Erskine and Sara came to town, but Lem was home, having returned to find a job. To him, Erskine and Sara seemed happy, healthy, and resplendent in new clothes. Wood walked with a fine, firm step and reminisced about his New York days without "mush or sentiment." Yet, at dinner, as Lem sniped to Mary in a letter, Wood "put on one of those exhibition performances, with a flock of agitated waiters hovering around," anxious to fulfill his every request. Sara spent her time madly sprinting around town for meetings and sending flowers or leather-bound books to friends. Lem resented how the pair spent money so profligately. By the time they sailed, Sara was a wreck and Erskine angry because she had completely exhausted herself.[11]

Their steamer departed in January 1924. Sara spent the entire trip either in her berth or "like a half-squashed worm" in a deck chair due to seasickness and the flu, which also felled Erskine. After sixteen days at sea, the ship docked in Naples, where in the distance Mount Vesuvius puffed its purple-black breath into the sky, turning the sunrise into bands of gold and saffron.[12] The three moved on to Sorrento, the destination Steffens had recommended for a prolonged stay. Cocumella, a charming old convent reconstituted as a modern hotel, became their base of operations for six weeks. Eventually, the trio ventured out to Pompeii, Amalfi, Sicily, and Syracuse. Sara loved the serene Doric columns of Sicily's Grecian ruins against a sky "too blue to believe." In Syracuse they attended plays at the famous Greek theater. During intermission, a young Italian man insisted they meet the actors. Sara assumed the invitation had been extended because of Erskine's distinguished appearance—he *looked* like a poet, and the Greeks, unlike Americans, venerated poets.[13]

When summer arrived they went to Rome, Florence, Vienna, Paris, and London. At Harriet Monroe's insistence they sought out Ezra Pound in Paris, discovering shared views regarding politics, capitalism, and American parochialism. Yet Pound's experimental poetry and Wood's fondness for older forms set them apart. Pound also admired James Joyce's newly published *Ulysses*; Wood could not abide it. To American literary expatriates writing in 1920s

Paris, Erskine seemed a fascinating man with the right political sensibilities, but his old-fashioned tastes meant he neither shared an affinity with nor applauded the Lost Generation's literary work.[14]

More simpatico was the relationship with Lincoln Steffens and his lover, a young aspiring writer from England named Ella Winter. The couples rendez-voused in Florence and immediately the women bonded. Ella and Sara both lived, unmarried, with men thirty years their senior, and both aspired to literary careers, which their partners encouraged. Steffens thought Sara and Erskine had achieved heaven on earth. He was working toward that end himself, and the fact that Ella became pregnant added to Steffens's exuberance. A few months later, Sara, Erskine, and Kay served as witnesses to Lincoln and Ella's wedding in Paris. The following November the bride gave birth to a son.[15]

By that time, Europe was losing its appeal for Sara and Erskine. Cities seemed crowded and dirty. They could not find the solitude they craved, and Erskine concluded that anyone who left California in search of the Fountain of Youth and Happy Isles was a fool. Also, traveling and touring proved anti-thetical to writing. They dashed about all the time while their poetry produc-tion and money ebbed.

Concern over finances cast a particular shadow. The U.S. Treasury Depart-ment rejected Erskine's claim that money he had earned from his land grant commission was not taxable because he had completed the work before the federal government instituted an income tax in 1913. True, he did not receive payment until 1918, five years after the law went into effect, but he did not believe it fair to assess work fulfilled before the law existed. The government disagreed and demanded $150,000 (more than $2.2 million today) in back taxes. The issue so vexed Erskine that he decided to return home to fight it. If he failed to win, all dreams for a quiet place to write—let alone basic financial security for himself, Sara, and his Portland family—would be dashed. They left Europe in August.[16] Although it took until April 1927 for a final ruling on the tax case, it came down in Wood's favor. The Treasury Department even concluded he had overpaid his taxes by $21,000. They owed him a refund.[17]

Sara and Erskine did not regret the early return to California. They now realized The Cats was their paradise. Its rough little mountain vineyard, lovely live oaks, and simple shack with three rooms and a stone fireplace in the kitchen would become their permanent home. It took leaving to realize its importance and its beauty. In springtime they marveled at nature's variety of wildflowers and marked the succession of blossoming trees, beginning with the almonds and followed by apricots and prunes. Wild hyacinths covered the hillsides in blue. In late fall, purple-black olives nestled among silvery branches, and golden apples and quinces hung among the yellowing, thinning leaves. And then there was the wildlife. Sara would not allow Vincent Marengo, their caretaker, gardener, and vintner, to shoot anything that might eat their grapes or vegetables, so he asked for a dog to help keep the critters at bay. A six-month-old German shepherd named Chum joined the family, as did goats Dora and Juno. Not long after she came to The Cats, Juno gave birth to twins, which Sara named Alcaeus and Sappho.

In the fall they made their own wine, despite the Eighteenth Amendment, which, between 1920 and 1933, banned the sale, transport, import, and production of alcoholic beverages in the United States. "How like the American mutt people," Erskine wrote of Prohibition, to ban liquor for all "because a relative few will be hurt by . . . freedom." He reveled in growing, harvesting, fermenting, and imbibing his own grapes, and defying the federal government. He risked little, however, since he was not selling the wine.

To the properties' natural attributes, Wood added artistic ones. Marengo and sculptor Robert Paine constructed several seating areas on the property, including a circular concrete seat and table resting under the live oaks. On a wall behind it Erskine inscribed, "True worship is Poetry. Poetry is Worship." Another seat on the crown of the hill contained Sara's and Erskine's palm prints, their initials, and those of Erskine's daughter Lisa, her husband Kirk, their children, and Kay.[18] Erskine wanted a dramatic entrance for the property, so he commissioned two very large, imposing stone cats to sit just off the highway at its junction with the lane leading up to their home. Paine, who had worked with the famed Augustus Saint-Gaudens, jumped at the opportunity. In place of a hefty commission, he asked only for day wages and the opportunity to stay in the shack on the property. It took several years to complete the project, and to this day the striking cats on their pedestals, the combination measuring over twenty feet high, still mark the entrance to the estate.[19]

As Sara and Erskine shook off "the mildew of Europe" and found their property "the homiest feeling place" in the world, they decided they needed one more thing: a bigger house. They wanted enough bedrooms for themselves, Kay, and their servants; a separate study for when they could not work outside; a place for all their books; and a solarium. But they wanted to keep it simple. Erskine thought (naively) a concrete building would dispense with painting and repairs for one hundred years. He hired a Berkeley-based architect named Walter Steilberg to design the new house, and in early January 1925 excavation began.[20]

By late November the couple left their Russian Hill house for good and moved into The Cats. "We started out to build a house for all time and we certainly are doing it," Erskine noted with much satisfaction, even as winter rains seeped through the concrete blocks and the house sometimes seemed like a "money devouring monster." Seeking additional privacy, Erskine bought several more parcels of contiguous land, and well into 1928 he poured more time and money into landscaping and terracing the property. In the end, their new home was hardly the simple monastic house Wood had claimed he wanted. Built in a U-shape and into the hillside so it would blend in with its environment, it contained five rooms (three bedrooms, a kitchen, and a very large open-concept living/dining room). Pergolas bordered each wing, and a courtyard with a tiled patio and fountain sat in the middle. French doors led out from the living room to an east-facing balcony. Bookcases filled with Wood's beautifully bound volumes lined the walls of that central room. His art and Persian rugs added to the rich effect. The perfectly flat rooftop contained a solarium that caused endless problems, as Steilberg never did get it watertight.[21]

Still, Wood was not finished. He commissioned more sculpture. Ralph Stackpole's enormous primeval woman, called "Maia," hung against the outside chimney facing the courtyard. Stackpole also contributed a medallion of a mother and child, set into the interior fireplace. Beniamino Bufano's bronze relief depicting Sara and Erskine seated beneath the tree of Poetry found its place in the living room. Bufano also sculpted a figure of a boy and a girl for the outside fountain. Later, Wood commissioned two more pieces: large renditions of his head and Sara's, both rather Stalinesque in appearance. Sara hated hers.

Curving concrete retaining walls set off terraced gardens above the house on its west side. Marengo oversaw the planting and care of shrubs, flowers, and olive, lemon, and grapefruit trees, and, of course, the vineyard. Erskine and Sara built a small Greek theater just off the courtyard. It was beginning, indeed, to seem like heaven on earth—isolated and peaceful, yet close enough to San Francisco to visit and host friends, attend concerts and lectures, and see their doctors, and not too far from the artist colony of Carmel. In time, though, such proximity meant people, often uninvited, could easily find them. So, they constructed yet another separate structure for their study, this one up the hill from the main house. It contained two rooms, one for each poet; a little closet where they stored their daily lunches of fruit, French bread, and Monterey Jack cheese; a small one-burner stove for tea; and a washbasin and toilet. It offered sufficient distance from the main house so that servants could honestly say neither Erskine nor Sara were "at home" when unexpected visitors stopped in.[22]

Fifteen years after first meeting, Sara and Erskine finally achieved a tranquil life together. Furious, resentful, and sorrowful spouses and children who did not understand them weighed less heavily on their hearts. Controversies over other lovers disappeared. Debates about whether free love meant monogamy ended. What each had long dreamed of, and what Sara in particular had long fought for, came to fruition. Wood provided the means, but it would never have materialized without Sara's iron-clad determination to make it happen—forgiving Wood, again and again, his dishonesty and failure to live up to their ideals; backpedaling when their swords crossed; and refusing to accept break-ups when he threatened them. The place became a symbol and a physical manifestation of their commitment to one another and to their hard-won relationship built on free love. It also represented their mutual dependency. A day or two alone quickly sent both Erskine and Sara into a tailspin.[23]

Yet they were never truly alone. They hired help. Erskine knew that he could not write and simultaneously manage home, landscaping, and winery without servants. For him, a country life did not mean giving up privileges of class. He bemoaned the time it took to cook, wash dishes, make beds, clean house, and maintain house and grounds, as such tasks left no opportunity for contemplation and creative work. Vincent Marengo solved the problem, since he took care of the outside work and then married another Italian immigrant, Mary, who covered the domestic chores. The Marengos' labor made Sara's and Erskine's ideal life possible. The couple did not, however, acknowledge the irony that their version of anarchism and personal fulfillment rested upon the labor of others—people for whom Erskine's escapism would never be possible. Only rich, propertied people could achieve this kind of freedom and autonomy.

Still, Erskine appreciated and respected Vincent's talents in the vineyard and had an easygoing relationship with Mary. Sara maintained a more reserved, formal relationship with the pair, although she helped Mary prepare for her citizenship exam and then hosted a big celebration on the estate when she became an American. The couples were close enough with each other that Sara and Erskine stood as witnesses to Vincent and Mary's wedding on The Cats property, and Erskine constructed a separate domicile for the Marengos in a gatehouse down the road and out of sight of his own house. He even bequeathed $9,000 to the couple so that upon his death they could acquire a home of their own, off the property. Sara made sure they received it. Sara and Erskine thought the Marengos "marvelous," "extraordinary," and "gay and happy," although Mary occasionally displayed bouts of melancholy.

It is more difficult to know what the Marengos thought of Erskine and Sara, but their long years of service suggest they were relatively satisfied working at The Cats.[24] That said, the Marengos never sat down for dinner with the guests, and Sara once said outright that their "taste was [not] cultivated enough" to participate in the parties. Neither Wood nor Sara could shake their tendencies toward condescension and snobbery. The distinctions that came with money, class, and employer/employee status remained intact.[25]

In 1926, Wood marked his seventy-fourth birthday alone with Sara at The Cats. On Russian Hill, they had often celebrated such occasions with a host of friends, many delivering speeches or poems dedicated to the guest of honor. Now, just Sara satisfied him. As he reflected on his life that day, Erskine admitted he and Sara had brought sorrow to others in their determination to create this life, but he believed the end justified it all. "Our own great and flawless happiness would be justification enough," Erskine told Sara. Then he added, "Everyone is happier than would have been possible under a cloak of lies."[26]

Katherine agreed . . . eventually. She believed her mother and Erskine became the ideal couple at The Cats. She knew Erskine had engaged in liaisons with many beautiful, intelligent women, yet none of them fulfilled him as Sara did. And, of course, Erskine was everything to Sara. As Kay grew into adulthood and could better understand the choices her mother had made, she loved being in their company.[27]

Albert Ehrgott might have found it difficult to stomach Wood's conclusion that everyone was happier in the long run, yet by the mid-1920s, even he had moved on. In March 1925, he married Mabel Dewitt at the Thousand Oaks Baptist Church in Berkeley. The marriage was happy but short-lived. Albert died on June 15, 1929, at age sixty-six. On his deathbed, he asked Katherine to tell Sara he forgave her. Whether Kay relayed the message, or how Sara reacted to it, remains unrecorded.[28]

His death, though undoubtedly painful for Katherine, had one small silver lining: she did not have to choose between her father's Baptist church or The Cats as the venue for her own wedding the following September. During her freshman year at the University of Wisconsin, she had met a graduate student, Jim Caldwell, and quickly fell in love. When he moved to Harvard to earn a Ph.D. in literature, she transferred to Radcliffe to be near him while continuing her own studies. In summer 1925, Kay brought Caldwell to The Cats to meet Sara and Erskine. They approved, finding in him a "gentle poetic nature" and a "little touch of aristocracy." He was a literary type, though an academic rather than a poet.[29]

Four years later, Kay and Jim wed, choosing marriage over free love. Sara did not mind. In fact, opposed as both she and Erskine were to formal marriage sanctified by church or state, they threw themselves into this wedding wholeheartedly. It is more than a little ironic that a couple who openly eschewed marriage should do so, but they did it for their love of Kay. Erskine, ever the arbiter of taste, oversaw everything. He picked out the mother-of-the-bride dress that Sara wore; supervised Kay's choices of silver, linen, and lingerie; and drew the design for her monogrammed silver, even though the salesman cautioned his style was "not the latest." The ever-confident Wood shook him off, insisting "beauty is beauty. If a thing is right, neither fashion or time can make it wrong."[30]

On the wedding day, September 1 (also Sara's forty-seventh birthday), The Cats looked like a fairyland. Neighbor, friend, and former senator James Phelan sent a truckload of flowers—vases and jars teaming with blue delphinium and pink gladiolas. Baskets of blooms graced every pedestal surrounding the little Greek theater, the site of the ceremony. The day was "clear as a Mexican opal" when the bride, Sara, and Pops descended a set of stairs to the massive old oak where the groom waited with Dr. Louis Newman, rabbi of Temple Emanuel in San Francisco. Newman agreed there was no need for the ceremony to include theology or what Erskine considered "superstition." Instead, the rabbi read some "poetry" from the Bible and the couple exchanged simple vows, which did not include any promise on the bride's part that she would unconditionally obey her husband. Nor did they pledge to love each other until death. Kay also insisted on keeping her own name, being very much her mother's daughter in this respect. The pianist played "Ode to Joy" and then, joined by a violinist, part of Handel's Sonata in D Major. Sara and Erskine each read a poem and then the ceremony concluded, having lasted just a few minutes.[31]

Guests flowed in and out of the house until waiters served dinner in the courtyard, which was festooned with electric bulbs offering warm light as afternoon slipped into a gentle, fragrant dusk. Celebrants toasted bride and groom with Erskine's own Burgundy vintage 1922. It was, Sara and Erskine concluded, "the most beautiful wedding in the world . . . all bathed in love."[32] It must have helped that Kay would not be going far. The English Department at the University of California, Berkeley, had recently hired Caldwell as an assistant professor, and the couple would live relatively close by.

———

About one month before the wedding, newspaperman John D. Barry had watched Sara and Erskine stroll down a San Francisco street, completely absorbed in one another. It surprised him to find the couple in the city and away from The Cats. They were a striking pair: Erskine with his kind, surprisingly youthful face framed by long, thick white hair and trimmed beard; Sara, smaller, younger, and with a sweet demeanor and a light in her eyes that suggested an inner glow. It seemed to Barry the couple lived "in eternity." The courage with which they had broken from their pasts and started anew, doing what they thought most worthwhile—writing poetry—made them especially notable. Incredibly productive, they published their poetry in magazines and books, working, Barry noted, "at the top of their bent."[33]

Poetry had first brought Sara and Erskine together, and poetry sustained them for thirty-four years. Sara's belief in Erskine's poetic genius partly explained why she put him before all other people, causes, and her own writing. Erskine had long justified his relationship with Sara on the basis of poetry as well. She offered encouragement, understanding, inspiration, and much-needed editorial assistance. They found their greatest connection through verse, and, finally, living at The Cats allowed them the time and place to devote to writing.

By the late twenties, Erskine knew his most productive poetic years had passed. He still sought to publish that work, however, possibly with major houses and for national audiences. Sara also wanted his talents recognized. That would validate her taste and salve the wounds she had suffered in championing and devoting herself to him. Erskine, though, recognized his limitations as a poet. He did not believe literary fame was "something [the] stars . . . intended" for him. It did not help that he refused to study poetic technique. "I am sure the rhapsodists, bards and troubadours," Erskine once wrote, "never had a lesson any more than the grosbeak." He would not abide rules of any kind, especially those that violated self-expression.[34] Applause mattered little, he claimed, compared to the satisfaction the act of writing offered.

Yet, he did want wider audiences, so he revised *The Poet in the Desert*, and in 1929 New York's radical Vanguard Press published it. For this edition, Erskine strengthened the anti-imperialist and antiwar messages, expanded the already lengthy poem by three sections, and added more interpretive lines. He replaced Victorian phrasing with more modern diction. While his verse sometimes echoed Whitman, its sentimentality, verbosity, and even a touch of the pompous detracted from the overall effect. Too much preaching remained.

Still, *The Poet in the Desert* turned out to be Erskine's most important contribution to American poetry. Sections eventually found their way into a few anthologies, but Erskine never achieved recognition as a great poet. His reputation was strongest during his lifetime and in the Pacific Northwest; after he died, it faded quickly.[35]

He received greater critical and financial returns from a collection of satirical essays he had begun writing in the 1910s and eventually published in book form as *Heavenly Discourse* and *Earthly Discourse*. These projects originated with an antiwar essay Wood wrote for Max Eastman's *The Masses*. Written in the form of a dialogue, the witty satire pleased both Eastman and contributor John Reed, who asked for more. Erskine obliged, eventually producing about forty pieces that skewered marriage, evangelical Christianity, patriotism, sexual prudery, censorship, bigotry, and Theodore Roosevelt's militancy and jingoism. In the piece on marriage, God and Jesus stroll through the universe using stars as steppingstones. Jesus asks God if he and "mother" ever married. God answered, "Holy Smoke! What are you talking about?" Jesus explains that on Earth men and women must receive a license from church and state to marry and have children. Without that license, their children would be "bastards." God finds this preposterous. While this may seem tame to twenty-first-century sensibilities, this type of writing shocked readers one hundred years ago. When the essay first appeared in *The Masses*, issues had to be removed from newsstands because censors deemed it blasphemous.[36]

In other dialogues, Erskine parodied U.S. Postal Inspector and morality crusader Anthony Comstock, evangelist Billy Sunday, and newspaperman William Randolph Hearst. He employed mockery, burlesque, irony, and even slapstick to puncture dogmas, beliefs, and oppressive policies. Meanwhile, Wood's God, who cannot be bothered with Earth—"that little pill"—calls for "freedom, freedom, always freedom." Other social philosophers and reformers with ideas akin to Erskine's, including Voltaire, Mark Twain, Thomas Paine, Margaret Fuller, Mary Wollstonecraft, and Socrates, also "participate" in the dialogues.[37]

Vanguard published *Heavenly Discourse* in 1927. The book received mixed reviews. What mattered more to Erskine and his publisher, though, was readers' reactions. They loved it. The first edition became Vanguard Press's bestseller. In 1944 it went into its twenty-fifth printing, and in 1945 Penguin Books bought the reprint rights. Erskine delighted in commercial success and young peoples' enthusiasm for his book, even as he knew his work was not great literature but propaganda that converted no one. His essays served as "a bludgeon which will hit where Swift and Voltaire would miss—the average young mind." Only those who already agreed with the book's sentiments praised it, but he was glad it gave them courage to help spread the book's ideas.[38]

Hoping to capitalize on the success of *Heavenly Discourse*, and under pressure from his publisher, Erskine published a sequel, *Earthly Discourse*, in 1937. It contained eleven dialogues of various lengths that take place on earth and focus primarily on contemporary issues and personalities. God, Saint Peter, and Satan appear, as do Hitler, Edward VIII of England and his lover Wallis Simpson, William Randolph Hearst (again), and the justices of the United States Supreme Court. Two-thirds of the book concentrates on the Court's *Marbury v. Madison* case of 1803, which allowed judicial review of congressional legislation. Another focuses on the more recent Angelo Herndon case, in which an African American man was convicted for his efforts to organize white and black workers in the South. Unfortunately, *Earthly Discourse* did not resonate with readers. Even Erskine admitted it was "as dry as a law brief."[39]

Grabhorn Press published his last book, *Sonnets to Sappho*, in 1939. He had asked poet, critic, and Columbia University professor Mark Van Doren to shop the work around New York in 1926, but it attracted no attention. Thirteen years later, Grabhorn printed it in a lovely rendition of bookmaker's art. After that, Erskine's literary productivity declined, in part because, among other health problems, his eyesight dimmed. Yet he still had much to say. "Why can't I have another twenty years?" he wrote a friend. "I would only be 107—not so very old—look at those darned Jews—Methuselah, for instance." Among his projects were a history of his father's role in the conquest of California, and his own autobiography. He tried to write but struggled with his near illegible handwriting, and so he switched to using an early dictation machine called an Ediphone, filling cylinders with memories. Unfortuantely, he had covered only his youth before his time ran out.[40]

Just as Sara promoted Erskine's literary work, Erskine returned the favor during their years at The Cats. If not as euphoric about her talent as she was of his, he was equally dedicated to seeing her poetry in print. Sara's verses appeared in *The Worker's Monthly*, *The Harp*, *The Minaret*, *Equal Rights*, *The Liberator*, *The New Masses*, *Overland Monthly*, and *Good Housekeeping*. Relationships, death, and nature's beauty dominated thematically. Not surprisingly, her love for Erskine inspired many poems, including "Waiting," which appeared in *The Measure*.

> The hush of my heart as I wait for him
> Is the hush of the night
> As she waits for the moon.
> And the thrill of my body watching for him
> Watching for the noon . . .

Her son's death inspired "To a Young Son," published in *The Nation* in 1925.

> For me the feet of time stood still
> Beside the place you lay with death.
> My future fell asleep and will
> Only awake if wakes your breath . . .

Nor did she ignore her daughter. Her poem "To Kay" appeared in *Poetry* magazine and opened with these lines:

> A shy deep stream of somber water,
> Little daughter, little daughter;
> Not the surface skimming brook,
> Running where all others look,
> Or frankly spilling out your soul
> Into the overflowing bowl . . . [41]

Sara embraced the identity of "woman poet," believing women filled a "vacuum in poetry" with their "subtler, more penetrating interpretations of eternal values." Ever a feminist, she championed women poets, who refused to be silenced. "The liberation of the lip is an essential part of 'equal rights,'" she wrote, including under that label the right to speak openly about sexuality. Sara believed she spoke for all women, although she wanted to be heard, and read, by men as well.[42]

She also wanted to publish a book of her poetry. In fall 1926, Erskine and Sara visited New York, hoping to sell Sara's *The Pale Woman*. Mark Van Doren, then working on the *Nation*'s staff, agreed to take it under his wing. He offered the manuscript to Harper and several other publishers, with no success. An editor at Dutton thought the volume included "just awful" poems. It wasn't that the poetry itself was bad but that the subject matter was unprintable—"Mary Magdalene to her Unborn Child" was about abortion, for example. Abortion was not only difficult, dangerous, and painful, it remained illegal at this time (although Sara and others in her circle knew it was always available to them through their class privilege). To talk or write about it publicly also remained firmly taboo.

Finally, New York printer William Edwin Rudge published the book in 1927. Sara dedicated the volume to Albert Field and Katherine. One poem, "The Passing," addressed the heartbreak of miscarriage. Others mourned the loss of Albert. Yet others celebrated love and, of course, Erskine.

> Had we not clutched Love flying by
> Where had you been? Where had I?
>
> I had been dead, destroyed by duty;
> You, tantalized by proffered beauty
>
> Snatched away would fumble song,
> Striking discord all day long.
>
> Love, like century flowers, may come
> Once in a life time and be gone . . . .
> Ah, but we caught her speeding wing
> And I am alive to hear you sing.[43]

The book's tone ranged from pessimistic, sorrowful, and brooding to warm, passionate, and buoyant. Her verses addressed issues and experiences that appealed to women. Her voice was feminine and sensitive but also, at times, trite, didactic, and sentimental. It pleased Sara that readers understood her intention to offer a woman's voice, but the book did not fly off the shelves. Stores struggled to keep Erskine's *Heavenly Discourse* in stock while *The Pale Woman* sold slowly, if at all. This did not cause great concern. Sara and Erskine wanted their books out in the world; the money from sales never motivated them.[44]

Sara immediately began her next project, a long poem on Barabbas, the biblical character who, while being crucified next to Christ, was set free. She researched the story and then, over several years, composed the poem, consciously focusing on form and technique. William Rose Benét, editor of the *Saturday Review*, and a poet in his own right, agreed to help find a publisher. After Harper and Brothers, Farrar and Rinehart, Houghton Mifflin, and Simon and Schuster turned it down, Albert and Charles Boni published it in 1932. That a New York house did so, in the depth of the Great Depression, was remarkable. Benét's influence no doubt helped, as did California friend and well-known poet Robinson Jeffers, whose endorsement appeared on the back cover: "The poem is epic . . . jeweled with lovely imagery and shining words . . . . It is a majestic poem."[45]

Some agreed with Jeffers, including the Commonwealth Club of California, which bestowed a gold medal on *Barabbas* as the best book written by a California author that year. Praise, however, was not universal. *Poetry*'s reviewer slammed it in spite of Jeffers's endorsement, which the reviewer found frankly puzzling. The reviewer concluded that Field's ambition exceeded her ability, her imagined details failed to convince, her choice of stanza form seemed monotonous, and the poem was scarce on beautiful language.[46]

Sara's urge to write burned steady nevertheless, however, and so, in 1936, her third book of poetry appeared, published by Random House thanks again to Benét, who brought it to founder Bennett Cerf. *Darkling Plain*, which revisited themes of love and beauty and included numerous sonnets inspired by Erskine, revealed the same strengths and weaknesses of all her poetry: Sara's verses displayed delicacy and precision, but she overwrote, lacked distinction in her phrasing, and relied too often on the words "azure," "trans-lucent," "heavenly," and "immortal." One reviewer sourly noted, "What she has given us here is not a darkling plain but a gloomy thicket." Surprisingly, Random House asked her to produce another book of poetry. She never did. This was the last book of her own poetry Sara published.[47]

By the mid-thirties, the couple was done writing, but they had found another way to create poetry: through how they lived. Sara and Erskine spent enor-mous sums of money creating an atmosphere of beauty for everyday—not just special—occasions. They wanted to transform their home, and their very lives, into works of art. Guests appreciated this, perhaps none more than Ella Winter and Lincoln Steffens, who had repatriated to California in the late 1920s. Of Sara and The Cats, Ella wrote, "You are like your own opal ring in those sur-roundings." Assuming Erskine had built the house for Sara, Ella compared it to the tower Robinson Jeffers had built for his wife, Una, in nearby Carmel—"a monument to your love that only a lover could make."[48]

Steffens heaped even more effusive praise on the place. "Los Gatos is a work of art," he wrote Erskine, "and has the extraordinary effect of . . . making [me, as a guest] also beautiful, as music and poetry do." The Cats, he went on, "expresses you & Sarah [sic] more completely than anything you two have ever written . . . . You are, both of you . . . beautiful works of art." He believed humans can evoke beauty in the way they live; "that is what you have proven, that is what you illustrate."[49] What an affirmation of Erskine and Sara, together.

Other poets, including Robinson Jeffers, shared this assessment. Not par-ticularly social, Jeffers lived quietly in Carmel with his wife and their twin sons. Erskine did not yet know the man when he sent him a copy of *The Poet in the Desert* in 1925, but Jeffers liked its "brilliant white imagination, like a wind over a desert vision as wide as a vulture's." He then sent Erskine a copy of his *Tamar and Other Poems*, the book that had skyrocketed Jeffers's reputation and made him one of the nation's most highly regarded poets of the 1920s and 1930s. Wood did not always find Jeffers's subjects (such as incest and degeneracy) to his taste, but he knew the poet's originality and imagina-tive power made him a luminary. The men agreed poetry should explore big, philosophical themes. Jeffers also generously complimented Sara's poetry. He especially liked the more personal verses in *The Pale Woman*. The poem "Had We Not Clutched Love Flying By," he thought, was "triumphant in its Shelleyan lyrical power." Sara, no doubt, enjoyed the comparison.[50]

What the Jefferses most valued about Erskine and Sara, however, was the way they *lived*, the artistry in their existences, an assessment that echoed that of their friend Steffens. "Your mingled lives are a beautiful thing for all of us to keep & hold in our hearts," Una told Sara. After one "golden day" at The Cats, Una urged Sara and Erskine to write their memoirs. "Your life has been interesting & full, vivid & full of integrity." Una thought the story of their relationship especially fascinating.[51]

Another poet who agreed that Sara and Erskine's greatest achievement was the life they had built together was William Rose Benét, who not only said as much but made a point to publicize that appraisal. He appreciated their poetry and invited both to contribute to an anthology of the best living poets in America, in which their work would stand alongside that of T. S. Eliot, Jeffers, Carl Sandburg, Edna St. Vincent Millay, and Ezra Pound. Yet, more than anything, he admired their life in California. "There is no place in this mad world like 'The Cats' or any presence like the presence of you two." A weekend visit there had been like "one's dream of a highly intelligent heaven." Benét, who was just a few years younger than Sara, considered Erskine "a second father" and called him "Zeus." "Why can't you both live forever?" he wrote. "The world needs you. And there will be no others like you."[52]

Benét eventually featured Erskine and Sara in a section of his book-length semi-autobiographical poem *The Dust Which Is God* (1941). Their home, he explained, "hung like a hawk's nest over the town below." The "older man a rebel sage" greeted visitors with "loving laughter."

> And at his shoulder
> gracious and beautiful with silver hair
> and the world's kindest eyes and bravery
> known to the gods alone stood the fit comrade
> to one so good and great . . .

In the "blue evening" they sipped wine on the patio or in big chairs before grand windows as they talked and read aloud. "Zeus" might quote Thomas Jefferson or explain how the Russians could still accomplish economic freedom. An individualist, Erskine hungered for any movement that would eliminate special privilege, inequality, and injustice. But then the old man, an intellectual anarchist, concluded they could not save the world that night, so they should enjoy their wine, talk of vineyards, and muse how little interest the stars took in mankind.

> After a week when Raymond [Benét]
> left them   he felt the enrichment of his spirit
> from the man of wisdom and unwithering youth
> and her of deep compassion and love   He left them
>
> reluctantly   and from the car he waved
> farewell while he saw them stand together
> on the high steps.[53]

Sara and Erskine must have loved having their hideaway immortalized in this way. That Benét won the Pulitzer Prize for this poem made its reach even wider and their part in the story even more satisfying.

Nineteen

AFTER ERSKINE

WHILE ERSKINE, AT LAST, REALIZED HIS LONG-DEFERRED DREAM IN CALIFORNIA, his Portland family only gradually readjusted to life without him. Erskine's powerful personality, steady demeanor, and capacity to handle problems calmly, not to mention his love and emotional and financial support, had lasted well into his children's adulthoods, but his letters could not replace his physical presence. They missed him. Nanny and Kitty would not have agreed with Erskine's birthday assertion that everyone's life was better now that he and Sara lived together.

In October 1924, Kitty Beck committed suicide. She had been living in Seattle with George Vanderveer, whom some people considered the Clarence Darrow of the Pacific Northwest. He had gained national fame (or notoriety) as an attorney for Industrial Workers of the World defendants. A brilliant trial lawyer with a strong streak of cynicism, Vanderveer also liked poetry, including Erskine's. When Kitty met him, he must have struck her as a man with at least some of Erskine's attributes, political commitments, and ideals. Sadly, he lacked Erskine's discipline when it came to drinking. Kitty, yet again, became involved with a deep-in-debt alcoholic.

Married when he met Kitty, Vanderveer divorced his wife in 1922. Then he and Kitty, with checkbook in hand, built a beautiful home on Lake Burien, south of Seattle. Both drank heavily. When Erskine visited Kitty in fall 1924, he found her in great distress and urged her to stop drinking. A few days later, she wrote out the words "Kitty Beck—sometimes known as Kitty Vanderveer" and secured them above her bed. Then she lay down, wrapped herself tight in a tent of blankets, inhaled chloroform, and died. Her sister sent Kitty's suicide note to Erskine. It read:

> I cannot be happy under conditions existing and this in no
> way means any criticism of Van. He has a life's purpose and I have
> nothing, just as Bunch [her nickname for Erskine] suggests. I wanted

to quit many years before, so you must not feel that Van is to blame. Keep all this quiet as possible. Cremate me without any sort of service or dress, rapped [*sic*] in a sheet. Give my love to Bunch. I can say no more. Get Mr. Wood to let you have the Land Grant [money] and retire.

K[1]

Certainly Vanderveer factored largely in the suicide, yet Erskine shared some responsibility, too. For years he had been everything to her, the center and purpose of her life. Sara's entrance into Erskine's world many years before had altered but not terminated their affair, yet when Erskine departed Portland in 1918, Kitty was left behind, and her disastrous relationship with Vanderveer followed. Erskine's disapproval of her drinking may have been the final straw.

That, at least, was Marie Equi's conclusion. Kitty's suicide, two years after Janina Klecan's, horrified the scrappy doctor, who believed Erskine's treatment of women disgraceful and destructive. These suicides proved it. She circulated rumors in Portland that Erskine had taken everything from Kitty, including her already shattered self-respect. Kitty's sister, Emily "Sissy" Seaman, disagreed and said the suicide was more likely a result of Vanderveer having stolen Kitty's assets, including the trust Erskine had established for her. George, not Erskine, had "morally murdered" her. Whatever the truth of the matter, it was a sad and sordid end—one Erskine had long predicted. In the moment, though, his reaction seemed muted. Two months after Kitty's death he dashed off a note to Sissy, saying he hoped to see her in California some day and to learn more details of Kitty's death. If he felt remorse or responsibility for the suicide, he left no record of it. He offered no reminiscences of Kitty's long service and devotion to him. He expressed no outward grief.[2]

Problems with his son Berwick, and his sense of responsibility for all his children, could not so easily be put aside. The family continued to turn to him in crisis, and he always answered the call. Throughout his adult life Berwick struggled financially. He also had an alcohol problem. By 1922, he had given up farming in eastern Oregon (where his father had staked him) and moved to Portland to sell bonds. Erskine helped again, purchasing bonds to provide

Berwick a commission. Two years later Berwick started his own company, Redfield and Wood, using Wood's 419 office. Erskine offered stock as collateral for a loan Berwick and his partner took out, but otherwise they managed to keep their heads above water on their own.[3]

Then came the stock market crash of October 1929, which destroyed Berwick's firm and cost his extended family members dearly. Berwick lost all shares of the bank stock that his brother Max's widow and children depended upon for income. More catastrophically, he lost $35,000 of his mother's money, which she had given him to invest on her behalf as he thought best. Berwick had used it as collateral to buy more stocks, a decision his brother Erskine believed bordered on the criminally negligent. Berwick never should have exposed his mother to such serious risk. His "gambler's psychology" showed complete recklessness and disregard for Nanny's (and their father's) property. It also revealed, Erskine told his father, Berwick's "grossest incompetence."[4]

Things deteriorated further. Berwick's drinking turned deadly. On Thanksgiving Eve 1930, while driving home from a party, an inebriated Berwick killed a man who stepped in front of his car on a dark country road. The accident threw the family into protection mode, at enormous expense to Erskine, who paid the dead man's family a sizeable sum "to buy peace." According to Sara, this cost Erskine "another $12,000," but it is difficult to determine the total expenditure the father spent on this disaster. A grand jury decided not to prosecute Berwick for involuntary manslaughter, perhaps out of courtesy to his influential father and family. Although relieved, a furious Erskine told his son and daughter-in-law Alice that this was not an exoneration and that their lives had been a "failure—in every sense." Parental advice and money could not protect them from themselves; they had to accept responsibility for the tragedy or else end in "wretchedness." They must also abstain from alcohol. If ever tempted to drink again, Erskine hoped that the "dead body on the highway would rise before them," although he doubted Berwick and Alice would change. The "tides of life and heredity"—a reference to Erskine's own father's alcoholism—"are too strong."[5]

Nanny remained the other perpetual Wood family heartache. Feeling abandoned, she nevertheless acted with dignity and never uttered a word against Erskine publicly, but privately she was more forthright. Still, she corresponded with her husband through the 1920s and into the 1930s, writing mostly about their children and grandchildren. When, in 1924, Erskine again asked for a divorce so both could live truthfully and freely and set an "example to the world and help future generations to a larger, nobler and saner view" of marriage and divorce, she did not reply. Meanwhile, the emotional repercussions of her husband's decision to leave her fell primarily on her son Erskine, who lived next door. He took full responsibility for her and shared her resentment about the desertion.[6]

Occasionally Erskine's anger toward his father came roaring out. Most summers, when Wood returned to Oregon he joined the family on their property along the Metolius River. Mostly, relations remained cordial, even loving. During one visit, for example, the patriarch used his time there to pen a charming, poetic "Testament of Charles Erskine Scott Wood" intended for the grandchildren, bequeathing something befitting each child's personality:

> To Erskine Biddle Wood, called Erskineson,
>
> I give all the trout in the Metolius,
>
> The pretty dottings their bright sides upon,
>
> And the red streak;—the sudden splash and fuss
>
> When quick they show a golden-gleaming side . . .

> To Rebecca Biddle Wood, or Happy Becks,
>
> I give the birds that mostly here frequent;
>
> The gentle doves, small heads and irised necks
>
> That coo so soft when the long day is spent . . .

> And to each one hereafter to be born;
>
> I give green earth, blue sky, beauty of night,
>
> The scarlet sunsets and the golden morn;
>
> The black, strange universe with stars alight.
>
> And we left questioning every distant spark;

I would give something to take out the fright

From hearts lost in the vast celestial dark,

The never-answered questions of the soul;

But that I cannot. I can only give

The truth by which the Universe must live.

Beauty is Love, and Love the unknown Whole.[7]

During these summer sojourns, the grandchildren gathered around the campfire at night, giving Erskine their adoring and eager attention as he talked about Chief Joseph and told Indian tales. Unsatisfied, though, he continued to wish Sara could be there and that his family would accept her. Knowing that Sara's presence would devastate Nanny, the children would not comply with Erskine's request. His son Erskine, in particular, not only insisted Sara stay away but said he did not want his father to even mention her name during their time together.

And this is where things stood in 1927, the year daughter Nan suggested Sara pick up Erskine in nearby Bend, rather than fetching him from Portland as usual. Erskine interpreted this as an invitation for Sara to stay on Nan's side on the river. When her brother learned of the plan, he became furious with both his sister and his father. Sara did not come to Bend after all, but the situation precipitated a family crisis. Erskine returned to California upset. Nearly ten years after he had left Portland, the fissure within the family—and the heartbreak and resentment it caused—remained visceral and raw.[8]

Not surprisingly, the two Erskines hashed this out in writing, each staking his position with rock-solid self-confidence and an equal measure of self-righteousness. Erskine complained his father always pushed Sara on them, while Sara herself did not wish to intrude. Further, the younger Erskine opposed the idea of his parents' divorce, in light of his mother's feelings about it. "Much better an honest and open un-lawful alliance [with Sara]," he told his father. It also disturbed the son that his father referred to Sara as "Mrs. Wood." Beyond the fact that it upset him and his siblings, the younger Erskine argued that it insulted Sara, whom he saw as neither a liar nor a hypocrite when it came to her status as Wood's lover rather than his wife. In fact, she displayed courage about their status as free lovers. Above all, Erskine wanted his father to understand how much he had hurt the family. He felt it would be wrong to keep himself silent on this matter and suppress a "resentment that would grow until it burst."[9]

Wood characteristically responded with a lawyerly brief and a philosophical treatise on free love before his letter turned more personal, focusing on Nanny's determination to punish him for living his own life and on Erskine's "rigid" loyalty to her. He thought Nanny was compounding everyone's grief by refusing to accept her place in his heart as the companion of his youth and the mother of his children, even as she acceded to Sara the role of companion of his old age. He urged his son to "breathe in love, not hate; [breathe in] tolerance, forgiveness, understanding, freedom of soul." Lisa had demonstrated how to do this. Even Nanny admitted that Lisa's love for Sara took nothing away from her mother. As patriarch, Erskine would do all he could to make his children's lives happier, give all he could . . . "except my soul." He hoped Erskine would come to California one day, but he himself would never visit the family in Portland again. Erskine did not reply, but Wood, of course, relented on that last point.[10]

Indeed, things could have been different between the Erskines. Lisa, who lived in the San Francisco Bay Area, had pursued an alternative stance on the family division. She became close to Sara and did not hide the relationship from her mother nor see it as an act of disloyalty. She refused to allow Nanny to interpret her daughter's feelings as betrayal. More, she urged her mother to grant Erskine the divorce. Nanny's fear the grandchildren would think less of her struck Lisa as nonsense. The children loved both grandfather "Gaga" and Nanny. They also knew Sara brought Erskine happiness and that he was living according to his honest beliefs and principles. Lisa believed her mother would achieve peace of mind if she agreed to divorce, and therefore encouraged her to follow that course. Nanny would not, but neither did she break off her relationship with her daughter.[11]

By the early 1930s, Nanny's health failed. She suffered from uremic poisoning and experienced periods of cognitive confusion. She became largely bedridden, though she managed a few last letters to her husband in 1932. "I wish you a happy birthday with our children," she wrote in February. Nanny never forgot his birthday, loving him to the end.

That end came December 18, 1933, when she was seventy-eight years old. Her children discussed appropriate wording for her headstone, and although they initially they agreed on "Nanny Moale Wood," followed by her birthdate, birthplace, and death date and place, her son Erskine reconsidered after they dispersed. He wanted to add "Wife of Charles Erskine Scott Wood," and so he did, setting in stone the role, identity, and status she had maintained for most of her life.[12] Nanny had for years accused Erskine of always getting his way. The divorce was one thing, however, that she could, and did, deny him. By the time of her death, he no longer harbored ill will toward her about this.

While the family gathered in Portland for Nanny's funeral, Erskine (who was recovering from a serious illness and unable to travel) walked with Sara to their favorite bench on The Cats property. Between ten o'clock and noon, the time of the services, Erskine regaled Sara with stories of Nanny's many good qualities, her devotion to him, and how she was a favorite at his army posts. He talked about their children's births. He remembered the sorrow they had shared when their infant daughter, Katherine Gordon, had died. Sara listened in sympathetic silence.

She decided to write a condolence letter to the younger Erskine, admitting some timidity in doing so, not knowing if a word from her would be welcome. She sent it anyway, certain Erskine now felt peace even in pain because he was such a "devoted son, leaving no room for remorse, no . . . failure to show [his mother] love and render her service." Sara hoped he would now visit his father, and she invited him to "feel his home and mine is a refuge for you—a place where you will find love and gentle understanding always."[13] It was a time for weeping and a time for a new beginning.

Indeed, relationships between the couple and their children improved considerably in the 1930s and 1940s. After Nanny's death, no longer having to "choose" between their parents, Erskine and Nan visited The Cats, as did other children and grandchildren. Sara and Erskine traveled to Portland in September 1935 to celebrate three grandchildren's weddings taking place within a few weeks of one another. Sara feared the Woods might rebuff her, but they were cordial. Several years later the couple returned to Portland and even stayed at Erskine's home. Five years after Nanny's death, her son finally accepted his father's relationship with Sara, and the day they left, Erskine wrote a note of appreciation to his father for having made the long trip in spite of his health problems. It showed "courage and enterprise . . . [;] how much the memory of it will always mean to me."[14]

Meanwhile, Sara's family grew. In February 1932 Kay gave birth to a daughter. She named the baby Sara. The new grandmother, just shy of fifty years old, was smitten. In fact, Kay concluded, her mother thought no one more wonderful in the world than granddaughter Sara, with the possible exceptions of C. E. S. Wood and the deceased Albert Field. Four years later, Kay and Jim added a son named Daniel to their family.[15]

Sara also welcomed her siblings to The Cats. Mary and Lem had moved east in the 1920s, where neither found professional satisfaction or happiness and Mary experienced periodic bouts of depression. Physical distance meant the sisters, who had shared so much in the past, now saw one another only rarely, but Mary did visit The Cats in 1933. She marveled at the beautiful estate and its owners: "Erskine, weathered and seasoned as the great oaks themselves, . . . Sara the spirit of the place—the sky and water to Erskine's earth." She loved them both "dearly, deeply" but could not resist a few jabs, suggesting Sara's "'Lady Bountiful' attitude" reflected a troubled conscience. Sara tried, Mary claimed, to overcome guilt regarding her good fortune by being munificent. Yet there were limits. When Mary hinted she wanted to stay longer, Sara said no. Mary then confided to Lem she had tired of being there and felt like "just a 'relation on a visit.'" A bit more graciously, she admitted visitors inundated the place and took their toll on Sara's stamina.[16]

Mary's assessment of Erskine remained consistently favorable. She found him "very beautiful—a god among men—still mentally alert and still . . . in love with life." He also became, before the end of 1933, the one thing that kept the Partons from losing everything. The Depression hit the couple hard. Lem retained his job but could not keep up payments on their two mortgages, for a city townhouse and a country place in Snedens Landing, New York. They lost the former, including all the equity they had in it, and would have lost the other place, for which they owed delinquent taxes, if Erskine had not taken over the deed at the Partons' request. While Mary and Lem appreciated Erskine's generosity, it probably stung to ask for his help, but they did and Erskine kindly agreed.

Even Erskine could not evade the world's economic troubles, however, and the Great Depression took its toll on his wealth, too. As his income shrunk and his expenses rose, he considered selling some of his art treasures, but their values had fallen so precipitously that he decided to wait until the market improved. Instead, he took out loans, to his son Erskine's alarm. He also had to pay for others' mistakes and even treachery. The most damaging financial hit came from within the Wood family. After Max's death, Erskine appointed son-in-law David Honeyman (Nan's husband) as trustee for the trust funds of both the Wood family and Kitty Beck. (Kitty's sister Sissy now owned the trust Erskine had set up for her.) In 1941 it became clear Honeyman had embezzled money from the trusts. These funds represented a significant chunk of Erskine's lifetime earnings, and to have a son-in-law steal and squander them infuriated him. It particularly outraged Erskine that Honeyman had taken $30,000 of Max's sons' funds and $10,000 of Lisa's money.

Erskine pushed for legal action. His son Erskine, however, wanted to tread lightly, considering the scoundrel was his sister's husband. On that point, Wood had little sympathy. Surely, he thought, Nan would not ask the family to let this go "at the expense of justice to Max's children." Nan, however, offered no apology. Her brother hoped for an out-of-court settlement, but that did not happen. Now ninety years old, essentially blind, and in failing health, Erskine left the legal process to the other Erskine, though his mind remained sharp and his righteous anger strong. Most grievously, Honeyman had "robbed the helpless and the orphan ruthlessly. This latter, to me, is his greatest crime." In the end, the court concluded Honeyman had mismanaged the trust. He appealed, which led to further legal expenses, but the court ultimately awarded the family $10,000. Family fighting about money . . . it was a sad conclusion to a tragic situation that would have broken Erskine's heart had he lived to see it.[17] Death spared him this fate.

When Erskine reached his eighties, time finally caught up with his body. After undergoing a prostatectomy in 1934, he told a friend, "Man is a machine that soon begins to break down and when once the collapse has begun there is no end . . . till the tank is out of gas and the old engine stops." Sure enough, in 1937, eighty-five-year-old Erskine suffered a massive heart attack. Doctors held out little hope for his recovery, but with tender nursing from Lisa and Sara, Erskine survived. He returned to The Cats two months later.[18]

Through months of recuperation, Sara knew something troubled Erskine. Finally, he revealed his concern. Had he died, Sara could have experienced "complications" regarding money and property, and so he concluded they must protect her financial future by marrying. Shocked, Sara thought that, legal definitions aside, it would be an affront to their principles—"an indignity impossible to face"—to see their relationship as anything less than that of husband and wife in spirit and commitment, especially after all they had experienced in the name of free love. She did not concern herself with legal matters or care what others thought about their relationship. Long ago, they had committed to living together openly; marrying now was unthinkable. Of course, Nanny's refusal to divorce had made marriage impossible while she was alive, but that was not the point. When Nanny died, it never occurred to either of them to "legalize" their love.[19]

Now, Erskine changed his mind. Ever the lawyer, he believed the risk to Sara's security too important to ignore. So, she relented, with the proviso that their wedding remain secret, since it represented such a reversal of their bedrock beliefs. They asked a young San Francisco rabbi, Jacob Weinstein, to officiate. On January 20, 1938, a ceremony was held at The Cats, the only witnesses being Kay and Jim, Lisa and her husband Kirk, and the rabbi's wife. With tact, tenderness, and as little ritual as possible, the rabbi offered a few remarks before reading Sara's poem "Evening Affirmation":

> Our love did not build around light
> For its firm fruit's pit.
> The source of both day and night
> Is the heart of it.

Weinstein then read Erskine's poem "What Shall I Say of You," ending with the lines, "When you go the god of me sinks, O pure and passionate priestess." The rabbi then concluded, "I would feel myself sacreligiously [sic] presumptuous to feel that I . . . had any divine authority to pronounce you husband and wife. Your lives have done that in a manner that has been an example of true marriage far more powerfully than the lives of many whose marriage was, from the first, legalized." The best he could offer was that, by virtue of civil authority vested in him, they were now husband and wife in the eyes of California law, as they had long been "in the eyes of the divine law of the kingdom of heaven." Wood presented Sara with a ruby ring set in heavy Chinese gold.

Sara later admitted that the "hour we had both rather dreaded"—a rather dismal description of one's wedding day—had "proved one of the most beautiful in our lives together." That was it. They did not broadcast the marriage and never celebrated an anniversary. They saw their wedding as a legal necessity and nothing more.[20] It was also a remarkable concession. After decades of dismissing marriage sanctified by church or state and pouring onto paper his heartfelt belief in free love, Erskine had bowed to cold convention and laws of property. Practical considerations shoved philosophical principle aside. It was, of course, not the first time Erskine's actions contradicted his convictions; the marriage became just one more paradox in a life full of them.

Erskine's mortality continued to weigh upon the couple as the quality of his life diminished. Sara became constant caretaker; Erskine, the dependent. The routine of working in their studio ebbed. Sara wanted Erskine to devote any vitality he could still muster to creative work, but his eyesight and energy had so weakened that he could manage little writing. Her own writing nosedived as well.

The Cats remained their haven, offering up one golden day after another, with gardens springing to life in late winter, the sight of a deer in the grove, or an immense rattlesnake by the Marengos' house in the summer—all of it evoking wonder. Sara woke early one May morning to witness a total eclipse of the sun. The moon appeared as a copper disc surrounded by a thin rim of pale light. At the moment of totality, she claimed, "A sharp shudder passed over the earth, shaking the trees with a low moan."[21]

The beauty of their home, however, could not fend off the gloomy news of war in Europe, soon followed by Japan's attack on Pearl Harbor and the United States' entrance into the conflict. These developments wore heavily on Sara. Long a committed pacifist, she had opposed World War I as a conflict of unvarnished imperialism, but this war was different. The rise of fascism, its commitment to world conquest, and Hitler's pure evil horrified her.[22] To relent on her pacifist ideals made her soul sick, but the Nazis gave her no choice.

Erskine, too, mobilized one last time, in opposition not to the war but to the homegrown injustice that was arising in its wake. For many years he had purchased treasures from an Asian art and antique shop in San Francisco's Chinatown run by Takezo Shiota.[23] Japan-born Shiota had arrived in the United States in 1894 at age nineteen and built his business by catering to white Americans and appraising Asian art for Bay Area museums. He built a home in San Mateo, and Erskine and Sara hosted the Shiota family at The Cats. On December 8, 1941, the day after the Pearl Harbor attack, Takezo's world shattered. Literally overnight the federal government declared him, along with thousands of others of Japanese descent, an "enemy alien." They sent him first to an internment camp in Missoula, Montana, then to one at Fort Sill, Oklahoma, and finally to Camp Livingston, in Louisiana.

The hysteria mixed with racism that swept the entire nation after Pearl Harbor claimed Shiota as one of its victims. In adherence to President Roosevelt's February 1942 Executive Order 9066, the federal government eventually rounded up over 110,000 people of Japanese ancestry, mostly from coastal states, and imprisoned them in concentration camps in the interior. The reasoning behind the order? That people of Japanese ancestry—including men, women, and children, even those who were natural-born citizens of the United States—posed a security risk to the nation. In March, the government sent the remainder of the Shiota family, including the American-born citizen children, to an internment camp in Poston, Arizona. They had not seen their father since his arrest.[24]

Erskine and Sara provided the Shiotas with support through letters of encouragement and gifts of fruit and chocolates. The family also hoped Erskine would use his legal and literary talents to help their father achieve a rehearing. "Your friendly words," son Jutaro Shiota explained, "may speed his release and help him to rejoin his family."[25] Of course, Wood obliged. As the son of the first surgeon general of the navy, and as the self-proclaimed oldest living graduate of West Point, he related the history of his relationship with Shiota and insisted that during Shiota's forty-three years in San Francisco he had earned the respect of all who knew him. He had never expressed disloyalty to the United States. Keeping things low-key and personal, Erskine offered no lengthy treatise on the questionable legality of Shiota's detainment or incarceration. Not long after, the Shiota family received word that their father would receive a rehearing in March 1943. They believed Wood responsible for this small victory.[26] Erskine also served as a reference for the Shiota children so they could find employment outside the camp. One ended up in Cincinnati, one in New York, and another in Hartford, Connecticut.[27] As for Takezo, the government finally allowed him to join his family in Arizona. He died not long after. His last wish—to return home to San Francisco—went unfulfilled. Not even Wood's powers of persuasion could remedy that.[28]

On January 17, 1944, Erskine began experiencing labored breathing. Sara sent for the doctor, who informed her this was the beginning of the end. Erskine had been in slow, steady decline for several years by this time. Nevertheless, this news stunned Sara, who went looking for Wood and found him lying on a west-facing window seat in the living room. Suspecting nothing, he held her close. Sara never revealed to him what the doctor had told her. That night he ate a hearty dinner and chuckled as she read aloud a chapter from his *Earthly Discourse*. The following day he did not wake until late afternoon, and he was weak and indifferent to food. At that point, Sara alerted family members, who quickly made their way to The Cats to say their goodbyes.[29] Erskine, not realizing what was happening, expressed love and good humor to those who came to his bedside, recognizing each by name and clasping their hands. At night Kay's husband, Jim Caldwell, noted how Wood tossed and turned. When asked why he did not sleep, Wood wryly responded, "What's the use?" and they both laughed.

Several days later, on January 22, 1944, at 2:10 p.m., Erskine died. Sara believed he neither suffered nor was conscious of his impending death. Still, "for those of us who loved the out-worn cloak that had wrapped his great spirit," Sara wrote to her stepson Erskine, "it was difficult to see the prolonged wracking of his body." With one last deep breath, the body had surrendered and set Wood free. Vincent and Mary Marengo wept openly. "We have lost a Father," they told Sara.[30]

Surprisingly for a pair who seemed so often to consider their mortality, Erskine and Sara never discussed plans for their funerals or the disposition of their bodies. She did not know if he wanted a gravesite or preferred crema-tion, the "purification by fire" he praised in *The Poet in the Desert*. Sara turned to Erskine's sonnets, looking for guidance. She stumbled upon this:

> If any would for me build a true bier
>
> Bring my dumb ashes to a pleasant spot
>
> And scatter them without despairing tear
>
> About a young oak. So by time forgot
>
> I shall be joyous in the strong oak's veins
>
> And laugh from out his leaves to the blue sky,
>
> Rejoice in summer sun and winter rains
>
> And know perhaps a gentler ecstasy
>
> Than this world gives. Birds frolic in the boughs
>
> And breezes play. And so the seasons pass.
>
> Lovers I know will come to kiss their vows
>
> And lie awhile upon the whispering grass.
>
> And some who knew me may come here to give
>
> A petal of the heart while yet they live.

As if receiving direct word from Erskine himself, Sara knew exactly what to do. On February 20, what would have been his ninety-second birthday, nearby family and a few close friends scattered his ashes around the great oak in The Cats' grove. Sara asked that her ashes, too, be eventually scattered there, as a symbol of the couple's undying unity.[31]

Many years before, Erskine had written to Sara about separation from one another, and she gave that letter special treatment when transferring the couple's correspondence to the Huntington Library four decades later. The letter, from June 20, 1915, had been taken out of chronological order and placed at the very end of the hundreds of letters Erskine had written to Sara over the course of their relationship. While it's possible the placement was the result of a filing oversight or mistake, one might also consider that Sara may have intended the letter to be read as Erskine's final message to her, and to future researchers, concerning his death and how he wanted Sara to cope.

Treasure the memories, he urged her, for they will be sweet and comforting. As poets, they should find in separation's sorrow new ways of living, new strength. Out of the sadness, "make new poetry . . . . We love each other as I think only poets can love . . . and though we be far apart . . . the thought we have been given a treasure not commonly given will comfort us. Be brave, be strong my beloved."[32] She tried. Yet Erskine's death, after a relationship of such intensity and longevity, left her diminished. He had been the center of her life for so long, a solo existence would never have the richness of purpose, or poetry, that characterized their partnership.

Obituaries appeared on both coasts, shorter ones in the *New York Times* and the *New York Herald Tribune*, and longer ones in the *Saturday Review*, the *Oregon Daily Journal*, the *San Francisco Chronicle*, and the *Los Gatos Mail-News*.[33] As to the scattering of Erskine's remains at the base of the old oak tree, William Rose Benét wrote Sara of the perfection of that decision. Now he would always be a part of that tree, "like a wood god in the spring." To have known them both, he added, had been one of the great experiences of his life.[34]

Benét and others wondered if Sara would remain at The Cats. Sara never considered leaving. First, she was not old, being only sixty-one when Wood died, and she believed she could handle management of the place. Happily, the Marengos agreed to stay on to help. They too had put much of their own lives into the property, and though others had tried to lure them away, offering twice the price Erskine paid them, they continued in her employ. Erskine had made Sara promise, in turn, never to desert them. More importantly, she did not want to give up all she and Erskine had built together. The Cats both symbolized and embodied their love. To give it up was unthinkable.[35]

Sara also had work to do on Erskine's unfinished poetry. Above all, she wanted to fortify his reputation as a poet. To that end, she undertook several projects. First, she wanted to publish his collected poems. Second, she gathered as many of his literary manuscripts, diaries, letters, and other papers to create an archive of Erskine's life and work. Finally, she wanted that life immortalized in a biography. These projects kept her busy for the next ten years.[36]

About one month after Wood died, Leslie Bliss of Southern California's Huntington Library contacted Sara. The library collected books by California authors as part of its larger mission to preserve the state's history, and Bliss hoped Sara would complete their Wood/Field holdings by gifting first editions of their printed works. Then, Bliss asked for more: their manuscripts and letters.[37] Aware that Sara hoped to preserve Wood's long-term reputation, Bliss provided advice on collecting materials for a future biography. One task was to gather letters Wood had sent to others, and Sara doggedly pursued the task, promising not to exclude a single letter from the collection, regardless of its content. She would not censor or whitewash their personal failings, blemishes, hypocrisies, or deceits. To her great credit, Sara kept that promise. Erskine had anticipated such a collection long before—telling her, early on, to save all their letters, certain their lives as pioneers of free love would interest future generations. Sara succeeded beyond Wood's dreams.[38]

But who would write the biography? Sara wanted anthropologist Oscar Lewis, an expert on the West and a good writer.[39] That plan never materialized. Not long after the Lewis option was off the table, Edwin Bingham, a young University of Oregon history professor, contacted Sara about writing Erskine's life. Cautious, she informed him the project would be "complex," requiring both a historian and an "artist" in the literary sense. Before giving her blessing, Sara wanted to see samples of Bingham's prose.[40] He forwarded several chapters of his dissertation, in which Sara detected not just literary potential but also "the inevitable academic touch," which she hoped he could put aside. Having no other options, she gave Bingham her support and promised he would not have "a meddling old lady on [his] hands to criticize [his] every paragraph."[41] If Bingham was not "the knight in shining armor" Sara had hoped for, he would do a solid "if not brilliant" book.[42] In the end, Bingham never completed it.[43]

Sara did, however, pull together a volume of Erskine's poetry, which Vanguard Press published as *The Collected Poems of Charles Erskine Scott Wood* in

1949.[44] With that, Sara concluded her nearly forty-year effort to convince the world of Erskine's poetic talent. Occasionally, she submitted one of her own poems to the *New Yorker*, but the magazine turned them down. Without Erskine's inspiration and encouragement, the fire to produce and publish her work was extinguished.[45]

———————

These projects could not extinguish Sara's loneliness, although she rarely recorded such feelings. For a woman who had continually poured her emotional state onto paper for years, this is remarkable. Only occasionally did she admit that to ignore "the emptiness here in this house and the heaviness here in my breast would be the denial of my very existence, so deep, so true is the pain . . . . This is the last, the lonliest [*sic*] ascent." She missed Erskine's warm company, brilliant conversation, and touch.[46] Often, the simple act of walking up the road to The Cats sparked grief, even as it provided rich memories and solace. On January 22, 1957, thirteen years after Erskine's death, and on what would have been his one hundred fifth birthday, family members gathered to pay homage while Sara confided to her diary that her sorrow had not dimmed. Rather, eagerness to join him had grown.[47]

Sara attempted suicide on two occasions. The first time, a hysterical Vincent Marengo called Kay to tell her Sara had swallowed a bottle's worth of sleeping pills. Her bathroom, in fact, was full of sedatives. After recovering, Sara promised the Marengos she would not stockpile medications again. But she did, including not only pills but drugs she injected with needles. The substances changed her personality, made her difficult to live with, and further undermined her overall health.

While the first suicide attempt frightened everyone, the second infuriated the Marengos and Kay, who felt guilty about her anger but could not hide it. These emotions were hard for Sara to take because, Kay believed, "if ever anybody wanted adulation it was she." The suicide attempts added to the strain between mother and daughter that had never completely disappeared. Kay's therapist recommended a psychiatrist for Sara in San Francisco. Sara went to at least one appointment but did not stick with it.[48]

The rich social network Erskine and Sara had built in California, however, and the presence of Kay, Erskine's daughter Lisa, and their respective families in the Bay Area, helped reduce the grief and isolation. For many years Sara continued to host twenty or more people for Thanksgiving dinner. Birthdays and a celebration of Kay and Jim's twenty-fifty wedding anniversary also brought merriment to The Cats. Sara acquired another German Shepherd, named Barda, who eventually produced puppies. Barda's unbridled joy every time Sara returned home helped dull the pain of Erskine's absence.[49] In addition, she continued to spend time in Carmel with friends and attend cultural events in San Francisco.

One other thing offered Sara solace in the years after Erskine's death: religion or, more accurately, spirituality. She had long ago moved away from traditional Christianity but remained a seeker of Truth and transcendent meaning in life. In the 1940s, she became a follower of the Ramakrishna movement, a product of the nineteenth-century Hindu Renaissance. Founder Sri Ramakrishna's teachings included the Vedanta, one of six traditional schools of Hindu philosophy that blended Kali worship, Vaishnavism, Tantrism, and Western humanitarianism.[50]

Swami Vivekananda brought the Ramakrishna movement to the United States when he was invited to the first World's Parliament of Religions, held in 1893 during the World's Columbian Exposition in Chicago. He stayed for three years, establishing several Vedanta centers in the United States, some of which remain in operation to this day. His central message was: Every soul is potentially divine, and one's divinity can be discerned through work, worship, or philosophy. Doctrines, dogmas, rituals, and temples mattered little. The American form of Vedantism emphasized that all individual souls, through rigorous spiritual effort, could eventually merge into One Absolutely Everlasting Blissful Intelligence. Humans were not born sinners destined for hell. The Western version of the philosophy also diverged from more orthodox Hinduism by addressing ethics, social responsibility, and humanitarian aid.

Many Americans drawn to Vedanta centers were educated middle- or upper-class women. They also tended to be fallen-away Christians. The earliest and most enduring Ramakrishna centers cropped up on both coasts, with California eventually boasting the greatest numbers. Sometime around 1939 a friend introduced Sara to Vivekananda's writings, and by 1945 she had joined the San Francisco Vedanta Society, one of the largest and most dynamic Ramakrishna centers in the nation. She remained a member for thirty-seven years.[51] The Ramakrishna emphasis on universalism and individualism matched with reason and social responsibility appealed to Sara. She found the philosophy both intellectually satisfying and pragmatic, applicable to everyday life. It was a religion that turned inward *and* outward and provided the guidance and inspiration Sara had sought her entire life. Vedanta philosophy helped her swing beyond her narrow, confined life into the "reaches of far time and space." But the greatest lesson of Vedanta, Sara thought, was the "Unity or Oneness which is Love's supreme manifestation."[52] The movement provided Sara one more benefit: it brought her into contact with a new generation of seekers, including Alan Watts, who became dean of San Francisco's American Academy of Asian Studies and a figure associated with the 1960s counterculture. She invited Watts to The Cats and gave him her library on Vedantic thought.[53]

Spiritual sustenance and family support, pleasure in nature's beauty and music, dogs and visits with longtime friends, work to secure Wood's reputation in the literary world—all of these things helped Sara pass the years after Erskine's death. But Sara's days at The Cats eventually came to a close. To leave that beloved place became just one of many endings that shaped her final years.

Twenty
ENDINGS

THE BEAUTIFUL, BURDENSOME CATS, SO ESSENTIAL TO SARA'S HAPPINESS AND identity, was also a serious draw on her financial resources. As early as 1947, she began considering selling the property. Its sale would sever her from what was both the most material and the most symbolic manifestation of her life's love. To hand it over to strangers would end its purpose: demonstrating how to craft a life of poetry and beauty. Yet, as Sara and the Marengos aged, she had little choice.

Just around the time of Erskine's last decline, hidden but chronic problems emerged all over the property. The concrete block structure continually leaked and ruined the electric wiring. Seepages from the flat roof threatened the expensive Philippine mahogany ceiling underneath. Rectifying these problems meant dipping into stocks Erskine had intended as Sara's old-age security, but it had to be done.[1]

The grounds, too, required constant care. In summer 1946 a plague of moths laid millions of eggs in The Cats's live oak trees, destroying the oak where Erskine's ashes had been scattered. Sara had to spray the entire grove with DDT.[2] Most dispiriting, on Halloween someone splattered red paint on one of the estate's great stone cats. A similar act had occurred seventeen years before, and after Erskine complained in the local newspaper about the desecration, the town of Los Gatos promised to keep a police officer on guard every Halloween thereafter. That pledge had been long forgotten. Angry and heartbroken, Sara asked the local newspaper to reprint Erskine's original communication. This time Sara received no word of public regret, no offer to protect the statue, and no funds to restore the vandalized cat.[3]

Then, in early January 1952, a terrible storm destroyed the road between the highway and the house, and Sara could no longer put off the "enforced selling of this precious place." She invested $1,000, a significant sum, to advertise the property in the nationally distributed *Previews*, a lavish pamphlet that included photographs. By fall, realtors and potential buyers began visiting the property, an experience Sara found "distasteful." "Well, courage," she wrote in her diary, "it must be this way."[4]

The Cats did not sell quickly. In spring 1954, nearly two years after Sara first put the property up for sale, a couple bid $30,000 (around $278,000 today). Sara regretfully could not accept their offer, but she thought them worthy of the place. She determined another couple—a "strange pair [from] the motion picture world"—to be totally unacceptable. The woman was "a fancy blonde, not by birth" and her partner was "a dark, rough looking man with an accent I could not place." Happily, they made no offer.[5]

Finalizing the sale had become increasingly more imperative after the Marengos had retired in 1953 and Sara's efforts to replace them proved difficult. It took three tries to find suitable employees.[6] In July 1954, Latvian immigrants Fred and Anna Lesinski came to work for Sara. She paid them more than she had the previous help, knowing she would lose "my excellent Latvian couple" if she did not. That year they assisted her in pulling off a beautiful Thanksgiving dinner for thirty-two guests, the last of its kind.[7]

As 1955 began, the *Previews* people believed The Cats would sell that year. Sure enough, in March, Fred Hampton, a retired oil company executive, offered $37,500 cash ($360,000 today) and Sara took it. Friends and family sent condolences, treating the sale like a death in the family. Sara had lived in that house for thirty years. Mary acknowledged the heartbreak of uprooting one's home, its treasures, and the "entangling memories [which] reach deep in the soil of one's life." Lincoln Steffens's widow, Ella Winter, put it best, reprising some of Steffens's own thoughts about the place and its owners from many years before, and surely capturing Sara's own perspective:

> It hurts so to have you & the Cats separate . . . . All we can say is that always we must think of you at The Cats—as one thinks of you & Erskine together . . . . You became The Cats & they were you & we felt the thrill & joy of anticipation of two such beautiful personalities the moment we saw the proud disdainful stone creatures sitting there at their portal.

Then, she added, "Where will you go? Where will you be?"[8]

Sara considered moving back to San Francisco, but the thought of living in a high-rise apartment filled her with "cold dismay." She decided instead on a small house in Oakland, not far from Kay and Jim, but not too near. As for the mournful process of leaving The Cats forever, Sara left no record. Perhaps she was too busy, too depressed, or unable to find words to adequately express the loss. All three probably played a role in the silence over the wrenching experience.

On September 1, with the move behind Sara, Kay and Jim hosted a special surprise celebration for her seventy-third birthday, to remind her that she had not left everything behind. Friends from Los Gatos, Carmel, San Rafael, San Francisco, and the East Bay attended. In the pattern long ago set by Erskine and Sara, guests presented speeches, read poems, and performed music in her honor. The Marengos visited several weeks later, but everybody knew the greater physical distance between Sara and all of her dear friends meant future get-togethers would be rare.[9]

Nor could the occasional party or short visit make up for the greater losses she endured, and the ones still to come. Una Jeffers, William Rose Benét, Emma Wold, and the younger Erskine's wife Becky all died in 1950.[10] Lisa passed away in 1958, three months after becoming ill. "On this day the lovliest [*sic*] human being, save one, it has been to my everlasting blessing to know—our Lisa . . . slipped from the confinement of her so-long painful body about 4:20 in the afternoon," Sara wrote in her diary. "Try for courage as I do, I am desolate with Lisa's going."[11] More than any other woman, Lisa had provided Sara with unswerving support, love, and companionship during her later years in California. Although Sara had become, technically, Lisa's stepmother, the relationship between the two women, just three years apart in age, had none of the complexities and tensions of that between Kay and her mother. Lisa seemed more akin to a sister or best friend than a daughter.

As for Sara's own sisters, they lived long, though not particularly happy, lives. Relationships among the Field women had often proved rocky, fraught with jealousies and resentments. Mary, however, had been a role model as a young intellectual, writer, and free lover, and she was an emotional rock to Sara, especially in the early years of her affair with Wood. Occasional flashes of temper could never sever the ties that bound them. Mary's end did not come until 1969. It was, however, a protracted, painful process. When Lemuel Parton died in 1942, his daughter, Margaret, moved to New York to provide Mary some emotional support. By the late 1940s, Margaret was a talented *New York Herald* foreign correspondent in Asia. There, she met her first husband. The marriage did not last, but it produced a son, Lemuel Britton, whom Mary helped raise when Margaret came home and juggled a flourishing career as a journalist, magazine editor, and freelance writer. In time, Margaret also bore primary caretaker responsibility for Mary, who was in her eighties by the early 1960s and was not aging gracefully.[12]

As Mary began demonstrating serious symptoms of dementia, she agreed, under great duress, to live in a place called Glen Riddle, under supervision. Still spirited, Mary escaped several times. Once she scrambled onto a train and rode along until the conductor, disturbed by the old woman's physical condition and presuming she should not be traveling alone in such a state, took her off and sent her back. Meanwhile, she wrote letters to her siblings complaining about Margaret's terrible treatment of her.[13]

In 1962 Margaret remarried, and for a time Mary lived with the couple. She suffered several small strokes, and the dementia worsened. Her hostility toward Margaret, her grandson, and her new son-in-law intensified. She often became confused, one night wandering outside in thirty-degree weather, flimsily dressed. Finally, she knocked on the door, and when Margaret opened it said, "Why Margaret . . . . What a lovely surprise." On a separate occasion, Mary believed she was on Russian Hill. And yet another time, she did not recognize Margaret, thought she was in an institution, and begged to go across the street to "her sister's" home. Mary became incontinent. She expressed fears of being abandoned by her mother or burning in hell, as her father had predicted she would. She accused everyone of stealing from her.[14]

Margaret had no one to turn to but Sara. She hated to bring these problems to her "frail" aunt, but she needed to share them with someone who knew Mary well. Sara could do little except send encouraging letters and occasionally call on the phone.[15] Eventually, Margaret arranged for her mother to live in a nursing home, from which Mary, in very shaky handwriting, sent a heartrending message to Sara. Crazy with despair and loneliness, and restricted to a wheelchair because she had broken a hip and a leg, Mary claimed that

Margaret could end the torture if she would only allow Mary to return to her home. "But she does not want me—her mother! The years I cared tenderly for her!" She ended with, "Darling, this small note is crammed full of love . . . . I love you!!!"[16] Margaret dutifully visited her mother several times a week until Mary died on July 3, 1969, at age ninety-one.

All was not loss, however. Sara continued to participate in San Francisco's Vedanta Society, attend cultural and social events, and enjoy her family. She also began to receive notice from historians, not because she was the widow of Charles Erskine Scott Wood or a published poet in her own right but because of her suffrage activities. In 1959, historian Amelia Fry began a long series of oral history interviews with Sara for the Bancroft Library, at the University of California, Berkeley. Although the conversations proved wide-ranging and covered much of Sara's life, they focused primarily on her experiences as a suffragist. The 1915 cross-continental journey from San Francisco to Washington, D.C., of course, attracted particular attention. Fry published an article about it in the magazine *American West*. Not long after, Sara received a letter from John Harris Kirkley, who was working with Jeannette Rankin, a friend of Sara's, on political issues, including elimination of the Electoral College. Rankin, who in 1916 had become the first woman elected to Congress, still lived in Carmel. She and Sara had crossed paths in Washington during the suffrage fight, and now, many years later, Rankin sent her regards.

It was Kirkley, however, who spoke Sara's language and no doubt captured her heart when he described her historic automobile journey as one that made "the ideal real" and "the spirit flesh," for in that trip she portrayed "dramatically and physically, in the form of your own person and personality, the movement of emotion, mind, and spirit from West to East as the suffrage movement spread." He compared it to the best kind of poetry—one that combined form and content. Sara must have appreciated this. She was not only remembered, but remembered in a way she particularly valued: as a person who joined politics with poetry.[17]

Sara also experienced deep satisfaction in seeing old emotional wounds healed. As Kay and Sara both aged, their relationship mellowed. While Sara's health problems never ceased, Kay's capacity for sympathy increased. Her mother noted the change. She seemed more tender and caring. Sara attributed this to Kay having finally found happiness, and that, in turn, improved their relationship.[18]

Erskine Wood's regrets about his rocky relationship with his late father and Sara were equally poignant. In 1970, at age ninety-one, the younger Erskine began writing a book about his father. The oldest of Wood and Nanny's children, he was also the last to survive. Berwick had died several months before, and Nan had passed in her sleep just the night before Erskine penned an important letter to Sara, telling her the book project had led him to reread Wood's letters, including those written during the early years of his affair with Sara. In revisiting them, Erskine now realized his father's "desperate trials with me, and my cold failure to understand life and him." He deeply regretted the anguish he had caused Wood and Sara, to whom he now admitted, "I have an equal sorrow over my so long hostility to you." Erskine knew Sara had always understood that Erskine's unfriendliness toward her was a product of his loyalty to his mother. Still, he wished he had been more like his tender and loving sister Lisa.

He did find comfort in knowing that, as the years passed, he had softened toward the couple, reestablished a happier relationship with his father, and shared good times at The Cats. "How well I remember him with his kindly face, his blue eyes, Jovian locks, his humor and his stories, his joy in his quiet hillside, his vineyard, and wine barrels, Vincent and Mary, and of course," Erskine concluded, "most of all you—his beloved wife." A few years later, before turning this letter over to the Huntington Library, Kay wrote on it in pencil that it was of "inestimable meaning to S.B.F.W."[19]

Three and a half years later, in the summer of 1974, Sara Bard Field died after many years of frail health. She was ninety-one, the same age as Erskine at the time of his passing.[20] Unlike Erskine, Sara had no surviving spouse to spread the word about her death or to encourage their literary friends who were still living to write obituaries or memorials for various periodicals. The *Oakland Tribune* published only a short notice with the headline "Sara Wood, Early Suffragist, Dies." The article described her as a "former missionary" and "poetess" as well as suffragist. It devoted three paragraphs to the 1916 cross-country suffrage trip, followed by a brief mention of her husband Wood, her published books, and the honorary degree Mills College awarded her in

1933. It ended with information that friends could make memorial donations to the American Civil Liberties Union, the University of California, or the Save the Redwoods League.[21]

How inadequate is an obituary as a summary of one's life. The *Tribune's* outline falls pathetically short of conveying the vitality and meaning of Sara's existence. Happily, it was not the last or only word. Only months before Sara died, her niece Margaret Parton published a memoir. Sara and Erskine—but especially Sara, whom Margaret repeatedly identified as "my fairy-godmother aunt"—figure importantly in the story. Margaret's earliest memories of San Francisco, where she had been born, included her mother's "beautiful younger sister" who lived on Russian Hill with a man called "Pops." He wore a gardenia in his buttonhole, seemed to always carry opals and amethysts in the pockets of his gray tweed suit, and had white hair and a beard in which, when she sat on his lap, he encouraged Margaret to search for elves. Next to her parents, she loved Sara the most.[22] They had remained close until the Partons moved east.

Even with great geographical distance between them, however, Margaret felt she could always turn to Sara for support, advice, and love. Her aunt played a huge role in encouraging, as she wrote to Sara in 1950, a "special feeling for poetry, for beauty—both the beauty of art and flowers and gracious living and the beauty of the spirit—this you gave me above all." No one better understood the challenges of living with Mary. No one better understood Margaret's creative urges or encouraged them so wholeheartedly. No one better understood the agonizing pain of losing a teenage son, as Margaret did when her son Lem died from leukemia at age seventeen, that sad coincidence mirroring Sara's loss of Albert at nearly the same age. "Mothers who have lost sons in their first flush of young manhood have a particular sense of communion with each other, don't you think?" Margaret once asked Sara.[23]

For all of these reasons, Margaret wanted to immortalize Sara in the pages of her 1973 memoir. She did so in the description of a 1932 visit to The Cats when Margaret was eighteen years old. From the entrance on the red earthen road with its stone cats, up through the wild lilac, madrona, and manzanita to the grove of live oaks where wind chimes hung, and on to the front door, Margaret captured the feel and look of the place and brought it to life one more time. An apricot tree sat on one side of that door, ripe with fruit. At the top of the steps, Sara and Pops welcomed her into the house and a "month of enchantment."

Beauty caught the eye in all directions: the view from the living room's French windows toward Sara's secret garden and the Santa Clara Valley beyond, the bronze urn filled with white petunias sitting on the piano, pillows on the couch made from Persian saddlebags, the fine soaps in Sara and Erskine's bathroom with its sunken tub of green tiles, the dressers filled with satin and silk lingerie and the closets with brocaded capes chosen for their particular elegance.

Mornings began with fruit, toast, and coffee in the inner courtyard. A pergola heavy with purple and white grapes surrounded it on three sides. Its floor consisted of small broken tiles in all the colors of a paint box, creating a joyous effect. The fourth side opened up to a hillside with terraces, each edged with petunias. Another pergola dripped with fragrant wisteria on the last terrace. On the hill above the house Margaret found a cement table and bench, the latter with words etched into it reading "Temples were built in the hills for Gods . . . . This seat is for the contemplation of beauty which is true worship." Elsewhere, a pedestal that supported the busts of Erskine and Sara bore a line from one of Sara's poems—"Had we not clutched love flying by, where had you been? Where had I?"—and one of Erskine's: "I know for everyone, were he but bold, surely along some starry path his soul awaits him."

During the day, while Sara and Erskine worked on their poetry, Margaret amused herself by writing in her diary, reading, playing the piano, and sketching. The three reunited for a light lunch of salad, cheese, and fruit. Later in the day, they gathered for cocktails followed by dinner. In the evening, Sara read poetry out loud or they sat in the courtyard identifying constellations or marveling at the soft moonlight as Margaret inhaled the intermingled aromas of California: jasmine, orange and lemon trees, eucalyptus, and roses.

But it was not a completely idyllic experience. One day Margaret accidentally overheard Sara say to her Aunt Marion, "Yes, and considering that she was raised in an atmosphere of such easygoing slovenliness, isn't it surprising that Margaret keeps her fingernails clean?" This comment stunned Margaret. First, her mother was a good housekeeper. But more shocking and hurtful was the unvarnished condescension and even cruelty Sara expressed toward both

Mary and Margaret. How could her aunt be condescending and loving simultaneously? How explain this contradiction in Sara's character—a gracious, generous, kind, and encouraging woman who could also be mean-spirited? How could she be a champion of truth and honesty while secretly harboring such hostile feelings toward her niece?

Yet, even as Margaret related this story many years later, she also insisted the wound it opened no longer mattered. What did matter was that she "had finally balanced the sunlight against the shadow," having decided that most of the memories Sara gave her were "bathed in the light of the high noon of love," the others forgotten or rarely remembered. At the end of her month's stay, Margaret stood below the great oak doorway while Sara and Erskine bid her goodbye from the balcony above the apricot tree. They stood then, "arm in arm," as "in a sense, they stand now in my memory. And forever."[24]

Sara may very well have read this description of her life before she died, and if she did, she likely delighted in it. She would have appreciated its message, even the part that cast her in an unattractive light, revealing her capacity for pettiness and snobbery. It brought The Cats and her beloved Erskine back into focus for a new generation of readers. More, Margaret had accurately captured their love. It was as Margaret presented it—full of sunlight but also shadow, truth but also deception, beauty but also flashes of ugliness, satisfaction and self-realization but also selfishness.

Finally, Sara and Erskine would have seconded Mary Field Parton's view of life, written to her daughter Margaret when she was in college. It was the passage Margaret chose to conclude her memoir:

> I believe that life is worth having experienced. It holds moments of rare happiness, hours and hours of gentle peace, much pain, and if one is imaginative and vicarious, much more pain. Yet . . . it is good to live . . . for man stands on his hind legs and his face lifts to the stars.[25]

This serves as a useful coda for Sara and Erskine's story as well. They achieved moments of great happiness and peace but also suffered and caused much pain. They attempted to face, and reach, the stars and sometimes stumbled.

Poetry first brought them together, and it sustained their relationship for thirty-four years. Sara and Erskine believed poetry the highest form of human expression and its creation the greatest use of one's time. It lifted people above the drudgery and ugliness of everyday existence. It transformed life's anguish into Truth and Beauty. It also justified their love for one another, helping them evade responsibility for the grief it brought to others, explaining their special partnership while excusing their disloyalty. Sara and Erskine thought their commitment to poetry, the foundation of their joined lives, validated their love and ensured its immortality.

This is not to say their poetry stood the test of time. For years Sara insisted Erskine's poetry rivaled, even surpassed, Walt Whitman's. (Erskine knew better.) She encouraged him to polish his work and share it with the world, and he did enjoy the thrill of seeing his published work appear alongside T. S. Eliot and Ezra Pound in *Poetry* and in William Rose Benét's anthology, as well as in his own books. And yet, his verse spoke a fading language—one that suited nineteenth- rather than twentieth-century tastes. He disliked modernist poetry, and modernists found his work old-fashioned. He had missed his moment.

The burdensome Classical allusions and political sermonizing that weighed down Erskine's poetry were not evident in Sara's. Her style better fit modern sensibilities, but its quality, too, fell short of the work of her more talented contemporaries. Sara and Erskine's poetry, then, did not endure. Instead, it fairly quickly fell into obscurity.

The couple's political sensibilities proved more durable and relevant, even if their actions and accomplishments remain largely unknown today. Erskine and Sara stood at the forefront of progressive—even radical—change in an era that bristled with the vibrant possibility of political, economic, and social transformation. It was a moment in American history when radical change seemed not only possible but imminent. Erskine remained consistently committed to anti-imperialism, labor, women's rights, free speech, and his own brand of anarchism that vaunted personal liberty above all else throughout the decades of his long life. He never hesitated to speak out and devote considerable time and treasure to these issues.

Sara had found her opening into political activism mostly through the women's suffrage movement and lent her considerable voice to advancing the 1920 ratification of the Nineteenth Amendment—a huge success. She had gained fleeting national fame for her efforts, surpassing that of Erskine, who never breached his regional renown to obtain nationwide influence or recognition. Because she came out of the West and moved in and out of active campaigning, however, she is rarely mentioned in the pantheon of famous suffrage and feminist forebears, although her name circulated in the 1960s and 1970s, when she was still alive, among a new wave of feminists looking for role models. Her oral history, stored at UC Berkeley's Bancroft Library, remains an important piece of suffrage history, particularly because of its western context.

That Sara and Erskine's public stances and political values did not always jibe with their personal choices does not discount the importance of their work. To be sure, they had their contemporary critics, ranging from conservative Portland journalists to anarchist Emma Goldman. Erskine came under attack for the apparent inconsistencies between his devotion to justice for workers, on the one hand, and his legal work defending corporations, on the other. That he enjoyed luxury, expressed distaste for the poor, and depended on the labor of others to achieve his own freedom opened him up to reproach as well. He shrugged off such criticism. Other aspects of his life, including bearing economic responsibility for his family, he believed, explained the first contradiction; his undeniable generosity to many others, he thought, helped blunt the failings of the second.

Sara's inability to break through her thoughtlessly crude ideas about race and class eroded her standing as a forward-thinking feminist. Later in life, her positions on race evolved, but during the height of her suffrage endeavors she did not recognize these shortcomings. Her primary goal in life—to create a home with Erskine—and her practice of falling back on the suffrage movement only when Erskine demurred allows room to doubt her commitment to feminism, equal rights, and suffrage. Sara herself, however, would not have seen a contradiction. True, Erskine always came first, but her dedication to these other goals remained firm, and she steadfastly insisted that her lover embrace her values regarding women's power. The home they eventually created centered on mutual respect, freedom, and equality.

Sara's immersion in the suffrage movement, in the company of talented, ambitious, and independent women, refined her aspirations regarding equal-ity. Participation in the more radical branch of the movement gave her the confidence to demand and gain more power in her relationship with Erskine. Initially she deferred to his greater sophistication, experience, and presumed wisdom, yet her early resistance to patriarchy in her childhood home and then again in her marriage to Albert Ehrgott made her ripe for revolt against its appearance in her free-love relationship. With newfound self-assurance and self-possession, Sara challenged Erskine—particularly his dishonesty, hypoc-risy, and infidelity—and bent him to a more equal partnership. If not a perfect match, the two achieved a life together that brought mutual happiness, har-mony, and peace.

Suffrage success notwithstanding, Erskine and Sara's generation of radi-cal activists, for all their optimism and energy, did not transform the United States into an anarchistic or socialist utopia. In fact, by 1918 and the end of World War I, such aspirations would be crushed and crushed again. Yet many of their positions and ideas have since become accepted—although not always uncontested—elements of contemporary American political life. They helped plant big seeds that eventually bore fruit. It took a century of action and reac-tion, followed by more of the same, and the process was often brutally slow and discouraging. That many of the issues remain current struggles demon-strates how challenging it is to foster social, economic, and political justice. No progress could have been achieved, however, without activists such as Sara and Erskine, people who took the risks inherent in challenging entrenched power: articulating their goals, pushing them forward as far as possible, and then passing them on to others who, when the political climate once again proved propitious, would move them still farther down the road.

Sara and Erskine also did not become the celebrated pioneers of free love they always hoped to be. They did, however, anticipate the decline in marriage as the sole structure for partnership, and they openly advocated the right of any husband or wife to leave a marriage that lacks love. Since their day, legal requirements for divorce have been greatly liberalized, and the con-cept of shared custody of children is much more common. Restraints on women who seek both family and meaningful work outside the home, as well as reproductive rights, have eased considerably. None of this makes divorce, child custody cases, or unwanted pregnancies less heartbreaking, of course, and unrequited love, infidelity, dishonesty, and deception still cause pain, disrupt families, and harm children. No one can prevent people from changing their hearts and minds, leaving spouses behind and unsettling families. Sara and Erskine, however, wanted to make these behaviors less catastrophic for those involved by at least removing the legal and social strictures that trapped people in permanently unhappy marriages.

Their story does not provide an unblemished model on negotiating such treacherous territory. They fell short of their own ideals regarding honesty and integrity. Their love was not always beautiful, and it was never perfect. But it was vital, full, and sometimes brave. They ultimately lived the life they had long envisioned—one of freedom and responsibility, artistry and love. By their example, they urge others to do the same.

ACKNOWLEDGMENTS

This book had a long gestation period, beginning, I now realize, with Professor Lewis O. Saum, of the University of Washington's History Department, who strongly suggested I investigate, for my doctoral dissertation, nineteenth-century U.S. army officers' reflections on the topic of going to war against Native Americans. It was a startling, totally unexpected proposal, since I was interested in the intersection between women's and Native American history and was absolutely uninterested in and uninformed about military history. Nevertheless, I followed Saum's lead, and that led me to Charles Erskine Scott Wood, an unorthodox post–Civil War army officer and the central male figure in the story I tell here.

While reading Wood's army diaries and correspondence at the Huntington Library, I discovered a huge trove of letters between Wood and Sara Bard Field, written between 1911 and the 1930s. Who was this woman? And what generated such an enormous archive? Intrigued, I dipped into a box or two and quickly learned theirs was an intriguing story of free love, radicalism, and family. It was not until several decades and several books later, however, that I returned to Erskine and Sara and decided to tell their story. I am grateful to Lew, now gone, for pushing me into new territory and teaching me to always be on the lookout for the surprises that inevitably come in the study of human beings.

The Huntington Library and its staff have been central supporters of this book. Their massive C. E. S. Wood Collection, which includes thousands of letters exchanged among the principal figures, their families, and famous friends, meant I needed to spend significant time in San Marino. Happily, the Huntington's Research Department, then headed by Dr. Roy Ritchie, awarded me a *Los Angeles Times* Distinguished Fellowship, which allowed me to spend an academic year there, finishing one book and getting a solid start on the research for this one. That year and all subsequent visits were enriched by both Roy's personal encouragement and the help of Peter Blodgett, the H. Russell Smith Foundation Curator of Western American History, whose deep knowledge of the collection and the Wood/Field story (not to mention his friendship) were invaluable. A coterie of other Fellows—historians and literary scholars including Kevin Leonard, Elliott West, Carl and Jane Smith, and Susan Gilman—generously offered suggestions as I began the early stages of the project. Sharon Strom, Fred Weaver, Carl and Jane Smith, Malcolm Rohrbough, Sarah Hanley, Carol and François Rigolot, Helen and Daniel Horowitz, Bob and Pat Smith, and other participants in the Emeriti Seminars offered the same in the project's later stage. Throughout it all, and especially important, was the staff of the Reader Services Department, who located and lugged to the reading room manuscript box after manuscript box for my perusal.

Additional research took me to smaller collections, including the C. E. S. Wood Papers at the Bancroft Library, where Teresa Salazar graciously aided me. Doug Erickson, Jeremy Skinner, and Paul Merchant, all archivists with the Special Collections of Lewis and Clark College, also proved extremely hospitable and helpful. I am particularly grateful for the personal tour Paul Merchant, who created the guide to the Wood Family Collection, gave me of Wood-related sites in Portland. Archivists at the University of Oregon's Special Collections in Eugene and the Oregon Historical Society in Portland also made my research excursions smooth and profitable.

My academic home, Southern Methodist University, provided significant financial resources and sabbatical leaves to complete the research and turn my mounds of material into a manuscript. Being named the 2011 Dedman Family Distinguished Professor and then University Distinguished Professor of History proved particularly invaluable. I am especially appreciative of support from former College of Arts and Sciences dean William Tsutsui, History Department chairs James Hopkins, Kathleen Wellman, and Andy Graybill, and my Clements Center for Southwest Studies colleagues Andy Graybill, Neil Foley, Ruth Ann Elmore, and the late David J. Weber.

Early on I realized this was a story best told as a narrative and pitched to a general readership. I want to thank the many people—who are *not* academics—who said upon learning about this project, "Now *that's* a book I would like to read!" Some of these people are friends and family members. Others are strangers I happened to sit next to on an airplane or meet at a party. The turn to a trade rather than academic approach required adjustments, however. Conversations about Erskine and Sara with family members, including Loy and Trisha Righter Lack, Ron and Bonnie Righter Sanders, my late father Atwood Smith, brother Brian Smith, and sister Barbara SilverSmith, helped redirect me to the issues that might matter less in academic life but more in "real" life. Barbara, always a huge supporter of my work, valiantly read an early, much-too-long draft and offered helpful advice on trimming. Over the years, friends such as Marly and the late Dan Merrill, Ken and Betty Down, David Wallace Adams, and Mike and Connie Cassity have kindly engaged in conversations about this project. Thanks to all.

I have had the pleasure of meeting some of C. E. S. Wood's descendants. I especially enjoyed the opportunity to attend one of Erskine and Sandy Wood's Welcome Dinners at Wood's Landing along the Columbia River. Every spring the Wood family hosts the Nez Perce Tribal Council and other tribal members who come to nearby Fort Vancouver, Washington, to participate in the Chief Red Heart Memorial Ceremony. It was a magical evening. Mary Wood and Sara Wood Smith have encouraged my longstanding interest in their great-grandfather. C. E. S. Wood, I am certain, would applaud his family's sustained relationships with Nez Perce people and their hospitality to me and support of my work regarding his relationship with Sara Bard Field. I hope all of the Woods will someday come to the Huntington Library to read Erskine's letters to, and about, his family. Although he left Portland, he never stopped loving his family, as those letters so touchingly demonstrate. Sadly, I was unable to locate any of Sara's descendants.

Historians Dan Sharfstein and Louis Warren offered useful advice, counsel, and introductions regarding trade publishing. John Demos provided a particularly important boost to my confidence regarding this particular story and the value of the narrative approach at a moment when my confidence was flagging. Peter Blodgett introduced me to Chris Rogers, who became my agent, believed in the project, and found the right publishing home. Steve Wasserman, publisher and executive director of Heyday, and anonymous readers supplied excellent direction on how to transform a sprawling manuscript into a much more readable and interesting book. I am also appreciative of Heyday staff members Gayle Wattawa, Ashley Ingram, Diane Lee, Emmerich Anklam, and Lisa K. Marietta for their contributions during the book production stage.

Finally, my husband, Robert W. Righter, has been with me throughout—patiently listening to the stories I brought home from the archives, accompanying me on research trips, reading drafts, and always encouraging me. I owe him much more than a dedication, but at least that is a start in recognizing how important and treasured he is—not simply to this book but to my life. Sara and Erskine would completely understand.

A NOTE ON SOURCES

When an emissary from Southern California's Huntington Library approached Sara Bard Field about donating Charles Erskine Scott Wood's papers, he probably assumed most of the materials would relate to Wood and Sara's literary and political endeavors. Sara's gift to the Huntington, however, included much more. The original donation came to 312 boxes of materials, including approximately twenty-seven hundred letters Wood and Field wrote to each other, documenting in impeccable detail their thirty-four-year love affair. Most letters were handwritten, long, and unique. Even as they covered familiar ground and returned to unresolved issues, they found new ways to express their thoughts and their hearts.

Sara also handed over to the Huntington hundreds of letters the couple wrote to and received from family members and close friends. Still, there was more to come. Eventually Sara's daughter, Katherine Field Caldwell, donated 44 additional boxes of letters and materials. This massive collection provided the scholarly foundation for this book.

Other, smaller collections offered additional sources. Wood's son Erskine gifted the Lewis and Clark College Library's Special Collections with the Wood Family Papers, which offer insight into the Portland Woods' side of the story. Sara's niece Margaret Parton donated the Mary Field Parton Papers to the University of Oregon's Special Collections, and these were especially useful for information regarding the Field family and Sara's pre-Erskine life. Finally, the Bancroft Library, at the University of California, Berkeley, holds a small but important C. E. S. Wood Collection that includes letters between Wood and his son Erskine, Wood and Clarence Darrow and, of course, Wood and Sara.

C. E. S. Wood's biographer relied primarily on the Huntington Collection and focused primarily on his political and literary life. Without Erskine and Sara's belief that their correspondence would interest later generations, their determination to save all of their correspondence, and the commitment of archivists to acquire and preserve the letters, Sara's story, her free-love affair, and its impact on the Wood and Field families would have been lost.

ABBREVIATIONS TO NOTES

This list of abbreviations provides the key for the endnotes, identifying individual correspondents and the archives where the original sources now reside.

AB	Alva Belmont
AE	Albert Ehrgott
AF	Annie Field
AFE	Albert Field Ehrgott
AP	Alice Paul
BB	Blanche Brown
BW	Berwick Wood
CD	Clarence Darrow
CESW	Charles Erskine Scott Wood
CESWBL	Charles Erskine Scott Wood Papers, Bancroft Library, Berkeley, California
CESWHL	Charles Erskine Scott Wood Papers, Huntington Library, San Marino, California
CESWHLA	Charles Erskine Scott Wood Papers Addenda, Huntington Library, San Marino, California
CTD	The Cat's Diary, CESWHL
EB	Edwin Bingham
ES	Emily "Sissy" Seaman
EW	Erskine Wood
FO	Fremont Older
GG	Gilson Gardner
GT	Genevieve Taggard
GW	George West
HJ	Homer Johannsen
IR	Ida Rauh
JE	Julia Emory
JS	Jutaro Shiota
KE	Katherine Ehrgott
LB	Leslie Bliss

LP	Lemuel Parton
LS	Lincoln Steffens
LW	Lisa Wood
ME	Marie Equi
MF	Mary Field Parton
MP	Margaret Parton
MPP	Margaret Parton Papers, Special Collections, University of Oregon, Eugene, Oregon
MVD	Mark Van Doren
MW	Max Wood
NMSW	Nanny Moale Smith Wood
NW	Nan Wood
RJ	Robinson Jeffers
SBF	Sara Bard Field
SBFA	Sara Bard Field autobiography manuscript, CESWHL
SBFOH	*Sara Bard Field: Poet and Suffragist.* Transcript of an oral history interview conducted by Amelia R. Fry, California Oral History Project, Bancroft Library, University of California, Berkeley
SD	Sara Bard Field diaries
TS	Takezo Shiota
TW	Emma (Thelma) Wold
UJ	Una Jeffers
WA	C. E. S. Wood autobiography manuscript, CESWHL
WD	C. E. S. Wood diaries, CESWHL
WFP	Wood Family Papers, Lewis and Clark College Library, Portland, Oregon
WMW	William Maxwell Wood
WRB	William Rose Benét

NOTES

Manuscript sources are identified by folder number/box number.

ONE

1. WA, 3/6 and 19/6, CESWHL.
2. WMW to CESW, December 28, 1870, 37/284; and WMW to CESW, May 8, 1873, 38/284. Both CESWHL.
3. WA, 1/6 and 9/6, CESWHL.
4. WMW to CESW, December 28, 1879, 37/284, CESWHL.
5. WA, 1/6 and 9/6, CESWHL; Hamburger, *Two Rooms*, 10–22; and Sharfstein, *Thunder in the Mountains*, 119–26.
6. Hamburger, 26–27.
7. Ibid., 27–31.
8. WA, 9/6 and 22/6, CESWHL.
9. Ibid., 9/6 and 39/6, CESWHL.
10. Ibid., 32/6, 35/6, and 39/6, CESWHL.
11. Ibid., 37/6 and 44/6, CESWHL.
12. Hamburger, 34–35.
13. Ibid., 39–40; Smith, *Reimagining Indians*, 23–26 and 33; Sharfstein, 192–200; and CESW to Lute Pease, February 22, 1928, 57/235, CESWHL.
14. C. E. S. Wood, "Among the Thlinkits in Alaska," *Century Monthly* 46 (July 1882): 323–29.
15. Sharfstein, 115–20, 132–35, and 179–82.
16. WD, June 27 and July 17, 1877, box 26, CESWHL.
17. Smith, *Reimagining Indians*, 26–27; and Sharfstein, 399–402.
18. Smith, *Reimagining Indians*, 27.
19. CESW to NMSW, December 25, 1875, 10/243; CESW to NMSW, December 31, 1875, 11/243; CESW to NMSW, March 5, 1875, 15/243; CESW to NMSW, March 8, 1878, 16/243; and CESW to NMSW, June 14, 1878, 19/243. All CESWHL.
20. CESW to NMSW, December 27, 1877, 13/243, CESWHL.
21. NMSW to CESW, [ca. 1878], 7/260, CESWHL.
22. NMSW, "Personal Recollections of Nannie Moale Wood," WFP; and CESW to NMSW, March 12, 1878, 17/243, CESWHL.
23. Hamburger, 68–72; and NMSW, "Personal Recollections," WFP.
24. Hamburger, 72–74; NMSW, "Personal Recollections," WFP; CESW to NMSW, February 24, 181, 20/243, CESWHL; and CESW to NMSW, January 12, 1883, 21/243, CESWHL.
25. Hamburger, 73–74.
26. Ibid., 79–83.
27. Ibid., 85–86.
28. Bingham and Barnes, *Wood Works*, 12.
29. Hamburger, 84–86 and 94–98.
30. CESW to Mr. Pearmain, May 21, 1913, 44/235, CESWHL.
31. "A Versatile Citizen," *Oregonian*, November 30, 1909; and Hamburger, 143–46 and 149–52.
32. Hamburger, 87–88 and 90–93.
33. WD, August 6, 1893; September 9, 1887; and October 6, [1887], 6/26, CESWHL.
34. WD, [August 1896], 11/26, CESWHL.
35. Wood, *Life*, 55.
36. Ibid., 107–9 and 110–18.
37. CESW to EW, April 24, 1897, box 7, CESWBL.

38.	CESW to NW, January 30, 1907, 27/233, CESWHL.
39.	WD, August [1894], 4/27; WD, [1893], 6/26; and WD, [March 1908], 8/27. All CESWHL.
40.	CESW to NMSW, September 10, 1893, 24/243, CESWHL.
41.	Hamburger, 115; Erskine Wood, *Life*, 132–33; and EW to CESW, December 29, 1899, and December 6, 1901, box 6, CESWBL.
42.	EW to CESW, December 9, 1905, box 6, CESWBL.

TWO

1.	SBFOH; SBFA, 11/80, CESWHL; and MP biography ms., 5–11/38, MPP.
2.	SBFA, 11/80, CESWHL.
3.	Ibid.
4.	SBFOH.
5.	Ibid. The "basso profundo" phrase comes from SBFA, 11/80, CESWHL.
6.	MP biography ms., 5/38, MPP. A letter Mary wrote several months after Sara's wedding suggests a less critical view of marriage. MF to Alice Field, November 9, 1900, 5/1, MPP.
7.	SBFOH.
8.	Ibid; SBF to Alice Field, December 12, 1902, MPP; and AE to Alice Field, December 24, 1900, 5/1, MPP.
9.	SBFOH. Mrs. Tilly's first name is unknown.
10.	Ibid.
11.	Ibid.
12.	Ibid.
13.	Ibid.
14.	Ibid.
15.	Ibid.
16.	Ibid.
17.	MP biography ms., 5–11/38; and MF to "Mr dear Dr. Taylor," [1906], 9/1. Both MPP.
18.	MF to CESW, January 16, 1914, 18/180, CESWHL.
19.	SBFOH; and MF to CESW, [January 17, 1913], 7/180, CESWHL.

THREE

1.	SBFOH; and Hamburger, 157.
2.	SBFOH; and Hamburger, 158.
3.	SBFOH.
4.	Ibid.
5.	SBFOH; and Hamburger, 159.
6.	SBFOH; and Hamburger, 160.
7.	SBFOH.
8.	Ibid.
9.	SBF to CESW, [September 1, 1911], 4/266, CESWHL. Sara did not date many of these early letters. In this one, however, she mentions it is her birthday.
10.	SBF to CESW, [July 1911], two letters, 1a/266, CESWHL. Other exuberant, breathless love letters to Erskine can be found in folders 1–4/266, CESWHL.
11.	SBF to CESW, [1911,] 1a/266, CESWHL.
12.	SBF to CESW, two letters, [1911], 1a/266; and SBF to CESW, [September 5, 1911], 4/266. All CESWHL.

13. SBF to CESW, August 11, 1911, 3/266; SBF to CESW, [1911], 1a/266; SBF to CESW ["Friday evening," 1911], 1a/266; and SBF to CESW, "Monday evening" [September 1911], 3/266. All CESWHL.
14. SBF to CESW, "Thursday morning," [1911], 1a/266, CESWHL.
15. SBF to CESW, [August 1911], 1a/266; SBF to CESW, "Tuesday night," [September 1911], 4/266; and SBF to CESW, [August 1911], 3/266. All CESWHL.
16. CESW to SBF, [August 1911], 3/244; and CESW to SBF, August 18, 1911, 4/244. Both CESWHL.
17. CESW to SBF, September 8 and September 10, 1911, 5/244, CESWHL.
18. SBF to CESW, [September 1911], 3/266; SBF to CESW, September 5, 1911, 4/266; and SBF to CESW, [August 1911], 1a/266. All CESWHL.
19. SBF to CESW, [September 1911], 8/266, CESWHL.
20. SBF to CESW, "Tuesday morning," [September 1911], 8/266, CESWHL.

FOUR

1. SBF to CESW, [October 1911], 5/266; and CESW to SBF, October 6, 1911, 8/244. Both CESWHL.
2. Farrell, *Clarence Darrow*, 206–12.
3. Hamburger, 164.
4. CESW to SBF, September 8, 1911, 5/244; and SBF to CESW, [September 1911], 8/266. Both CESWHL.
5. SBF to CESW, [October 1911] and October 5, 1911, 5/266, CESWHL; and SBF to CESW, October 10, 1911, 23/32, CESWHLA.
6. CESW to SBF, October 6, 1911, 9/244, CESWHL.
7. SBF to CESW, [October 1911], 5/266, CESWHL.
8. Farrell, 87–89, 91, 92–93, and 121–22.
9. McRae, *Last Trials*, 21; Farrell, 200–205; and MP biograpghy ms., 5–11/38, MPP.
10. McRae, 22; MF to SBF, June 1, 1909, 1/18; and MF to SBF, [July 1909,] 2/181. Both CESWHL.
11. MP biograpghy ms., 5/38, MPP; CD to MF, July 26, 1910, 4/2, MPP; and McRae, 22.
12. MF to SBF, [October 1910], 6/181, CESWHL.
13. SBF to CESW, [October 1911], 5/266, CESWHL.
14. Lincoln Steffens made the same observation about Darrow, in the context of the McNamara trial: Steffens, *Autobiography*, 658–80.
15. SBF to CESW, [October 26, 1911] and [October 1911], 5/266, CESWHL; SBF to AE, October 14, 1911, 3/263, CESWHL; and Farrell, 94–95 and endnote on 485. On Darrow's jesting on women's issues, see SBF to CESW, [November 6, 1911], 26/32, CESWHLA.
16. CESW to SBF, October 16, 1911, 15/244, CESWHL.
17. Ibid.
18. SBF to CESW, [October 1911], 5/266; and SBF to AE, November 5, 1911, 5/263. Both CESWHL.
19. CESW to SBF, October 17, 1911, 17/244; and CESW to SBF, October 25, 1911, 20/244. Both CESWHL.
20. SBF to CESW, [October 1911], 5/266, CESWHL.
21. SBF to CESW, [October 26, 1911], [October 21, 1911], and [October 1911], 5/266, CESWHL; SBF to CESW, [1911], 8/266, CESWHL; and SBF to CESW, October 21, 1911, 24/32, CESWHLA.
22. Earl Harding to SBF, November 10, 1911, 55/14, CESWHLA.

23. SBF to CESW, [October 26, 1911], and [October 21, 1911], 5/266; and SBF to CESW, [November 11, 1911], 6/266. All CESWHL.

24. SBF to CESW, [October 29, 1911], 6/266; and SBF to AE, [postmarked October 31, 1911], 21/263. Both CESWHL.

25. CESW to SBF, October 14, 1911, 13/244; CESW to SBF, October 25, 1911, 20/244; and CESW to SBF, November 3, 1911, 28/244. All CESWHL.

26. CESW to SBF, October 17, 1911, 17/266; CESW to SBF, November 18, 1911, 18/266; CESW to SBF, October 25, 1911, 20/266; CESW to SBF, October 28, 1911, 21/266; CESW to SBF, [October 1911], 25/266; and CESW to SBF, November 3, 1911, 28/266. All CESWHL.

27. "Woman Writes Impression of Great Trial[;] Vividly Describes Scene in the Courtroom," October 17, 1911; "Describes Trial's Principals[;] Portland Woman Writes Entertainingly About Chief Actors in Famous McNamara Case," October 24, 1911; and "All Jailors Love M'Namara Boys, Especially John," November 4, 1911. All *Oregon Daily Journal*.

28. October 29, 1911, *Oregon Daily Journal*.

29. SBF to CESW, [November 6, 1911], 26/32, CESWHLA; and SBF to AE, November 5, 1911, 4/263, CESWHL.

30. Farrell, 212–14 and 226–33; and Steffens, 661–80.

31. SBF to CESW, December 4 and December 8, 1911, 7/266, CESWHL.

FIVE

1. SBF to AE, [1911], 12/263; and SBF to CESW, December 6, 1911, 7/266. Both CESWHL.

2. SBF to AE, October 14, 1911, 3/263; and SBF to AE, October 31, 1911, 4/263. Both CESWHL.

3. SBF to AE, October 31, 1911, 4/263; and SBF to AE, November 9, 1911, 6/263. Both CESWHL.

4. SBF to AE, [1911], 15/263; SBF to AE, [1911], 9/263; and SBF to CESW, [October 26, 1911], 5/266. All CESWHL. See also Albert's letter to Wood, quoted in Hamburger, 177.

5. SBF to AE, October 14, 1911, 3/263; SBF to AE, [1911], 9/263; SBF to AE, [1911], 10/263; SBF to AE, [1911], 11/263; and SBF to AE, [1911], 13/263. All CESWHL.

6. SBF to CESW, [October 1911], 5/266; and SBF to AE, [1911], 17/263. Both CESWHL.

7. CESW to SBF, October 28, 1911, 21/244; SBF to AE, [1911], 18/263; SBF to CESW, [November 6, 1911], 26/32; SBF to CESW, [November 24, 1911], 28/32; and SBF to CESW, [November 25, 1911], 29/32. All CESWHL.

8. SBF to CESW, [October 26, 1911], 5/266; and CESW to SBF, October 18, 1911, 18/244. Both CESWHL.

9. CESW to SBF, "Thanksgiving Day," 1911, 33/244; and CESW to SBF, November 25, 1911, 36/244. Both CESWHL.

10. CESW to SBF, November 27, 1917, 50/244, CESWHL.

11. CESW to SBF, November 26, 1911, 40/244; and CESW to SBF, November 27, 1911, 50/244. Both CESWHL.

12. CESW to SBF, November 28, 1911, 44/244, CESWHL.

13. SBF to CESW, [October 1911], 5/266; CESW to SBF, September 8, 1911, 5/244; CESW to SBF, November 3, 1911, 28/244; and SBF to CESW, [October 1911], 5/266. All CESWHL. Although the last letter has a note indicating that it was likely sent in October, it was written in response to Wood's letter of November 3.

14. SBF to CESW, [November 1911], 6/266, CESWHL.
15. CESW to SBF, "Thanksgiving Day," 1911, 33/244; CESW to SFB, November 26, 1911, 40/244; and CESW to SBF, November 27, 1911, 50/244. All CESWHL.
16. CESW to SBF, November 28, 1911, 43/244; and CESW to SBF, December 4, 1911, 57/244. Both CESWHL.
17. SBF to CESW, "Wednesday noon," [November 1911], 5/266; and CESW to SBF, December 4, 1911, 57/244. Both CESWHL.
18. SBF to CESW, December 4, December 6, December 7, and December 8, 1911, 7/266, CESWHL.
19. SBF to CESW, [December 6, 1911], and December 8, 1911, 7/266; CESW to SBF, [November 1911], 51/244; and CESW to SBF, December 4, 1911, 57/244. All CESWHL.

SIX

1. SBF to CESW, [April 1912], 2/267, CESWHL.
2. Mead, *How the Vote Was Won*, 5.
3. SBF to CESW, [April 1912], 2/267, CESWHL. This was not the only occasion on which Sara made such comments regarding African Americans. See also SBF to CESW, October 30, 1912, 8/267, CESWHL. Sara's distaste for people of color also extended to Asian Americans, as evidenced by, for instance, her telling Wood about a "horrid" train trip when an "old Jap behind me went to sleep and snored like a whole litter of pigs." SBF to CESW, March 27, 1912, 1/267, CESWHL.
4. Lunardini, *From Equal Suffrage*, 8.
5. SBFOH.
6. "College Equal Suffragists, Chinese Women Dine Together," *Oregon Daily Journal*, April 12, 1912; and "Chinese Women Dine with White," *Morning Oregonian*, April 12, 1912. Copies found in "Scrap Book Containing Clippings About Trips and Speeches Made by Mother," box 34, CESWHL.
7. For more on Duniway, see Mead, *How the Vote Was Won*; Moynihan, *Rebel for Rights*; and "Women Suffrage in Oregon," in *The Oregon Encyclopedia*, www.oregonencyclopedia.org, accessed March 12, 2018.
8. For Albert's Men's Equal Suffrage League appointment, see *Sunday Oregonian*, March 10, 1912.
9. SBFOH.
10. SBF to CESW, April 20, 1912, and [April 17, 1912], 2/267, CESWHL.
11. SBF to CESW, March 29, 1912, 1/267, CESWHL; and "Mrs. Ehrgott Is Not Fat Woman," *Pendleton Livewire*, March 28, 1912.
12. Newspaper accounts of Sara's suffrage presentations can be found in "Scrap Book Containing Clippings," box 34, CESWHL.
13. Ibid.
14. SBF to CESW, March 27 and March 29, 1912, 1/267; SBF to CESW, May 14, 1912, 3/267; SBF to CESW, September 6, 1912, 7/267; and SBF to CESW, September 16, 1912, 7/267. All CESWHL.
15. SBF to CESW, October 22, 1912, 8/267, CESWHL.
16. SBF to CESW, March 27, 1912, 1/267; SBF to CESW, May 10, 1912, 3/267; and SBF to CESW, August 29, 1912, 6/267. All CESWHL.
17. SBF to CESW, May 10, 1912, 2/267; SBF to CESW, May 13, 1912, 3/267; and SBF to CESW, September 5, 1912, 7/267. All CESWHL.

18. SBF to CESW, May 13, 1912, 3/267; SBF to CESW, March 27, 1912, 1/267; and SBF to CESW, March 30, 1912, 1/267. All CESWHL.

19. SBFOH; CESW to SBF, May 13, 1912, 84/244, CESWHL; and "Scrap Book Containing Clippings," box 34, CESWHL.

20. SBF to CESW, October 22, 1912, 8/267, CESWHL.

21. Hamburger, 175; and CESW to SBF, October 17, 1912, 21/245, CESWHL.

22. CESW to SBF, September 24, 1912, 11/245, CESWHL; CESW to SBF, October 1, 1912, 16/245, CESWHL; and Hamburger, 175.

23. CESW to SBF, October 16, 1912, 19/245, CESWHL.

24. CESW to SBF, October 17, 1912, 20/245; CESW to SBF, October 17, 1912, 21/245; and CESW to SBF, October 18, 1912, 22/245. All CESWHL.

25. "Scrap Book Containing Clippings," box 34, CESWHL.

26. CESW to SBF, March 1912, 68/244; CESW to SBF, April 11, 1912, 71/244; CESW to SBF, April 1912, 81/245; CESW to SBF, September 24, 1912, 11/245; CESW to SBF, September 15, 1912, 6/245; CESW to SBF, October 18, 1912, 22/245; and SBF to CESW, [April 18, 1912], 2/267. All CESWHL.

27. SBF to CESW, [April 18, 1912], 2/267, CESWHL.

28. SBF to CESW, April 17, 1912, 2/267; CESW to SBF, April 18, 1912, 77/244; and CESW to SBF, April 20, 1912, 80/44. All CESWHL.

29. SBF to CESW, April 17 and April 22, 1912, 2/267, CESWHL.

30. The suicide comments begin in July and last well into September. See SBF to CESW, [1912], 3/267; SBF to CESW, [June 1912], 4/267; SBF to CESW, July 10, July 15, and July 17, and August 27, 1912, 5/267; SBF to CESW, August 29, 1912, and "Wed. morning in the woods," [1912], 6/267; and SBF to CESW, September 1, September 5, and September 7, 1912, 7/267. All CESWHL.

31. Rickie Solinger, *Pregnancy and Power: A Short History of Reproductive Politics in America* (New York: New York University Press, revised edition, 2019).

32. SBF to CESW, September 18, 1912, 7/267, CESWHL.

33. CESW to SBF, September 1, 1912, 1/245; CESW to SBF, September 8, 1912, 2/245; CESW to SBF, September 9, 1912, 3/245; and CESW to SBF, September "10 or 11," 1912, 4/245. All CESWHL.

34. CESW to SBF, September 15, 1912, 6/245, CESWHL.

35. CESW to SBF, September 16, 1912, 7/245; CESW to SBF, September 20, 1912, 8/245; CESW to SBF, September 22, 1912, 9/245; CESW to SBF, September 23, 1912, 10/245; SBF to CESW, September 11, 1912, 7/267; and SBF to CESW, September 14 and 23, 1912, 12/267. All CESWHL.

36. SBF to CESW, September 11, 1912, 7/267, CESWHL.

37. SBF to CESW, September 23, 1912, 7/267, CESWHL.

38. Ibid.

39. Ibid.

40. Ibid.

41. CESW to SBF, September 25, 1912, 12/245, CESWHL.

42. SBF to CESW, September 30, 1912, 7/267; and CESW to SBF, September 30, 1912, 14/245. Both CESWHL.

SEVEN

1. *Morning Oregonian*, March 12, April 27, July 27, and July 31, 1910, and January 23, 1911.

2. *Morning Oregonian*, November 21, 1911, and January 27, 1912; and *Sunday Oregonian*, February 18, 1912.
3. *Morning Oregonian*, March 20, March 23, and May 20, 1912.
4. *Sunday Oregonian*, March 24, 1912.
5. CESW to SBF, [April 1912], 80/245; CESW to SBF, September 25, 1912, 12/245; and SBF to CESW, [April 24, 1912], 2/267. All CESWHL.
6. CESW to SBF, March 27, 1912, 65/244; and CESW to SBF, April 23, 1912, 81/244. Both CESWHL.
7. SBF to CESW, [April 1912], 2/267, CESWHL.
8. SBF to CESW, May 10 and May 13, 1912, 3/267; SBF to CESW, July 10, 1912, 5/267; and SBF to CESW, September 6, 1912, 7/267. All CESWHL.
9. SBF to CESW, May 10, and May 13, 1912, 3/267; SBF to CESW, July 10, 1912, 5/267; and SBF to CESW, September 6, 1912, 7/267. All CESWHL.
10. SBF to CESW, April 22, 1912, 2/267; and SBF to CESW, August 29, 1912, 6/267. Both CESWHL.
11. SBF to CESW, September 16, 1912, 7/267, CESWHL.
12. AE to SBF, July 26, 1912, 29/130; and AE to SBF, July 29, 1912, 30/130. Both CESWHL.
13. AE to SBF, July 29, 1912, 30/130, CESWHL.
14. Ibid.
15. AE to SBF, August 1, 1912, 31/130, CESWHL.
16. AE to CESW, July 21 and August 5, 1912, box 2, CESWBL.
17. SBF to CESW, September 3 and September 14, 1912, 7/267, CESWHL.
18. This story comes from a deposition Emma Wold made in the context of Sara and Albert's divorce proceedings, found in 15/26, CESWHLA.
19. CESW to SBF, October 1, 1912, 15/245, CESWHL; and AE to CESW, October 4, 1912, box 2, CESWBL.
20. CESW to SBF, October 1, 1912, 15/245, CESWHL; and AE to CESW, October 4, 1912, box 2, CESWBL.
21. SBF to CESW, [October 2, 1912], and October 3, 1912, 8/267, CESWHL.
22. SBF to CESW, October 3, 1912, 8/267, CESWHL.
23. CESW to SBF, October 16, 1912, 19/245; and SBF to CESW, [October 30, 1912], 8/267. Both CESWHL.
24. SBFOH.
25. SBF to CESW, [November 26, 1912], [November 28, 1912], "Thanksgiving Day," 1912, and November 30, 1912, 1/268, CESWHL.
26. "History of Las Encinas Hospital," brochure distributed by the hospital, which still operates in Pasadena.
27. SBF to CESW, [December 5, 1912], [December 8, 1912], and [December 9, 1912], 2/268, CESWHL; CESW to SBF, November 30, 1912, 40/245, CESWHL; and SBF diary, January 4, 1913, box 34, CESWHLA.
28. SBF to CESW, [December 8, 1912], 2/268; CESW to SBF, December 7, 1912, 58/245; and CESW to SBF, December 11 and December 12, 1912, 62/245. All CESWHL.
29. Promissory notes for these loans can be found in 19/130, CESWHL.
30. AE to CESW, November 14, 1912, 21/130, CESWHL.
31. Helen Ladd Corbett to CESW, two letters, one with no date, the other dated May 6, no year, box 2, CESWBL; and Hamburger, 198.
32. SBF to CESW, December 11 and December 15, 1912, 2/268. Both CESWHL.
33. CESW to BW, June 5, 1912, box 7; and CESW to BW, May 12, 1913, box 6. Both CESWBL.

34. CESW to SBF, December 19, 1912, 70/245; and CESW to SBF, December 22, 1912, 71/245. Both CESWHL.
35. SBF to CESW, December 8 and December 11, 1912, 2/268, CESWHL.
36. SBF to CESW, December 15, 1912, 2/268; and CESW to SBF, December 17, 1912, 68/245. Both CESWHL.
37. SBF to CESW, December 19 and ["Christmas Day"], 1912, 2/268; CESW to SBF, December 22, 1912, 71/245; and CESW to SBF, [December 1912], 78/245. All CESWHL.
38. SBF to CESW, [December 22, 1912], and ["Christmas Day"], 1912, 2/268, CESWHL.

EIGHT

1.   Farrell, 234–81; and MP biography ms., 5–11/38, MPP.
2.   CD to CESW, February 20 and February 23, [1912], "Clarence Darrow" folder, CESWBL; CD to CESW, March 1, [1912], 41/126, CESWHL; and CD to SBF, October 6, 1918, 52/126, CESWHL.
3.   CESW to SBF, April 12, 1912, 73/244, CESWHL.
4.   Ibid.
5.   MF to SBF, [1912], 10/181; MF to SBF, [1912], 12/181; and MF to CESW, August 6, 1912, 6/180. All CESWHL.
6.   Farrell, 239–63.
7.   MF diary, "The Labor Leaders," 1/58, MPP.
8.   MF to SBF, [1912], 10/181, CESWHL; MF to CESW, [1912], 8/180, CESWHL; MF to CESW, August 6, 1912, 6/180, CESWHL; and Farrell, 264.
9.   SBF to CESW, September 6, 1912, 7/267, CESWHL; and Farrell, 266–67.
10. SBF to CESW, September 7, 1912, 7/267, CESWHL.
11. SBF to CESW, September 12, 1912, 7/267, CESWHL.
12. MF to CESW, [1912], 7/180; and MF to SBF, [November 1912], 10/181. Both CESWHL.
13. MF to LP, [1912], 5/2, MPP.
14. Ibid.; MF to SBF, [1912], 10/181, CESWHL; and Farrell, 270.
15. MF to CESW, [1912], 8/180; MF to SBF, [1912], 7/181; and MF to SBF, [1912], 8/181. All CESWHL.
16. Draft letter, MF to AE, [January 1913], 3/180; AE to MF, January 15, 1913, 14/130; and AE to MF, January 15, 1913, 14/130. All CESWHL.
17. CESW to AE, December 28, 1912, 36/229, CESWHL.
18. AE to CESW, January 3, 1913, 22/130; and AE to CESW, January 15, 1913, 24/130. Both CESWHL.
19. CESW to George Field, January 15, 1913, 35/230, CESWHL.
20. CES to SBF, January 17, 1913, 1/246; and CES to SBF, March 11, March 20, and March 24, 1913, 3/246. All CESWHL.
21. SBF to CESW, January 14, January 16, January 22, 1913, and [January 1913], 1/269; and SBF to CESW, February 27, 1913, 2/269. All CESWHL.
22. MP biography ms., 6/38; and MF to LP, [February 1913], 5/2. Both MPP.
23. Steffens, 700–701.
24. MF to LP, [January/February 1913], 5/2, MPP.
25. Farrell, 270–77.
26. MF to LP, [March 1913], 5/2, MPP; and SBF to CESW, March 9, 1913, 3/269, CESWHL.
27. SFB to CESW, April 4 and April 8, 1913, 1/270, CESWHL.
28. MF to LP, [January 1913] and [February 1913], 5/2, MPP.

29. MF to LP, September 1, 1912, 5/2, MPP.
30. LP to MF, [ca. 1913], 2/6, MPP.
31. MF to SBF, [October 1912], 5/2, MPP.
32. MF to LP, [February 1913], 5/2; and MP biography ms., 6/38. Both MPP.
33. SBF to CESW, January 14 and January 16, 1913, 1/269; and SBF to CESW, April 8, 1913, 1/270. All CESWHL.
34. MF to CESW, [April 2, 1913], 13/180; and SBF to CESW, April 8, 1913, 1/270. Both CESWHL.
35. MP biography ms., 5/38, MPP.

NINE

1.   CESW to EW, April 27, 1897, folder "Before 1900," box 7, CESWBL; and Smith, *Reimagining Indians*, 37.
2.   Riley, *Divorce*, 1–8.
3.   Ibid., 85–87 and 124.
4.   Ibid., 135–37.
5.   SBF to CESW, January 1, 1913, 1/269, CESWHL.
6.   FO to CESW, June 21, 1912, 44/177, CESWHL.
7.   CESW to FO, June 26, 1912, 31/235, CESWHL.
8.   FO to CESW, October 14, 1912, 46/177; FO to CESW, January 1, 1913, 47/177; FO to CESW, May 12, 1913, 48/177; FO to CESW, October 6, 1913, 49/177; Cora Older to CESW, October 29, 1912, 29/177; FO to CESW, [1912], 30/177; FO to CESW, September 4, 1913, 32/177; FO to CESW, [1913], 36/177; and CESW to FO, June 26, 1912, 31/235. All CESWHL.
9.   SBF to CESW, January 16, 1913, 1/269; and SBF to CESW, March 4, 1913, 3/269. Both CESWHL.
10. SBF to CESW, March 28, 1913, 3/269, CESWHL.
11. SBF to CESW, March 4, 1913, 3/269; and SBF to CESW, [January 1913], 1/269. Both CESWHL.
12. MF to CESW, [January 1913], 10/180, CESWHL.
13. MF to CESW, [January 17, 1913], 9/180, CESWHL.
14. Ibid.
15. MF to CESW, [January 17, 1913], 9/180; and SBF diary, January 16 and January 19, 1913, box 34, CESWHL.
16. SBF to CESW, March 24, 1913, 3/269, CESWHL.
17. SBF to CESW, March 18, 1913, 3/269, CESWHL.
18. SBF to CESW, March 19, March 24, and March 25, 1913, 3/269, CESWHL.
19. MF to CESW, [April 1913], 13/180, CESWHL.
20. SBF to CESW, March 28, 1913, 3/269, CESWHL.
21. CESW to SBF, March 28, 1913, 3/246, CESWHL.
22. CESW to SBF, March 10, 1913, 3/246, CESWHL.
23. CESW to SBF, January 17, January 18, and January 19, 1913, 1/246, CESWHL.
24. WD, February 7 and February 8, 1913, box 28, CESWHL; and SD, February 7 and February 8, 1913, box 34, CESWHLA.
25. CESW diary, February 9 and February 10, 1913, box 28, CESWHL; and SBF diary, February 8, February 9, February 10, and February 11, 1913, box 34, CESWHLA.
26. WD, February 12, February 14, February 17, February 19, February 20, February 22, and February 24, 1913, box 28, CESWHL; and CESW to SBF, February 1913, 2/46, CESWHL.

27. SBF to CESW, February 22 and February 27, 1913, 2/269; and CESW to SBF, February 23 and February 25, 1913, 2/246. All CESWHL.

28. CESW to SBF, April 19, 1913, 61/26, CESWHL.

29. SBF to CESW, April 28, folder 1/270; May 7, May 17, and May 19, 1913, 2/270; and AE to MF, May 1, 1913, 15/130. All CESWHL.

30. Shamberger, *The Story of Goldfield*.

31. SD, May 22, 1913, box 34, CESWHLA; SBF to CESW, May 23, 1913, 2/270, CESWHL; and SBF to CESW, June 3, 1913, 3/270, CESWHL. For examples of letters in which Sara chronicles her depression as well as physical maladies, see SBF to CESW, June 25, June 27, and June 29, 1913, 3/270, CESWHL.

32. SBF to CESW, March 31, 1913, 3/269; SBF to CESW, April 1 and April 16, 1913, 1/270; and SBF to CESW, June 5, June 19, and June 23, 1913, 3/270. All CESWHL.

33. SBF to CESW, July 25, 1913, 4/270; MF to SBF, [July 8, 1913], 14/181, CESWHL; and MF to SBF, [December 1913], 17/181. All CESWHL.

34. Bingham and Barnes, *Wood Works*, 238.

35. CESW to SBF, June 8 and June 22, 1913, 6/246, CESWHL.

36. SBF to CESW, June 14, June 16, and June 30, 1913, 2/270; SBF to CESW, September 21, 1931, 2/271; SBF to CESW, October 2, October 8, and October 14, 1913, 3/271; and SBF to CESW, November 4, 1914, 4/271. All CESWHL.

37. CESW to SBF, September 21, 1913, 1/247; CESW to SBF, October 15 and October 16, 1913, 2/247; CESW to SBF, November 8, 1913, 3/247; CESW to SBF, June 17, 1913, 6/246; and CESW to SBF, July 29, 1913, 7/246. All CESWHL.

38. "Goldfield, Nev., Celebration July 4 Is Big Event Not Soon Forgotten," *Oregonian*, July 13, 1913, p. 15.

39. CESW to SBF, October 8, 1913, 2/247; and CESW to SBF December 10, 1913, 4/247. Both CESWHL.

40. MF to CESW, [1913], 16/180; and SBF to CESW, June 3, 1913, 3/270. Both CESWHL.

41. SBF to CESW, June 10, June 19, and June 23, 1913, 3/270; and CESW to SBF, June 19, 1913, 6/246. All CESWHL.

42. SBF to CESW, June 10 and June 27, 1913, 3/270, CESWHL.

43. SBF to CESW, June 8, June 17, and June 25, 1913, 3/270; and SBF to CESW, July 6, 1913, 4/270. All CESWHL.

44. SBF to CESW, August 21, 1913, 1/271; and SBF to CESW, September 13 and September 17, 1913, 2/271. All CESWHL.

45. SBF to CESW, June 22, 1913, 3/270, CESWHL.

46. MF to CESW, [1913], 28/180, CESWHL.

47. SBF to CESW, November 28 and November 30, 1913, 4/271; and SBF to CESW, [November 1913], 2/247. All CESWHL.

48. SBF to CESW, December 3, 1913, 5/271, CESWHL.

49. SBF to CESW, November 20, 1913, 4/271; and SBF to CESW, December 3, December 4, and December 10, 1913, 5/271. All CESWHL.

50. CESW to SBF, February 18, 1914, 32/27a, CESWHLA; MF to CESW, [February 21, 1914], 21/180, CESWHL; MF to CESW, [1914], 29/180, CESWHL; and CESW to SBF, February 28, 1914, 7/247, CESWHL.

51. SBF to CESW, September 29, 1914, 1/274; and CESW to SBF, September 30, 1914, 4/274. See also CESW to SBF, October 1, October 2, and October 7, 1914, 5/274. All CESWHL.

52. SBF to CESW, [March 7, 1914], 3/272; and SBF to CESW, May 26, 1914, 5/272. All CESWHL.

53. CESW to SBF, May 29 and May 30, 1914, 10/247, CESWHL.

TEN

1. CESW to SBF, September 2, September 20, and September 27, 1914, 4/248, CESWHL.
2. Hamburger, 189 and 195–96; CESW to SBF, July 20 and July 27, 1913, 7/246, CESWHL; and CESW to SBF, September 27, 1914, 4/248, CESWHL.
3. CESW to SBF, September 27, 1914, 4/248, CESWHL.
4. SBF to CESW, August 22 and August 26, 1914, 3/273, CESWHL.
5. CESW to SBF, March 23, 1914, 7/247, CESWHL.
6. CESW to SBF, July 22, July 24, and July 26, 1914, 2/248, CESWHL.
7. SBF to CESW, June 26 and June 27, 1914, 1/273; and SBF and CESW, July 5 and July 24, 1914, 2/273. All CESWHL.
8. MF to SBF, [1914], 40/81; and MF to SBF, [1914], 45/81. Both CESWHL.
9. SBF to CESW, April 9 and April 18, 1915, 2/249, CESWHL.
10. SBF to CESW, April 28, 1915, 2/275; SBF and CESW, July 23, July 29, and July 31, 1915, 2/276; and SBF to CESW, August 3 and August 21, 1915, 3/276. All CESWHL.
11. SBF to CESW, August 26 and August 30, 1914, 3/273; and CESW to SBF, September 1, 1914, 4/248. All CESWHL.
12. SBF to CESW, March 2, 1914, 3/272; SBF to CESW, October 17, 1914, 2/274; SBF to CESW, November 9, 1914, 3/274; and SBF to CESW, December 13, 1914, 4/274. All CESWHL.
13. SBF to CESW, March 16 and March 21, 1914, 3/272; SBF to CESW, June 15, June 18, and June 20, 1914, 1/273; SBF to CESW, July 2, 1914, 2/273; and SBF to CESW, August 25, 1914, 3/273. All CESWHL.
14. SBF to CESW, September 22 and September 26, 1914, 1/274; SBF to CESW, October 17, October 21, October 24, October 26, October 30, and October 31, 1914, 2/274; and SBF to CESW, November 3, November 9, and November 10, 3/274. All CESWHL.
15. CESW to SBF, November 3, November 5, November 7, and November 12, 1914, 6/248, CESWHL.
16. SBF to CESW, September 10, 1914, 1/274; SBF to CESW, October 9, 1914, 2/274; and SBF to CESW, November 9, 1914, 3/274. All CESWHL.
17. CESW to SBF, January 7, 1915, 1/249, CESWHL.
18. CESW to SBF, January 25, 1915, 1/249, CESWHL.
19. SBF to CESW, April 15, April 16, and April 19, 1915, 2/275, CESWHL.
20. CESW to SBF, April 16, April 20, April 23, and April 25, 1915, 2/249, CESWHL.
21. SBF to CESW, April 22, 1915, 2/249, CESWHL.
22. CESW to SBF, May 2, 1915, 3/249; and SBF to CESW, May 5, 1915, 3/275. Both CESWHL.

ELEVEN

1. SBF to CESW, January 23, 1915, 1/275; and SBF to CESW, [July 1, 1915], 2/276. Both CESWHL.
2. Markwyn, *Empress San Francisco*; and Moore, *Empire on Display*, 4.
3. Zahniser and Fry, *Alice Paul*, 1–2.
4. Ibid., 46–47, 53, 66–67, 73, 86, and 104–5.
5. Ibid., 104–5, 119–21, 125–30, and 145–49; and Lemay, *Votes for Women*, 167-86.
6. Zahniser and Fry, 163–68, 178–81, and 191–92.
7. Ibid., 192–209.
8. SBFOH; and SBF to CESW, July 15, 1914, 2/276, CESWHL.

9. Zahniser and Fry, 225–26.
10. Ibid., 295; and SBF to CESW, July 8, 1915, 2/276, CESWHL.
11. SBFOH; and SBF to CESW, July 29, 1915, 2/276, CESWHL.
12. SBF to CESW, July 15, July 23, and [July 25], 1915, 2/276, CESWHL.
13. SBF to CESW, July 8 and July 15, 1915, 2/276, CESWHL.
14. CESW to SBF, January 2, 1915, 1/249; CESW to SBF, June 26 and June 27, 1915, 4/249; and CESW to SBF, July 14 and July 22, 1915, 5/249. All CESWHL.
15. CESW to SBF, July 31, 1915, 5/249; and CESW to SBF, [August 11, 1915], 6/249. Both CESWHL.
16. SBFOH.
17. Ibid.
18. Zahnhiser and Fry, 227.
19. SBFOH; and SBF to CESW, September 5, 1915, 4/276, CESWHL.
20. SBF to CESW, September 1, September 5, and September 9, 1915, 4/276, CESWHL.
21. CESW to SBF, September 8, 1915, 1/250, CESWHL.
22. CESW to SBF, "Tuesday night," 1915, 2/250, CESWHL.
23. CESW to SBF, September 26, 1915, 1/250, CESWHL.
24. Zahniser and Fry, 227.
25. Scharff, *Taking the Wheel*, 76–77.
26. Ibid., 13–26.
27. SBFOH.
28. SBF to CESW, September 27, 1915, 4/276, CESWHL.
29. SBFOH.
30. "Women's Envoy Is Greeted Here," *Deseret Evening News*, October 5, 1915, in "Scrap Book," 1/292, CESWHL.
31. SBFOH.
32. Ibid.
33. Ibid.; and "Called on the Governor," *Nebraska State Journal*, October 28, 1915, in "Scrap Book," 1/292, CESWHL.
34. SBFOH; "Women Lose Way To Meeting Here," *Topeka Daily Capital*, October 25, 1915; and "The Suffrage Car Gets In," *Kansas City [Missouri] Star*, October 21, 1915. All in "Scrap Book," 1/292, CESWHL.
35. SBFOH.
36. "Called on the Governor," *Nebraska State Journal*, October 28, 1915; "A Symbolic Crew of Suffragists," *Lincoln [Nebraska] Daily Star*, October 28, 1915; and "Suff Envoys Get Cold Reception," *Omaha Bee*, October 28, 1915. All in "Scrap Book," 1/292, CESWHL.
37. "Greetings to Sara Bard Field," by Frank Walsh, *Kansas City Post*, no dates, in "Scrap Book," 1/292, CESWHL.
38. SBFOH.
39. SBF to CESW, November 3 and November 7, 1915, 1/277, CESWHL.
40. SBF to CESW, November 15 and November 19, 1915, 1/277, CESWHL.
41. CESW to SBF, October 1 and October 17, 1915, 2/250, CESWHL.
42. CESW to SBF, November 15 and November 22, 1915, 3/250, CESWHL.
43. CESW to SBF, October 8, 1915, "Tuesday" [between October 8 and October 12], and October 12, 1915, 2/250; and SBF to CESW, November 25, 1915, 1/277. All CESWHL.
44. SBFOH; and SBF to CESW, November 19, 1915, 1/277, CESWHL.
45. SBFOH; and SBF to CESW, November 9, November 15, and November 19, 1915, 1/277, CESWHL.

46. SBFOH; and SBF to CESW, November 25 and November 29, 1915, 1/277, CESWHL.
47. "President Greets Suffrage Envoys," clipping from unidentified newspaper, December 6, 1915, in "Scrap Book," 1/292, CESWHL. Representative James Brynes called upon the Speaker of the House to investigate the Congressional Union for Woman Suffrage's campaign fund, as there were particular concerns that Alva Belmont was proposing to make a $10,000 contribution to create an active lobby. "The corridors," Brynes complained, "are beginning to resemble the shopping districts during millinery openings." See "Congress Inquires Into 'Suff' Lobby," clipping from unidentified newspaper, no date, in "Scrap Book," 1/292, CESWHL.
48. SBF to CESW, December 10, 1915, 2/277, CESWHL.
49. SBF to CESW, December 10 and December 18, 1915, 2/277, CESWHL.
50. SBF to CESW, December 9 and December 21, 1915, 2/277, CESWHL.

TWELVE

1. CESW to SBF, December 21 and December 26, 1915, 4/250, CESWHL.
2. SBF to CESW, December 25, 1915, 2/277, CESWHL.
3. CESW to SBF, November 6, November 11, and November 12, 1915, 3/250; and CESW to SBF December 16, 1915, 4/250. All CESWHL.
4. GW to SBF, February 19, 1916, 42/216; GW to SBF, December 24, 1915, 43/216; GW to SBF, "Friday evening," 50/216; GW to SBF, undated, 53/216; GW to SBF, "Monday afternoon," 54/216; and GW to SBF, January 4, 1916, 56/216. All CESWHL.
5. GW to SBF, undated, 53/216; GW to SBF, "Monday afternoon," 54/216; GW to SBF, February 12, 1916, 57/216; and GW to SBF, [June 1916], 62/216. All CESWHL.
6. SBF to CESW, December 30, 1915, 2/277; and January 2, 1916, 4/277. Both CESWHL.
7. CESW to SBF, November 15, November 22, November 28, and November 29, 1915, 3/250; and CESW to SBF, December 5, December 14, December 18, and December 26, 1915, 4/250. All CESWHL.
8. CESW to SBF, April 9 and April 14, 1915, 2/249, CESWHL.
9. CESW to SBF, April 19, April 21, April 23, and April 28, 1915, 2/249; and CESW to SBF, May 4, May 13, May 15, and May 19, 1915, 3/249. All CESWHL.
10. SBF to CESW, April 16 and April 21, 1915, 2/275; and CESW to SBF, April 23, 1915, 2/249. All CESWHL.
11. SBF to CESW, May 9 and May 10, 1915, 3/275; and SBF to CESW, June 27, 1915, 1/276. All CESWHL.
12. Stansell, *American Moderns*, 227.
13. SBF to CESW, November 29, 1915, 1/277, CESWHL.
14. CESW to SBF, November 22, 3/250; and CESW to SBF, December 1, 1915, 4/250. Both CESWHL.
15. SBF to CESW, January 2 and January 19, 1916, 4/277; SBF to CESW, February 2 and February 6, 1916, 5/277; SBF to CESW, July 19, 1916, 3/278; SBF to CESW, September 12, 1916, 5/278; and CESW to SBF, January 25, 1916, 16/250. All CESWHL.
16. Irmscher, *Max Eastman*, 1–8 and 84–85.
17. Irmscher, 117–22; and Eastman, *Enjoyment of Living*, 342–58, 483–93, and 511–18.
18. Irmscher, 85–90, 94, 106–7, 117–23, 133–35, and 140–62; SBF to CESW, September 19, 1917, 4/280, CESWHL; and Eastman, 570.
19. Irmscher, 117–18; Eastman, 575; SBF to CESW, September 19, 1917, 4/280, CESWHL; and SBF to CESW, October 6, 1917, 1/281, CESWHL.
20. Eastman, 577; and Stansell, 267.

21. SBF to CESW, January 2, 1916, 4/277; and SBF to CESW, October 6, 1916, 6/278. Both CESWHL.

22. SBF to CESW, January 2, 1916, 4/277; SBF to CESW, January 7, 1917, 3/279; CESW to SBF, January 8 and January 12, 1917, 8/251; and CESW to SBF, August 27, 1917, 3/252. All CESWHL.

23. SBF to CESW, October 13, 1916, 6/278, CESWHL.

24. CESW to SBF, January 12 and January 18, 1915, 1/249; and CESW to SBF, April 6 and April 17, 1915, 2/249. All CESWHL.

25. CESW to SBF, April 17, 1916, 8/250, CESWHL.

26. CESW to SBF, April 18, April 19, and April 21, 1916, 8/250, CESWHL.

27. CESW to SBF, April 16, April 18, April 23, and April 26, 1916, 6/277, CESWHL.

28. CESW to SBF, April 28 and "Monday" [April 1916], 8/250; CESW to SBF, [May 1915] and May 3, 1916, 9/250; and SBF to CESW, April 18, 1916, 6/277. All CESWHL.

29. CESW to SBF, [May 1916], 9/250, CESWHL; SBF to CESW, April 24 and April 26, 1916, 6/277, CESWHL; SBF to CESW, May 3 and May 10, 1/278, CESWHL; and Hamburger, 233.

30. SBF to CESW, June 1, 1916, 2/278, CESWHL.

31. SBF to CESW, June 1 and June 2, 1916, 2/278, CESWHL.

32. SBF to CESW, June 4 and June 8, 1916, 2/278, CESWHL; and Zahniser and Fry, 239–43.

33. SBF to CESW, June 11 and June 18, 1916, 2/278, CESWHL; and Zahniser and Fry, 243–44.

34. SBF to CESW, June 18, 1916, 2/278, CESWHL.

35. SBF to CESW, June 27, 1916, 2/278, CESWHL.

36. GW to SBF, [1916], 61/216; GW to SBF, [June 1916], 63/216; and GW to SBF, [June 1916] and [June 1916], 71/216. All CESWHL.

37. GW to SBF, [June 1916], 74/216, CESWHL.

38. GG to SBF, August 8, 1916, 4/142; GG to SBF, September 24, 1916, 5/142; GG to SBF, September 26, 1916, 6/142; and GG to SBF, September 29, 1916, 7/142. All CESWHL.

39. SBF to CESW, June 27, 1916, 2/278; and CESW to SBF, July 3, 1916, 1/251. Both CESWHL.

40. SBF to CESW, July 18, [July 19], and July 23, 1916, 3/278, CESWHL.

41. SBF to CESW, July 25, [July 26], and July 30, 1916, 3/278, CESWHL.

42. CESW to SBF, July 20 and July 25, 1916, 1/251; and CESW to SBF, August 2, 1916, 2/251. All CESWHL.

43. CESW to SBF, August 2, August 5, August 6, and August 7, 1916, 2/251, CESWHL.

44. SBF to CESW, August 7, August 12, August 14, and August 16, 1916, 2/278, CESWHL.

45. CESW to SBF, August 8, August 9, [August 20], and [August 21], 1916, 2/251; CESW to SBF, September 2, September 8, and "Sat night," 1916, 3/251; and SBF to CESW, September 12 and September 13, 1916, 5/278. All CESWHL.

46. SBF to CESW, September 21, 1916, 5/278, CESWHL.

47. SBF to CESW, September 24, 1916, 5/278, CESWHL.

48. SBF to CESW, November 3, [November 9], November 11, and November 15, 1916, 1/279, CESWHL.

THIRTEEN

1. CES to SBF, November 6, 1916, 5/251, CESWHL.

2. CESW to SBF, August 7 and August 8, 1916, 2/251; and CESW to SBF, September 7, 1912, 3/251. All CESWHL.

3. CESW to SBF, September 3 and September 7, 1916, 3/251; and CESW to SBF, October 5 and October 14, 1916, 4/251. All CESWHL.

4. CESW to SBF, October 11, 2016, 4/251, CESWHL.

5. CESW to SBF, October 13 and October 14, 1916, 4/251, CESWHL.

6. CESW to SBF, January 29, 1916, 6/250; and WD, January 1, January 22, and February 17, 1916, 2/28. All CESWHL.

7. SBF to CESW, February 6, 1916, 5/277; and SBF to CESW, April 19, 1916, 6/277. Both CESWHL.

8. CESW to SBF, July 3, 1916, 1/251; and SBF to CESW, July 9, 1916, 3/278. Both CESWHL.

9. SBF to CESW, August 12, 1916, 4/278, CESWHL.

10. SBF to CESW, August 18, 1916, 4/278; and SBF to CESW, October 10 and October 13, 1916, 6/278. All CESWHL.

11. CESW to SBF, "June 1916," 10/250; and SBF to CESW, [September 3, 1916], 5/278. Both CESWHL.

12. SBF to CESW, [September 10, 1916], 5/278, CESWHL.

13. SBF to CESW, September [10], September 12, and September 21, 1916, 5/278; and SBF to CESW, October 9, 1916, 6/278. All CESWHL.

14. "Woman's Party Speakers to Hold Special Meetings in Twin Falls," *Twin Falls [Idaho] News*; "Sara Bard Field Severe on Wilson," *Salt Lake Tribune*, October 10, 1916, 6/278; and SBF to CESW, October 3 and October 6, 1916, 6/278, CESWHL.

15. SBF to CESW, October 10, October 14, October 16, and October 18, 1916, 6/278, CESWHL.

16. SBFOH; and CESW to SBF, November 9, 1916, 5/251, CESWHL.

17. SBF to CESW, November 9, November 11, and November 13, 1916, 1/279, CESWHL.

18. SBF to CESW, November 18, 1916, 1/279, CESWHL.

19. Hamburger, 220.

20. Ibid., 221.

21. SBF to CESW, July 1, 1915, 2/276, CESWHL.

22. CESW to SBF, July 10, 1915, 5/249, CESWHL.

23. SBF to CESW, July 21, July 23, July 26, and July 31, 1915, 2/276; and SBF to CESW, August 5, 1915, 3/276. All CESWHL.

24. CESW to SBF, July 30 and July 31, 1915, 5/249, CESWHL.

25. SBF to CESW, August 5, 1915, 3/276, CESWHL.

26. SBF to CESW, August 13, 1915, 3/276, CESWHL; CESW to SBF, August 9, 1915, 6/249, CESWHL; CESW to SBF, September 4, 2015, 1/250, CESWHL; and Hamburger, 222.

27. SBF to CESW, August 8, 1915, 3/276, CESWHL.

28. Hamburger, 240–41; and CESW to SBF, November 7, November 9, November 10, and November 16, 1916, 5/251, CESWHL.

29. Hamburger, 236–37; and CESW to SBF, June 18, June 19, June 21, June 23, and June 24, 1916, 10/250, CESWHL.

30. CESW to SBF, no date, September 19, and September 25, 1916, 3/251, CESWHL.

31. SBF to CESW, September 15, September 16, and September 21, 1916, 5/278, CESWHL.

FOURTEEN

1. CESW to NW, June 7, 1915, 19/254, CESWHL.

2. CESW to EW, July 25, 1915, letter 4.1, box 4, WFP. This is a draft of the letter. For a summary of Wood's arguments to Erskine, see CESW to SBF, July 24, 1915, 5/249, CESWHL.

3. WD, March 6, 1916, 2/28, CESWHL.
4. CESW to NW, July 29, 1915, 29/233, CESWHL.
5. LW to CESW, October 19, 1915, 21/197; and CESW to SBF, October 21, 1915, 2/250. Both CESWHL.
6. SBF to CESW, March 25, 1917, 5/279; and SBF to CESW, October 10, 1917, 1/281. Both CESWHL.
7. SBF to CESW, September 3, 1916, 5/278; SBF to CESW, October 2, 1916, 6/278; and SBF to CESW, November 20, 1916, 1/279. All CESWHL.
8. SBF to CESW, June 15, 1917, 1/280, CESWHL.
9. SBF to CESW, July 29, 1917, 2/280, CESWHL.
10. SBF to CESW, November 21, 1917, 2/281; SBF to CESW, July 25, 1918, 7/281; and SBF to CESW, August 13, 1918, 1/282. All CESWHL.
11. SBF to CESW, March 27 and March 28, 1917, 5/279; and SBF to CESW, May 5, 1917, 1/281. All CESWHL.
12. SBF to CESW, May 5 and [May] 1915, 3/275; SBF to CESW, July 21, 1915, 2/276; SBF to CESW, June 1, 1916, 2/278; SBF to CESW, July 18, July 19, July 25, and July 30, 1916, 3/278; and SBF to CESW, September 7, 1916, 5/278. All CESWHL.
13. CESW to SBF, July 24, 1917, 2/280; CESW to SBF, December 22, December 23, and December 28, 6/252; SBF to CESW, June 12, 1917, 1/280; SBF to CESW, July 25, 1915, 2/276; and SBF to CESW, September 1, 2015, 4/276. All CESWHL.
14. SBF to CESW, June 12, 1917, 1/280, CESWHL.
15. CESW to SBF, April 6, 1915, 2/249; CESW and SBF, June 25, 1915, 4/249; CESW to SBF, July 3, 1915, 5/249; and CESW to SBF, November 6, 1915, 3/250. All CESWHL.
16. SBF to CESW, July 3 and July 6, 1915, 2/276, CESWHL.
17. SBF to CESW, November 3, November 12, November 15, and November 18, 1916, 1/279; and SBF to CESW, December 2 and December 4, 1916, 2/27. All CESWHL. Erskine supported the overdose idea, too.
18. WD, November 27, November 28, December 5, and December 24, 1916, 2/28, CESWHL.
19. SBF to CESW, August 21, 1915, 2/276; and SBF to CESW, September 3, 1916, 5/278. Both CESWHL.
20. Stevens, *Jailed for Freedom*, 43–52.
21. SBF to CESW, November 11 and November 18, 1916, 1/279; and SBF to CESW, December 14, December 21, and [December 25], 1916, 2/279. All CESWHL.
22. WD, December 19, December 20, and December 22, 1916, 2/28; and CESW to SBF, December 23, 1916, 6/251. All CESWHL.
23. SBF to CESW, December 25, 1916, 2/279, CESWHL.
24. CESW to SBF, December 28, 1916, 6/251, CESWHL.
25. SBF to CESW, December 28, 1916, 2/279; and CESW to SBF, December 28 and December 29, 1916, 6/251. All CESWHL.
26. SBF to CESW, December 30, 1916, 2/279, CESWHL.

FIFTEEN

1. Stevens, 43–52; SBFOH, 360; and SBF to CESW, December 28, 1916, 2/279, CESWHL.
2. Stevens, 55–56; SBF to CESW, January 10, 1917, 3/279, CESWHL; and SBFOH.
3. Zahniser and Fry, 255–60.
4. Ibid., 262–68.

5. Zahniser and Fry, 271–72; Stevens, 105–12; and SBF to CESW, July 24, 1917, 2/280, CESWHL.

6. SBF to CESW, July 20, 1917, 2/280, CESWHL.

7. SBF to CESW, August 30, 1917, 3/280, CESWHL. The Alice Paul story comes from SBFOH, in an account recorded many years after the event. Sara's letters from 1917 do not relate this story.

8. CESW to SBF, January 4 and January 15, 1917, 8/251, CESWHL.

9. Stevens, 124; and CESW to SBF, "Saturday—Sept. 1917" and "Tuesday—Sept.," 1917, 4/252, CESWHL.

10. CESW to SBF, "Saturday," [September 1917,] 4/252, CESWHL.

11. SBF to CESW, September 10, September 13, September 19, September 20, and September 28, 1917, 4/280, CESWHL.

12. Stevens, 226; and Zahniser and Fry, 284–95 and 308–16.

13. Hoffert, *Alva Vanderbilt Belmont*, ix and x–xii.

14. SBF to CESW, August 16 and August 21, 1915, 3/276, CESWHL; and SBFOH.

15. SBF to CESW, November 25, 1915, 1/277; and SBF to CESW, December 10 and December 18, 1915, 2/277. All CESWHL.

16. CESW to SBF, December 14, December 18, and December 26, 1915, 4/250; and CESW to SBF, May 12, 1917, 1/252. All CESWHL.

17. SBF to CESW, July 25 and July 27, 1917, 2/280, CESWHL.

18. Hoffert, 25–48.

19. Ibid., 50–106.

20. SBF to CESW, July 27 and July 29, 1917, 2/280, CESWHL; and SBFOH.

21. SBFOH.

22. Ibid.

23. SBF to CESW, July 31, 1917, 2/280, CESWHL.

24. SBF to CESW, July 27 and 29, 2/280, CESWHL.

25. SBF to CESW, August 13, 1917, 3/280, CESWHL; and SBFOH.

26. SBF to CESW, August 14 and August 15, 1917, 3/280, CESWHL.

27. SBF to CESW, July 31, 1917, 2/280; and SBF to CESW, August 2, 1917, 3/280. Both CESWHL.

28. Ibid.

29. SBF to CESW, October 13, 1917, 1/281, CESWHL.

30. Hoffert, 126–36.

31. SBF to CESW, November 21, 1917, 2/281, CESWHL.

32. CESW to SBF, October 24, 1917, 4/252; and CESW to SBF, November 27, 1917, 5/252. Both CESWHL.

33. SBFOH.

34. SBF to CESW, July 20 and July 27, 1917, 2/280; and SBF to CESW, August 30, 1917, 3/280. All CESWHL.

35. CESW to SBF, April 3, 1917, 11/251, CESWHL.

36. CESW to SBF, April 6 and April 8, 1917, 11/251, CESWHL.

37. Hamburger, 245–46; and Irmscher, 132.

38. Hamburger, 246–47; and CESW to SBF, July 20 and July 22, 1917, 2/252, CESWHL.

39. Hamburger, 248–49; and SBF to CESW, August 17, 1917, 3/252, CESWHL.

40. CESW to SBF, August 13 and August 25, 1917, 3/252, CESWHL.

41. CESW to SBF, September 22, 1917, 4/252, CESWHL.

42. CESW to SBF, November 20, 1917, 5/252, CESWHL.

43. SBF to CESW, January 21, 1917, 3/279; SBF to CESW, April 15, 1917, 6/279; and SBF to CESW, June 12, 1917, 1/280. All CESWHL.

44. SBF to CESW, June 14 and June 15, 1917, 1/280, CESWHL.
45. Aronson, *Crystal Eastman*, 173–76.
46. Hamburger, 249; SBF to CESW, August 30, 1917, 3/280, CESWHL; and SBF to CESW, September 1 and September 4, 1917, 4/280, CESWHL.
47. SBF to CESW, October 8, 1917, 1/281, CESWHL.
48. CESW to SBF, October 13, 1917, 4/252, CESWHL.

SIXTEEN

1. SBF to CESW, March 26, 1917, 5/279; and SBF to CESW, November 21, 1917, 2/281. Both CESWHL.
2. CESW to SBF, "Friday pm" and April 23, 1918, 8/252, CESWHL.
3. CESW to SBF, July 24 and July 25, 1918, 9/252, CESWHL.
4. CESW to SBF, August 4, August 9, August 11, and August 13, 1918, 10/252, CESWHL.
5. CESW to SBF, April 23, 1918, 8/252; CESW to SBF, July 15, 1918, and [July 1918], 9/252; and CESW to SBF, August 11, 1918, and "Friday," 10/252. All CESWHL.
6. SBF to CESW, July 30, 1918, 7/281; SBF to CESW, August 3, August 12, and August 14, 1/282; and CESW to SBF, August 16, 1918, 10/252. All CESWHL.
7. SBF to CESW, July 26, 1918, 7/281, CESWHL.
8. AFE to HJ, September 7, 1918, 15/131; and AFE to SBF, [March 1918,] 66/133, CESWHL.
9. AFE to SBF, [March 1918], 62/133; and AFE to HJ, September 7, 1918, 15/131. Both CESWHL.
10. SBF to CESW, July 22, 1918, 7/281; AFE to SBF, [September 1, 1917], 57/133; and AFE to CESW, [1914], 27/131. All CESWHL.
11. AFE to SBF, [September 1, 1917], 57/133; AFE to SBF, [March 1918], 62/133; and AFE to SBF, [August 1918], 65/133. All CESWHL.
12. AFE to CESW, July 29, 1918, 43/131, CESWHL. The letter was signed: "Lovingly your Son Albert Field."
13. AFE to CESW, July 29, 1918, 43/131, CESWHL.
14. AFE to CESW, [March 27, 1913], 23/131; and CESW to AFE, March 29, 1913, 40/229. Both CESWHL.
15. AFE to CESW, February 23, 1915, 29/131; AFE to CESW, [June 27, 1915], 31/131; AFE to CESW, [June 25, 1916], 34/131; AFE to CESW, July 20, 1916, 35/131; AFE to CESW, [ca. 1916], 36/131; AFE to CESW, [December 24, 1917], 39/131; and AFE to CESW, February 2, 1918, 41/131. All CESWHL.
16. AE to CESW, March 22, 1918, 25/130, CESWHL.
17. CESW to AE, April 1, 1918, 38/229, CESWHL.
18. AE to CESW, June 25, 1918, 26/130, CESWHL.
19. SBF to AE, October 6, 1918, 27/263, CESWHL.
20. CESW to MW, October 28, 1918, 31/254, CESWHL; SBFOH; and Caldwell, "Family," 36–39.
21. Caldwell, 39.
22. CESW to MW, October 28, 1918, 31/254; and AE to SBF, December 6, 1918, 48/130. Both CESWHL.
23. AE to SBF, December 6, 1918, 48/130, CESWHL.
24. CESW to MW, October 28, 1918, 31/254, CESWHL; AE to SBF, December 6, 1918, 48/130, CESWHL; and Caldwell, 40–42.
25. Caldwell, 41–42.
26. AE to SBF, November 21, 1918, 47/130, CESWHL.

27.   AE to SBF, December 6, 1918, 48/130, CESWHL.
28.   Hamburger, 264; and SBFOH.
29.   IR to SBF, October 25, 1918, 69/187; IR to SBF, November 15, 1918, 71/187; CD to
       SBF, November 16, 1918, 53/126; and AB to SBF, January 5, 1919, 11/101. All CESWHL.
30.   AF to SBF, [1918], 4/13; AF to SBF, January 27, 1919, 6/13; AF to MF, December 19,
       1918, 3/13; and AF to Marion Field Green, January 7, 1919, 3/13. All CESWHL.
31.   HJ to SBF, December 6, 1918, 27/158, CESWHL.
32.   SBF to TW, [November 26, 1918,] 69/265; SBF to TW, January 21, 1919, 70/265;
       and TW to SBF, [October 1918,] 40/220. All CESWHL.
33.   SBFOH; and SBF to CESW, November 29, 1918, 4/282, CESWHL.
34.   SBF to CESW, September 5 and September 6, 1919, 6/282; SBF to CESW, August 5,
       August 12, August 15, and August 25, 1919, 5/282; and SBF to CESW, October 6
       and October 9, 1919, 1/283. All CESWHL. Sara's letter of October 6, 1919, was
       twenty-one pages long.
35.   SBF to TW, March 4, 1920, 72/265; and CESW to SBF, June 3, 1921, 3/253.
       Both CESWHL.

SEVENTEEN

1.   Hamburger, 277–78.
2.   Ibid., 267.
3.   Ibid., 266; and CESW to George Foster Peabody, October 15, 1919, 43/235, CESWHL.
4.   CESW to George Foster Peabody, October 15, 1919, 43/235, CESWHL; CESW to
       Louis Post, November 5, 1918, 70/235, CESWHL; and Hamburger, 265–66.
5.   Helquist, *Marie Equi*, 142–43 and 158–61.
6.   Ibid., 162–67.
7.   Ibid., 171–79.
8.   Ibid., 181–82; CESW to A. Mitchell Palmer, April 28, 1919, 39/40, CESWHL; and
       CESW to A. Mitchell Palmer, April 29, 1919, 40/235, CESWHL.
9.   Helquist, 183–86; and Hamburger, 271–75.
10.   Helquist, 186–88; and CESW to ME, March 10, 1920, 32/230, CESWHL.
11.   Helquist, 190; and ME to SBF, April 4, 1921, 52/135, CESWHL.
12.   Helquist, 201–6; CESW to ME, March 10, 1920, 32/230, CESWHL; CESW to
       Louis Post, October 20, 1919, 71/235, CESWHL; Helquist, 209–14; and Hamburger,
       275.
13.   TW to SBF, May 19, 1920, 57/221; TW to SBF, September 2, 1920, 58/221; and AP
       to SBF, December 19, 1920, 34/183. All CESWHL.
14.   SBF to CESW, February 5, February 6, February 15, and February 16, 1921, 2/283,
       CESWHL.
15.   SBF to CESW, [February 22], 1921, 2/283, CESWHL.
16.   Ibid.; Hamburger, 284–85; SBFOH; and Caldwell, 51–55. Crystal Eastman
       was equally disgusted with Paul's stonewalling of the conference and resistance
       to broadening the NWP's goals, but Eastman eventually supported the focus on the
       Equal Rights Amendment, which to this day remains unratified. See Aronson,
       227–30 and 235–43.
17.   CESW to SBF, May 25 and May 27, 1921, 2/253, CESWHL.
18.   EW to CESW, November 5, 1920, 75/256, CESWHL.
19.   CESW to SBF, May 31, 1921, 1/253; CESW to SBF, July 9, 1921, 4/253; CESW to
       SBF, June 3, June 6, June 7, and June 10, 1921, 3/253. All CESWHL.
20.   CESW to SBF, June 26, 1921, 3/253, CESWHL. This letter is thirty-two pages long.

21. Ibid.
22. Cox, *Sympathetic History*, 2–20; McGarry, *Ghosts*, 1–21 and 98–99; Goldsmith, *Other Powers*, xi and 35–48; and Strom, *Fortune*, 146–54.
23. SBF to TW, March 4, 1920, 7/265, CESWHL.
24. JE to SBF, May 17, 1921, 9/135; JE to SBF, September 23, 1921, 12/135; JE to SBF, [1921], 13/135; and JE to SBF, [1921], 16/135. All CESWHL.
25. JE to SBF, [1921], 17/135, CESWHL.
26. This automatic writing message can be found in 32/263, CESWHL.
27. CESW to SBF, June 13, 1921, 3/253; and CESW to SBF, July 20, 1921, 4/253. Both CESWHL.
28. "Albert Field Ehrgott's Memory Book," box 79, CESWHL.
29. "Oh, Grave, Where Is Thy Victory," written in June 1919, 8/92, CESWHL.
30. Neither Sara nor Erskine wrote about this catastrophic period of their life together. Only Kay's memoir provides any insight into it. See Caldwell, 45–49.
31. CESW to MW, November 21, 1919, 34/254, CESWHL.
32. MW to "Dearest Dad," August 23, 1918, 11/285, CESWHL.
33. CESW to SBF, November 2, 1921, 43/27; and CESW to SBF, [November 1921], 44/27. Both CESWHLA.
34. CESW to SBF, November 3, 1921, 45/27, CESWHLA.
35. CESW to LW, November 8, 1921, 23/237, CESWHL.
36. Ibid.
37. CESW to SBF, November 10, 1921, 52/27; and CESW to SBF, November 16, 1921, 58/27. Both CESWHLA.
38. CESW to SBF, November 8, 1921, 50/27; CESW to SBF, November 17, 1921, 59/27; and CESW to SBF, November 18, 1921, 60/27. All CESWHLA.
39. CESW to SBF, June 13, 1921, 3/253, CESWHL.
40. Hamburger, 294; and BW to CESW, October 17, 1922, 41/224, CESWHL.

EIGHTEEN

1. The phrase "glittering array" is Sara's. See SBFOH.
2. Ibid.; and Caldwell, 61–77.
3. SBFOH.
4. LP to MF, [1920], 7/3, MPP.
5. LP to MF, [no date], 7/3; and LP to MF, [1922], 2/4. Both MPP.
6. LS to CESW and SBF, August 30, 1922, 3/200, CESWHL.
7. SBFOH.
8. CTD, December 10 and December 11, 1923, 4/28, CESWHL.
9. CTD, [December 1923], 4/28, CESWHL.
10. SD, December 22, December 25, December 26, December 27, and December 31, 1923, and January 2, January 5, and January 8, 1924, 2/84, CESWHL. For information on the Stevens/Malone relationship, which ended in divorce several years after this visit, see Hoffert, 150–58.
11. LP to MF, January 3 and January 12, 1924, 5/4, MPP; and SBF to TW, March 15, 1924, 75/265, CESWHL.
12. SD, January–June 1924, 2/84; SBF to TW, March 15, 1924, 75/265, CESWHL; and SBFOH.
13. Caldwell, 85–95; and SBFOH.
14. Hamburger, 299.

15. LS to CESW, May 23, 1924, 6/200, CESWHL; LS to CESW, October 4, 1924, folder 7/200, CESWHL; LS to CESW, March 14, 1925, 8/200, CESWHL; and Hamburger, 298.

16. CESW to GT, April 9, 1924, 2/238, CESWHL; SBFOH; and Hamburger, 298.

17. Hamburger, 305.

18. CTD, May 5, May 14, and December 19, 1923, 4/28, CESWHL.

19. SBFOH; and CTD, May 5, 1923, 4/28, CESWHL. The cat statues were in place by May 1923.

20. CTD, [November 1924] and December 8, 1925, 4/28, CESWHL.

21. CTD, October 28 and November 21, 1925, and January 6, January 10, and January 11, 1928, 4/28, CESWHL; CESW to KE, January 20, 1926, 61/27A, CESWHLA; Hamburger, 302–3; and SBFOH.

22. Hamburger, 302–3; and SBFOH.

23. This last comment comes almost verbatim from SBFOH.

24. For a more critical assessment of the relationship between Erskine and Sara and the Marengos, see Frank, *Local Girl*, 115–76.

25. CTD, January 3, 1926, 4/28; SBFOH; and Frank, 87–176.

26. CTD, February 20, 1926, 4/28, CESWHL.

27. Caldwell, 82–83.

28. Wood noted Ehrgott's marriage on March 18, 1925, in CTD, 4/28, CESWHL. Albert's deathbed forgiveness of Sara comes from Caldwell, 83.

29. SBFOH.

30. Wood and Field, *A Beautiful Wedding*, 18, 23–24, and 80. Copy in CESWHL.

31. Ibid., 7–15.

32. Ibid., 71–74 and 43.

33. John Barry, "On a Mountain Top," *San Francisco News*, August 7, 1929, box 310, CESWHL.

34. CESW to WRB, February 4, 1932, 23/277, CESWHL.

35. Bingham and Barnes, 299; for reviews, see box 208, CESWHL.

36. Bingham and Barnes, 265–88.

37. Ibid., 267.

38. Ibid., 267–68; for reviews, see box 209, CESWHL; and see also WD, 4/28, CESWHL; CESW to MVD, April 28, 1927, 47/238, CESWHL; CESW to MVD, February 28, 56/238, CESWHL; and CESW to MVD, March 22, 1928, 58/238, CESWHL.

39. Bingham and Barnes, 304–12; CESW to Caro Weir, June 1, 1937, 23/230, CESWHL; and CESW to BB, January 3, 1937, 11/228, CESWHL.

40. CESW to BB, January 19, 1939, 20/228, CESWHL; CESW to BB, April 25, 1939, 21/228, CESWHL; Hamburger, 344–48; and Bingham and Barnes, 312–13.

41. These poems can be found in "Scrap Book," 2/292, CESWHL.

42. SBF, "The Man-Handling of Poetry," *Equal Rights*, May 23, 1925; and SBF, "Genevieve Taggard," *Equal Rights*, July 27, 1925. Both in "Scrap Book," 2/292, CESWHL.

43. Field, *Pale Woman*, 23–24.

44. Reviews in "Scrap Book," 2/292; CESW to MVD, December 28, 1927, 73/238; and CESW to MVD, November 21, 1927, 53/238. All CESWHL.

45. WRB to SBF, January 31, 1932, 35/102, CESWHL; and Field, *Barabbas*, back jacket cover.

46. Reviews in box 310, CESWHL.

47. WRB to SBF, December 9, 1935, 41/102, CESWHL; and reviews in box 310, CESWHL.
48. Ella Winter to SBF, October 7, 1927, 8/220, CESWHL.
49. LS to CESW, February 13, 1929, 13/200, CESWHL.
50. WD, December 30, 1927, 4/28; SBF to CESW, July 3, 1928, 8/283; RJ to SBF, December 16, 1927, 9/157; and RJ to SBF, June 20, [1933], 8/283. All CESWHL.
51. UJ to SBF, October 19, 1933, 64/157; UJ to SBF, April 16, 1936, 75/157; and UJ to SBF, [November 1937], 81/157. All CESWHL.
52. WRB to CESW, [1933], 3/102; WRB to CESW, May 31, 1938, 18/102; WRB to CESW, April 20, 1940, 19/102; WRB to CESW, March 1, 1938, 20/102; WRB to SBF, [June 1936], 45/102; and WRB to SBF, August 14, 1938, 52/102. All CESWHL.
53. Benét, *Dust Which Is God.*

NINETEEN

1. ES to CESW, October 30, 1924, 5/195, CESWHL.
2. ES to CESW, December 2, 1924, 6/195; ES to CESW, [1924], 7/195; ES to CESW, [1924], 8/195; ES to CESW, January 10, 1925, 10/195; and CESW to ES, December 10, 1924, 1/237. All CESWHL.
3. BW to CESW, January 3, 1922, 39/224, CESWHL; BW to CESW, September 13, 1922, 40/224, CESWHL; and BW to CESW, October 17, 1922, 41/224, CESWHL. For other letters from BW to CESW, see 45–53/224, CESWHL; and BW to CESW, February 27, 1924, 3/24, CESWHLA.
4. BW to CESW, November 11, 1929, 55/224; EW to CESW, July 10, 1930, 39/257; and EW to CESW, July 17, 1930, 40/257. All CESWHL.
5. CESW to EW, January 30, 1931, 43/4, WFP; SBF to Alice Field, January 21, 1931, 10/5, MPP; and EW to CESW, June 16, 1941, 52/257, CESWHL.
6. NMSW to CESW letters from the 1920s can be found in boxes 260 and 261, CESWHL. See also CESW to NW, July 11, 1924, 39/26, CESWHLA.
7. Copy of *The Testament of Charles Erskine Scott Wood*, WFP.
8. SBF, "Notes Concerning the Letter of Charles Erskine Scott Wood to his son, Erskine, July 22, 1927," 2/92, CESWHL.
9. EW to CESW, July 12, 1927, 30/257, CESWHL.
10. CESW to EW, July 22, 1927, 51/242, CESWHL.
11. LW to NMSW, [1924], 60/197, CESWHL.
12. EW to CESW, July 17, 1931, 43/257, CESWHL; EW to CESW, October 21, 1932, 14/28, CESWHLA; NMSW to CESW, [February 1930], 13/261, CESWHL; NMSW to CESW, February 9, 1932, 14/261, CESWHL; and EW to CESW, February 19, 1934, 16/28, CESWHLA.
13. CESW to Rebecca Biddle Wood, December 22, 1933, 70/4; and SBF to EW, December 28, 1933, 71/4. Both WFP.
14. CESW to Caro Weir, September 7, 1935, 20/230; and EW to CESW, August 19, 1938, 47/257. Both CESWHL.
15. WD, February 1 and February 10, 1932, 4/28, CESWHL; and Caldwell, 149–50.
16. MF to MP, [August 1933], 4/6; and MF to LP, [August 1933], 4/5. Both MPP.
17. CESW to EW, September 15, 1941, 52/242; CESW to EW, June 16, 1942, 54/242; EW to SBF, December 22, 1942, 2/237; CESW to EW, March 2, 1943, 55/242; CESW to EW, March 4, 1943, 55/242; CESW to EW, March 5, 1942, 56/242; EW to SBF, September 15, 1944, 13/258; EW to SBF, August 16, 1945, 20/258; and Myrtle Wood to EW, [1947], 24/126. All CESWHL.

18. CESW to Ellen Van Volkenburg Browne, May 24, 1934, 15/24, CESWHL.
19. SBF to WRB, November 30, 1949, 34/262, CESWHL.
20. Ibid.
21. SD, May 13, May 14, and May 24, 1938, box 34, CESWHLA.
22. SBF to Frank Olmstead, December 5, 1942, 15/265, CESWHL.
23. TS to CESW, February 13, 1912, 67/195; TS to CESW, [1917], 68/195; TS to CESW, March 19, 1926, 71/195; and JS to CESW, September 20, 1938, 73/195. All CESWHL.
24. This biographical information on Shiota comes from Fumi Shiota to the Honorable Frank J. Hennessy, February 26, 1943, contained in a letter from Fumi Shiota to "Col. And Mrs. Wood," March 6, 1943, 59/195, CESWHL.
25. JS to CESW and SBF, December 20, 1942, 61/195; JS to CESW, December 22, 1942, 62/195; and JS to CESW, January 15, 1943, 63/195. All CESWHL.
26. JS to CESW and SBF, January 26, 1943, 64/195; JS to CESW, February 20, 1943, 65/195; and CESW to Leo Silverstein, January 22, 1943, 7/237. All CESWHL.
27. Fumi Shiota to SBF and CESW, March 6, 1943, 59/159; and JS to SBF and CESW, February 20, 1943, 65/195. Both CESWHL.
28. JS to SBF, February 20, 1944, 66/195, CESWHL.
29. SBF memorandum book, January 17 and January 18, 1944; see also SD, 1944, box 85, CESWHL.
30. SBF to EW, February 9, 1944, 1/284; and SD, January 22, 1944, box 85. Both CESWHL.
31. SD, January 22, 1944, box 85, CESWHL.
32. CESW to SBF, June 20, [1915], 7/253, CESWHL.
33. Copy of obituary in WRB to SBF, January 23, 1944, 55/102, CESWHL.
34. WRB to SBF, [May 1944], 59/102, CESWHL.
35. SBF to EW, February 9, 1944, 1/284, CESWHL.
36. Ibid.
37. LB to SBF, February 19, 1944, 34/154, CESWHL.
38. SBF to WRB, November 30, 1949, folder 34/262, CESWHL.
39. SBF to Bennett Cerf, September 18, 1952, 77/262, CESWHL; and SBF to Robert Glass Cleland, August 7, 1952, 78/262, CESWHL. See also SBF to LB, August 7, 1952, 39/262, in which she states, "I shall not cease from effort as long as I am here to make it. The Biography *must* be done!"
40. SBF to EB, January 25, 1953, 35/262, CESWHL.
41. SBF to EB, February 17, 1953, 36/262, CESWHL.
42. SBF to Vera Allen, June 3, 1952, 22/262; SBF to Robert Glass Cleland, November 24, 1953, 79/262; SBF to Monroe Deutsch, June 3, 1953, 84/262; and SD, March 9, 1954, box 34. All CESWHL.
43. SD, June 18, September 15, and September 16, 1954, box 34; and SD, January 8, 1957, 3/86. All CESWHL.
44. SD, October 20, 1947, box 34, CESWHLA; SBF to Jim Henle, November 9, 1947, 27/264, CESWHL; and SBF to Jim Henle, June 13, 1948, 31/264, CESWHL.
45. Sara noted in her diary on July 16, 1945 (SD, 2/85, CESWHL), that when she returned to poetry she felt rusty—"'the divine effluvia' seems spent." See also SD, July 20, 1949, 5/85, CESWHL.
46. SD, February 1 and August 14, 1945, 2/85, CESWHL.
47. SD, February 2, 1948, 4/85; and SD, February 20, 1957, 3/86. Both CESWHL.
48. Caldwell, 160–62.
49. SD, February 2, 1948, 4/85, CESWHL.
50. Jackson, *Vedanta,* 67–107.

51. SBF to Swami Madhavananda, January 5, 1945, 10/265, CESWHL. This letter included a financial contribution in Erskine's memory and was sent "with my deepest gratitude to the Master for the light he has brought to me."
52. SBF to "Tashie" [one of Erskine's granddaughters], August 6, 1947, 53/264, CESWHL.
53. SBF to Alan Watts, March 9, 1954, 64/265; SD, December 11, 1944, 1/85; SD, September 25, 1955, 2/86; SD, June 6, 1948, 4/85; SD, October 10, 1947, box 34; and SD, July 2, 1950, 6/85. All CESWHL.

TWENTY

1. SBF to C.P.A. Mart Building [a contractor], March 18, 1943, 45/265; SBF to Tashie, August 6, 1947, 53/264; and SBF to Jim Henle, October 29, 1947, 26/264. All CESWHL.
2. SBF to Tashie, August 6, 1947, 53/264, CESWHL.
3. SD, November 6 and November 8, 1947, box 34, CESWHLA; and SBF to Jim Henle, November 9, 1947, 27/264, CESWHL. For Sara's letter to the *Los Gatos Mail-News*, see 56/264, CESWHL.
4. SD, July 21, July 22, July 26, July 29, September 15, and September 29, 1952, 1/86; and SBF to Vera Allen, June 3, 1953, 22/262. All CESWHL.
5. SD, March 6 and September 22, 1954, box 34, CESWHLA.
6. SD, January 12, January 15, January 16, January 20, and April 18, 1954, box 34, CESWHLA.
7. SD, May 1, June 5, July 16, August 13, August 18, August 24, November 17, November 22, and November 26, 1954, box 34, CESWHLA.
8. MP to SBF, April 29, 1955, 80/182; and Ella Winter to SBF, May 26, 1955, 19/220. Both CESWHL.
9. SD, May 27, September 1, September 2, and September 3, 1955, 2/86, CESWHL.
10. SD, March 18, 1949, 5/85; and SD, June 11 and June 12, 1950, 6/85. All CESWHL.
11. SD, August 20, August 22, and November 22, 1958, box 24, CESWHLA.
12. Parton, *Journey*, 70–87.
13. MP to SBF, August 31, 1962, 9/5, CESWLA.
14. MP to SBF, August 31, 1962, 9/5; MP to SBF, [1962], 10/5; MP to SBF, November 11, 1963, 12/5; MP to SBF, November 15, 1963, 13/5; and MP to SBF, January 2, 1964, 14/5. All CESWLA.
15. MP to SBF, November 15, 1963, 13/5, CESWHLA.
16. MP to SBF, August 2, 1962, 82/182, CESWHL.
17. SD, October 2, 1959, 4/86; John Harris Kirkley to SBF, August 17, 1972, 40/160. Both CESWHL.
18. SD, September 9, 1959, 4/86, CESWHL.
19. EW to SBF, December 11, 1970, 27/258, CESWHL.
20. Caldwell, 162.
21. "Sara Wood, Early Suffragist, Dies," *Oakland Tribune*, June 18, 1974, E21.
22. Parton, 9.
23. MP to SBF, November 19, 1950, 56/154; MP to SBF, November 28, 1970, 65/154; and MP to SBF, February 22, 1972, 68/154. All CESWHL.
24. Parton, 33–39.
25. Ibid., 241.

SELECTED BIBLIOGRAPHY

Aronson, Amy. *Crystal Eastman: A Revolutionary Life*. New York: Oxford University Press, 2020.

Avrich, Paul, and Karen Avrich. *Sasha and Emma: The Anarchist Odyssey of Alexander Berkman and Emma Goldman*. Cambridge: The Belknap Press of Harvard University Press, 2012.

Baker, Jean. *Margaret Sanger: A Life of Passion*. New York: Hill and Wang, 2011.

Benét, William Rose. *The Dust Which Is God*. New York: Dodd, Mead and Co., 1941.

Bingham, Edwin. "Oregon's Romantic Rebels: John Reed and Charles Erskine Scott Wood." *Pacific Northwest Quarterly* 50 (July 1959): 77–90.

Bingham, Edwin, and Tim Barnes. *Wood Works: The Life and Writings of Charles Erskine Scott Wood*. Corvallis: Oregon State University Press, 1997.

Boag, Peter. *Same-Sex Affairs: Constructing and Controlling Homosexuality in the Pacific Northwest*. Berkeley: University of California Press, 2013.

Burke, Carolyn. *Foursome: Alfred Stieglitz, Georgia O'Keefe, Paul Strand, Rebecca Salsbury*. New York: Alfred A. Knopf, 2019.

Cahill, Cathleen. *Recasting the Vote: How Women of Color Transformed the Suffrage Movement*. Chapel Hill: University of North Carolina Press, 2020.

Caldwell, Katherine Field. "Family and Berkeley Memories, and the Study and Profession of Asian Art." Oral history conducted in 1992 and 1993 by Suzanne B. Riess, Regional Oral History Office, Bancroft Library, University of California, Berkeley, 1993. Transcript available at https://archive.org/details/familyberkelymem00fielrich/mode/2up.

Celello, Kristin. *Making Marriage Work: A History of Marriage and Divorce in the Twentieth-Century United States*. Chapel Hill: University of North Carolina, 2009.

Coontz, Stephanie. *Marriage, a History: How Love Conquered Marriage*. New York: Penguin Books, 2005.

———. *The Way We Never Were: American Families and the Nostalgia Trap*. New York: Basic Books, 2000.

Cox, Robert S. *A Sympathetic History of American Spiritualism*. Charlottesville: University of Virginia Press, 2003.

Dinesen, Isak. *On Modern Marriage and Other Observations*. New York: St. Martin's Press, 1977.

Dubois, Ellen Carol. *Suffrage: Women's Long Battle for the Vote*. New York: Simon and Schuster, 2020.

Eastman, Max. *Enjoyment of Living*. New York: Harpers, 1948.

Farrell, John A. *Clarence Darrow: Attorney for the Damned.* New York: Vintage Books, 2011.

Field, Sara Bard. *Barabbas: A Dramatic Narrative.* New York: Albert and Charles Boni, 1932.

———. *Darkling Plain.* New York: Random House, 1936.

———. *The Pale Woman and Other Poems.* New York: William Edwin Rudge, 1927.

———. *Sara Bard Field: Poet and Suffragist.* Interview conducted by Amelia R. Fry, 1959–1963. Transcript available from the Regional Oral History Project, Bancroft Library, University of California, Berkeley.

Fishbein, Leslie. *Rebels in Bohemia: The Radicals of The Masses, 1911–1917.* Chapel Hill: University of North Carolina Press, 1982.

Frank, Dana. *Local Girl Makes History: Exploring Northern California's Kitsch Monuments.* San Francisco: City Lights Foundation, 2007.

Goldsmith, Barbara. *Other Powers: The Age of Suffrage, Spiritualism, and the Scandalous Victoria Woodhull.* New York: Alfred Knopf, 1998.

Hamburger, Robert. *Two Rooms: The Life of Charles Erskine Scott Wood.* Lincoln: University of Nebraska Press, 1998.

Hartog, Hendrik. *Man and Wife in America: A History.* Cambridge: Harvard University Press, 2000.

Helquist, Michael. *Marie Equi: Radical Politics and Outlaw Passions.* Corvallis: Oregon State University Press, 2015.

Hoffert, Sylvia. *Alva Vanderbilt Belmont: Unlikely Champion of Women's Rights.* Bloomington: Indiana University Press, 2012.

Irmscher, Christopher. *Max Eastman: A Life.* New Haven: Yale University Press, 2017.

Jackson, Carl T. *Vedanta for the West: The Ramakrishna Movement in the United States.* Bloomington: Indiana University Press, 2004.

Kersten, Andrew E. *Clarence Darrow: American Iconoclast.* New York: Hill and Wang, 2011.

Lemay, Kate Clarke. *Votes for Women! A Portrait of Persistence.* Washington, D.C.: National Portrait Gallery, Smithsonian Institution in cooperation with Princeton University Press, 2019.

Lunardini, Christine E. *From Equal Suffrage to Equal Rights: Alice Paul and the National Woman's Party.* New York: New York University Press, 1986.

Markwyn, Abigail M. *Empress San Francisco: The Pacific West, The Great West and California at the Panama-Pacific International Exposition.* Lincoln: University of Nebraska Press, 2014.

McCarter, Jeremy. *Young Radicals in the War for American Ideals.* New York: Random House, 2017.

McGarry, Molly. *Ghosts of Futures Past: Spiritualism and the Cultural Politics of Nineteenth-Century America*. Berkeley: University of California Press, 2008.

McRae, Donald. *The Last Trials of Clarence Darrow*. New York: William Morrow, 2009.

Mead, Rebecca J. *How the Vote Was Won: Woman Suffrage in the Western United States, 1868–1914*. New York: New York University Press, 2004.

Miller, Nina. *Making Love Modern: The Intimate Public Worlds of New York's Literary Women*. New York: Oxford University Press, 1998.

Moore, Sarah J. *Empire on Display: San Francisco's Panama-Pacific International Exposition of 1915*. Norman: University of Oklahoma Press, 2013.

Moynihan, Ruth Barnes. *Rebel for Rights: Abigail Scott Duniway*. New Haven: Yale University Press, 1983.

O'Toole, Patricia. *The Five of Hearts: An Intimate Portrait of Henry Adams and His Friends*. New York: Simon and Schuster, 1990.

Parton, Margaret. *Journey through a Lighted Room*. New York: Viking Press, 1977.

Riley, Glenda. *Divorce: An American Tradition*. New York: Oxford University Press, 1991.

Rose, Phyllis. *Parallel Lives: Five Victorian Marriages*. New York: Vintage Books, 1983.

Rosenstone, Robert A. *Romantic Revolutionary: A Biography of John Reed*. New York: Vintage Books, 1975.

Sandweiss, Martha A. *Passing Strange: A Gilded Age Tale of Love and Deception Across the Color Line*. New York: Penguin Press, 2009.

Scharff, Virginia. *Taking the Wheel: Women and the Coming of the Motor Age*. Albuquerque: University of New Mexico Press, 1991.

Shamberger, Hugh A. *The Story of Goldfield*. Carson City, NV: 1982.

Sharfstein, Daniel J. *Thunder in the Mountains: Chief Joseph, Oliver Otis Howard, and the Nez Perce War*. New York: Norton, 2016.

Smith, Sherry L. *Reimagining Indians: Native Americans Through Anglo Eyes, 1880–1940*. New York: Oxford University Press, 2000.

———. *The View from Officers' Row: Army Perceptions of Western Indians*. Tucson: University of Arizona Press, 1990.

Stansell, Christine. *American Moderns: Bohemian New York and the Creation of a New Century*. New York: Henry Holt and Co., 2000.

Steffens, Lincoln. *The Autobiography of Lincoln Steffens*. New York: Harcourt, Brace and Company, 1931.

Stevens, Doris. *Jailed for Freedom*. New York: Liveright Publishing, 1920.

Strom, Sharon Hartman. *Fortune, Fame, and Desire: Promoting the Self in the Long Nineteenth Century*. Lanham, MD: Rowman and Littlefield, 2016.

Wood, C. E. S. *The Collected Poems of Charles Erskine Scott Wood*. New York: Vanguard Press, 1949.

———. *Earthly Discourse*. New York: Vanguard Press, 1937.

———. *Heavenly Discourse*. New York: Vanguard Press, 1927.

———. *Poems from the Ranges*. San Francisco: Lantern Press, 1929.

———. *The Poet in the Desert*. Portland, 1918.

———. *Sonnets to Sappho*. San Francisco: Grabhorn Press, 1939.

Wood, C. E. S., and Sara Bard Field. *A Beautiful Wedding*. Self-published, 1929.

———. *Maia, A Sonnet Sequence*. Portland: F. W. Baltes, 1918.

Wood, Erskine. *The Life of Charles Erskine Scott Wood*. Portland: Published by Erskine Wood, 1978.

Zahniser, J. D., and Amelia R. Fry. *Alice Paul: Claiming Power*. New York: Oxford University Press, 2014.

INDEX

ABOUT THE AUTHOR

Sherry L. Smith is a University Distinguished Professor of History (Emerita) at Southern Methodist University. She now lives in Moose, Wyoming, and Pasadena, California, with her husband, Robert W. Righter (also a historian) and their English Setter named Una. A historian of the American West and Native America, Smith's other books include *Hippies, Indians, and the Fight for Red Power* and *Reimagining Indians: Native Americans through Anglo Eyes, 1880–1940*, both published by Oxford University Press. She is a past president of the Western History Association and received the *Los Angeles Times* Distinguished Fellowship at the Huntington Library, which supported research for *Bohemians West*. Smith has also been honored with fellowships from the National Endowment for the Humanities, the Fulbright Foundation, and Yale University's Beinecke Library.